Genetic Algorithms in Search, Optimization, and Machine Learning

FR-53917
FET B CSCT

Genetic Algorithms in Search, Optimization, and Machine Learning

David E. Goldberg
The University of Alabama

PEARSON

Copyright © 1989 by Pearson Education, Inc.
This edition is published by arrangement with Pearson Education, Inc. and Dorling Kindersley Publishing, Inc.

ISBN 978-81-775-8829-3

First Impression, 2006
Eighteenth Impression, 2013
Nineteenth Impression, 2014

Published by Dorling Kindersley (India) Pvt. Ltd., licensees of Pearson Education in South Asia.

Head Office: 7th Floor, Knowledge Boulevard, A-8(A), Sector-62, Noida – 201309, U.P, India.
Registered Office: 11 Community Centre, Panchsheel Park, New Delhi 110 017, India.

Printed in India by Saurabh Printers Pvt. Ltd.

Foreword

I first encountered David Goldberg as a young, PhD-bound Civil Engineer inquiring about my course *Introduction to Adaptive Systems*. He was something of an anomaly becuase his severely practical field experience in the gas-pipeline industry, and his evident interest in that industry, did not seem to dampen his interest in what was, after all, an abstract course involving a lot of "biological stuff." After he enrolled in the course, I soon realized that his expressed interests in control, gas pipelines, and AI were the surface tell-tales of a wide-ranging curiosity and a talent for careful analysis. He was, and is, an engineer interested in building, but he was, and is, equally interested in ideas.

Not long thereafter, Dave asked if I would be willing to co-chair (with Ben Wylie, the chairman of our Civil Engineering Department) a dissertation investigating the use of genetic algorithms and classifier systems in the control of gas-pipeline transmission. My first reaction was that this was too difficult a problem for a dissertation—there are no closed analytic solutions to even simple versions of the problem, and actual operation involves long, craftsmanlike apprenticeships. Dave persisted, and in a surprisingly short time produced a dissertation that, in turn, produced for him a 1985 NSF Presidential Young Investigator Award. So much for my intuition as to what constitutes a reasonable dissertation.

In the past few years GAs have gone from an arcane subject known to a few of my students, and their students, to a subject engaging the curiosity of many different research communities including researchers in economics, political science, psychology, linguistics, immunology, biology, and computer science. A major reason for this interest is that GAs really work. GAs offer robust procedures that can exploit massively parallel architectures and, applied to classifier systems, they provide a new route toward an understanding of intelligence and adaptation. David Goldberg's book provides a turnpike into this territory.

One cannot be around David Goldberg for long without being infected by his enthusiasm and energy. That enthusiasm comes across in this book. It is also an embodiment of his passion for clear explanations and carefully worked examples. His book does an exceptional job of making the methods of GAs and classifier systems available to a wide audience. Dave is deeply interested in the intellectual problems of GAs and classifier systems, but he is interested even more in seeing these systems used. This book, I think, will be instrumental in realizing that ambition.

John Holland
Ann Arbor, Michigan

Preface

This book is about genetic algorithms (GAs)—search procedures based on the mechanics of natural selection and natural genetics. In writing it, I have tried to bring together the computer techniques, mathematical tools, and research results that will enable you to apply genetic algorithms to problems in your field. If you choose to do so, you will join a growing group of researchers and practitioners who have come to appreciate the natural analogues, mathematical analyses, and computer techniques comprised by the genetic algorithm methodology.

The book is designed to be a textbook and a self-study guide. I have tested the draft text in a one semester, senior-level undergraduate/first-year graduate course devoted to genetic algorithms. Although the students came from different backgrounds (biochemistry, chemical engineering, computer science, electrical engineering, engineering mechanics, English, mathematics, mechanical engineering, and physics) and had wide differences in mathematical and computational maturity, they all acquired an understanding of the basic algorithm and its theory of operation. To reach such a diverse audience, the tone of the book is intentionally casual, and rigor has almost always been sacrificed in the interest of building intuition and understanding. Worked out examples illustrate major topics, and computer assignments are available at the end of each chapter.

I have minimized the mathematics, genetics, and computer background required to read this book. An understanding of introductory college-level mathematics (algebra and a little calculus) is assumed. Elementary notions of counting and finite probability are used, and Appendix A summarizes the important concepts briefly. I assume no particular knowledge of genetics and define all required genetic terminology and concepts within the text. Last, some computer programming ability is necessary. If you have programmed a computer in any language, you should be able to follow the computer examples I present. All computer code in this book is written in Pascal, and Appendix B presents a brief introduction to the essentials of that language.

Although I have not explicitly subdivided the book into separate parts, the chapters may be grouped in two major categories: those dealing with search and optimization and those dealing with machine learning.

The first five chapters are devoted to genetic algorithms in search and optimization. Chapter 1 introduces the topic of genetic search; it also describes a simple genetic algorithm and illustrates the GA's application through a hand calculation. Chapter 2 introduces the essential theoretical basis of GAs, covering topics including schemata, the fundamental theorem, and extended analysis. If you dislike theory, you can safely skip Chapter 2 without excessive loss of continuity; however, before doing so, I suggest you try reading it anyway. The mathematical underpinnings of GAs are not difficult to follow, but their ramifications are subtle; some attention to analysis early in the study of GAs promotes fuller understanding of algorithm power. Chapter 3 introduces computer implementation of genetic algorithms through example. Specifically, a Pascal code called the simple genetic algorithm (SGA) is presented along with a number of extensions. Chapter 4 presents a historical account of early genetic algorithms together with a potpourri of current applications. Chapter 5 examines more advanced genetic operators and presents a number of applications illustrating their use. These include applications of micro- and macro-level operators as well as hybrid techniques.

Chapters 6 and 7 present the application of genetic algorithms in machine learning systems. Chapter 6 gives a generic description of one type of genetics-based machine learning (GBML) system, a classifier system. The theory of operation of such a system is briefly reviewed, and one Pascal implementation called the simple classifier system (SCS) is presented and applied to the learning of a boolean function. Chapter 7 rounds out the picture of GBML by presenting a historical review of early GBML systems together with a selective survey of other current systems and topics.

ACKNOWLEDGMENTS

In writing acknowledgments for a book on genetic algorithms, there is no question who should get top billing. I thank John H. Holland from the University of Michigan for his encouragement of this project and for giving birth to the infant we now recognize as the genetic algorithms movement. It hasn't been easy nurturing such a child. At times she showed signs of stunted intellectual growth, and the other kids on the block haven't always treated her very nicely. Nonetheless, John stood by his baby with the quiet confidence only a father can possess, knowing that his daughter would one day take her rightful place in the community of ideas.

I also thank two men who have influenced me in more ways than they know: E. Benjamin Wylie and William D. Jordan. Ben Wylie was my dissertation adviser in Civil Engineering at the University of Michigan. When I approached him with the idea for a dissertation about gas pipelines and genetic algorithms, he was appropriately skeptical; but he gave me the rope and taught me the research and organizational skills necessary not to hang myself. Bill Jordan was my Department Head in Engineering Mechanics at The University of Alabama (he retired in 1986). He was and continues to be a model of teaching quality and administrative fairness that I still strive to emulate.

I thank my colleagues in the Department of Engineering Mechanics at Alabama, A. E. Carden, C. H. Chang, C. R. Evces, S. C. Gambrell, J. L. Hill, S. E. Jones, D. C. Raney, and H. B. Wilson, for their encouragement and support. I also thank my many colleagues in the genetic algorithms community. Particular thanks are due Stewart Wilson at the Rowland Institute for Science for providing special encouragement and a sympathetic ear on numerous occasions.

I thank my students (the notorious Bama Gene Hackers), including C. L. Bridges, K. Deb, C. L. Karr, C. H. Kuo, R. Lingle, Jr., M. P. Samtani, P. Segrest, T. Sivapalan, R. E. Smith, and M. Valenzuela-Rendon, for lots of long hours and hard work. I also recognize the workmanlike assistance rendered by a string of right-hand persons: A. L. Thomas, S. Damsky, B. Korb, and K. Y. Lee.

I acknowledge the editorial assistance provided by Sarah Bane Wood at Alabama. I am also grateful to the team at Addison-Wesley, including Peter Gordon, Helen Goldstein, Helen Wythe, and Cynthia Benn, for providing expert advice and assistance during this project.

I thank the reviewers, Ken De Jong, John Holland, and Stewart Wilson, for their comments and suggestions.

A number of individuals and organizations have granted permission to reprint or adapt materials originally printed elsewhere. I gratefully acknowledge the permission granted by the following individuals: L. B. Booker, G. E. P. Box, K. A. De Jong, S. Forrest, J. J. Grefenstette, J. H. Holland, J. D. Schaffer, S. F. Smith, and S. W. Wilson. I also acknowledge the permission granted by the following organizations: Academic Press, Academic Press London Ltd. (*Journal of Theoretical Biology*), the American Society of Civil Engineers, the Association for Computing Machinery, the Conference Committee of the International Conference on Genetic Algorithms, Kluwer Academic Publishers (*Machine Learning*), North-Holland Physics Publishing, the Royal Statistical Society (*Journal of the Royal Statistical Society, C*), and John Wiley and Sons, Inc.

I thank my spouse and still best friend, Mary Ann, for her patience and assistance. There were more than a few evenings and weekends I didn't come home when I said I would, and she proofread the manuscript, judiciously separating my tolerable quips from my unacceptable quirks. Untold numbers of readers would thank you, Nary (sic), if they knew the fate they have been spared by your sound judgment.

This material is based upon work supported by the National Science Foundation under Grant MSM-8451610. I am also grateful for research support provided by the Alabama Research Institute, Digital Equipment Corporation, Intel

Corporation, Mr. Peter Prater, the Rowland Institute for Science, Texas Instruments Incorporated, and The University of Alabama.

Last, it has become a cliche in textbooks and monographs; after thanking one and all for their assistance, the author gallantly accepts blame for all remaining errors in the text. This is usually done with no small amount of pomp and circumstance—a ritualistic incantation to ward off the evil spirits of error. I will forgo this exercise and close these acknowledgments by paraphrasing a piece of graffiti that I first spotted on the third floor of the West Engineering Building at the University of Michigan:

To err is human. To really foul up, use a computer.

Unfortunately, in writing this book, I find myself subject to both of these sources of error, and no doubt many mistakes remain. I can only take comfort in knowing that error is the one inevitable side effect of our human past and the probable destiny of our artificially intelligent future.

Contents

FOREWORD iii
PREFACE v

1 A GENTLE INTRODUCTION TO GENETIC ALGORITHMS 1

What Are Genetic Algorithms?   1
Robustness of Traditional Optimization and Search Methods   2
The Goals of Optimization   6
How Are Genetic Algorithms Different from Traditional Methods?   7
A Simple Genetic Algorithm   10
Genetic Algorithms at Work—a Simulation by hand   15
Grist for the Search Mill—Important Similarities   18
Similarity Templates (Schemata)   19
Learning the Lingo   21
Summary   22
Problems   23
Computer Assignments   25

2 GENETIC ALGORITHMS REVISITED: MATHEMATICAL FOUNDATIONS 27

Who Shall Live and Who Shall Die? The Fundamental Theorem   28
Schema Processing at Work: An Example by Hand Revisited   33
The Two-armed and k-armed Bandit Problem   36
How Many Schemata Are Processed Usefully?   40

The Building Block Hypothesis   41
Another Perspective: The Minimal Deceptive Problem   46
Schemata Revisited: Similarity Templates as Hyperplanes   53
Summary   54
Problems   55
Computer Assignments   56

**3   COMPUTER IMPLEMENTATION OF
A GENETIC ALGORITHM   59**

Data Structures   60
Reproduction, Crossover, and Mutation   62
A Time to Reproduce, a Time to Cross   66
Get with the Main Program   68
How Well Does it Work?   70
Mapping Objective Functions to Fitness Form   75
Fitness Scaling   76
Codings   80
A Multiparameter, Mapped, Fixed-Point Coding   82
Discretization   84
Constraints   85
Summary   86
Problems   87
Computer Assignments   88

4   SOME APPLICATIONS OF GENETIC ALGORITHMS   89

The Rise of Genetic Algorithms   89
Genetic Algorithm Applications of Historical Interest   92
De Jong and Function Optimization   106
Improvements in Basic Technique   120
Current Applications of Genetic Algorithms   125
Summary   142
Problems   143
Computer Assignments   145

**5   ADVANCED OPERATORS AND TECHNIQUES IN
GENETIC SEARCH   147**

Dominance, Diploidy, and Abeyance   148
Inversion and Other Reordering Operators   166

Other Micro-operators   179
Niche and Speciation   185
Multiobjective Optimization   197
Knowledge-Based Techniques   201
Genetic Algorithms and Parallel Processors   208
Summary   212
Problems   213
Computer Assignments   214

6 INTRODUCTION TO GENETICS-BASED MACHINE LEARNING 217

Genetics-Based Machine Learning: Whence It Came   218
What is a Classifier System?   221
Rule and Message System   223
Apportionment of Credit: The Bucket Brigade   225
Genetic Algorithm   229
A Simple Classifier System in Pascal   230
Results Using the Simple Classifier System   245
Summary   256
Problems   258
Computer Assignments   259

7 APPLICATIONS OF GENETICS-BASED MACHINE LEARNING 261

The Rise of GBML   261
Development of CS-1, the First Classifier System   265
Smith's Poker Player   270
Other Early GBML Efforts   276
A Potpourri of Current Applications   293
Summary   304
Problems   306
Computer Assignments   307

8 A LOOK BACK, A GLANCE AHEAD 309

APPENDIXES 313

A **A REVIEW OF COMBINATORICS
   AND ELEMENTARY PROBABILITY 313**

Counting   313
Permutations   314
Combinations   316
Binomial Theorem   316
Events and Spaces   317
Axioms of Probability   318
Equally Likely Outcomes   319
Conditional Probability   321
Partitions of an Event   321
Bayes' Rule   322
Independent Events   322
Two Probability Distributions: Bernoulli and Binomial   323
Expected Value of a Random Variable   323
Limit Theorems   324
Summary   324
Problems   325

B **PASCAL WITH RANDOM NUMBER GENERATION FOR
   FORTRAN, BASIC, AND COBOL PROGRAMMERS 327**

Simple1: An Extremely Simple Code   327
Simple2: Functions, Procedures, and More I/O   330
Let's Do Something   332
Last Stop Before Freeway   338
Summary   341

C **A SIMPLE GENETIC ALGORITHM
   (SGA) IN PASCAL 343**

D **A SIMPLE CLASSIFIER SYSTEM
   (SCS) IN PASCAL 351**

E **PARTITION COEFFICIENT TRANSFORMS FOR
   PROBLEM-CODING ANALYSIS 373**

Partition Coefficient Transform   374
An Example: $f(x) = x^2$ on Three Bits a Day   375
What do the Partition Coefficients Mean?   376

Using Partition Coefficients to Analyze Deceptive Problems   377
Designing GA-Deceptive Problems with Partition Coefficients   377
Summary   378
Problems   378
Computer Assignments   379

BIBLIOGRAPHY   381
INDEX   403

1 | A Gentle Introduction to Genetic Algorithms

In this chapter, we introduce genetic algorithms: what they are, where they came from, and how they compare to and differ from other search procedures. We illustrate how they work with a hand calculation, and we start to understand their power through the concept of a schema or similarity template.

WHAT ARE GENETIC ALGORITHMS?

Genetic algorithms are search algorithms based on the mechanics of natural selection and natural genetics. They combine survival of the fittest among string structures with a structured yet randomized information exchange to form a search algorithm with some of the innovative flair of human search. In every generation, a new set of artificial creatures (strings) is created using bits and pieces of the fittest of the old; an occasional new part is tried for good measure. While randomized, genetic algorithms are no simple random walk. They efficiently exploit historical information to speculate on new search points with expected improved performance.

Genetic algorithms have been developed by John Holland, his colleagues, and his students at the University of Michigan. The goals of their research have been twofold: (1) to abstract and rigorously explain the adaptive processes of natural systems, and (2) to design artificial systems software that retains the important mechanisms of natural systems. This approach has led to important discoveries in both natural and artificial systems science.

The central theme of research on genetic algorithms has been *robustness*, the balance between efficiency and efficacy necessary for survival in many different environments. The implications of robustness for artificial systems are manifold. If artificial systems can be made more robust, costly redesigns can be reduced or eliminated. If higher levels of adaptation can be achieved, existing systems can perform their functions longer and better. Designers of artificial systems—both software and hardware, whether engineering systems, computer systems, or business systems—can only marvel at the robustness, the efficiency, and the flexibility of biological systems. Features for self-repair, self-guidance, and reproduction are the rule in biological systems, whereas they barely exist in the most sophisticated artificial systems.

Thus, we are drawn to an interesting conclusion: where robust performance is desired (and where is it not?), nature does it better; the secrets of adaptation and survival are best learned from the careful study of biological example. Yet we do not accept the genetic algorithm method by appeal to this beauty-of-nature argument alone. Genetic algorithms are theoretically and empirically proven to provide robust search in complex spaces. The primary monograph on the topic is Holland's (1975) *Adaptation in Natural and Artificial Systems*. Many papers and dissertations establish the validity of the technique in function optimization and control applications. Having been established as a valid approach to problems requiring efficient and effective search, genetic algorithms are now finding more widespread application in business, scientific, and engineering circles. The reasons behind the growing numbers of applications are clear. These algorithms are computationally simple yet powerful in their search for improvement. Furthermore, they are not fundamentally limited by restrictive assumptions about the search space (assumptions concerning continuity, existence of derivatives, unimodality, and other matters). We will investigate the reasons behind these attractive qualities; but before this, we need to explore the robustness of more widely accepted search procedures.

ROBUSTNESS OF TRADITIONAL OPTIMIZATION AND SEARCH METHODS

This book is not a comparative study of search and optimization techniques. Nonetheless, it is important to question whether conventional search methods meet our robustness requirements. The current literature identifies three main types of search methods: calculus-based, enumerative, and random. Let us examine each type to see what conclusions may be drawn without formal testing.

Calculus-based methods have been studied heavily. These subdivide into two main classes: indirect and direct. Indirect methods seek local extrema by solving the usually nonlinear set of equations resulting from setting the gradient of the objective function equal to zero. This is the multidimensional generalization of the elementary calculus notion of extremal points, as illustrated in Fig. 1.1. Given a smooth, unconstrained function, finding a possible peak starts by restricting search to those points with slopes of zero in all directions. On the other hand,

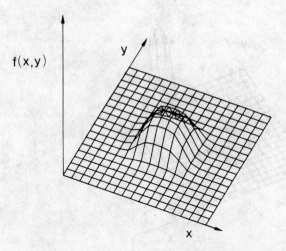

f(x,y)

y

x

FIGURE 1.1   The single-peak function is easy for calculus-based methods.

direct (search) methods seek local optima by hopping on the function and moving in a direction related to the local gradient. This is simply the notion of *hill-climbing*: to find the local best, climb the function in the steepest permissible direction. While both of these calculus-based methods have been improved, extended, hashed, and rehashed, some simple reasoning shows their lack of robustness.

First, both methods are local in scope; the optima they seek are the best in a neighborhood of the current point. For example, suppose that Fig. 1.1 shows a portion of the complete domain of interest; a more complete picture is shown in Fig. 1.2. Clearly, starting the search or zero-finding procedures in the neighborhood of the lower peak will cause us to miss the main event (the higher peak). Furthermore, once the lower peak is reached, further improvement must be sought through random restart or other trickery. Second, calculus-based methods depend upon the existence of derivatives (well-defined slope values). Even if we allow numerical approximation of derivatives, this is a severe shortcoming. Many practical parameter spaces have little respect for the notion of a derivative and the smoothness this implies. Theorists interested in optimization have been too willing to accept the legacy of the great eighteenth and nineteenth-century mathematicians who painted a clean world of quadratic objective functions, ideal constraints, and ever present derivatives. The real world of search is fraught with discontinuities and vast multimodal, noisy search spaces as depicted in a less calculus-friendly function in Fig. 1.3. It comes as no surprise that methods depending upon the restrictive requirements of continuity and derivative existence are unsuitable for all but a very limited problem domain. For this reason and

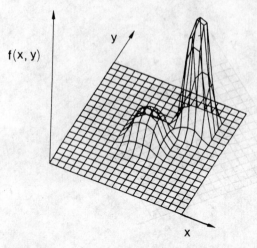

FIGURE 1.2 **The multiple-peak function causes a dilemma. Which hill should we climb?**

because of their inherently local scope of search, we must reject calculus-based methods. They are insufficiently robust in unintended domains.

   Enumerative schemes have been considered in many shapes and sizes. The idea is fairly straightforward; within a finite search space, or a discretized infinite search space, the search algorithm starts looking at objective function values at every point in the space, one at a time. Although the simplicity of this type of

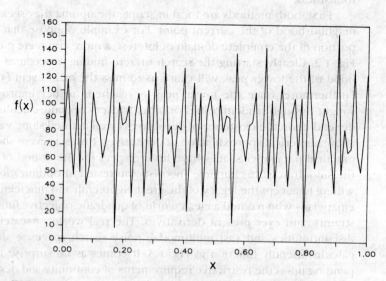

FIGURE 1.3 **Many functions are noisy and discontinuous and thus unsuitable for search by traditional methods.**

algorithm is attractive, and enumeration is a very human kind of search (when the number of possibilities is small), such schemes must ultimately be discounted in the robustness race for one simple reason: lack of efficiency. Many practical spaces are simply too large to search one at a time and still have a chance of using the information to some practical end. Even the highly touted enumerative scheme *dynamic programming* breaks down on problems of moderate size and complexity, suffering from a malady melodramatically labeled the "curse of dimensionality" by its creator (Bellman, 1961). We must conclude that less clever enumerative schemes are similarly, and more abundantly, cursed for real problems.

Random search algorithms have achieved increasing popularity as researchers have recognized the shortcomings of calculus-based and enumerative schemes. Yet, random walks and random schemes that search and save the best must also be discounted because of the efficiency requirement. Random searches, in the long run, can be expected to do no better than enumerative schemes. In our haste to discount strictly random search methods, we must be careful to separate them from randomized techniques. The genetic algorithm is an example of a search procedure that uses random choice as a tool to guide a highly exploitative search through a coding of a parameter space. Using random choice as a tool in a directed search process seems strange at first, but nature contains many examples. Another currently popular search technique, *simulated annealing*, uses random processes to help guide its form of search for minimal energy states. A recent book (Davis, 1987) explores the connections between simulated annealing and genetic algorithms. The important thing to recognize at this juncture is that randomized search does not necessarily imply directionless search.

While our discussion has been no exhaustive examination of the myriad methods of traditional optimization, we are left with a somewhat unsettling conclusion. conventional search methods are not robust. This does not imply that they are not useful. The schemes mentioned and countless hybrid combinations and permutations have been used successfully in many applications; however, as more complex problems are attacked, other methods will be necessary. To put this point in better perspective, inspect the problem spectrum of Fig. 1.4. In the figure a mythical effectiveness index is plotted across a problem continuum for a specialized scheme, an enumerative scheme; and an idealized robust scheme. The gradient technique performs well in its narrow problem class, as we expect, but it becomes highly inefficient (if useful at all) elsewhere. On the other hand, the enumerative scheme performs with egalitarian inefficiency across the spectrum of problems, as shown by the lower performance curve. Far more desirable would be a performance curve like the one labeled Robust Scheme. It would be worthwhile sacrificing peak performance on a particular problem to achieve a relatively high level of performance across the spectrum of problems. (Of course, with broad, efficient methods we can always create hybrid schemes that combine the best of the local search method with the more general robust scheme. We will have more to say about this possibility in Chapter 5.) We shall soon see how genetic algorithms help fill this robustness gap.

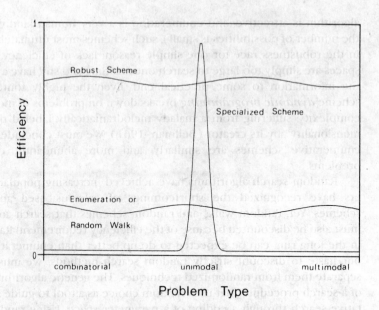

FIGURE 1.4   Many traditional schemes work well in a narrow problem domain. Enumerative schemes and random walks work equally inefficiently across a broad spectrum. A robust method works well across a broad spectrum of problems.

THE GOALS OF OPTIMIZATION

Before examining the mechanics and power of a simple genetic algorithm, we must be clearer about our goals when we say we want to optimize a function or a process. What are we trying to accomplish when we optimize? The conventional view is presented well by Beightler, Phillips, and Wilde (1979, p. 1):

> Man's longing for perfection finds expression in the theory of optimization. It studies how to describe and attain what is Best, once one knows how to measure and alter what is Good or Bad. . . . *Optimization theory* encompasses the quantitative study of optima and methods for finding them.

Thus optimization seeks to improve performance toward some optimal point or points. Note that this definition has two parts: (1) we seek improvement to approach some (2) optimal point. There is a clear distinction between the *process* of improvement and the *destination* or optimum itself. Yet, in judging optimization procedures we commonly focus solely upon convergence (does the method reach the optimum?) and forget entirely about interim performance. This emphasis stems from the origins of optimization in the calculus. It is not, however, a natural emphasis.

Consider a human decision maker, for example, a businessman. How do we judge his decisions? What criteria do we use to decide whether he has done a good or bad job? Usually we say he has done well when he makes adequate selections within the time and resources allotted. Goodness is judged relative to his competition. Does he produce a better widget? Does he get it to market more efficiently? With better promotion? We never judge a businessman by an attainment-of-the-best criterion; perfection is all too stern a taskmaster. As a result, we conclude that convergence to the best is not an issue in business or in most walks of life; we are only concerned with doing better relative to others. Thus, if we want more humanlike optimization tools, we are led to a reordering of the priorities of optimization. The most important goal of optimization is improvement. Can we get to some good, "satisficing" (Simon, 1969) level of performance quickly? Attainment of the optimum is much less important for complex systems. It would be nice to be perfect: meanwhile, we can only strive to improve. In the next chapter we watch the genetic algorithm for these qualities; here we outline some important differences between genetic algorithms and more traditional methods.

HOW ARE GENETIC ALGORITHMS DIFFERENT FROM TRADITIONAL METHODS?

In order for genetic algorithms to surpass their more traditional cousins in the quest for robustness, GAs must differ in some very fundamental ways. Genetic algorithms are different from more normal optimization and search procedures in four ways:

1. GAs work with a coding of the parameter set, not the parameters themselves.
2. GAs search from a population of points, not a single point.
3. GAs use payoff (objective function) information, not derivatives or other auxiliary knowledge.
4. GAs use probabilistic transition rules, not deterministic rules.

Genetic algorithms require the natural parameter set of the optimization problem to be coded as a finite-length string over some finite alphabet. As an example, consider the optimization problem posed in Fig. 1.5. We wish to maximize the function $f(x) = x^2$ on the integer interval [0, 31]. With more traditional methods we would be tempted to twiddle with the parameter x, turning it like the vertical hold knob on a television set, until we reached the highest objective function value. With GAs, the first step of our optimization process is to code the parameter x as a finite-length string. There are many ways to code the x parameter, and Chapter 3 examines some of these in detail. At the moment, let's consider an optimization problem where the coding comes a bit more naturally.

Consider the black box switching problem illustrated in Fig. 1.6. This problem concerns a black box device with a bank of five input switches. For every setting of the five switches, there is an output signal f, mathematically $f = f(s)$,

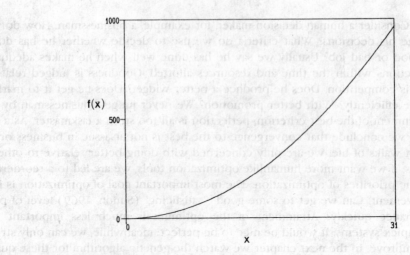

FIGURE 1.5   A simple function optimization example, the function $f(x) = x^2$ on the integer interval [0, 31].

where s is a particular setting of the five switches. The objective of the problem is to set the switches to obtain the maximum possible f value. With other methods of optimization we might work directly with the parameter set (the switch settings) and toggle switches from one setting to another using the transition rules of our particular method. With genetic algorithms, we first code the switches as a finite-length string. A simple code can be generated by considering a string of five 1's and 0's where each of the five switches is represented by a 1 if the switch is on and a 0 if the switch is off. With this coding, the string 11110 codes the setting where the first four switches are on and the fifth switch is off. Some of the codings introduced later will not be so obvious, but at this juncture we acknowledge that genetic algorithms use codings. Later it will be apparent

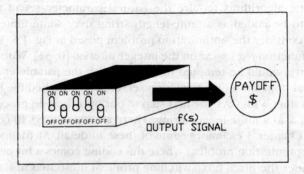

FIGURE 1.6   A black box optimization problem with five on-off switches illustrates the idea of a coding and a payoff measure. Genetic algorithms only require these two things: they don't need to know the workings of the black box.

that genetic algorithms exploit coding similarities in a very general way; as a result, they are largely unconstrained by the limitations of other methods (continuity, derivative existence, unimodality, and so on).

In many optimization methods, we move gingerly from a single point in the decision space to the next using some transition rule to determine the next point. This point-to-point method is dangerous because it is a perfect prescription for locating false peaks in multimodal (many-peaked) search spaces. By contrast, GAs work from a rich database of points simultaneously (a population of strings), climbing many peaks in parallel; thus, the probability of finding a false peak is reduced over methods that go point to point. As an example, let's consider our black box optimization problem (Fig. 1.6) again. Other techniques for solving this problem might start with one set of switch settings, apply some transition rules, and generate a new trial switch setting. A genetic algorithm starts with a population of strings and thereafter generates successive populations of strings. For example, in the five-switch problem, a random start using successive coin flips (head = 1, tail = 0) might generate the initial population of size $n = 4$ (small by genetic algorithm standards):

```
01101
11000
01000
10011
```

After this start, successive populations are generated using the genetic algorithm. By working from a population of well-adapted diversity instead of a single point, the genetic algorithm adheres to the old adage that there is safety in numbers; we will soon see how this parallel flavor contributes to a genetic algorithm's robustness.

Many search techniques require much auxiliary information in order to work properly. For example, gradient techniques need derivatives (calculated analytically or numerically) in order to be able to climb the current peak, and other local search procedures like the greedy techniques of combinatorial optimization (Lawler, 1976; Syslo, Deo, and Kowalik, 1983) require access to most if not all tabular parameters. By contrast, genetic algorithms have no need for all this auxiliary information: GAs are blind. To perform an effective search for better and better structures, they only require payoff values (objective function values) associated with individual strings. This characteristic makes a GA a more canonical method than many search schemes. After all, every search problem has a metric (or metrics) relevant to the search; however, different search problems have vastly different forms of auxiliary information. Only if we refuse to use this auxiliary information can we hope to develop the broadly based schemes we desire. On the other hand, the refusal to use specific knowledge when it does exist can place an upper bound on the performance of an algorithm when it goes head to head with methods designed for that problem. Chapter 5 examines ways to use nonpayoff information in so-called knowledge-directed genetic algorithms; however, at this juncture we stress the importance of the blindness assumption to pure genetic algorithm robustness.

Unlike many methods, GAs use probabilistic transition rules to guide their search. To persons familiar with deterministic methods this seems odd, but the use of probability does not suggest that the method is some simple random search; this is not decision making at the toss of a coin. Genetic algorithms use random choice as a tool to guide a search toward regions of the search space with likely improvement.

Taken together, these four differences—direct use of a coding, search from a population, blindness to auxiliary information, and randomized operators—contribute to a genetic algorithm's robustness and resulting advantage over other more commonly used techniques. The next section introduces a simple three-operator genetic algorithm.

A SIMPLE GENETIC ALGORITHM

The mechanics of a simple genetic algorithm are surprisingly simple, involving nothing more complex than copying strings and swapping partial strings. The explanation of why this simple process works is much more subtle and powerful. Simplicity of operation and power of effect are two of the main attractions of the genetic algorithm approach.

The previous section pointed out how genetic algorithms process populations of strings. Recalling the black box switching problem, remember that the initial population had four strings:

```
01101
11000
01000
10011
```

Also recall that this population was chosen at random through 20 successive flips of an unbiased coin. We now must define a set of simple operations that take this initial population and generate successive populations that (we hope) improve over time.

A simple genetic algorithm that yields good results in many practical problems is composed of three operators:

1. Reproduction
2. Crossover
3. Mutation

Reproduction is a process in which individual strings are copied according to their objective function values, f (biologists call this function the fitness function). Intuitively, we can think of the function f as some measure of profit, utility, or goodness that we want to maximize. Copying strings according to their fitness values means that strings with a higher value have a higher probability of contributing one or more offspring in the next generation. This operator, of course, is an artificial version of natural selection, a Darwinian survival of the fittest

TABLE 1.1 **Sample Problem Strings and Fitness Values**

No.	String	Fitness	% of Total
1	01101	169	14.4
2	11000	576	49.2
3	01000	64	5.5
4	10011	361	30.9
Total		1170	100.0

among string creatures. In natural populations fitness is determined by a creature's ability to survive predators, pestilence, and the other obstacles to adulthood and subsequent reproduction. In our unabashedly artificial setting, the objective function is the final arbiter of the string-creature's life or death.

The reproduction operator may be implemented in algorithmic form in a number of ways. Perhaps the easiest is to create a biased roulette wheel where each current string in the population has a roulette wheel slot sized in proportion to its fitness. Suppose the sample population of four strings in the black box problem has objective or fitness function values f as shown in Table 1.1 (for now we accept these values as the output of some unknown and arbitrary black box—later we will examine a function and coding that generate these same values).

Summing the fitness over all four strings, we obtain a total of 1170. The percentage of population total fitness is also shown in the table. The corresponding weighted roulette wheel for this generation's reproduction is shown in Fig. 1.7. To reproduce, we simply spin the weighted roulette wheel thus defined four times. For the example problem, string number 1 has a fitness value of 169, which represents 14.4 percent of the total fitness. As a result, string 1 is given 14.4 percent of the biased roulette wheel, and each spin turns up string 1 with prob-

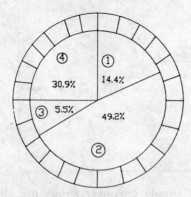

FIGURE 1.7 **Simple reproduction allocates offspring strings using a roulette wheel with slots sized according to fitness. The sample wheel is sized for the problem of Tables 1.1 and 1.2.**

ability 0.144. Each time we require another offspring, a simple spin of the weighted roulette wheel yields the reproduction candidate. In this way, more highly fit strings have a higher number of offspring in the succeeding generation. Once a string has been selected for reproduction, an exact replica of the string is made. This string is then entered into a mating pool, a tentative new population, for further genetic operator action.

After reproduction, simple crossover (Fig. 1.8) may proceed in two steps. First, members of the newly reproduced strings in the mating pool are mated at random. Second, each pair of strings undergoes crossing over as follows: an integer position k along the string is selected uniformly at random between 1 and the string length less one $[1, l - 1]$. Two new strings are created by swapping all characters between positions $k + 1$ and l inclusively. For example, consider strings A_1 and A_2 from our example initial population:

$$A_1 = 0\ 1\ 1\ 0\ |\ 1$$
$$A_2 = 1\ 1\ 0\ 0\ |\ 0$$

Suppose in choosing a random number between 1 and 4, we obtain a $k = 4$ (as indicated by the separator symbol $|$). The resulting crossover yields two new strings where the prime ($'$) means the strings are part of the new generation:

$$A'_1 = 0\ 1\ 1\ 0\ 0$$
$$A'_2 = 1\ 1\ 0\ 0\ 1$$

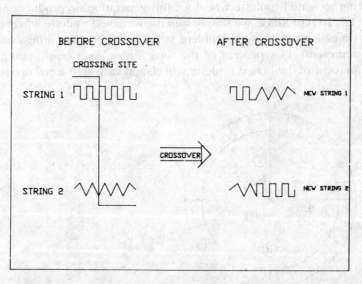

FIGURE 1.8 A schematic of simple crossover shows the alignment of two strings and the partial exchange of information, using a cross site chosen at random.

The mechanics of reproduction and crossover are surprisingly simple, involving random number generation, string copies, and some partial string exchanges. Nonetheless, the combined emphasis of reproduction and the structured, though randomized, information exchange of crossover give genetic algorithms much of their power. At first this seems surprising. How can two such simple (and computationally trivial) operators result in anything useful, let alone a rapid and robust search mechanism? Furthermore, doesn't it seem a little strange that chance should play such a fundamental role in a directed search process? We will examine a partial answer to the first of these two questions in a moment; the answer to the second question was well recognized by the mathematician J. Hadamard (1949, p. 29):

> We shall see a little later that the possibility of imputing discovery to pure chance is already excluded. . . . On the contrary, that there is an intervention of chance but also a necessary work of unconsciousness, the latter implying and not contradicting the former. . . . Indeed, it is obvious that invention or discovery, be it in mathematics or anywhere else takes place by combining ideas.

Hadamard suggests that even though discovery is not a result—cannot be a result—of pure chance, it is almost certainly guided by directed serendipity. Furthermore, Hadamard hints that a proper role for chance in a more humanlike discovery mechanism is to cause the juxtaposition of different notions. It is interesting that genetic algorithms adopt Hadamard's mix of direction and chance in a manner that efficiently builds new solutions from the best partial solutions of previous trials.

To see this, consider a population of n strings (perhaps the four-string population for the black box problem) over some appropriate alphabet, coded so that each is a complete *idea* or prescription for performing a particular task (in this case, each string is one complete switch-setting idea). Substrings within each string (idea) contain various *notions* of what is important or relevant to the task. Viewed in this way, the population contains not just a sample of n ideas; rather, it contains a multitude of notions and rankings of those notions for task performance. Genetic algorithms ruthlessly exploit this wealth of information by (1) reproducing high-quality notions according to their performance and (2) crossing these notions with many other high-performance notions from other strings. Thus, the action of crossover with previous reproduction speculates on new ideas constructed from the high-performance building blocks (notions) of past trials. In passing, we note that despite the somewhat fuzzy definition of a notion, we have not limited a notion to simple linear combinations of single features or pairs of features. Biologists have long recognized that evolution must efficiently process the epistasis (positionwise nonlinearity) that arises in nature. In a similar manner, the notion processing of genetic algorithms must effectively process notions even when they depend upon their component features in highly nonlinear and complex ways.

Exchanging of notions to form new ideas is appealing intuitively, if we think in terms of the process of *innovation*. What is an innovative idea? As Hadamard suggests, most often it is a juxtaposition of things that have worked well in the past. In much the same way, reproduction and crossover combine to search potentially pregnant new ideas. This experience of emphasis and crossing is analogous to the human interaction many of us have observed at a trade show or scientific conference. At a widget conference, for example, various widget experts from around the world gather to discuss the latest in widget technology. After the lecture sessions, they all pair off around the bar to exchange widget stories. Well-known widget experts, of course, are in greater demand and exchange more ideas, thoughts, and notions with their lesser known widget colleagues. When the show ends, the widget people return to their widget laboratories to try out a surfeit of widget innovations. The process of reproduction and crossover in a genetic algorithm is this kind of exchange. High-performance notions are repeatedly tested and exchanged in the search for better and better performance.

If reproduction according to fitness combined with crossover gives genetic algorithms the bulk of their processing power, what then is the purpose of the mutation operator? Not surprisingly, there is much confusion about the role of mutation in genetics (both natural and artificial). Perhaps it is the result of too many B movies detailing the exploits of mutant eggplants that consume mass quantities of Tokyo or Chicago, but whatever the cause for the confusion, we find that mutation plays a decidedly secondary role in the operation of genetic algorithms. Mutation is needed because, even though reproduction and crossover effectively search and recombine extant notions, occasionally they may become overzealous and lose some potentially useful genetic material (1's or 0's at particular locations). In artificial genetic systems, the mutation operator protects against such an irrecoverable loss. In the simple GA, mutation is the occasional (with small probability) random alteration of the value of a string position. In the binary coding of the black box problem, this simply means changing a 1 to a 0 and vice versa. By itself, mutation is a random walk through the string space. When used sparingly with reproduction and crossover, it is an insurance policy against premature loss of important notions.

That the mutation operator plays a secondary role in the simple GA, we simply note that the frequency of mutation to obtain good results in empirical genetic algorithm studies is on the order of one mutation per thousand bit (position) transfers. Mutation rates are similarly small (or smaller) in natural populations, leading us to conclude that mutation is appropriately considered as a secondary mechanism of genetic algorithm adaptation.

Other genetic operators and reproductive plans have been abstracted from the study of biological example. However, the three examined in this section, reproduction, simple crossover, and mutation, have proved to be both computationally simple and effective in attacking a number of important optimization problems. In the next section, we perform a hand simulation of the simple genetic algorithm to demonstrate both its mechanics and its power.

GENETIC ALGORITHMS AT WORK—A SIMULATION BY HAND

Let's apply our simple genetic algorithm to a particular optimization problem step by step. Consider the problem of maximizing the function $f(x) = x^2$, where x is permitted to vary between 0 and 31, a function displayed earlier as Fig. 1.5. To use a genetic algorithm we must first code the decision variables of our problem as some finite-length string. For this problem, we will code the variable x simply as a binary unsigned integer of length 5. Before we proceed with the simulation, let's briefly review the notion of a binary integer. As decadigited creatures, we have little problem handling base 10 integers and arithmetic. For example, the five-digit number 53,095 may be thought of as

$$5 \cdot 10 + 3 \cdot 10^3 + 0 \cdot 10^2 + 9 \cdot 10^1 + 5 \cdot 1 = 53,095.$$

In base 2 arithmetic, we of course only have two digits to work with, 0 and 1, and as an example the number 10,011 decodes to the base 10 number

$$1 \cdot 2^4 + 0 \cdot 2^3 + 0 \cdot 2^2 + 1 \cdot 2^1 + 1 \cdot 2^0 = 16 + 2 + 1 = 19.$$

With a five-bit (*binary digit*) unsigned integer we can obtain numbers between 0 (00000) and 31 (11111). With a well-defined objective function and coding, we now simulate a single generation of a genetic algorithm with reproduction, crossover, and mutation.

To start off, we select an initial population at random. We select a population of size 4 by tossing a fair coin 20 times. We can skip this step by using the initial population created in this way earlier for the black box switching problem. Looking at this population, shown on the left-hand side of Table 1.2, we observe that the decoded x values are presented along with the fitness or objective function values $f(x)$. To make sure we know how the fitness values $f(x)$ are calculated from the string representation, let's take a look at the third string of the initial population, string 01000. Decoding this string as an unsigned binary integer, we note that there is a single one in the $2^3 = 8$'s position. Hence for string 01000 we obtain $x = 8$. To calculate the fitness or objective function we simply square the x value and obtain the resulting fitness value $f(x) = 64$. Other x and $f(x)$ values may be obtained similarly.

You may notice that the fitness or objective function values are the same as the black box values (compare Tables 1.1 and 1.2). This is no coincidence, and the black box optimization problem was well represented by the particular function, $f(x)$, and coding we are now using. Of course, the genetic algorithm need not know any of this; it is just as happy to optimize some arbitrary switching function (or any other finite coding and function for that matter) as some polynomial function with straightforward binary coding. This discussion simply reinforces one of the strengths of the genetic algorithm: by exploiting similarities in codings, genetic algorithms can deal effectively with a broader class of functions than can many other procedures.

A generation of the genetic algorithm begins with reproduction. We select the mating pool of the next generation by spinning the weighted roulette wheel

TABLE 1.2 A Genetic Algorithm by Hand

String No.	Initial Population (Randomly Generated)	x Value (Unsigned Integer)	$f(x)$ x^2	pselect$_i$ $\frac{f_i}{\Sigma f}$	Expected count $\frac{f_i}{\bar{f}}$	Actual Count (from Roulette Wheel)
1	0 1 1 0 1	13	169	0.14	0.58	1
2	1 1 0 0 0	24	576	0.49	1.97	2
3	0 1 0 0 0	8	64	0.06	0.22	0
4	1 0 0 1 1	19	361	0.31	1.23	1
Sum			1170	1.00	4.00	4.0
Average			293	0.25	1.00	1.0
Max			576	0.49	1.97	2.0

(shown in Fig. 1.7) four times. Actual simulation of this process using coin tosses has resulted in string 1 and string 4 receiving one copy in the mating pool, string 2 receiving two copies, and string 3 receiving no copies, as shown in the center of Table 1.2. Comparing this with the expected number of copies ($n \cdot$pselect$_i$) we have obtained what we should expect: the best get more copies, the average stay even, and the worst die off.

With an active pool of strings looking for mates, simple crossover proceeds in two steps: (1) strings are mated randomly, using coin tosses to pair off the happy couples, and (2) mated string couples cross over, using coin tosses to select the crossing sites. Referring again to Table 1.2, random choice of mates has selected the second string in the mating pool to be mated with the first. With a crossing site of 4, the two strings 01101 and 11000 cross and yield two new strings 01100 and 11001. The remaining two strings in the mating pool are crossed at site 2; the resulting strings may be checked in the table.

The last operator, mutation, is performed on a bit-by-bit basis. We assume that the probability of mutation in this test is 0.001. With 20 transferred bit positions we should expect $20 \cdot 0.001 = 0.02$ bits to undergo mutation during a given generation. Simulation of this process indicates that no bits undergo mutation for this probability value. As a result, no bit positions are changed from 0 to 1 or vice versa during this generation.

Following reproduction, crossover, and mutation, the new population is ready to be tested. To do this, we simply decode the new strings created by the simple genetic algorithm and calculate the fitness function values from the x values thus decoded. The results of a single generation of the simulation are shown at the right of Table 1.2. While drawing concrete conclusions from a single trial of a stochastic process is, at best, a risky business, we start to see how genetic algorithms combine high-performance notions to achieve better performance. In the table, note how both the maximal and average performance have improved in the new population. The population average fitness has improved from 293 to

TABLE 1.2 (*Continued*)

Mating Pool after Reproduction (Cross Site Shown)	Mate $\begin{pmatrix} \text{Randomly} \\ \text{Selected} \end{pmatrix}$	Crossover Site $\begin{pmatrix} \text{Randomly} \\ \text{Selected} \end{pmatrix}$	New Population	x Value	$f(x)$ x^2
0 1 1 0 | 1	2	4	0 1 1 0 0	12	144
1 1 0 0 | 0	1	4	1 1 0 0 1	25	625
1 1 | 0 0 0	4	2	1 1 0 1 1	27	729
1 0 | 0 1 1	3	2	1 0 0 0 0	16	256
					1754
					439
					729

NOTES:

1) Initial population chosen by four repetitions of five coin tosses where heads = 1, tails = 0.

2) Reproduction performed through 1 part in 8 simulation of roulette wheel selection (three coin tosses).

3) Crossover performed through binary decoding of 2 coin tosses (TT = 00_2 = 0 = cross site 1, HH = 11_2 = 3 = cross site 4).

4) Crossover probability assumed to be unity p_c = 1.0.

5) Mutation probability assumed to be 0.001, p_m = 0.001, Expected mutations = 5·4·0.001 = 0.02. No mutations expected during a single generation. None simulated.

439 in one generation. The maximum fitness has increased from 576 to 729 during that same period. Although random processes help cause these happy circumstances, we start to see that this improvement is no fluke. The best string of the first generation (11000) receives two copies because of its high, above-average performance. When this combines at random with the next highest string (10011) and is crossed at location 2 (again at random), one of the resulting strings (11011) proves to be a very good choice indeed.

This event is an excellent illustration of the ideas and notions analogy developed in the previous section. In this case, the resulting good idea is the combination of two above-average notions, namely the substrings 11––– and –––11. Although the argument is still somewhat heuristic, we start to see how genetic algorithms effect a robust search. In the next section, we expand our understanding of these concepts by analyzing genetic algorithms in terms of schemata or similarity templates.

The intuitive viewpoint developed thus far has much appeal. We have compared the genetic algorithm with certain human search processes commonly called innovative or creative. Furthermore, hand simulation of the simple genetic algorithm has given us some confidence that indeed something interesting is going on here. Yet, something is missing. What is being processed by genetic algorithms and how do we know whether processing it (whatever it is) will lead to optimal or near optimal results in a particular problem? Clearly, as scientists.

engineers, and business managers we need to understand the what and the how of genetic algorithm performance.

To obtain this understanding, we examine the raw data available for any search procedure and discover that we can search more effectively if we exploit important similarities in the coding we use. This leads us to develop the important notion of a *similarity template,* or *schema.* This in turn leads us to a keystone of the genetic algorithm approach, the *building block hypothesis.*

GRIST FOR THE SEARCH MILL—IMPORTANT SIMILARITIES

For much too long we have ignored a fundamental question. In a search process given only payoff data (fitness values), what information is contained in a population of strings and their objective function values to help guide a directed search for improvement? To ask this question more clearly, consider the strings and fitness values originally displayed in Table 1.1 from the simulation of the previous section (the black box problem) and gathered below for convenience:

String	Fitness
01101	169
11000	576
01000	64
10011	361

What information is contained in this population to guide a directed search for improvement? On the face of it, there is not very much: four independent samples of different strings with their fitness values. As we stare at the page, however, quite naturally we start scanning up and down the string column, and we notice certain similarities among the strings. Exploring these similarities in more depth, we notice that certain string patterns seem highly associated with good performance. The longer we stare at the strings and their fitness values, the greater is the temptation to experiment with these high fitness associations. It seems perfectly reasonable to play mix and match with some of the substrings that are highly correlated with past success. For example, in the sample population, the strings starting with a 1 seem to be among the best. Might this be an important ingredient in optimizing this function? Certainly with our function $(f(x) = x^2)$ and our coding (a five-bit unsigned integer) we know it is (why is this true?). But, what are we doing here? Really, two separate things. First, we are seeking similarities among strings in the population. Second, we are looking for causal relationships between these similarities and high fitness. In so doing, we admit a wealth of new information to help guide a search. To see how much and precisely what information we admit, let us consider the important concept of a schema (plural, *schemata*), or similarity template.

SIMILARITY TEMPLATES (SCHEMATA)

In some sense we are no longer interested in strings as strings alone. Since important similarities among highly fit strings can help guide a search, we question how one string can be similar to its fellow strings. Specifically we ask, in what ways is a string a representative of other string classes with similarities at certain string positions? The framework of schemata provides the tool to answer these questions.

A schema (Holland, 1968, 1975) is a similarity template describing a subset of strings with similarities at certain string positions. For this discussion, let us once again limit ourselves without loss of generality to the binary alphabet {0,1}. We motivate a schema most easily by appending a special symbol to this alphabet; we add the * or *don't care* symbol. With this extended alphabet we can now create strings (schemata) over the ternary alphabet {0, 1, *}, and the meaning of the schema is clear if we think of it as a pattern matching device: a schema matches a particular string if at every location in the schema a 1 matches a 1 in the string, a 0 matches a 0, or a * matches either. As an example, consider the strings and schemata of length 5. The schema *0000 matches two strings, namely {10000, 00000}. As another example, the schema *111* describes a subset with four members {01110, 01111, 11110, 11111}. As one last example, the schema 0*1** matches any of the eight strings of length 5 that begin with a 0 and have a 1 in the third position. As you can start to see, the idea of a schema gives us a powerful and compact way to talk about all the well-defined similarities among finite-length strings over a finite alphabet. We should emphasize that the * is only a metasymbol (a symbol about other symbols); it is never explicitly processed by the genetic algorithm It is simply a notational device that allows description of all possible similarities among strings of a particular length and alphabet.

Counting the total number of possible schemata is an enlightening exercise. In the previous example, with $l = 5$, we note there are $3 \cdot 3 \cdot 3 \cdot 3 \cdot 3 = 3^5 = 243$ different similarity templates because each of the five positions may be a 0, 1, or * In general, for alphabets of cardinality (number of alphabet characters) k, there are $(k + 1)^l$ schemata. At first blush, it appears that schemata are making the search more difficult. For an alphabet with k elements there are only (only?) k^l different strings of length l. Why consider the $(k + 1)^l$ schemata and enlarge the space of concern? Put another way, the length 5 example now has only $2^5 = 32$ different alternative strings. Why make matters more difficult by considering $3^5 = 243$ schemata? In fact, the reasoning discussed in the previous section makes things easier. Do you recall glancing up and down the list of four strings and fitness values and trying to figure out what to do next? We recognized that if we considered the strings separately, then we only had four pieces of information;

however, when we considered the strings, their fitness values, and the similarities among the strings in the population, we admitted a wealth of new information to help direct our search. How much information do we admit by considering the similarities? The answer to this question is related to the number of unique schemata contained in the population. To count this quantity exactly requires knowledge of the strings in a particular population. To get a bound on the number of schemata in a particular population, we first count the number of schemata contained in an individual string, and then we get an upper bound on the total number of schemata in the population.

To see this, consider a single string of length 5: 11111, for example. This string is a member of 2^5 schemata because each position may take on its actual value or a don't care symbol. In general, a particular string contains 2^l schemata. As a result, a population of size n contains somewhere between 2^l and $n \cdot 2^l$ schemata, depending upon the population diversity. This fact verifies our earlier intuition. The original motivation for considering important similarities was to get more information to help guide our search. The counting argument shows that a wealth of information about important similarities is indeed contained in even moderately sized populations. We will examine how genetic algorithms effectively exploit this information. At this juncture, some parallel processing appears to be needed if we are to make use of all this information in a timely fashion.

These counting arguments are well and good, but where does this all lead? More pointedly, of the 2^l to $n \cdot 2^l$ schemata contained in a population, how many are actually processed in a useful manner by the genetic algorithm? To obtain the answer to this question, we consider the effect of reproduction, crossover, and mutation on the growth or decay of important schemata from generation to generation. The effect of reproduction on a particular schema is easy to determine; since more highly fit strings have higher probabilities of selection, on average we give an ever increasing number of samples to the observed best similarity patterns (this is a good thing to do, as is shown in the next chapter); however, reproduction alone samples no new points in the space. What then happens to a particular schema when crossover is introduced? Crossover leaves a schema unscathed if it does not cut the schema, but it may disrupt a schema when it does. For example, consider the two schemata 1***0 and **11*. The first is likely to be disrupted by crossover, whereas the second is relatively unlikely to be destroyed. As a result, schemata of short defining length are left alone by crossover and reproduced at a good sampling rate by reproduction operator. Mutation at normal, low rates does not disrupt a particular schema very frequently and we are left with a startling conclusion. Highly fit, short-defining-length schemata (we call them *building blocks*) are propagated generation to generation by giving exponentially increasing samples to the observed best; all this goes in parallel with no special bookkeeping or special memory other than our population of n strings. In the next chapter we will count how many schemata are processed usefully in each generation. It turns out that the number is something like n^3. This compares favorably with the number of function evaluations (n). Because this processing leverage is so important (and apparently unique to genetic algorithms), we give it a special name, *implicit parallelism*.

LEARNING THE LINGO

The power behind the simple operations of our genetic algorithm is at least intuitively clearer if we think of building blocks. Some questions remain: How do we know that building blocks lead to improvement? Why is it a near optimal strategy to give exponentially increasing samples to the best? How can we calculate the number of schemata usefully processed by the genetic algorithm? These questions are answered fully in the next chapter, but first we need to master the terminology used by researchers who work with genetic algorithms. Because genetic algorithms are rooted in both natural genetics and computer science, the terminology used in the GA literature is an unholy mix of the natural and the artificial. Until now we have focused on the artificial side of the genetic algorithm's ancestry and talked about strings, alphabets, string positions, and the like. We review the correspondence between these terms and their natural counterparts to connect with the growing GA literature and also to permit our own occasional slip of a natural utterance or two.

Roughly speaking, the *strings* of artificial genetic systems are analogous to *chromosomes* in biological systems. In natural systems, one or more chromosomes combine to form the total genetic prescription for the construction and operation of some organism. In natural systems the total genetic package is called the *genotype*. In artificial genetic systems the total package of strings is called a *structure* (in the early chapters of this book, the structure will consist of a single string, so the text refers to strings and structures interchangeably until it is necessary to differentiate between them). In natural systems, the organism formed by the interaction of the total genetic package with its environment is called the *phenotype*. In artificial genetic systems, the structures decode to form a particular *parameter set, solution alternative,* or *point* (in the solution space). The designer of an artificial genetic system has a variety of alternatives for coding both numeric and nonnumeric parameters. We will confront codings and coding principles in later chapters; for now, we stick to our consideration of GA and natural terminology.

In natural terminology, we say that chromosomes are composed of *genes*, which may take on some number of values called *alleles*. In genetics, the position of a gene (its *locus*) is identified separately from the gene's function. Thus, we can talk of a particular gene, for example an animal's eye color gene, its locus, position 10, and its allele value, blue eyes. In artificial genetic search we say that strings are composed of *features* or *detectors,* which take on different *values*. Features may be located at different *positions* on the string. The correspondence between natural and artificial terminology is summarized in Table 1.3.

Thus far, we have not distinguished between a gene (a particular character) and its locus (its position); the position of a bit in a string has determined its meaning (how it decodes) uniformly throughout a population and throughout time. For example, the string 10000 is decoded as a binary unsigned integer 16 (base 10) because implicitly the 1 is in the 16's place. It is not necessary to limit codings like this, however. A later chapter presents more advanced structures that treat locus and gene separately.

TABLE 1.3 Comparison of Natural and GA Terminology

Natural	Genetic Algorithm
chromosome	string
gene	feature, character, or detector
allele	feature value
locus	string position
genotype	structure
phenotype	parameter set, alternative solution, a decoded structure
epistasis	nonlinearity

SUMMARY

This chapter has laid the foundation for understanding genetic algorithms, their mechanics and their power. We are led to these methods by our search for robustness; natural systems are robust—efficient and efficacious—as they adapt to a wide variety of environments. By abstracting nature's adaptation algorithm of choice in artificial form we hope to achieve similar breadth of performance. In fact, genetic algorithms have demonstrated their capability in a number of analytical and empirical studies.

The chapter has presented the detailed mechanics of a simple, three-operator genetic algorithm. Genetic algorithms operate on populations of strings, with the string coded to represent some underlying parameter set. Reproduction, cross-over, and mutation are applied to successive string populations to create new string populations. These operators are simplicity itself, involving nothing more complex than random number generation, string copying, and partial string exchanging; yet, despite their simplicity, the resulting search performance is wide-ranging and impressive. Genetic algorithms realize an innovative notion exchange among strings and thus connect to our own ideas of human search or discovery. A simulation of one generation of the simple genetic algorithm has helped illustrate both the detail and the power of the method.

Four differences separate genetic algorithms from more conventional optimization techniques:

1. Direct manipulation of a coding
2. Search from a population, not a single point
3. Search via sampling, a blind search
4. Search using stochastic operators, not deterministic rules

Genetic algorithms manipulate decision or control variable representations at the string level to exploit similarities among high-performance strings. Other methods usually deal with functions and their control variables directly. Because genetic algorithms operate at the coding level, they are difficult to fool even when the function may be difficult for traditional schemes.

Genetic algorithms work from a population; many other methods work from a single point. In this way, GAs find safety in numbers. By maintaining a population of well-adapted sample points, the probability of reaching a false peak is reduced.

Genetic algorithms achieve much of their breadth by ignoring information except that concerning payoff. Other methods rely heavily on such information, and in problems where the necessary information is not available or difficult to obtain, these other techniques break down. GAs remain general by exploiting information available in any search problem. Genetic algorithms process similarities in the underlying coding together with information ranking the structures according to their survival capability in the current environment. By exploiting such widely available information, GAs may be applied in virtually any problem.

The transition rules of genetic algorithms are stochastic; many other methods have deterministic transition rules. A distinction exists, however, between the randomized operators of genetic algorithms and other methods that are simple random walks. Genetic algorithms use random choice to guide a highly exploitative search. This may seem unusual, using chance to achieve directed results (the best points), but nature is full of precedent.

We have started a more rigorous appraisal of genetic algorithm performance through the concept of schemata or similarity templates. A schema is a string over an extended alphabet, $\{0,1,*\}$ where the 0 and the 1 retain their normal meaning and the * is a wild card or don't care symbol. This notational device greatly simplifies the analysis of the genetic algorithm method because it explicitly recognizes all the possible similarities in a population of strings. We have discussed how building blocks—short, high-performance schemata—are combined to form strings with expected higher performance. This occurs because building blocks are sampled at near optimal rates and recombined via crossover. Mutation has little effect on these building blocks; like an insurance policy, it helps prevent the irrecoverable loss of potentially important genetic material.

The simple genetic algorithm studied in this chapter has much to recommend it. In the next chapter, we will analyze its operation more carefully. Following this, we will implement the simple GA in a short computer program and examine some applications in practical problems.

■ PROBLEMS

1.1. Consider a black box containing eight multiple-position switches. Switches 1 and 2 may be set in any of 16 positions. Switches 3, 4, and 5 are four-position switches, and switches 6–8 have only two positions. Calculate the number of unique switch settings possible for this black box device.

1.2. For the black box device of Problem 1.1, design a natural string coding that uses eight positions, one position for each switch. Count the number of switch settings represented by your coding and count the number of schemata or similarity templates inherent in your coding.

1.3. For the black box device of Problem 1.1, design a minimal binary coding for the eight switches and compare the number of schemata in this coding to a coding for Problem 1.2

1.4. Consider a binary string of length 11, and consider a schema, 1*********1. Under crossover with uniform crossover site selection, calculate a lower limit on the probability of this schema surviving crossover. Calculate survival probabilities under the same assumptions for the following schemata: ****10*****, 11*********, ***111*****, ****1*0****, **1***1**0*.

1.5. If the distance between the outermost alleles of a particular schema is called its *defining length* δ, derive an approximate expression for the survival probability of a particular schema of total length l and defining length δ under the operation of simple crossover.

1.6. Six strings have the following fitness function values: 5, 10, 15, 25, 50, 100. Under roulette wheel selection, calculate the expected number of copies of each string in the mating pool if a constant population size, $n = 6$, is maintained.

1.7. Instead of using roulette wheel selection during reproduction, suppose we define a copy count for each string, $ncount_i$ as follows: $ncount_i = f_i/\bar{f}$ where f_i is the fitness of the ith string and $\bar{f}$ is the average fitness of the population. The copy count is then used to generate the number of members of the mating pool by giving the integer part of $ncount_i$ copies to the ith string and an additional copy with probability equal to the fractional part of $ncount_i$. For example, with $f_i = 100$ and $\bar{f} = 80$, string i would receive an $ncount_i$ of 1.25, and thus would receive one copy with probability 1.0 and another copy with probability 0.25. Using the string fitness values in Problem 1.6, calculate the expected number of copies for each of the six strings. Calculate the total number of strings expected in the gene pool under this form of reproduction.

1.8. The form of reproduction discussed in Problem 1.7 is sometimes called reproduction with expected number control. In a short essay, explain why this is so. In what ways are roulette wheel selection and expected number control similar? In what ways are they different?

1.9. Suppose the probability of a mutation at a single bit position is 0.1. Calculate the probability of a 10-bit string surviving mutation without change. Calculate the probability of a 20-bit string surviving mutation without change. Recalculate the survival probabilities for both 10- and 20-bit strings when the mutation probability is 0.01.

1.10. Consider the strings and schemata of length 11. For the following schemata, calculate the probability of surviving mutation if the probability of mutation is 0.1 at a single bit position: ***1**0****, 1*********0, ***111*****, *1000010*11. Recalculate the survival probabilities for a mutation probability $p_m = 0.01$.

■ COMPUTER ASSIGNMENTS

A. One of the primitive functions required in doing genetic algorithms on a computer is the ability to generate pseudorandom numbers. The numbers are pseudorandom because as von Neumann once said, "Anyone who considers arithmetical methods of producing random digits is, of course, in a state of sin." As part of this assignment, go forth and sin some more. Use the random number generator given in Appendix B to create a program where you generate 1000 random numbers between 0 and 1. Keep track of how many numbers are generated in each of the four quartiles, 0–0.25, 0.25–0.5, 0.5–0.75, 0.75–1.0, and compare the actual counts with the expected number. Is the difference within reasonable limits? How can you quantify whether the difference is reasonable?

B. Suppose you have 10 strings with the following probabilities of selection in the next generation: 0.1, 0.2, 0.05, 0.15, 0.0, 0.11, 0.07, 0.04, 0.00, 0.12, 0.16. Given that these are the only possible alternatives, calculate whether the probabilities are consistent. Write a computer program that simulates roulette wheel selection for these 10 strings. Spin the wheel 1000 times and keep track of the number of selections for each string, comparing this number to the expected number of selections.

C. Write a function that generates a pseudorandom integer between some specified lower limit and some specified upper limit. Test the program by generating 1000 numbers between 3 and 12. Keep track of the quantity of each number selected and compare these figures to the expected quantities.

D. Create a procedure that receives two binary strings and a crossing site value, performs simple crossover, and returns two offspring strings. Test the program by crossing the following strings of length 10: 1011101011, 0000110100. Try crossing site values of − 3, 1, 6, and 20.

E. Create a function *mutation* that complements a particular bit value with specified mutation probability p_m. Test the function by performing 1000 calls to mutation using mutation probabilities p_m = 0.001, 0.01, 0.1. Compare the realized number of mutations to the expected number.

F. Using the simple crossover operator of Assignment D, repeatedly apply the crossover operator to strings contained within the following population of size $n = 200$ and $l = 5$:

    100 copies of 11100
    100 copies of 00011

Perform crossover ($p_c = 1.0$) for 50 generations without replacement under no selection. Compare the initial and final distributions of strings. Also compare the expected quantity of each string to the realized quantity in generation 50.

2 | Genetic Algorithms Revisited: Mathematical Foundations

The broad brush of Chapter 1 painted an accurate, if somewhat crude, picture of genetic algorithms and their mechanics and power. Perhaps these brush strokes appeal to your own sense of human discovery and search. That somehow a regular though randomized procedure can achieve some of the breadth and intuitive flair of human search seems almost too good to be true. That this discovery procedure should mirror the natural processes that created the species possessing the procedure is a recursion of which Godel, Escher, or Bach (Hofstadter, 1979) could each have been proud. Despite their intuitive appeal, and despite their symmetry, it is crucial that we back these fuzzy feelings and speculations about genetic algorithms using cold, mathematical facts.

Actually, we have already begun a more rigorous appraisal of GAs. Toward the end of the last chapter, the fundamental concept of a schema or similarity template was introduced. Quantitatively, we found that there are indeed a large number of similarities to exploit in a population of strings. Intuitively, we saw how genetic algorithms exploit in parallel the many similarities contained in building blocks or short, high-performance schemata. In this chapter, we make these observations more rigorous by doing several things. First, we count the schemata represented within a population of strings and consider which grow and which decay during any given generation. To do this, we consider the effect of reproduction, crossover, and mutation on a particular schema. This analysis leads to the fundamental theorem of genetic algorithms that quantifies these growth and decay rates more precisely; it also points to the mathematical form of this growth. This form is connected to an important and classical problem of decision theory, the two-armed bandit problem (and its extension, the k-armed bandit). The mathematical similarity between the optimal (minimal loss) solution to the two-armed and k-armed bandit and the equation describing the number of trials given to successive generations of schemata in the simple genetic algorithm is striking. Counting the number of schemata that are usefully processed by the simple genetic algorithm reveals tremendous leverage in the building block processing. Finally, we consider an important question: How do we know that combining building blocks leads to high performance in arbitrary problems? The question sparks our consideration of some relatively new tools of genetic algorithm analysis: schema transforms and the minimal deceptive problem.

WHO SHALL LIVE AND WHO SHALL DIE? THE FUNDAMENTAL THEOREM

The operation of genetic algorithms is remarkably straightforward. After all, we start with a random population of n strings, copy strings with some bias toward the best, mate and partially swap substrings, and mutate an occasional bit value for good measure. Even though genetic algorithms directly manipulate a population of strings in this straightforward manner, in Chapter 1 we started to recognize that this explicit processing of strings really causes the implicit processing of many schemata during each generation. To analyze the growth and decay of the many schemata contained in a population, we need some simple notation to add rigor to the discussion. We consider the operation of reproduction, crossover, and mutation on the schemata contained in the population.

We consider strings, without loss of generality, to be constructed over the binary alphabet $V = \{0, 1\}$. As a notational convenience, we refer to strings by capital letters and individual characters by lowercase letters subscripted by their position. For example, the seven-bit string $A = 0111000$ may be represented symbolically as follows:

$$A = a_1 a_2 a_3 a_4 a_5 a_6 a_-.$$

Here each of the a_i represents a single binary feature or detector (in accordance with natural analogy, we sometimes call the a_i's *genes*), where each feature may take on a value 1 or 0 (we sometimes call the a_i values *alleles*). In the particular string 0111000, a_1 is 0, a_2 is 1, a_3 is 1, etc. It is also possible to have strings where detectors are not ordered sequentially as in string A. For example a string A' could have the following ordering:

$$A' = a_2 a_6 a_1 a_3 a_- a_1 a_5.$$

A later chapter explores the effect of extending the representation to allow features to be located in a manner independent of their function. For now, assume that a feature's function may be determined by its position.

Meaningful genetic search requires a population of strings, and we consider a population of individual strings $A_j, j = 1, 2, \ldots, n$, contained in the population $A(t)$ at time (or generation) t where the boldface is used to denote a population.

Besides notation to describe populations, strings, bit positions, and alleles, we need convenient notation to describe the schemata contained in individual strings and populations. Let us consider a schema H taken from the three-letter alphabet $V+ = \{0, 1, *\}$. As discussed in the previous chapter, the additional symbol, the asterisk or star *, is a don't care or wild card symbol which matches either a 0 or a 1 at a particular position. For example, consider the length 7 schema $H = *11*0**$. Note that the string $A = 0111000$ discussed above is an example of the schema H, because the string alleles a_i match schema positions h_i at the fixed positions 2, 3, and 5.

From the results of the last chapter, recall that there are 3^l schemata or similarity defined over a binary string of length l. In general, for alphabets of cardinality k, there are $(k + 1)^l$ schemata. Furthermore, recall that in a string population with n members there are at most $n \cdot 2^l$ schemata contained in a population because each string is itself a representative of 2^l schemata. These counting arguments give us some feel for the magnitude of information being processed by genetic algorithms; however, to really understand the important building blocks of future solutions, we need to distinguish between different types of schemata.

All schemata are not created equal. Some are more specific than others. For example, the schema $011*1**$ is a more definite statement about important similarity than the schema $0******$. Furthermore, certain schema span more of the total string length than others. For example, the schema $1****1*$ spans a larger portion of the string than the schema $1*1****$. To quantify these ideas, we introduce two schema properties: schema *order* and *defining length*.

The order of a schema H, denoted by $o(H)$, is simply the number of fixed positions (in a binary alphabet, the number of 1's and 0's) present in the template. In the examples above, the order of the schema $011*1**$ is 4 (symbolically, $o(011*1**) = 4$), whereas the order of the schema $0******$ is 1.

The defining length of a schema H, denoted by $\delta(H)$, is the distance between the first and last specific string position. For example, the schema $011*1**$ has defining length $\delta = 4$ because the last specific position is 5 and the first specific position is 1, and the distance between them is $\delta(H) = 5 - 1 = 4$. In the other example (the schema $0******$), the defining length is particularly easy to calculate. Since there is only a single fixed position, the first and last specific positions are the same, and the defining length $\delta = 0$.

Schemata and their properties are interesting notational devices for rigorously discussing and classifying string similarities. More than this, they provide the basic means for analyzing the net effect of reproduction and genetic operators on building blocks contained within the population. Let us consider the individual and combined effect of reproduction, crossover, and mutation on schemata contained within a population of strings.

The effect of reproduction on the expected number of schemata in the population is particularly easy to determine. Suppose at a given time step t there are

m examples of a particular schema H contained within the population $A(t)$ where we write $m = m(H,t)$ (there are possibly different quantities of different schemata H at different times t). During reproduction, a string is copied according to its fitness, or more precisely a string A_i gets selected with probability $p_i = f_i/\Sigma f_j$. After picking a nonoverlapping population of size n with replacement from the population $A(t)$, we expect to have $m(H, t + 1)$ representatives of the schema H in the population at time $t + 1$ as given by the equation $m(H, t + 1) = m(H,t) \cdot n \cdot f(H)/\Sigma f_j$, where $f(H)$ is the average fitness of the strings representing schema H at time t. If we recognize that the average fitness of the entire population may be written as $\bar{f} = \Sigma f_j/n$ then we may rewrite the reproductive schema growth equation as follows:

$$m(H, t + 1) = m(H, t)\frac{f(H)}{\bar{f}}$$

In words, a particular schema grows as the ratio of the average fitness of the schema to the average fitness of the population. Put another way, schemata with fitness values above the population average will receive an increasing number of samples in the next generation, while schemata with fitness values below the population average will receive a decreasing number of samples. It is interesting to observe that this expected behavior is carried out with every schema H contained in a particular population A in parallel. In other words, all the schemata in a population grow or decay according to their schema averages under the operation of reproduction alone. In a moment, we examine why this might be a good thing to do. For the time being, simply note that many things go on in parallel with simple operations on the n strings in the population.

The effect of reproduction on the number of schemata is qualitatively clear; above-average schemata grow and below-average schemata die off. Can we learn anything else about the mathematical form of this growth (decay) from the schema difference equation? Suppose we assume that a particular schema H remains above average an amount $c\bar{f}$ with c a constant. Under this assumption we can rewrite the schema difference equation as follows:

$$m(H, t + 1) = m(H,t)\frac{(\bar{f} + c\bar{f})}{\bar{f}} = (1 + c) \cdot m(H, t).$$

Starting at $t = 0$ and assuming a stationary value of c, we obtain the equation

$$m(H, t) = m(H, 0) \cdot (1 + c)^t$$

Business-oriented readers will recognize this equation as the compound interest equation, and mathematically oriented readers will recognize a geometric progression or the discrete analog of an exponential form. The effect of reproduction is now quantitatively clear; reproduction allocates exponentially increasing (decreasing) numbers of trials to above- (below-) average schemata. We will connect this rate of schemata allocation to the multiarmed bandit problem, but for right now we will investigate how crossover and mutation affect this allocation of trials.

To some extent it is curious that reproduction can allocate exponentially increasing and decreasing numbers of schemata to future generations in parallel; many, many different schemata are sampled in parallel according to the same rule through the use of n simple reproduction operations. On the other hand, reproduction alone does nothing to promote exploration of new regions of the search space, since no new points are searched; if we only copy old structures without change, then how will we ever try anything new? This is where crossover steps in. Crossover is a structured yet randomized information exchange between strings. Crossover creates new structures with a minimum of disruption to the allocation strategy dictated by reproduction alone. This results in exponentially increasing (or decreasing) proportions of schemata in a population on many of the schemata contained in the population.

To see which schemata are affected by crossover and which are not, consider a particular string of length $l = 7$ and two representative schemata within that string:

$$A = 0\ 1\ 1\ 1\ 0\ 0\ 0$$
$$H_1 = *\ 1\ *\ *\ *\ *\ 0$$
$$H_2 = *\ *\ *\ 1\ 0\ *\ *$$

Clearly the two schemata H_1 and H_2 are represented in the string A, but to see the effect of crossover on the schemata, we first recall that simple crossover proceeds with the random selection of a mate, the random selection of a crossover site, and the exchange of substrings from the beginning of the string to the crossover site inclusively with the corresponding substring of the chosen mate. Suppose string A has been chosen for mating and crossover. In this string of length 7, suppose we roll a single die to choose the crossing site (there are six sites in a string of length 7). Further suppose that the die turns up a 3, meaning that the cross cut will take place between positions 3 and 4. The effect of this cross on our two schemata H_1 and H_2 can be seen easily in the following example, where the crossing site has been marked with the separator symbol $|$:

$$A = 0\ 1\ 1\ |\ 1\ 0\ 0\ 0$$
$$H_1 = *\ 1\ *\ |\ *\ *\ *\ 0$$
$$H_2 = *\ *\ *\ |\ 1\ 0\ *\ *$$

Unless string A's mate is identical to A at the fixed positions of the schema (a possibility that we conservatively ignore), the schema H_1 will be destroyed because the 1 at position 2 and the 0 at position 7 will be placed in different offspring (they are on opposite sides of the separator symbol marking the cross point, or cut point). It is equally clear that with the same cut point (between bits 3 and 4), schema H_2 will survive because the 1 at position 4 and the 0 at position 5 will be carried intact to a single offspring. Although we have used a specific cut point for illustration, it is clear that schema H_1 is less likely to survive crossover than schema H_2 because on average the cut point is more likely to fall between the extreme fixed positions. To quantify this observation, we note that schema H_1 has a defining length of 5. If the crossover site is selected uniformly at random among the $l - 1 = 7 - 1 = 6$ possible sites, then clearly schema H_1 is destroyed with probability $p_d = \delta(H_1)/(l - 1) = 5/6$ (it survives with probability $p_s = 1 - p_d = 1/6$). Similarly, the schema H_2 has defining length $\delta(H_2) = 1$, and it is destroyed during that one event in six where the cut site is selected to occur between positions 4 and 5 such that $p_d = 1/6$ or the survival probability is $p_s = 1 - p_d = 5/6$.

More generally, we see that a lower bound on crossover survival probability p_s can be calculated for any schema. Because a schema survives when the cross site falls outside the defining length, the survival probability under simple cross-over is $p_s = 1 - \delta(H)/(l - 1)$, since the schema is likely to be disrupted whenever a site within the defining length is selected from the $l - 1$ possible sites. If crossover is itself performed by random choice, say with probability p_c at a particular mating, the survival probability may be given by the expression

$$p_s \geq 1 - p_c \cdot \frac{\delta(H)}{l - 1},$$

which reduces to the earlier expression when $p_c = 1.0$.

The combined effect of reproduction and crossover may now be considered. As when we considered reproduction alone, we are interested in calculating the number of a particular schema H expected in the next generation. Assuming independence of the reproduction and crossover operations, we obtain the estimate:

$$m(H, t + 1) \geq m(H, t) \cdot \frac{f(H)}{\bar{f}} \left[1 - p_c \cdot \frac{\delta(H)}{l - 1} \right].$$

Comparing this to the previous expression for reproduction alone, the combined effect of crossover and reproduction is obtained by multiplying the expected number of schemata for reproduction alone by the survival probability under crossover p_s. Once again the effect of the operations is clear. Schema H grows or decays depending upon a multiplication factor. With both crossover and reproduction, that factor depends on two things: whether the schema is above or below the population average and whether the schema has relatively short or long defining length. Clearly, those schemata with both above-average observed performance and short defining lengths are going to be sampled at exponentially increasing rates.

The last operator to consider is mutation. Using our previous definition, mutation is the random alteration of a single position with probability p_m. In order for a schema H to survive, all of the specified positions must themselves survive. Therefore, since a single allele survives with probability $(1 - p_m)$, and since each of the mutations is statistically independent, a particular schema survives when each of the $o(H)$ fixed positions within the schema survives. Multiplying the survival probability $(1 - p_m)$ by itself $o(H)$ times, we obtain the probability of surviving mutation, $(1 - p_m)^{o(H)}$. For small values of p_m ($p_m << 1$), the schema survival probability may be approximated by the expression $1 - o(H) \cdot p_m$. We therefore conclude that a particular schema H receives an expected number of copies in the next generation under reproduction, crossover, and mutation as given by the following equation (ignoring small cross-product terms):

$$m(H,\ t + 1) \geqslant m(H,\ t) \cdot \frac{f(H)}{\bar{f}} \left[1\ -\ p_c \frac{\delta(H)}{l - 1}\ -\ o(H)p_m \right].$$

The addition of mutation changes our previous conclusions little. Short, low-order, above-average schemata receive exponentially increasing trials in subsequent generations. This conclusion is important, so important that we give it a special name: the *Schema Theorem,* or the Fundamental Theorem of Genetic Algorithms. Although the calculations that led us to prove the schema theorem were not too demanding, the theorem's implications are far reaching and subtle. To see this, we examine the effect of the three-operator genetic algorithm on schemata in a population through another visit to the hand-calculated GA of Chapter 1.

SCHEMA PROCESSING AT WORK: AN EXAMPLE BY HAND REVISITED

Chapter 1 demonstrated the mechanics of the simple GA through a hand calculation of a single generation. Let us return to that example, this time observing how the GA processes schemata—not individual strings—within the population. The hand calculation of Chapter 1 is reproduced in Table 2.1. In addition to the information presented earlier, we also keep a running count of three particular schemata, which we call H_1, H_2, and H_3, where $H_1 = 1****$, $H_2 = *10**$, and $H_3 = 1***0$.

Observe the effect of reproduction, crossover, and mutation on the first schema, H_1. During the reproduction phase, the strings are copied probabilistically according to their fitness values. Looking at the first column of the table, we notice that strings 2 and 4 are both representatives of the schema $1****$. After reproduction, we note that three copies of the schema have been produced (strings 2, 3, 4 in the mating pool column). Does this number correspond with the value predicted by the schema theorem? From the schema theorem we expect to have $m \cdot f(H)/\bar{f}$ copies. Calculating the schema average $f(H_1)$, we obtain $(576 + 361)/2 = 468.5$. Dividing this by the population average $\bar{f} = 293$ and multiplying by the number of H_1 schemata at time t, $m(H_1, t) = 2$, we obtain the expected number of H_1 schemata at time $t + 1$, $m(H,t + 1) = 2 \cdot 468.5/293 = 3.20$. Comparing this to the actual number of schemata (three), we see that we have the correct number of copies. Taking this one step further, we realize that crossover cannot have any further effect on this schema because a defining length $\delta(H_1) = 0$ prevents disruption of the single bit. Furthermore, with the mutation rate set at $p_m = 0.001$ we expect to have $m \cdot p_m = 3 \cdot 0.001 = 0.003$ or no bits changed within the three schema copies in the three strings. As a result, we ob-

TABLE 2.1   **GA Processing of Schemata—Hand Calculations**

String Processing

String No.	Initial Population $\left(\begin{array}{c}\text{Randomly}\\\text{Generated}\end{array}\right)$	x Value $\left(\begin{array}{c}\text{Unsigned}\\\text{Integer}\end{array}\right)$	$f(x)$ x^2	pselect$_i$ $\dfrac{f_i}{\Sigma f}$	Expected count $\dfrac{f_i}{\bar{f}}$	Actual Count $\left(\begin{array}{c}\text{from}\\\text{Roulette}\\\text{Wheel}\end{array}\right)$
1	0 1 1 0 1	13	169	0.14	0.58	1
2	1 1 0 0 0	24	576	0.49	1.97	2
3	0 1 0 0 0	8	64	0.06	0.22	0
4	1 0 0 1 1	19	361	0.31	1.23	1
Sum			1170	1.00	4.00	4.0
Average			293	0.25	1.00	1.0
Max			576	0.49	1.97	2.0

Schema Processing

		Before Reproduction	
		String Representatives	Schema Average Fitness $f(H)$
H_1	1 * * * *	2,4	469
H_2	* 1 0 * *	2,3	320
H_3	1 * * * 0	2	576

serve that for schema H_1, we do obtain the expected exponentially increasing number of schemata as predicted by the schema theorem.

So far, so good; but schema H_1 with its single fixed bit seems like something of a special case. What about the propagation of important similarities with longer defining lengths? For example consider the propagation of the schema H_2 = *10** and the schema H_3 = 1***0. Following reproduction and prior to crossover the replication of schemata is correct. The case of H_2 starts with two examples in the initial population and ends with two copies following reproduction. This agrees with the expected number of copies, $m(H_2) = 2 \cdot 320/293 = 2.18$, where 320 is the schema average and 293 is the population average fitness. The case of H_3 starts with a single example (string 2) and ends with two copies following reproduction (strings 2 and 3 in the string copies column). This agrees with the expected number of copies $m(H_3) = 1 \cdot 576/293 = 1.97$, where 576 is the schema's average fitness and 293 is the population's average fitness. The circumstances following crossover are a good bit different. Notice that for the short schema, schema H_2, the two copies are maintained even though crossover has

TABLE 2.1 (*Continued*)

			String Processing			

Mating Pool after Reproduction (Cross Site Shown)	Mate $\left(\begin{matrix}\text{Randomly}\\\text{Selected}\end{matrix}\right)$	Crossover Site $\left(\begin{matrix}\text{Randomly}\\\text{Selected}\end{matrix}\right)$	New Population	x Value	$f(x)$ x^2
0 1 1 0 | 1	2	4	0 1 1 0 0	12	144
1 1 0 0 | 0	1	4	1 1 0 0 1	25	625
1 1 | 0 0 0	4	2	1 1 0 1 1	27	729
1 0 | 0 1 1	3	2	1 0 0 0 0	16	256
Sum					1754
Average					439
Max					729

	Schema Processing				

After Reproduction			After All Operators		
Expected Count	Actual Count	String Representatives	Expected Count	Actual Count	String Representatives
3.20	3	2,3,4	3.20	3	2,3,4
2.18	2	2,3	1.64	2	2,3
1.97	2	2,3	0.0	1	4

occurred. Because the defining length is short we expect crossover to interrupt the process only one time in four ($l - 1 = 5 - 1 = 4$). As a result, the schema H_2 survives with high probability. The actual expected number of H_2 schemata is thus $m(H_2, t+1) = 2.18 \cdot 0.75 = 1.64$, and this compares well with the actual count of two schemata. H_3 is a schema of a different color. Because of the long defining length ($\delta(H_3) = 4$), crossover usually destroys this schema.

The hand calculation has confirmed the theory developed earlier in this chapter. Short, low-order schemata are given exponentially increasing or decreasing numbers of samples depending on a schema's average fitness. In a moment we will estimate the number of schemata that are processed in this way, but before we do, we must ask and answer a pressing question. Why should we give an exponentially increasing number of trials to the observed best schemata? In other words, why is this particular allocation strategy a good road to follow? The answer lies along what at first may seem like a detour, following a gambler among the slot machines of Las Vegas.

THE TWO-ARMED AND *K*-ARMED BANDIT PROBLEM

The effect of reproduction, crossover, and mutation are now both quantitatively and qualitatively clear. Schemata of short defining length, low order, and above average fitness (building blocks) receive exponentially increasing trials in future generations. This is a fact, beyond all question. Yet despite careful proof of this point, at least one nagging question remains: Why is this a good thing to do? More to the point, why should exponentially increasing samples be given to the observed best building blocks? This question leads to an important problem of statistical decision theory, the two-armed bandit problem and its extension, the *k*-armed bandit problem. Although this seems like a detour from our main concern (after all, we are trying to understand genetic algorithms, not minimize our gambling losses), we shall soon see that the optimal solution to the bandit problem is very similar in form to the exponential allocation of trials from our tripartite GA.

Suppose we have a two-armed slot machine, as depicted in Fig. 2.1 with two arms named LEFT and RIGHT. Furthermore, let's assume we know that one of the arms pays an award μ_1 with variance σ_1^2 and the other arm pays an award μ_2 with variance σ_2^2 where $\mu_1 \geq \mu_2$. Which arm should we play? Clearly, we would like to play the arm that pays off more frequently (the arm with payoff μ_1), but therein lies the rub. Since we don't know beforehand which arm is associated with the

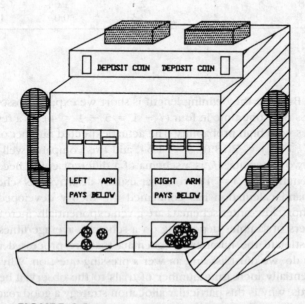

FIGURE 2.1 The two-armed bandit problem poses a dilemma: how do we search for the right answer (exploration) at the same time we use that information (exploitation)?

higher expected reward, we are faced with an interesting dilemma. Not only must we make a decision (more precisely, a sequence of decisions) about which arm to play, but we must at the same time collect information about which is the better arm. This trade-off between the exploration for knowledge and the exploitation of that knowledge is a recurrent and fundamentally important theme in adaptive systems theory. How we address this dilemma will say a lot about the ultimate success of our methods.

One way to approach the trade-off is to separate exploration from exploitation by first performing a single experiment and thereafter making a single irreversible decision that depends upon the outcome of the experiment. This is one approach of traditional decision theory that we can describe rigorously as follows. Suppose we have a total of N trials to allocate among the two arms. We first allocate an equal number of trials n ($2n < N$) trials to each of the two arms during the experimental phase. After the experiment, we allocate the remaining $N - 2n$ trials to the arm with best observed payoff. Assuming we know N, μ_1, μ_2, σ_1, and σ_2, we can calculate the expected loss (De Jong, 1975):

$$L(N,n) = |\mu_1 - \mu_2| \cdot [(N - n)q(n) + n(1 - q(n))],$$

where $q(n)$ is the probability that the worst arm is the observed best arm after n trials have been attempted on each machine. This probability is well approximated by the tail of the normal distribution:

$$q(n) \cong \frac{1}{\sqrt{2\pi}} \cdot \frac{e^{-x^2/2}}{x}, \qquad \text{where } x = \frac{\mu_1 - \mu_2}{\sqrt{\sigma_1^2 + \sigma_2^2}} \cdot \sqrt{n}.$$

From these equations we can see that two sources of loss are associated with the procedure. The first loss is a result of issuing n trials to the wrong arm during the experiment. The second is a result of choosing the arm associated with the lower payoff (μ_2) even after performing the experiment. We cannot be absolutely certain at the end of the experiment that we will pick the right arm, so we do expect occasionally to pick the wrong arm and incur a loss on the remaining $N - 2n$ trials during the exploration phase. We may solve for the optimal experiment size n^* by taking the derivative of the loss equation and setting it to zero. Figure 2.2 shows how the optimal experiment n^* size varies with the total number of trials N and c, the ratio of signal difference to noise, where $c = (\mu_1 - \mu_2)/(\sigma_1^2 + \sigma_2^2)^{0.5}$.

This simple procedure is easy to analyze, but there are no doubt better ways, perhaps optimal ways, to allocate the trials to the better arm. Holland (1975) has performed calculations that show how trials should be allocated between the two arms to minimize expected losses. This results in the allocation of n^* trials to the worse arm and $N - n^*$ trials to the better arm where n^* is given by the following equation:

$$n^* \cong b^2 \ln\left[\frac{N^2}{8\pi b^4 \ln N^2}\right], \qquad \text{where } b = \sigma_1/(\mu_1 - \mu_2).$$

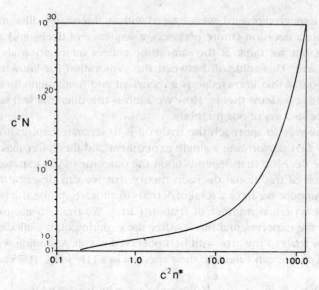

FIGURE 2.2 The modified total number of trials (c^2N) grows at a greater than exponential function of the modified optimal experiment size (c^2n^*) in the one-shot, decision-theory approach to the two-armed bandit problem.

Turning the equation around, we realize that the number of trials given to the observed better arm is given by the equation:

$$N - n^* \cong N \cong \sqrt{8\pi b^4 \ln N^2} \cdot e^{n^{*\,2b^2}}$$

In other words, to allocate trials optimally (in the sense of minimal expected loss), we should give slightly more than exponentially increasing trials to the observed best arm. Unfortunately, this strategy is unrealizable, as it requires knowledge of outcomes before they occur. Nonetheless, it forms an important bound on performance that a realizable strategy should try to approach. Certainly many strategies can approach this ideal. The experimental approach analyzed earlier showed how exponentially fewer trials were given to the worse arm as the number of trials increased. Another method that comes even closer to the ideal trial allocation is the three-operator genetic algorithm discussed earlier. The schema theorem guarantees giving at least an exponentially increasing number of trials to the observed best building blocks. In this way the genetic algorithm is a realizable yet near optimal procedure (Holland, 1973a, 1975) for searching among alternative solutions.

With a genetic algorithm we are no longer solving a simple two-armed bandit problem; in the usual genetic algorithm we consider the simultaneous solution of many multiarmed bandits. To make this point more forcefully, we first consider the form of the solution to a single k-armed bandit and then demonstrate that the usual genetic algorithm may be thought of as the composition of many such k-armed bandits.

The form of the bounding k-armed bandit solution was also discovered by Holland (1973a). The minimal expected loss solution to the allocation of trials to k competing arms is similar to the two-armed solution as it dictates that greater than exponentially increasing numbers of trials be given to the observed best of the k arms. This result is not surprising, but it does connect nicely to our notions of schema processing if we consider a set of competing schemata as a particular k-armed bandit. To see this connection, we define this notion of a competing set of schemata, and then count the number and size of the k-armed bandit problems being solved within a genetic algorithm of given string length.

Two schemata A and B with individual positions a_i and b_i are *competing* if at all positions $i = 1, 2, \ldots, l$ either $a_i = b_i = *$ or $a_i \neq *$, $b_i \neq *$, $a_i \neq b_i$ for at least one i value. For example, consider the set of eight schemata that compete at locations 2, 3, and 5 in the following strings of length 7:

```
* 0 0 * 0 * *
* 0 0 * 1 * *
* 0 1 * 0 * *
* 0 1 * 1 * *
* 1 0 * 0 * *
* 1 0 * 1 * *
* 1 1 * 0 * *
* 1 1 * 1 * *
```

There are eight competing schemata over the three positions 2, 3, and 5 because any of the three positions may take on either a 1 or a 0 ($2^3 = 8$).

We can start to see the connection to the k-armed bandit problem in our list of eight competing schemata. Since these schemata are defined over the same positions, they compete with one another for precious population slots. In order to allocate the population slots properly, we need to allocate exponentially increasing numbers to the observed best schemata just as we give exponentially increasing trials to the observed best arm in the k-armed bandit. One of the differences between our situation in a genetic algorithm and the vanilla flavored k-armed bandit is that we have a number of problems proceeding in parallel. For example, with three positions fixed over a string of length 7 there are $\binom{7}{3} = 35$ of the ($2^3 = 8$) eight-armed bandit problems. In general, for schemata of order j over strings of length l, there are $\binom{l}{j}$ different k_j-armed bandit problems, where

$k_j = 2^j$. Not all of the $\Sigma \binom{l}{j} = 2^l$ problems are played out equally well because crossover has a tendency to disrupt those bandits with long defining lengths as discussed earlier. In the next section, we count the number of schemata that are usefully processed by the genetic algorithm.

HOW MANY SCHEMATA ARE PROCESSED USEFULLY?

Our counting arguments thus far have indicated that we have somewhere between 2^l and $n \cdot 2^l$ schemata being processed in a string population with length l and size n. As we know, not all of these are processed with high probability because crossover destroys those with relatively long defining lengths. In this section we compute a lower bound on those schemata that are processed in a useful manner—those that are sampled at the desirable exponentially increasing rate.

The most widely quoted counting of effective schemata processing is Holland's well known, but poorly understood $O(n^3)$ estimate (Goldberg, 1985d). Simply stated, this estimate means that despite the processing of only n structures each generation, a genetic algorithm processes something like n^3 schemata. This result is so important, Holland has given it a special name, *implicit parallelism*. Even though each generation we perform computation proportional to the size of the population, we get useful processing of something like n^3 schemata in parallel with no special bookkeeping or memory other than the population itself. Let us rederive this estimate to understand its underlying assumptions and examine the source of this computational leverage.

Consider a population of n binary strings of length l. We consider only schemata that survive with a probability greater than p_s a constant. As a result, assuming the operation of simple crossover and a small mutation rate, we admit only those schemata with an error rate $\varepsilon < 1 - p_s$. This leads us to consider only those schemata with length $l_s < \varepsilon(l - 1) + 1$.

With a particular schema length, we can estimate a lower bound on the number of unique schemata processed by an initially random population of strings. To do this, we first count the number of schemata of length l_s or less. We then multiply this by an appropriate population size, chosen so we expect, on average, no more than one of each schema of length $l_s/2$. Suppose we wish to count the schemata of length l_s in the following string of length $l = 10$:

```
1 0 1 1 1 0 0 0 1 0
```

To do this we calculate the number of schemata in the first cell of 5,

```
|1 0 1 1 1|0 0 0 1 0
```

so the last bit in the cell is fixed. That is, we want all schemata of the form

```
|% % % % 1|* * * * *
```

where the stars * are don't care symbols and the percent signs % take on either the fixed value (the 1 or 0 at that position) or a don't care. Clearly there are $2^{(l_s - 1)}$ of these schemata because $l_s - 1 = 4$ positions can be fixed or take on the don't care. To count the total number of these, we simply slide the template of 5 along one space at a time:

```
1|0 1 1 1 0|0 0 1 0
```

We perform this trick a total of $l - l_s + 1$ times and we can estimate the total number of schema of length l_s or less as $2^{(l_s - 1)} \cdot (l - l_s + 1)$. This count is the number of such schemata in this particular string. To overestimate the number of such schemata in the whole population, we could simply multiply by the population size n and obtain the count $n \cdot 2^{(l_s - 1)} \cdot (l - l_s + 1)$. This obviously overestimates the correct count because surely there will be duplicates of low-order schemata in large populations. To refine the estimate, we pick a population size $n = 2^{l_s/2}$. By choosing in this manner, we expect to have one or fewer of all schemata of order $l_s/2$ or more. Recognizing that the number of schema is binomially distributed, we conclude that half are of higher order than $l_s/2$ and half are of smaller order. If we count only the higher order ones, we estimate a lower bound on the number of schemata as follows:

$$n_s \geqslant n(l - l_s + 1)2^{l_s - 2}.$$

This differs from the previous overestimate by a factor of 1/2. Furthermore, the restriction of the population size to the particular value $2^{l_s/2}$ results in the expression:

$$n_s = \frac{(l - l_s + 1)n^3}{4}$$

Since $n_s = Cn^3$, we conclude that the number of schemata is proportional to the cube of the population size and is thus of order n^3, $O(n^3)$.

Thus we see that despite the disruption of long, high-order schemata by crossover and mutation, genetic algorithms inherently process a large quantity of schemata while processing a relatively small quantity of strings.

THE BUILDING BLOCK HYPOTHESIS

The picture of genetic algorithms' performance is much clearer with the perspective afforded by schemata. Short, low-order, and highly fit schemata are sampled, recombined, and resampled to form strings of potentially higher fitness. In a way, by working with these particular schemata (the building blocks), we have reduced the complexity of our problem; instead of building high-performance strings by trying every conceivable combination, we construct better and better strings from the best partial solutions of past samplings.

Because highly fit schemata of low defining length and low order play such an important role in the action of genetic algorithms, we have already given them a special name: building blocks. Just as a child creates magnificent fortresses through the arrangement of simple blocks of wood, so does a genetic algorithm seek near optimal performance through the juxtaposition of short, low-order, high-performance schemata, or building blocks.

There is, however, one catch. Repeatedly Chapter 1 claimed that notions combine to form better ideas. Just now, it was claimed that building blocks combine to form better strings. While these claims seem perfectly reasonable, how do we know whether they hold true or not?

Certainly there is a growing body of empirical evidence to support these claims in a variety of problem classes. Starting two decades ago with two pioneering dissertations (Bagley, 1967; and Rosenberg, 1967) and continuing through the many genetic algorithm applications demonstrated at recent conferences devoted to genetic algorithms (Grefenstette, 1985a, 1987a), the building block hypothesis has held up in many different problem domains. Smooth, unimodal problems, noisy multimodal problems, and combinatorial optimization problems have all been attacked successfully using virtually the same reproduction-cross-over-mutation GA. While limited empirical evidence does no theory prove, it does suggest that genetic algorithms are appropriate for many of the types of problems we normally encounter.

More recently, Bethke (1981) has shed some light on this topic. Using Walsh functions and a clever transformation of schemata, he has devised an efficient analytical method for determining schema average fitness values using Walsh coefficients. This in turn permits us to identify whether, given a particular function and coding, building blocks combine to form optima or near optima. Holland (1987b) has extended Bethke's computation to the analysis of schema averages when the population is not uniformly distributed.

Bethke's and Holland's Walsh-schema transform work is beyond the scope of this discussion, although the interested reader should consult Appendix E, which briefly discusses some important results. Nonetheless, the concepts behind these discoveries are sufficiently important that we must try to understand the regularity implied in building block processing, at least from an intuitive, graphic viewpoint. To do this, let us return to the five-bit coding example we started in Chapter 1. Recall, in that problem we were trying to maximize the function $f(x) = x^2$ where x was coded as a five-bit unsigned integer. In this problem, what do the building blocks look like and how do they lead to better solutions when they are mixed with one another? Consider a simple schema, $H_1 = 1****$ What does this one-fixed-bit schema look like? The answer is shown in Fig. 2.3 as the shaded region of the domain. Apparently, a schema with the high-order bit set covers the upper half of the domain of interest. Similarly, the schema $H_2 = 0****$ covers the lower half. Other one-bit examples prove illuminating, for example the schema $H_3 = ****1$ shown in Fig. 2.4. This schema covers the half domain that decodes to an odd number ($00001 = 1, 00011 = 3, 00101 = 5$, etc.). The schema $H_4 = ***0*$ also covers half the domain, but in the manner shown in Fig. 2.5. It seems that a one-bit schema covers half the domain, but the frequency of oscillation depends on the position of the fixed bit.

Higher order building blocks are certainly of interest. Consider the schema $H_5 = 10***$ as depicted in Fig. 2.6. This schema covers the lower quarter of the upper half domain. Other two-bit schemata may be sketched similarly, such as the schema $H_6 = **1*1$ as shown in Fig. 2.7. Like schema H_5, it too covers a quarter domain (why is this?), but in a more broken-up fashion. For readers familiar with Fourier series, the periodicity of the different schemata is suggestive.

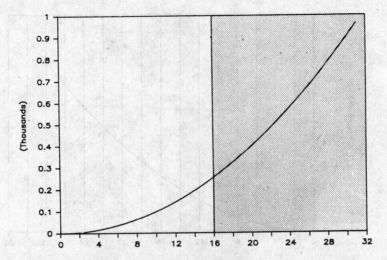

FIGURE 2.3 Sketch of schema 1**** overlaying the function $f(x) = x^2$.

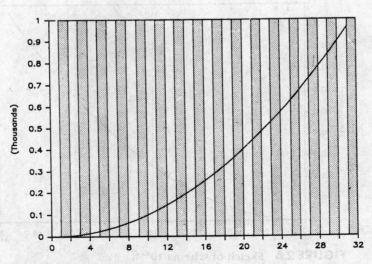

FIGURE 2.4 Sketch of schema ****1.

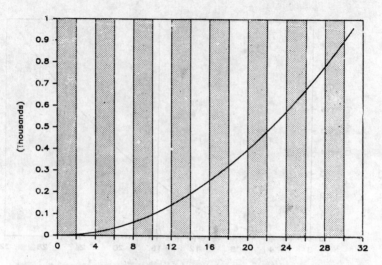

FIGURE 2.5   Sketch of schema ***0*.

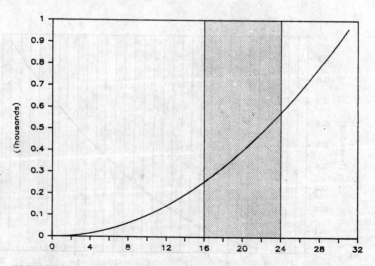

FIGURE 2.6   Sketch of schema 10***.

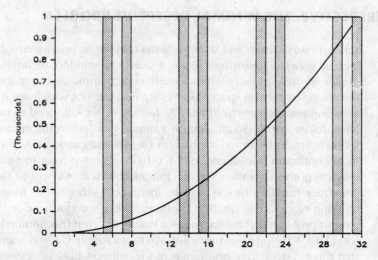

FIGURE 2.7   Sketch of schema **1*1.

In fact, it is this periodicity that permits the Walsh function analysis. Just as harmonic analysis determines physical properties through an examination of the relative magnitudes of Fourier coefficients, so does Walsh function analysis determine the expected static performance of a genetic algorithm through an analysis of the relative magnitudes of Walsh coefficients.

Although these transform methods are powerful mathematical tools for genetic algorithm analysis in specific cases, generalization of these results to arbitrary codings and functions has proved difficult. Bethke has generated a number of test cases that are provably misleading for the simple three-operator genetic algorithm (we call these coding-function combinations *GA-deceptive*). These results suggest that functions and codings that are GA-deceptive tend to contain isolated optima: the best points tend to be surrounded by the worst. Practically speaking, many of the functions encountered in the real world do not have this needle-in-the-haystack quality; there is usually some regularity in the function-coding combination—much like the regularity of one or more schemata—that may be exploited by the recombination of building blocks. Furthermore, we can argue that finding a needle in a haystack is going to be difficult regardless of the search technique adopted. Nevertheless, it is important to keep in mind that the simple genetic algorithm depends upon the recombination of building blocks to seek the best points. If the building blocks are misleading due to the coding used or the function itself, the problem may require long waiting times to arrive at near optimal solutions.

ANOTHER PERSPECTIVE: THE MINIMAL DECEPTIVE PROBLEM

Schema visualization and Walsh-schema transforms provide insight into the workings of genetic algorithms. From a practical standpoint, however, these techniques are at least as computationally cumbersome as an enumerative search of the discrete problem space. As a result, they are not widely used to analyze practical problems in genetic search. Nonetheless, we still need to understand better what makes a problem difficult for a simple GA. To investigate this matter further, let's construct the simplest problem that should cause a GA to diverge from the global optimum (Goldberg, 1987b). To do this, we want to violate the building block hypothesis in the extreme. Put another way, we would like to have short, low-order building blocks lead to incorrect (suboptimal) longer, higher order building blocks. The smallest problem where we can have such deception is a two-bit problem. In this section, we briefly develop this minimal deceptive problem (MDP). Despite our best efforts to fool a simple GA, it is somewhat surprising that this GA-deceptive problem is not usually GA-hard (does not usually diverge from the global optimum).

Suppose we have a set of four order-2 schemata over two defining positions, each schema associated with a fitness value as follows:

$$
\begin{array}{llllllllll}
* & * & * & 0 & * & * & * & * & 0 & * \qquad f_{00} \\
* & * & * & 0 & * & * & * & * & 1 & * \qquad f_{01} \\
* & * & * & 1 & * & * & * & * & 0 & * \qquad f_{10} \\
* & * & * & 1 & * & * & * & * & 1 & * \qquad f_{11} \\
\end{array}
$$

$$|\!\leftarrow \quad \delta(H) \quad \rightarrow|$$

The fitness values are schema averages, assumed to be constant with no variance (this last restriction may be lifted without changing our conclusions as we only consider expected performance). To start, let's assume that f_{11} is the global optimum:

$$f_{11} > f_{00}; \quad f_{11} > f_{01}; \quad f_{11} > f_{10}.$$

Since the problem is invariant to rotation or reflection in Hamming two-space, the assumption of a particular global optimum is irrelevant to the generality of our conclusions.

Next, we introduce the element of deception necessary to make this a tough problem for a simple genetic algorithm. To do this, we want a problem where one or both of the suboptimal, order-1 schemata are better than the optimal, order-1 schemata. Mathematically, we want one or both of the following conditions to hold:

$$f(0^*) > f(1^*);$$
$$f(^*0) > f(^*1).$$

In these expressions we have dropped consideration of all alleles other than the two defining positions, and the fitness expression implies an average over all strings contained within the specified similarity subset. Thus we would like the following two expressions to hold:

$$\frac{f(00) + f(01)}{2} > \frac{f(10) + f(11)}{2};$$

$$\frac{f(00) + f(10)}{2} > \frac{f(01) + f(11)}{2}.$$

Unfortunately, both expressions cannot hold simultaneously in the two-problem (if they do, point 11 cannot be the global optimum), and without loss of generality we assume that the first expression is true. Thus, the deceptive two-problem is specified by the globality condition (f_{11} is the best) and one deception condition (we choose $f(0^*) > f(1^*)$).

To put the problem into closer perspective, we normalize all fitness values with respect to the fitness of the complement of the global optimum as follows:

$$r = \frac{f_{11}}{f_{00}}; \qquad c = \frac{f_{01}}{f_{00}}; \qquad c' = \frac{f_{10}}{f_{00}}.$$

We may rewrite the globality condition in normalized form:

$$r > c; \qquad r > 1; \qquad r > c'.$$

We may also rewrite the deception condition in normalized form:

$$r < 1 + c - c'.$$

From these conditions, we may conclude a number of interesting facts:

$$c' < 1; \qquad c' < c.$$

From these, we recognize that there are two types of deceptive two-problem:

Type I: $f_{01} > f_{00}$ ($c > 1$).

Type II: $f_{00} \geq f_{01}$ ($c \leq 1$).

Figures 2.8 and 2.9 are representative sketches of these problems where the fitness is graphed as a function of two boolean variables. Both cases are deceptive, and it may be shown that neither case can be expressed as a linear combination of the individual allele values: neither case can be expressed in the form:

$$f(x_1 x_2) = b + \sum_{i=1}^{2} a_i x_i.$$

In the biologist's terms, we have an epistatic problem. Since it similarly may be proved that no one-bit problem can be deceptive, the deceptive, two-problem is the smallest possible deceptive problem: it is *the* minimal, deceptive problem (MDP). With the MDP defined, we now turn toward a complete schema analysis of its behavior.

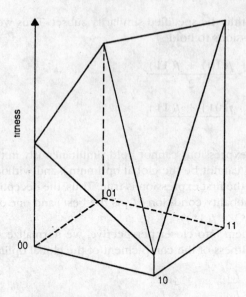

FIGURE 2.8   Sketch of Type I, minimal deceptive problem (MDP) $f_{01} > f_{00}$.

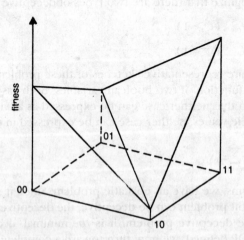

FIGURE 2.9   Sketch of Type II, minimal deceptive problem (MDP) $f_{00} > f_{01}$.

An Extended Schema Analysis of the Two-Problem

So far we have constructed a generalized two-bit problem that seems capable of misleading a genetic algorithm when the two defining bits of the problem become widely separated on the string. Judging from the schema theorem, we expect to have difficulty when the factor

$$\frac{f(11)}{\bar{f}}\left[1 - p_c \cdot \frac{\delta(11)}{l - 1}\right]$$

is less than or equal to 1 (assuming that $p_m = 0$). A more careful analysis requires us to consider the details of crossover more closely.

In an earlier section, we saw how the usual calculation of the expected number of schemata in the next generation is a lower bound. This is so because the derivation contains no source terms (one schema's loss is another's gain) and it assumes that we lose the schema whenever a cross occurs between the schema's outermost defining bits. In the two-problem this latter assumption is overly conservative, because the mating and crossing of noncomplementary pairs conserve the genetic material of the parents. For example, 00 crossed with 01 yields 01 and 00. The only time a loss of genetic material occurs is when complements mate and cross. In these cases, a 00 mated and crossed with a 11 yields the pair 01 and 10, and likewise, a 01 mated and crossed with a 10 yields the pair 11 and 00. The full crossover yield table is shown in Table 2.2 where an S is used to indicate that the offspring are the same as their parents.

In the yield table we see how complements lose material, although we also see how this loss shows up as a gain to the other complementary pair of schemata. Using this information, it is possible to write more accurate difference relationships for the expected proportion P of each of the four competing schemata. To do this we must account for the correct expected loss and gain of schemata due

TABLE 2.2 Crossover Yield Table in Two-Bit Problem

X	00	01	10	11
00	S	S	S	01 10
01	S	S	00 11	S
10	S	00 11	S	S
11	01 10	S	S	S

to crossover. Assuming proportionate reproduction, simple crossover, and random mating of the products of reproduction, we obtain the following autonomous, nonlinear, difference equations:

$$P_{11}^{t+1} = P_{11}^t \cdot \frac{f_{11}}{\bar{f}} \left[1 - p_c' \frac{f_{00}}{\bar{f}} P_{00}^t \right] + p_c' \frac{f_{01} f_{10}}{\bar{f}^2} P_{01}^t P_{10}^t;$$

$$P_{10}^{t+1} = P_{10}^t \cdot \frac{f_{10}}{\bar{f}} \left[1 - p_c' \frac{f_{01}}{\bar{f}} P_{01}^t \right] + p_c' \frac{f_{00} f_{11}}{\bar{f}^2} P_{00}^t P_{11}^t;$$

$$P_{01}^{t+1} = P_{01}^t \cdot \frac{f_{01}}{\bar{f}} \left[1 - p_c' \frac{f_{10}}{\bar{f}} P_{10}^t \right] + p_c' \frac{f_{00} f_{11}}{\bar{f}^2} P_{00}^t P_{11}^t;$$

$$P_{00}^{t+1} = P_{00}^t \cdot \frac{f_{00}}{\bar{f}} \left[1 - p_c' \frac{f_{11}}{\bar{f}} P_{11}^t \right] + p_c' \frac{f_{01} f_{10}}{\bar{f}^2} P_{01}^t P_{10}^t.$$

In these equations, the superscripts are time indexes, and the subscript binary numbers are schema indexes. The variable f is simply the current (generation t) population average fitness, which may be evaluated as follows:

$$\bar{f} = P_{00}^t f_{00} + P_{01}^t f_{01} + P_{10}^t f_{10} + P_{11}^t f_{11}.$$

The parameter p_c' is the probability of having a cross that falls between the two defining bits of the schema:

$$p_c' = p_c \cdot \frac{\delta(H)}{l-1}.$$

Together, these equations predict the expected proportions of the four schemata in the next generation. With specified initial proportions, we may follow the trajectory of the expected proportions through succeeding generations. A necessary condition for the convergence of the GA is that the expected proportion of optimal schemata must go to unity in the limit as generations continue:

$$\lim_{t \to \infty} P_{11}^t = 1.$$

To examine the behavior of these equations more carefully, we look at several numerical solutions of the extended schema equations for Type I and II problems. Some theoretical results are presented briefly without proof.

MDP Results

Figure 2.10 presents computational results for a representative Type I problem. At first, the optimum schema (schema 11) loses proportion; however, as schemata 10 and 00 lose proportion, the remaining battle is fought between schemata 11 and 01 alone, with 11 winning in the end. It may be shown that this result generalizes to any Type I problem with nonzero starting proportions of the four schemata. This result is surprising, as we originally designed the problem to cause divergence from the global optimum. In short, dynamic analysis tells us that the Type I minimal deceptive problem is not GA-hard.

Figures 2.11 and 2.12 present computational results for a Type II MDP. In Fig. 2.11 we see representative convergent results where (as in the Type I case) the solution converges to the optimum despite its initial deception. Not all Type II problems converge like this, however; when the complementary schema 00 has too great an initial proportion, schema 11 may be overwhelmed, with resulting convergence to the second best solution. Representative divergent results are shown in Fig. 2.12. Simple sufficient conditions for the convergence of a Type II problem may be derived (Goldberg, 1987b); it is surprising that all Type II problems converge to the best solution for most starting conditions.

Recent results (Bridges and Goldberg, 1987; Goldberg, 1987a) have extended the exact schema analysis to higher order problems. Other work along these lines may permit a constructive definition of the class of GA-hard problems. Of course, all of this work assumes a fixed coding. The addition of reordering operators such as inversion may be nature's answer to problems too difficult for a simple GA. We consider such operators and their analysis in Chapter 5.

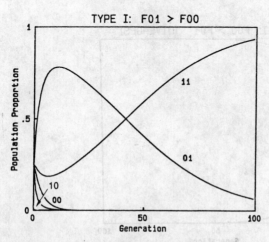

FIGURE 2.10 Numerical solution of a Type I, minimal deceptive problem (MDP): $r = 1.1, c = 1.05, c' = 0.0$.

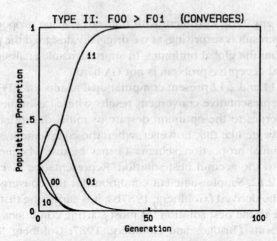

FIGURE 2.11 Numerical solution of a Type II, minimal deceptive problem that converges: $r = 1.1$, $c = 0.9$, $c' = 0.5$ with equal initial proportions.

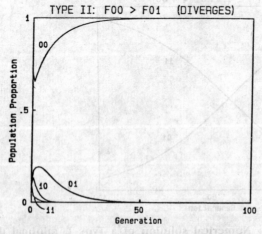

FIGURE 2.12 Numerical solution of a Type II, minimal deceptive problem that diverges: $r = 1.1$, $c = 0.9$, $c' = 0.5$ with unequal initial proportions.

SCHEMATA REVISITED: SIMILARITY TEMPLATES AS HYPERPLANES

Over the past two sections we have looked at schema processing from two perspectives: using schema visualization we have viewed schema processing as the manipulation of important periodicities, and under the minimal deceptive problem we have considered schema processing in a competitive, ecological setting. Another useful vantage point may be reached if we take a more geometric view of the underlying bit space.

To generate this geometrical vision of our search space, consider the strings and schemata of length $l = 3$. Because the string length is so short, it is easy to draw a picture of the search space (Fig. 2.13). In this representation, we view the space as a three-dimensional vector space. Points in the space are strings or schemata of order 3. Lines in the space, as indicated in the diagram, are schemata of order 2. Planes in the space are schemata of order 1, and the whole space is covered by the schema of order 0, the schema ***

This result generalizes to spaces of higher dimension where we must abandon the geometrical notions available to us in 3-space. Points, lines, and planes described by schemata in three dimensions generalize to hyperplanes of varying

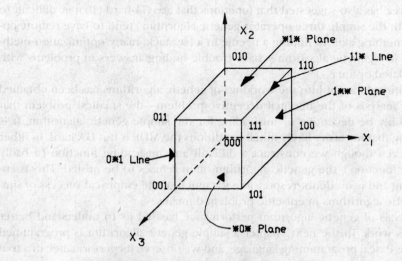

FIGURE 2.13 Visualization of schemata as hyperplanes in three-dimensional space.

dimension in n-space. Thus we can think of a genetic algorithm cutting across different hyperplanes to search for improved performance.

SUMMARY

In this chapter, we have undertaken a more rigorous appraisal of genetic algorithm performance using a more careful analysis of *schemata* (similarity templates). The primary result, embodied in the fundamental theorem of genetic algorithms says that high-performance, short-defining-length, low-order schemata receive at least exponentially increasing numbers of trials in successive generations. This occurs because reproduction allocates more copies to the best schemata and because simple crossover does not disturb short-defining-length schemata with high frequency. Since mutation is fairly infrequent, it has little effect on these important schemata. The exponential form of this trial allocation turns out to be a rational way to allocate trials, as it connects with the optimal solution to a two-armed bandit problem.

By processing similarities in this manner, a genetic algorithm reduces the complexity of arbitrary problems. In a sense, these highly fit, short, low-order schemata become the partial solutions to a problem (called building blocks), and a GA discovers new solutions by speculating on many combinations of the best partial solutions contained within the current population.

That building blocks do indeed lead to better performance is an underlying assumption of the simple genetic algorithm called the building block hypothesis. The Walsh-schema transform has provided us with an important tool for understanding whether particular problems are amenable to simple GA solution. Work in this area has also suggested that functions that are GA-hard (that is, difficult to solve with the simple three-operator genetic algorithm) tend to have remote optima, something akin to finding a needle in a haystack; many optimization methods, not just genetic algorithms, have trouble finding answers in problems with such isolated optima

Additional insight into the workings of genetic algorithms has been obtained through analysis of the minimal deceptive problem—the smallest problem that can possibly be deceptive or misleading for the simple genetic algorithm. It is surprising that for many likely initial conditions the MDP is not GA-hard. In other words, even though we construct a difficult and misleading function (a badly epistatic function), the genetic algorithm often refuses to be misled. This is encouraging and is no doubt responsible for much of the empirical success of simple genetic algorithms in epistatic problem domains.

Analysis of genetic algorithm performance has led us to understand better why GAs work. In the next chapter a simple genetic algorithm is programmed using the Pascal programming language, and we observe its performance in a trial problem.

▪ PROBLEMS

2.1. Consider three strings $A_1 = 11101111$, $A_2 = 00010100$, and $A_3 = 01000011$ and six schemata $H_1 = 1^{*******}$, $H_2 = 0^{*******}$, $H_3 = ^{******}11$, $H_4 = ^{***}0^*00^*$, $H_5 = 1^{*****}1^*$, and $H_6 = 1110^{**}1^*$. Which schemata are matched by which strings? What are the order and defining length of each of the schemata? Estimate the probability of survival of each schema under mutation when the probability of a single mutation is $p_m = 0.001$. Estimate the probability of survival of each schema under crossover when the probability of crossover $p_c = 0.85$.

2.2. A population contains the following strings and fitness values at generation 0:

#	String	Fitness
1	10001	20
2	11100	10
3	00011	5
4	01110	15

The probability of mutation is $p_m = 0.01$ and the probability of crossover is $p_c = 1.0$. Calculate the expected number of schemata of the form 1^{****} in generation 1. Estimate the expected number of schemata of the form $0^{**}1^*$ in generation 1.

2.3. Devise three methods of performing reproduction and calculate an estimate of the expected number of schemata in the next generation under each method.

2.4. Suppose we perform a crossoverlike operation where we pick two cross sites and exchange string material between the two sites.

```
x x x | x x | x x        x x x y y x x
                 →
y y y | y y | y y        y y y x x y y
```

Calculate a lower bound on the survival probability of a schema of defining length δ and order o under this operator. Recalculate the survival probability when we treat the string as a ring (when the left end is assumed to be adjacent to the right end).

2.5. How many unique schemata exist within strings of length $l = 10$, 20, and 30 when the underlying alphabet is binary? How many unique schemata of order 3 exist in binary strings of length $l = 10$, 20, and 30? Calculate reasonable upper and lower bounds on the number of schemata processed using strings of length $l = 10$, 20, and 30 when the population size $m = 50$. Assume a significant building block length equal to 10 percent of the total string length.

2.6. Suppose a schema H when present in a particular string causes the string to have a fitness 25 percent greater than the average fitness of the current population. If the destruction probabilities for this schema under mutation and crossover are negligible, and if a single representative of the schema is contained in the population at generation 0, determine when the schema H will overtake populations of size $n = 20, 50, 100,$ and 200.

2.7. Suppose a schema H when present in a particular string causes the string to have a fitness 10 percent less than the average fitness of the current population. If the destruction probabilities for this schema under mutation and crossover are negligible, and if representatives of the schema are contained in 60 percent of the population at generation 0, determine when the schema H will disappear from populations of size $n = 20, 50, 100,$ and 200.

2.8. A two-armed bandit pays equal awards with probabilities $p_1 = 0.7$ and $p_2 = 0.3$. Estimate the number of trials that should be given to the observed best arm after a total of 50 trials.

2.9. Derive a more accurate formula for calculating the number of unique schemata contained in a randomly generated initial population of size m when the string length is l. (*Hint*: Consider the probability of having no schemata of a particular order and use the complementary probability to count the number of schemata represented by one or more.)

2.10. Suppose a problem is coded as a single unsigned binary integer between 0 and 127 (base 10), where $0000000_2 = 0_{10}$, $1000000_2 = 64_{10}$, and $1111111 = 127$. Sketch the portion of the space covered by the following schemata: $1******$, $******0$, $111111*$, $10*****$, $*****01$, $**111**$.

■ COMPUTER ASSIGNMENTS

A. A fitness function for a single locus genetic algorithm is given by the function $f_1 = $ constant and $f_0 = $ constant. Derive the recursion relationship for the expected proportion of 1's under reproduction alone and reproduction with mutation in an infinitely large population. Program the finite difference relationship and calculate the expected proportion of 1's between generation 0 and 100 assuming equal proportions of 1's and 0's initially and a ratio of $f_1/f_0 = r = 1.1, 2, 10$.

B. Redo Problem A including mutation using mutation probability values of $p_m = 0.001, 0.01, 0.1$.

C. Consider an order 2 schema where we assume constant fitness values as follows:

```
**1***1**   f₁₁
**1***0**   f₁₀
**0***1**   f₀₁
**0***0**   f₀₀
```

Write finite difference relationships for the proportion of the four schemata (11, 10, 01, 00) under reproduction, crossover, and mutation. Be sure to use the correct loss and gain terms due to crossover. Program the finite difference relationships and simulate the performance of a large population with the f constants of Fig. 2.10. Compare and contrast results at p_m values of 0.001, 0.01, 0.1 to the results of Fig. 2.10.

D. For the function $f(x) = x^2$ on the integer interval $[0, 31]$ coded as a five-bit, unsigned binary integer. calculate the average fitness values for all 3^5 schemata. From this data, determine whether the function-coding is GA-deceptive or not.

E. Design a three-bit function that is GA-deceptive. Prove its deception by calculating all 3^3 schema averages.

3 | Computer Implementation of a Genetic Algorithm

When first approaching genetic algorithms, many users hesitate, not knowing where to start or how to begin. On the one hand, this aversive reaction seems strange. After all, in the first two chapters we have seen how genetic algorithms are mechanically quite simple, involving nothing more than random number generation, string copies, and partial string exchanges. On the other hand, for many business, scientific, and engineering users and programmers this stark simplicity is itself part of the problem; these individuals are familiar with using and programming high-level computer codes involving complex mathematics, interwoven databases, and intricate computations. Moreover, this same audience is most comfortable with the reassuring repeatability of deterministic computer programs. The direct manipulation of bit strings, the construction of custom codings, and even the randomness of GA operators can present a sequence of high hurdles that prevent effective application.

In this chapter, we leap these obstacles by first constructing the data structures and algorithms necessary to implement the simple genetic algorithm described earlier. Specifically, we write a Pascal computer code called the simple genetic algorithm (SGA), which contains nonoverlapping string populations, reproduction, crossover, and mutation applied to the optimization of a simple function of one variable coded as an unsigned binary integer. We also examine some implementation issues such as discretization of parameters, coding of strings, enforcement of constraints, and mapping of fitness that arise in applying GAs to particular problems.

DATA STRUCTURES

Genetic algorithms process populations of strings. Therefore it comes as no surprise that the primary data structure for the simple genetic algorithm is a string population. There are any number of ways to implement populations. For the SGA we choose the simplest; we construct a population as an array of individuals where each individual contains the phenotype (the decoded parameter or parameters), the genotype (the artificial chromosome or bit string), and the fitness (objective function) value along with other auxiliary information. A schematic of a population is shown in Fig. 3.1. The Pascal code of Fig. 3.2 declares a population type corresponding to this model. For readers unfamiliar with Pascal, the essentials of the language are presented in Appendix B; this appendix also presents some random number generation routines and utilities. Even without formal training, many readers should be able to decipher the essence of this code.

Referring to Fig. 3.2, we see the declaration of a number of constants: the maximum population size, *maxpop*, and the maximum string length, *maxstring*. These set upper bounds on the population size and the string length. Following the constant declarations, we declare the population itself, along with its components in the *type* block. As we can see, the type *population* is an *array* of type *individual* (indexed between 1 and *maxpop*). Type *individual* is a *record* composed of a type *chromosome* called *chrom*, a *real* variable called *fitness*, and a *real* type variable called *x*. These represent the artificial chromosome, the string fitness value, and the decoded parameter value *x* respectively. Digging further, we see that the type *chromosome* is itself an array of type *allele* (indexed between 1 and *maxstring*), which in this case is simply another name for the *boolean* type (a single bit, true or false).

INDIVIDUAL NUMBER	INDIVIDUALS			
	STRING	X	f(X)	OTHER
1	01111	15	225	
2	01001	9	81	
3	⋮	⋮	⋮	⋮
n	00111	7	49	

FIGURE 3.1   Schematic of a string population in a genetic algorithm.

```
const maxpop         = 100;
      maxstring      = 30;

type allele          = boolean; { Allele = bit position }
     chromosome      = array[1..maxstring] of allele; { String of bits }
     individual      = record
                         chrom:chromosome; { Genotype = bit string }
                         x:real;                { Phenotype = unsigned integer }
                         fitness:real;          { Objective function value }
                         parent1, parent2, xsite:integer; { parents & cross pt }
                       end;
     population       = array[1..maxpop] of individual;
```

FIGURE 3.2   A simple genetic algorithm, SGA, data type declarations in Pascal.

In the SGA, we apply genetic operators to an entire population at each generation, as shown in Fig. 3.3. To implement this operation cleanly, we utilize two nonoverlapping populations, thereby simplifying the birth of offspring and the replacement of parents. The declarations of the two populations *oldpop* and *newpop* are shown in Fig. 3.4 along with the declaration of a number of other global program variables. With these two populations, it is a simple matter to create new offspring from the members of *oldpop* using the genetic operators, place those new individuals in *newpop*, and set *oldpop* to *newpop* when we are

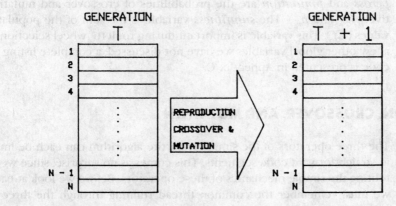

FIGURE 3.3   Schematic of nonoverlapping populations used in the SGA.

```
var   oldpop, newpop:population;              { Two non-overlapping populations }
      popsize, lchrom, gen, maxgen:integer;   { Integer global variables }
      pcross, pmutation, sumfitness:real;     { Real global variables }
      nmutation, ncross:integer;              { Integer statistics }
      avg, max, min:real;                     { Real statistics }
```

FIGURE 3.4   SGA global variable declarations in Pascal.

through. There are other, more storage-efficient methods of handling populations. We could maintain a single overlapping population and pay more careful attention to who replaces whom in successive populations. There is also no particular reason to keep the population size constant. Natural populations certainly change in size, and there may be motivation during artificial genetic search to permit population size variation from generation to generation. There is, however, stronger motivation in our current work to keep things simple, and this has guided the choice of nonoverlapping populations of constant size. In our machine learning work in later chapters we will need to come to terms with the population issue once more.

With our data structures designed and built, we need to understand the three operators—reproduction, crossover, and mutation—essential to SGA operation. Before we can do this, we need to define some of the more important global program variables that affect the operation of the entire code. Looking at Fig. 3.4 once again, we see a number of variables of type *integer*. Among them are the variables *popsize, lchrom,* and *gen.* These important variables correspond to what we have been calling population size (n), string length (l), and the generation counter (t). Additionally the variable *maxgen* is an upper limit on the number of generations. Also shown in Fig. 3.4 are a number of important global *real* variables: *pcross, pmutation, sumfitness, avg, max,* and *min.* The variables *pcross* and *pmutation* are the probabilities of crossover and mutation respectively (p_c and p_m). The *sumfitness* variable is the sum of the population fitness values (Σf). This variable is important during roulette wheel selection. There are a few other global variables we have not discussed; a complete listing of the SGA code is presented in Appendix C.

REPRODUCTION, CROSSOVER, AND MUTATION

The three operators of the simple tripartite algorithm can each be implemented in straightforward code segments. This comes as no surprise, since we have been touting the simple mechanics of these operators. Before we look at each routine, we must remember the common thread running through the three operators:

each depends on random choice. In the code segments that follow, we assume the existence of three random choice routines:

random   returns a real pseudorandom number between zero and one (a uniform random variable on the real interval [0, 1]).

flip   returns a boolean true value with specified probability (a Bernoulli random variable).

rnd   returns an *integer* value between specified lower and upper limits (a uniform random variable over a subset of adjacent integers).

A more complete discussion of these routines is contained in Appendix B where several programming examples are given.

In the simple genetic algorithm, reproduction is implemented in the function *select* as a linear search through a roulette wheel with slots weighted in proportion to string fitness values. In the code shown in Fig. 3.5, we see that *select* returns the population index value corresponding to the selected individual. To do this, the partial sum of the fitness values is accumulated in the real variable *partsum*. The real variable *rand* contains the location where the wheel has landed after a random spin according to the computation:

```
rand := random * sumfitness
```

Here the sum of the population fitnesses (calculated in the procedure *statistics*) is multiplied by the normalized pseudorandom number generated by *random*. Finally the *repeat-until* construct searches through the weighted roulette wheel until the partial sum is greater than or equal to the stopping point *rand*. The function returns with the current population index value *j* assigned to *select*.

```
function select(popsize:integer; sumfitness:real;
                var pop:population):integer;
{ Select a single individual via roulette wheel selection }
var rand, partsum:real; { Random point on wheel, partial sum }
    j:integer;              { population index }
begin
 partsum := 0.0; j := 0;        { Zero out counter and accumulator }
 rand := random * sumfitness; { Wheel point calc. uses random number [0,1] }
 repeat { Find wheel slot }
  j := j + 1;
  partsum := partsum + pop[j].fitness;
 until (partsum >= rand) or (j = popsize);
 { Return individual number }
 select := j;
end;
```

FIGURE 3.5 Function *select* implements roulette wheel selection.

This is perhaps the simplest way to implement selection. There are more efficient codes to implement this operator (a binary search will certainly speed things up), and there are many other ways to choose offspring with appropriate bias toward the best. We will examine some of these in later chapters, but for now we stay with this basic mechanism.

The code segment *select* gives us a straightforward way of choosing offspring for the next generation. From our previous descriptions, we know our next step is crossover. In SGA the crossover operator is implemented in a *procedure* that we, cleverly enough, have called *crossover* (Fig. 3.6). The routine *crossover* takes two parent strings called *parent1* and *parent2* and generates two offspring strings called *child1* and *child2*. The probabilities of crossover and mutation, *pcross* and *pmutation*, are passed to *crossover*, along with the string length *lchrom*, a crossover count accumulator *ncross*, and a mutation count accumulator *nmutation*.

Within *crossover* the operations mirror our description in Chapter 1. At the top of the routine, we determine whether we are going to perform crossover on the current pair of parent chromosomes. Specifically, we toss a biased coin that comes up heads (true) with probability *pcross*. The coin toss is simulated in the *boolean* function *flip*, where *flip* in turn calls on the pseudorandom number

```
procedure crossover(var parent1, parent2, child1, child2:chromosome;
                     var lchrom, ncross, nmutation, jcross:integer;
                     var pcross, pmutation:real);
{ Cross 2 parent strings, place in 2 child strings }
var j:integer;
begin
 if flip(pcross) then begin       { Do crossover with p(cross) }
   jcross := rnd(1,lchrom-1);      { Cross between 1 and l-1 }
   ncross := ncross + 1;          { Increment crossover counter }
  end else                        { Otherwise set cross site to force mutation }
   jcross := lchrom;
 { 1st exchange, 1 to 1 and 2 to 2 }
 for j := 1 to jcross do begin
   child1[j] := mutation(parent1[j], pmutation, nmutation);
   child2[j] := mutation(parent2[j], pmutation, nmutation);
  end;
 { 2nd exchange, 1 to 2 and 2 to 1 }
 if jcross<>lchrom then    { Skip if cross site is lchrom--no crossover }
  for j := jcross+1 to lchrom do begin
    child1[j] := mutation(parent2[j], pmutation, nmutation);
    child2[j] := mutation(parent1[j], pmutation, nmutation);
   end;
end;
```

FIGURE 3.6 Procedure *crossover* implements simple (single-point) crossover

routine *random*. If a cross is called for, a crossing site is selected between 1 and the last cross site. The crossing site is selected in the function *rnd*, which returns a pseudorandom *integer* between specified lower and upper limits (between 1 and *lchrom* − 1). If no cross is to be performed, the cross site is selected as *lchrom* (the full string length *l*) so a bit-by-bit mutation will take place despite the absence of a cross. Finally, the partial exchange of crossover is carried out in the two *for-do* constructs at the end of the code. The first *for-do* handles the partial transfer of bits between *parent1* and *child1* and between *parent2* and *child2*. The second *for-do* construct handles the transfer and partial exchange of material between *parent1* and *child2* and between *parent2* and *child1*. In all cases, a bit-by-bit mutation is carried out by the *boolean* (or allelean) function *mutation*.

Mutation at a point is carried out by *mutation* as shown in Fig. 3.7. This function uses the function *flip* (the biased coin toss) to determine whether or not to change a true to a false (a 1 to a 0) or vice versa. Of course the function *flip* will only come up heads (true) *pmutation* percent of the time as a result of the call to the pseudorandom number generator *random* within *flip* itself. The function also keeps tabs on the number of mutations by incrementing the variable *nmutation*. As with reproduction, there are ways to improve our simple mutation operator. For example, it would be possible to avoid much random number generation if we decided when the next mutation should occur rather than calling *flip* each time. Again, in this chapter, we avoid sophisticated niceties and stick with the basics.

The three main pieces of our genetic algorithm puzzle have proven to be none too puzzling. We have seen in this section how the three may be easily coded and easily understood. The next section continues piecing together the bigger GA picture as we coordinate reproduction, crossover, and mutation in a single generation.

```
function mutation(alleleval:allele; pmutation:real;
                  var nmutation:integer):allele;
{ Mutate an allele w/ pmutation, count number of mutations }
var mutate:boolean;
begin
 mutate := flip(pmutation);   { Flip the biased coin }
 if mutate then begin
   nmutation := nmutation + 1;
   mutation := not alleleval; { Change bit value }
 end else
   mutation := alleleval;     { No change }
end;
```

FIGURE 3.7 Function *mutation* implements a single-bit, point mutation.

A TIME TO REPRODUCE, A TIME TO CROSS

With the Big Three designed and built, creating a new population from an old one is no big deal. The proper sequencing is shown in Fig. 3.8 in the procedure *generation.* Starting at an individual index *j* = 1 and continuing until the population size, *popsize,* has been exceeded, we pick two mates, *mate1* and *mate2,* using successive calls to *select.* We cross and mutate the chromosomes using *crossover* (which itself contains the necessary invocations of *mutation*). In a final flurry of mad activity, we decode the pair of *chromosomes,* evaluate the objective (fitness) function values, and increment the population index *j* by 2.

Having already examined *select, crossover,* and *mutation* in detail, we need only concern ourselves with the two problem-dependent routines hinted at above. For any problem we must create a procedure that decodes the string to

```
procedure generation;
( Create a new generation through select, crossover, and mutation )
( Note: generation assumes an even-numbered popsize              )
var j, mate1, mate2, jcross:integer;
begin
 j := 1;
 repeat    ( select, crossover, and mutation until newpop is filled )
  mate1 := select(popsize, sumfitness, oldpop); ( pick pair of mates )
  mate2 := select(popsize, sumfitness, oldpop);
  ( Crossover and mutation - mutation embedded within crossover )
  crossover(oldpop[mate1].chrom, oldpop[mate2].chrom,
            newpop[j   ].chrom, newpop[j + 1].chrom,
            lchrom, ncross, nmutation, jcross, pcross, pmutation);
  ( Decode string, evaluate fitness, & record parentage data on both children )
  with newpop[j  ] do begin
    x := decode(chrom, lchrom);
    fitness := objfunc(x);
    parent1 := mate1;
    parent2 := mate2;
    xsite   := jcross;
  end;
  with newpop[j+1] do begin
    x := decode(chrom, lchrom);
    fitness := objfunc(x);
    parent1 := mate1;
    parent2 := mate2;
    xsite   := jcross;
  end;
  ( Increment population index )
  j := j + 2;
 until j>popsize
end;
```

FIGURE 3.8 Procedure *generation* generates a new population from the previous population.

create a parameter or set of parameters appropriate for that problem. We must also create a procedure that receives the parameter or set of parameters thus decoded and evaluate the figure of merit or objective function value associated with the given parameter set. These routines, which we call *decode* and *objfunc,* are the two places where the GA rubber meets the applications road. For different problems we will often need different decoding routines (although later on in this chapter we will examine some standard routines that have proven useful in a number of studies), and in different problems we will always need a different fitness function routine. Having said this, it is still useful to look at a particular decoding routine and a particular fitness function. To be consistent with work earlier in this book, we will continue to use binary unsigned integer coding, and we will continue to use a simple power function as the fitness function; however, we will increase the value of the exponent, using the function $f(x) = x^{10}$.

SGA uses the decoding routine shown in Fig. 3.9, the function *decode.* In this function, a single *chromosome* is decoded starting at the low-order bit (position 1) and mapped right to left by accumulating the current power of 2— stored in the variable *poweroftwo*—when the appropriate bit is set (value is true). The accumulated value, stored in the variable *accum,* is finally returned by the function *decode.*

The objective function used in SGA is a simple power function, similar to the function used in Chapter 1. In SGA we evaluate the function $f(x) = (x/coeff)^{10}$ The actual value of *coeff* is chosen to normalize the x parameter when a bit string of length *lchrom* = 30 is chosen. Thus $coeff = 2^{30} - 1 = 1073741823.0$. Since the x value has been normalized, the maximum value of the function will be $f(x) = 1.0$ when $x = 2^{30} - 1$ for the case when *lchrom* = 30. A straightforward implementation of the power function is presented in Fig. 3.10 as the function *objfunc.*

```
function decode(chrom:chromosome; lbits:integer):real;
{ Decode string as unsigned binary integer - true=1, false=0 }
var j:integer;
      accum, powerof2:real;
begin
 accum := 0.0; powerof2 := 1;
 for j := 1 to lbits do begin
   if chrom[j] then accum := accum + powerof2;
   powerof2 := powerof2 * 2;
   end;
 decode := accum;
end;
```

FIGURE 3.9 Function *decode* decodes a binary string as a single, unsigned integer.

```
function objfunc(x:real):real;
{ Fitness function - f(x) - x**n }
const coef - 1073741823.0; { Coefficient to normalize domain }
        n - 10;          { Power of x }
begin objfunc := power( x/coef, n ) end;
```

FIGURE 3.10   Function *objfunc* calculates the fitness function $f(x) = cx^{10}$ from the decoded parameter *x*.

GET WITH THE MAIN PROGRAM

We have described the data structures. We have built the genetic operators. We have decoded the strings, and we have figured the fitness values. Now is the time to wrap a ribbon around this parcel, test it, and ship it on for further use. In Fig. 3.11 we see the main program of SGA. At the top of the code, we start innocently enough by setting the generation counter to 0, *gen* := 0. We build steam as we read in program data, initialize a random population, calculate initial population statistics, and print out a special initial report using the procedure *initialize*. We won't dwell on the initialization code here. The interested reader should refer to Appendix C, which contains a complete copy of the SGA code.

At long last, with necessary preliminaries complete, we hit the main loop contained within the *repeat-until* construct. In rapid succession we increment the generation counter, generate a new generation in *generation*, calculate new generation statistics in *statistics*, print out the generation report in *report*, and advance the population in one fell swoop:

```
oldpop := newpop;
```

All this continues, step after relentless step, until the generation counter exceeds the maximum, thereby forcing the machinery to a grinding halt.

In our rush to see the big picture, we have missed some important details. The statistical routine *statistics* (Fig. 3.12) calculates the average, maximum, and minimum fitness values; it also calculates the *sumfitness* required by the roulette wheel. This version of *statistics* is again something of a minimally acceptable solution. Many other interesting population statistics could and probably should be tracked. For example, allele convergence statistics are often tabulated during a generation. Best string so far or best *k* strings so far could be stored for future reference. Population standard deviation or even population histograms might also be of interest in doing more detailed run postmortems. The separation of statistical functions in the routine statistics permits the easy addition of any or all of these computations.

```
begin       { Main program }
 gen := 0;    { Set things up }
 initialize;
 repeat       { Main iterative loop }
  gen := gen + 1;
  generation;
  statistics(popsize, max, avg, min, sumfitness, newpop);
  report(gen);
  oldpop := newpop; { advance the generation }
 until (gen >= maxgen)
end.         { End main program }
```

FIGURE 3.11 **Main program for a simple genetic algorithm, SGA.**

The procedure *report* presents the full population report, including strings, fitnesses, and parameter values. A listing of *report* and its single subprocedure *writechrom* are presented in Fig. 3.13. Once again, a wide array of tabular and graphic reporting options may be useful in genetic algorithm work. The simple *report* procedure is a good tool because it permits side-by-side comparison of consecutive generations. In turn, this allows checking of operators and analysis of the events leading to the construction of the best individuals.

```
procedure statistics(popsize:integer;
                     var max,avg,min,sumfitness:real;
                     var pop:population);
{ Calculate population statistics }
var j:integer;
begin
 { Initialize }
 sumfitness := pop[1].fitness;
 min        := pop[1].fitness;
 max        := pop[1].fitness;
 { Loop for max, min, sumfitness }
 for j := 2 to popsize do with pop[j] do begin
   sumfitness := sumfitness + fitness; { Accumulate fitness sum }
   if fitness>max then max := fitness; { New max }
   if fitness<min then min := fitness; { New min }
   end;
 { Calculate average }
 avg := sumfitness/popsize;
end;
```

FIGURE 3.12 **Procedure *statistics* calculates important population statistics.**

```
{ report.sga: contains writechrom, report }

procedure writechrom(var out:text; chrom:chromosome; lchrom:integer);
{ Write a chromosome as a string of 1's (true's) and 0's (false's) }
var j:integer;
begin
 for j := lchrom downto 1 do
   if chrom[j] then write(out,'1')
     else write(out,'0');
end;

procedure report(gen:integer);
{ Write the population report }
const linelength = 132;
var j:integer;
begin
 repchar(lst,'-',linelength); writeln(lst);
 repchar(lst,' ',50); writeln(lst,'Population Report');
 repchar(lst,' ',23);   write(lst,'Generation ',gen-1:2);
 repchar(lst,' ',57); writeln(lst,'Generation ',gen:2);
 writeln(lst);
   write(lst,' #                   string                x    fitness');
   write(lst,'          # parents xsite');
 writeln(lst,   '                 string                x    fitness');
 repchar(lst,'-',linelength); writeln(lst);
 for j := 1 to popsize do begin
 write(lst,j:2,') ');
   { Old string }
   with oldpop[j] do begin
     writechrom(lst,chrom,lchrom);
     write(lst,' ', x:10, ' ', fitness:6:4, '       |');
    end;
   { New string }
   with newpop[j] do begin
     write(lst,'       ', j:2, ') (', parent1:2, ',', parent2:2, ')
              xsite:2,'        ');
     writechrom(lst,chrom,lchrom);
     writeln(lst, ' ',x:10,' ', fitness:6:4);
    end;
 end;
 repchar(lst,'-',linelength); writeln(lst);
 { Generation statistics and accumulated values }
 writeln(lst,' Note: Generation ', gen:2, ' & Accumulated Statistics: '
          ,' max=', max:6:4,',  min=', min:6:4, ',  avg=', avg:6:4, ',  sum='
          ,sumfitness:6:4, ',  nmutation=', nmutation, ',  ncross= ', ncross);
 repchar(lst,'-',linelength); writeln(lst);
 page(lst);
end;
```

FIGURE 3.13 Procedures *report* and *writechrom* implement population reports.

HOW WELL DOES IT WORK?

We have trudged through the SGA code, step by step, inch by inch, gaining a better feel for some of the ins and outs of genetic algorithm programming. Of course, this is not the only way to skin a GA cat, and a number of public domain codes are available with numerous bells and whistles for effective optimization in a variety of domains (Booker and De Jong, 1985; De Jong, 1982; Grefenstette, 1984a, 1984b). Actually, we will be adding several important features of our own in this and later chapters. Let us resist temptation and hold off the fancy features. In this section, we stick with the bare-bones GA and see how well it works.

We have already specified our simple test problem. The bit string decodes as an unsigned 30-bit integer. The fitness function f is the power function $f(x) = (x/c)^n$, where c has been chosen to normalize x, and n has been chosen as 10. Some of you may cry foul, wondering why we have chosen a different function from the one followed in Chapters 1 and 2 ($f(x) = x^2$). Actually, we have changed the problem to make things tougher for the GA, as illustrated in Fig. 3.14. With the larger exponent, the average function value is lower, and a smaller proportion of the domain maps to values above some specified quantity. As a result, the random starting population will not contain very good points to begin; this is a better test of GA performance.

To specify our computer simulations more precisely, let's choose a trial set of GA parameters. In De Jong's (1975) study of genetic algorithms in function optimization, a series of parametric studies across a five-function suite of problems suggested that good GA performance requires the choice of a high crossover probability, a low mutation probability (inversely proportional to the population size), and a moderate population size. Following these suggestions we adopt the following parameters for our first computer simulations:

$pmutation$ = 0.0333   (probability of mutation)
$pcross$ = 0.6   (probability of crossover)
$popsize$ = 30   (population size, n)

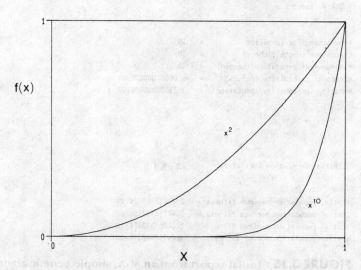

FIGURE 3.14   Comparison of the functions x^2 and x^{10} on the unit interval.

The string length for the hand simulations of a genetic algorithm in Chapter 1 was short (short by genetic algorithm standards): $l = 5$. This translated into a ridiculously small space with only $2^5 = 32$ points, where there was little practical need for genetic search. Any enumerative search or random walk would have found good points quickly. Of course, at that time our aim was pedagogical clarity, and the size of the search space was of little interest. Now that we are interested in seeing a stiffer test of GA performance, the string length is increased and the exponent of the test function is increased. With a string length $lchrom = 30$, the search space is much larger and random walk or enumeration should not be so profitable. With $lchrom = 30$ there are $2^{30} = 1.07(10^{10})$ points. With over 1.07 billion points in the space, one-at-a-time methods are unlikely to do very much very quickly. Moreover, the increase in exponent has adjusted the space so that only 1.05 percent of the points have a value greater than 0.9, as shown in Fig. 3.14. These two modifications make the problem a better test of GA performance.

We start the simple genetic algorithm and let it run for seven generations. The statistical report for the run is shown in Fig. 3.15 and the initial generation (gen = 0) and the first generation are shown side by side in Fig. 3.16. The initial population starts out with a population average fitness of 0.0347. The average fitness of the function on the specified interval may be calculated to be 0.0909. In some sense, we have been unlucky (but not unrealistically so) in our random choice of a population. Additionally glancing at our best member fitness in the initial population, $f_{max} = 0.2824$, we should expect to have $30(1 - 0.2824^{0.1}) = 3.56$ or approximately four strings in a random population of 30 with fitness

```
SGA Parameters
...............

Population size (popsize)          =   30
Chromosome length (lchrom)         =   30
Maximum # of generation (maxgen)   =   10
Crossover probability (pcross)     =   6.0000000000E-01
Mutation  probability (pmutation)  =   3.3300000000E-02




Initial Generation Statistics
.............................

Initial population maximum fitness =   2.8241322532E-01
Initial population average fitness =   3.4715832788E-02
Initial population minimum fitness =   1.1406151375E-10
Initial population sum of fitness  =   1.0414749837E+00
```

FIGURE 3.15 Initial report from an SGA, simple genetic algorithm, run.

Population Report

	Generation 0						Generation 1		
#	string	x	fitness		#	parents xsite	string	x	fitness
1)	111000011001100000101111110100	9.4621E+08	0.2824	|	1)	(1,19) 30	111000011001100000101101110100	9.4621E+08	0.2824
2)	110011001011010111000000100001	8.5862E+08	0.1069	|	2)	(1,19) 30	110101011110001110010011000101	8.9712E+08	0.1658
3)	010101111001011110000010001101	3.6739E+08	0.0000	|	3)	(23,19) 19	110101011100000011010110000001	8.9655E+08	0.1647
4)	011001111000011101101111011010	4.3423E+08	0.0001	|	4)	(23,19) 19	111111001000000010010011000101	1.0591E+09	0.8715
5)	011111111010010101011010110110	5.3539E+08	0.0009	|	5)	(19, 1) 11	111000011001100001001100101	9.4621E+08	0.2824
6)	101101111001000011000101101101	7.6993E+08	0.0359	|	6)	(19, 1) 11	110101011110000100011111110100	8.9707E+08	0.1657
7)	000110101111000010010111110000	1.1312E+08	0.0000	|	7)	(16, 1) 6	111000011001100000101111100100	9.4621E+08	0.2824
8)	010100111010111010001111100010	3.5099E+08	0.0000	|	8)	(16, 1) 6	110011010101011001001011100100	8.6132E+08	0.1103
9)	011011001110001010011110000101	4.5670E+08	0.0002	|	9)	(23,17) 30	101111000100000100111011110010	7.9071E+08	0.0469
10)	010011010110101000001101011011	3.2470E+08	0.0000	|	10)	(23,17) 30	110011101001000100001110110011	8.6640E+08	0.1170
11)	010111011010101011001101000010	3.9287E+08	0.0000	|	11)	(6,26) 30	101101100010001000010101101	7.6783E+08	0.0350
12)	010011010011001010110010001110	3.2379E+08	0.0000	|	12)	(6,26) 30	110010000101010100110110011110	8.4026E+08	0.0861
13)	110000100101101110100000100111	8.1520E+08	0.0636	|	13)	(2,19) 10	110101011101000100100000100001	8.9720E+08	0.1659
14)	010110001001111101000100110001	3.7171E+08	0.0000	|	14)	(2,19) 10	110011011011010111000011000101	8.6281E+08	0.1122
15)	010101111110000101101110010110	3.8538E+08	0.0000	|	15)	(17,17) 26	110011111001000100011100100101	8.7060E+08	0.1228
16)	110011010101010010011001100000	8.6129E+08	0.1103	|	16)	(17,17) 26	110010111101000010011100100011	8.5487E+08	0.1023
17)	110011111101000100011100100111	8.7165E+08	0.1243	|	17)	(19,17) 30	110101011110000100011000111	8.9707E+08	0.1657
18)	100000000100010111100101011100	5.3802E+08	0.0010	|	18)	(19,17) 30	110011111010000001110100011	8.7163E+08	0.1243
19)	110101011110000100100111000100	8.9707E+08	0.1657	|	19)	(19,19) 24	110101011110000100011000101	8.9707E+08	0.1657
20)	010011111000010001000011011101	3.3352E+08	0.0000	|	20)	(19,19) 24	110101011110000100011000101	8.9707E+08	0.1657
21)	001101011100110111010010000011	2.2567E+08	0.0000	|	21)	(26,17) 30	110010000101010100110110011110	8.4026E+08	0.0861
22)	000110011111000001100100110110	1.0880E+08	0.0000	|	22)	(26,17) 30	110000111110100001110010001011	8.2132E+08	0.0686
23)	101111001000000011110110000011	7.9064E+08	0.0469	|	23)	(23, 1) 3	111000011001100000001111110000	9.4621E+08	0.2824
24)	011101110000110001010011001011	4.9533E+08	0.0004	|	24)	(23, 1) 3	101111001000000011110100010100	7.9064E+08	0.0469
25)	010110111010001101010001010010	3.8436E+08	0.0000	|	25)	(27, 1) 10	110000011001100001001110011	8.1199E+08	0.0612
26)	110010000101010100110110011011	8.4026E+08	0.0861	|	26)	(27, 1) 10	101001100001010101011110100	6.9660E+08	0.0132
27)	101001100101110101001001100011	6.9778E+08	0.0134	|	27)	(1,17) 25	110010001001100000101111110100	8.4135E+08	0.0873
28)	100011110111010000100000110010	6.0169E+08	0.0031	|	28)	(1,17) 25	111001111101000010011100100011	9.7231E+08	0.3707
29)	010010100010000100001101100011	3.1092E+08	0.0000	|	29)	(1,19) 23	110101010100100000101111110100	8.9378E+08	0.1597
30)	001011001111001110010101100011	1.8854E+08	0.0000	|	30)	(1,19) 23	111000011110000000100011000101	9.4739E+08	0.2859

Note: Generation 1 & Accumulated Statistics: max=0.8715, min=0.0132, avg=0.1732, sum=5.1967, nmutation=35, ncross= 10

FIGURE 3.16 SGA run, generation report $t = 0$–1.

greater than 0.2824. We have not only been unlucky on average, we have been unlucky at the top. Despite the unfortunate initial depression of the population, once the genetic algorithm gets started, it quickly finds good performance, as we can see vividly after the first round of reproduction, crossover, and mutation. In the first generation, a very good string is found with fitness 0.8715. As the run continues, further improvement is found in both maximum and average population fitness as demonstrated in Fig. 3.17. Toward the end of the run, a form of convergence is observed as displayed in Fig. 3.18. In generation 7, if we scan up and down the bit strings we notice that there is a fair amount of agreement at

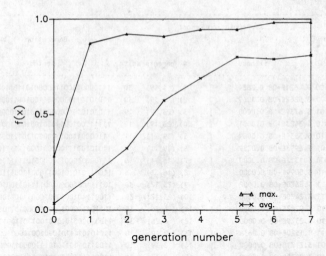

FIGURE 3.17 SGA run, best-of-generation (max) results and generation average (avg) results to generation 7.

most bit positions. This has occurred even though we have not reached the best point in the space; we have gotten close, however. In generation 6 an individual has appeared with fitness $f = 0.9807$. This is near optimal but not optimal (this point is in the top 0.19 percent of the points in the space). Convergent behavior without guarantee of optimality bothers many people who approach genetic algorithms from other, more traditional, optimization backgrounds. There are ways to slow down this *premature convergence,* as it has been called, and we shall look at some of these methods in this and later chapters; however, the fact of the matter is that genetic algorithms have no convergence guarantees in arbitrary problems. They do sort out interesting areas of a space quickly, but they are a weak method, without the guarantees of more convergent procedures. This does not reduce their utility. Quite the contrary, more convergent methods sacrifice globality and flexibility for their convergence. Additionally, many methods are limited to a narrow class of problem. As a result, genetic algorithms can be used where more convergent techniques dare not tread. Moreover, if you are solving problems where known local, but convergent, methods exist, the idea of a hybrid scheme is natural. Start your search using a genetic algorithm to sort out the interesting hills in your problem. Once the GA ferrets out the best regions, then take your locally convergent scheme and climb the local peaks. In this way, you can combine the globality and parallelism of the GA with the more convergent behavior of the local technique. In a moment we will look at one practical way of reducing the premature convergence problem through fitness scaling. First we must devise techniques to transform arbitrary objective functions to proper fitness function form.

```
.................................................................................................
                              Population Report
               Generation  6                                    Generation  7

#          string             x      fitness   | #   parents xsite        string             x      fitness
.................................................................................................
 1) 1111000110100100101011111000? 1.0135E+09 0.5615 |  1) ( 8, 6)   7  111111001011000000101111000100 1.0599E+09 0.8779
 2) 111111001000010001001111110011 1.0592E+09 0.8726 |  2) ( 8, 6)   7  111111001000000010011011101100 1.0591E+09 0.8715
 3) 111111001000000010011111110100 1.0591E+09 0.8715 |  3) ( 9,24)   9  111111001000000010011010100111 1.0591E+09 0.8715
 4) 111110011110000000101111100100 1.0481E+09 0.7849 |  4) ( 9,24)   9  111111101000000010000111110111 1.0675E+09 0.9430
 5) 111111001101100001101111010110 1.0605E+09 0.8834 |  5) ( 6,18)   3  111111011000011110101111100100 1.0633E+09 0.9070
 6) 111111001011000000101111101100 1.0599E+09 0.8779 |  6) ( 6,18)   3  111110001011000000111111101100 1.0431E+09 0.7484
 7) 111111001001100000101111101100 1.0595E+09 0.8747 |  7) (10,22)  22  101110011100000010011111110111 7.7910E+08 0.0405
 8) 111111001000000010011011000100 1.0591E+09 0.8715 |  8) (10,22)  22  111111001111010000101111100100 1.0610E+09 0.8872
 9) 111111101000000010000011100111 1.0675E+09 0.9430 |  9) (15,15)  30  111110011010000010011111110001 1.0470E+09 0.7772
10) 111111001100000010011111110111 1.0601E+09 0.8801 | 10) (15,15)  30  111110011010000010011111111001 1.0470E+09 0.7772
11) 111111001000000010011111110111 1.0591E+09 0.8715 | 11) (12,12)   5  111111111000000000111111010001 1.0716E+09 0.9807
12) 111111101000000010011111110001 1.0675E+09 0.9430 | 12) (12,12)   5  111111101000000010011111110001 1.0675E+09 0.9430
13) 110101011000000010000011000101 9.9616E+08 0.4724 | 13) (26,16)  15  111111001010000000101101110111 1.0596E+09 0.8757
14) 111111001001110000101111110000 1.0595E+09 0.8752 | 14) (26,16)  15  111110010110000010101111100100 1.0460E+09 0.7694
15) 111110011010000000101111110000 1.0470E+09 0.7772 | 15) (20, 1)  30  111111001000000010010011000100 1.0591E+09 0.8715
16) 111111001010000001010111100100 1.0596E+09 0.8758 | 16) (20, 1)  30  111100011010010010101011111100 1.0135E+09 0.5615
17) 111110011110000001100111101111 1.0481E+09 0.7850 | 17) ( 9,10)  30  111111101000000010011011100111 1.0675E+09 0.9430
18) 111111011000001110101111100100 1.0633E+09 0.9070 | 18) ( 9,10)  30  111111001100000010011111110111 1.0601E+09 0.8801
19) 111111001000000010011111110000 1.0591E+09 0.8715 | 19) ( 3, 8)  14  111111011000000010011111110100 1.0633E+09 0.9066
20) 111111001000000010010011000101 1.0591E+09 0.8715 | 20) ( 3, 8)  14  111111001000000010011011000100 1.0591E+09 0.8715
21) 111110011110000010101111110000 1.0481E+09 0.7850 | 21) ( 1,26)   8  111110010110000000111011001100 1.0460E+09 0.7694
22) 101110011110010010101111100100 7.7969E+08 0.0408 | 22) ( 1,26)   8  111100011010010010101111111111 1.0135E+09 0.5615
23) 111111101000000010011111110000 1.0675E+09 0.9430 | 23) (18,20)  30  110110110000001110101111100100 9.9621E+08 0.4726
24) 111111001000000010011111110111 1.0591E+09 0.8715 | 24) (18,20)  30  111111001000000010010010000101 1.0591E+09 0.8715
25) 111111111000000010011111100100 1.0717E+09 0.9807 | 25) (14,30)   3  111111001001100001011111100000 1.0595E+09 0.8747
26) 111110010110000000101111110111 1.0460E+09 0.7694 | 26) (14,30)   3  111111001001110001011110100100 1.0595E+09 0.8752
27) 111111001001110001101111110000 1.0595E+09 0.8752 | 27) (23, 3)  18  111111001001000010011111110000 1.0593E+09 0.8736
28) 011110011000010010000011000101 5.0968E+08 0.0006 | 28) (23, 3)  18  111111101100000010011111110100 1.0685E+09 0.9523
29) 111110011000000010011011110001 1.0601E+09 0.8801 | 29) (24, 2)  30  111111001000000010001111110111 1.0591E+09 0.8720
30) 111111001001100000101111100100 1.0595E+09 0.8747 | 30) (24, 2)  30  111111001000100010011111110011 1.0592E+09 0.8726
.................................................................................................
Note: Generation  7 & Accumulated Statistics:  max=0.9807,  min=0.0405,  avg=0.8100,  sum=24.2997,  nmutation=201,  ncross= 71
.................................................................................................
```

FIGURE 3.18 SGA run, generation report $t = 6–7$.

MAPPING OBJECTIVE FUNCTIONS TO FITNESS FORM

In many problems, the objective is more naturally stated as the minimization of some cost function $g(x)$ rather than the maximization of some utility or profit function $u(x)$. Even if the problem is naturally stated in maximization form, this alone does not guarantee that the utility function will be nonnegative for all x as we require in fitness function (recall that a fitness function must be a nonnegative figure of merit). As a result, it is often necessary to map the underlying natural objective function to a fitness function form through one or more mappings.

The duality of cost minimization and profit maximization is well known. In normal operations research work, to transform a minimization problem to a maximization problem we simply multiply the cost function by a minus one. In genetic algorithm work, this operation alone is insufficient because the measure thus obtained is not guaranteed to be nonnegative in all instances. With GAs the following cost-to-fitness transformation is commonly used:

$$f(x) = C_{max} - g(x) \quad \text{when } g(x) < C_{max},$$
$$= 0 \quad \quad \quad \text{otherwise.}$$

There are a variety of ways to choose the coefficient C_{max}. C_{max} may be taken as an input coefficient, as the largest g value observed thus far, as the largest g value in the current population, or the largest of the last k generations. Perhaps more appropriately, C_{max} should vary depending on the population variance. We will consider this last possibility in Chapter 4.

When the natural objective function formulation is a profit or utility function we have no difficulty with the direction of the function: maximized profit or utility leads to desired performance. We may still have a problem with negative utility function $u(x)$ values. To overcome this, we simply transform fitness according to the equation:

$$f(x) = u(x) + C_{min} \quad \text{when } u(x) + C_{min} > 0,$$
$$= 0 \quad \quad \quad \text{otherwise.}$$

We may choose C_{min} as an input coefficient, as the absolute value of the worst u value in the current or last k generations, or as a function of the population variance. We postpone further consideration of these possibilities to a later chapter.

All this monkeying about with objective functions should arouse suspicion about the underlying relationship between objective functions and fitness functions. In nature, fitness (the number of offspring that survive to reproduction) is a tautology. Large numbers of offspring survive because they are fit, and they are fit because large numbers of offspring survive. Survival in natural populations is the ultimate and only taskmaster of any import. By contradistinction, in genetic algorithm work we have the opportunity and perhaps the duty to regulate the level of competition among members of the population to achieve the interim and ultimate algorithm performance we desire. This is precisely what we do when we perform fitness scaling.

FITNESS SCALING

Regulation of the number of copies is especially important in small population genetic algorithms. At the start of GA runs it is common to have a few extraordinary individuals in a population of mediocre colleagues. If left to the normal selection rule ($pselect_i = f_i/\Sigma f$), the extraordinary individuals would take over a significant proportion of the finite population in a single generation, and this is undesirable, a leading cause of premature convergence. Later on during a run we have a very different problem. Late in a run, there may still be significant diversity within the population; however, the population average fitness may be close to the population best fitness. If this situation is left alone, average members and best members get nearly the same number of copies in future generations, and the survival of the fittest necessary for improvement becomes a random walk among the mediocre. In both cases, at the beginning of the run and as the run matures, fitness scaling can help.

One useful scaling procedure is linear scaling. Let us define the raw fitness f and the scaled fitness f'. Linear scaling requires a linear relationship between f' and f as follows:

$$f' = af + b.$$

The coefficients a and b may be chosen in a number of ways; however, in all cases we want the average scaled fitness f'_{avg} to be equal to the average raw fitness f_{avg} because subsequent use of the selection procedure will insure that each average population member contributes one expected offspring to the next generation. To control the number of offspring given to the population member with maximum raw fitness, we choose the other scaling relationship to obtain a scaled maximum fitness, $f'_{max} = C_{mult} \cdot f_{avg}$, where C_{mult} is the number of expected copies desired for the best population member. For typical small populations ($n = 50$ to 100) a $C_{mult} = 1.2$ to 2 has been used successfully.

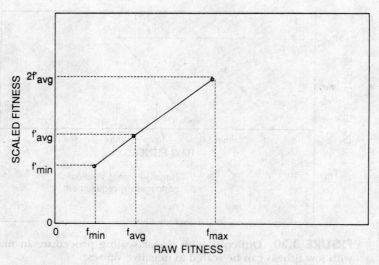

FIGURE 3.19 Linear scaling under normal conditions.

Toward the end of a run, this choice of C_{mult} stretches the raw fitness significantly. This may in turn cause difficulty in applying the linear scaling rule as shown in Fig. 3.19. As we can see, at first there is no problem applying the linear scaling rule, because the few extraordinary individuals get scaled down and the lowly members of the population get scaled up. The more difficult situation is shown in Fig. 3.20. This type of situation is common in a mature run when a few lethals (bad strings) are far below the population average and maximum, which are relatively close together. If the scaling rule is applied in this situation, the stretching required on the relatively close average and maximum raw fitness values causes the low fitness values to go negative after scaling. A number of solutions are available to solve this problem; here, when we cannot scale to the desired C_{mult}, we still maintain equality of the raw and scaled fitness averages and we map the minimum raw fitness f_{min} to a scaled fitness $f'_{min} = 0$.

The simple scaling procedure may easily be added to the simple genetic algorithm code through the use of three routines shown in Fig. 3.21: *prescale, scale,* and *scalepop*. The procedure *prescale* takes the average, maximum, and minimum raw fitness values, called *umax, uavg,* and *umin,* and calculates linear scaling coefficients a and b based on the logic described above. If it is possible to scale to the desired multiple, C_{mult} (in the code it is called *fmultiple*), then that is the computation performed. Otherwise, scaling is performed by pivoting about the average value and stretching the fitness until the minimum value maps to zero. The procedure *scalepop* is called after the preparation routine *prescale* to

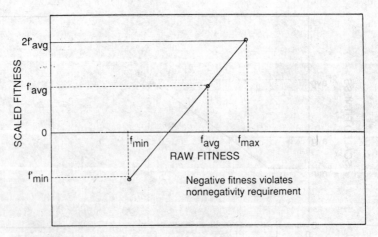

FIGURE 3.20 Difficulty with linear scaling procedure in mature run. Points with low fitness can be scaled to negative values.

```
{ scale.sga: contains prescale, scale, scalepop for scaling fitnesses }

procedure prescale(umax, uavg, umin:real; var a, b:real);
{ Calculate scaling coefficients for linear scaling }
const fmultiple = 2.0;       { Fitness multiple is 2 }
var   delta:real;            { Divisor }
begin
 if umin > (fmultiple*uavg - umax) / (fmultiple - 1.0) { Non-negative test }
    then begin   { Normal Scaling }
         delta := umax - uavg;
         a := (fmultiple - 1.0) * uavg / delta;
         b := uavg * (umax - fmultiple*uavg) / delta;
       end else begin   { Scale as much as possible }
         delta := uavg - umin;
         a := uavg / delta;
         b := -umin * uavg / delta;
         end;
end;

function scale(u, a, b:real):real;
{ Scale an objective function value }
begin  scale := a * u + b end;

procedure scalepop(popsize:integer; var max, avg, min, sumfitness:real;
                    var pop:population);
{ Scale entire population }
var j:integer;
    a, b:real;      { slope & intercept for linear equation }
begin
 prescale(max, avg, min, a, b);  { Get slope and intercept for function }
 sumfitness := 0.0;
 for j := 1 to popsize do with pop[j] do begin
   fitness := scale(objective, a, b);
   sumfitness := sumfitness + fitness;
   end;
end;
```

FIGURE 3.21 Scaling routines: procedure *prescale*, function *scale*, and procedure *scalepop*.

scale all the individual raw fitness values using the simple function *scale*. Here we have assumed that the raw fitness values are stored in the *individual* record in a real value called *objective* (*pop[j].objective*). The scaled fitness is placed in the real parameter *fitness*, and the sum of the fitness values *sumfitness* is recalculated. Installation and testing of the scaling procedure is left as an exercise.

In this way, simple scaling helps prevent the early domination of extraordinary individuals, while it later on encourages a healthy competition among near equals. This does not complete our examination of the possible objective function transformations, and we shall return to some more examples in Chapter 4. At the moment, we examine some of the coding options available to us in GA work beyond the simple codings we have used thus far.

CODINGS

We only have examined a very limited number of string coding alternatives for mapping a finite-length string to the parameters of an optimization problem. We have introduced a simple binary coding in response to a simple binary switching problem. In this coding we have concatenated a string of 0's and 1's coding, where the ith 0 (or 1) has meant that the ith switch is off (or on). We have also decoded a binary string as an unsigned integer where the string $A = a_l a_{l-1} \cdots a_2 a_1$ has decoded to the parameter value $x = \Sigma a_i \cdot 2^{i-1}$. Although these codings have given us some flexibility, they do not provide the variety of options we require to tackle the spectrum of problems we face in science, business, and engineering. In this section, we examine two fundamental principles of genetic algorithm coding to help guide our coding design in different problems. Later on we will look at a multiparameter, mapped, binary string coding that has proved and should continue to prove useful in a variety of problems.

In one sense, coding a problem for genetic search is no problem because the genetic algorithm programmer is limited largely by his imagination. As we saw in the last chapter, genetic algorithms exploit similarities in arbitrary codings as long as building blocks (short, high-performance schemata) lead to near optima. In another sense, this freedom of choice is a mixed blessing to the new user; the array of possible coding alternatives is both invigorating and bewildering. Given this freedom, how does a new user choose a good coding? Fortunately, genetic algorithms are forgiving because they are robust, and in that sense there is usually no need to agonize over coding decisions. Additionally, we offer two basic principles for choosing a GA coding: the *principle of meaningful building blocks* and the *principle of minimal alphabets*.

The principle of meaningful building blocks is simply this:

> **The user should select a coding so that short, low-order schemata are relevant to the underlying problem and relatively unrelated to schemata over other fixed positions.**

Although this principle can be checked rigorously using the Walsh analysis mentioned in Chapter 2, this procedure is rarely practical and as a result, coding design for meaningful building blocks is something of an art. Nonetheless, when we design a coding we should check the distances between related bit positions. Chapter 5 presents ways to rearrange the ordering of a string coding, as well as several operators that search for good codings while they search for good solutions.

The second coding rule, the principle of minimal alphabets, is simply stated:

> **The user should select the smallest alphabet that permits a natural expression of the problem.**

Until now we have been almost obsessed with the idea of binary codings. Has this been accidental or has there been method to our coding madness? That there has been method can be best illustrated by returning to our tired but illustrative

TABLE 3.1 Comparison of Binary and Nonbinary String Populations

Binary String	Value X	Nonbinary String	Fitness
0 1 1 0 1	13	N	169
1 1 0 0 0	24	Y	576
0 1 0 0 0	8	I	64
1 0 0 1 1	19	T	361

five-bit example started in Chapter 1. In Table 3.1, we see the same old four binary strings with their same old fitness values (which we obtained by decoding the strings as unsigned binary integers and thereby evaluated the fitness according to the relation $f(x) = x^2$). Recall that one of our original motivations for considering schemata was the natural attempt to associate high fitness with similarities among strings in the population. In the table, we also consider a nonbinary coding. In fact, we consider an extreme example. Consider a one-to-one mapping of the binary integers $[0, 31]$ to the 32-letter alphabet consisting of the 26 letter alphabet {A–Z} and the six digits {1–6}, as shown in Table 3.2.

In the binary case, as we scan the list (Table 3.1), the hunt for important similarities is made possible by the small cardinality of the alphabet. In the nonbinary case, as we scan the list we only have the four single-letter strings and their fitness values; there are no coding similarities to exploit. This is surely an extreme example, but the same principle holds true in less flagrant cases.

To see this a bit more mathematically, we should really compare the number of schemata available in a binary coding to the number of schemata available in a nonbinary coding. Of course, both the binary and nonbinary codings should

TABLE 3.2 Binary and Nonbinary Coding Correspondence

Binary	Nonbinary
0 0 0 0 0	A
0 0 0 0 1	B
.	.
.	.
.	.
1 1 0 0 1	Z
1 1 0 1 0	1
1 1 0 1 1	2
.	.
.	.
1 1 1 1 1	6

code the same number of alternatives; however, the different alphabet cardinalities require different string lengths. For equality of the number of points in each space, we require $2^l = k^{l'}$, where l is the binary code string length and l' is the nonbinary code string length. The number of schemata for each coding may then be calculated using the respective string length: 3^l in the binary case and $(k + 1)^{l'}$ in the nonbinary case. It is easy to show that the binary alphabet offers the maximum number of schemata per bit of information of any coding. Since these similarities are the essence of our search, when we design a code we should maximize the number of them available for the GA to exploit.

A MULTIPARAMETER, MAPPED, FIXED-POINT CODING

Our two principles give us some clues for designing effective codings for simple genetic algorithms. They do not, however, suggest practical methods for coding a particular problem. One successfully used method of coding multiparameter optimization problems of real parameters is the concatenated, multiparameter, mapped, fixed-point coding.

We have already considered an unsigned fixed-point integer coding; however, what happens if we are not very much interested in a parameter $x \in [0, 2^l]$? One way to circumvent this apparent limitation is to map the decoded unsigned integer linearly from $[0, 2^l]$ to a specified interval $[U_{min}, U_{max}]$. In this way, we can carefully control the range and precision of the decision variables. The precision of this mapped coding may be calculated:

$$\pi = \frac{U_{max} - U_{min}}{2^l - 1}$$

SINGLE U_1 PARAMETER (l_1 = 4)

```
0 0 0 0 ——→ Umin
1 1 1 1 ——→ Umax
others map linearly in between
```

MULTIPARAMETER CODING (10 parameters)

```
0 0 0 1 | 0 1 0 1 |  . . .  | 1 1 0 0 | 1 1 1 1 |
  U1    |   U2    |  . . .  |   U9    |   U10   |
```

FIGURE 3.22 Multiparameter code constructed from concatenated, mapped, fixed-point codes.

To construct a multiparameter coding, we can simply concatenate as many single-parameter codings as we require. Of course, each coding may have its own sublength, its own U_{max} and U_{min} values, as represented in Fig. 3.22.

A set of coding routines that implements the concatenated, mapped, fixed-point coding is presented in Fig. 3.23. The single-parameter routine decode dis-

```
type parmparm   = record        { parameters of the parameter }
                      lparm:integer; { length of the parameter }
                      parameter, maxparm, minparm:real; { parameter & range }
                    end;
     parmspecs  = array[1..maxparms] of parmparm;

var  parms:parmspecs;

procedure extract_parm(var chromfrom, chromto:chromosome;
                       var jposition, lchrom, lparm:integer);
{ Extract a substring from a full string }
var j, jtarget:integer;
begin
 j := 1;
 jtarget := jposition + lparm - 1;
 if jtarget > lchrom then jtarget := lchrom; { Clamp if excessive }
 while (jposition <= jtarget) do begin
   chromto[j] := chromfrom[jposition];
   jposition := jposition + 1;
   j := j + 1;
  end;
end;

function map_parm(x, maxparm, minparm, fullscale:real):real;
{ Map an unsigned binary integer to range [minparm,maxparm] }
begin map_parm := minparm + (maxparm - minparm)/fullscale*x end;

procedure decode_parms(var nparms, lchrom:integer;
                       var chrom:chromosome;
                       var parms:parmspecs);
var j, jposition:integer;
    chromtemp:chromosome; { Temporary string buffer }
begin
 j := 1; { Parameter counter }
 jposition := 1; { String position counter }
 repeat
  with parms[j] do if lparm>0 then begin
    extract_parm(chrom, chromtemp, jposition, lchrom, lparm);
    parameter := map_parm( decode(chromtemp, lparm),
                           maxparm, minparm, power(2.0, lparm)-1.0 );
   end else parameter := 0.0;
  j := j + 1;
 until j > nparms;
end;
```

FIGURE 3.23 Coding routines for use in SGA: procedure *extract_parm*, function *map_parm*, and procedure *decode_parms*.

cussed earlier is used by the new routines to decode a subparameter string as a binary unsigned integer. The procedure *extract_parm* removes a substring from a full string, the routine *map_parm* maps the unsigned integer to the range [*minparm, maxparm*], and the routine *decode_parms* coordinates the decoding of all *nparms* parameters. The installation and testing of these procedures is left as an exercise.

DISCRETIZATION

The discretization of a parameter optimization problem with real parameters is not the only type of discretization that may be required to perform genetic algorithm search. Many optimization problems, more properly optimal control problems, have not just a single control parameter but rather a control function that must be specified at every point in some continuum—a functional. To apply genetic algorithms to these problems, they first must be reduced to finite parameter form before parameter coding may take place.

This form of discretization may be illustrated easily with an example. Suppose we wish to minimize the time of travel of a bicycle between two points, and suppose further that we can apply a force f as a function of time $f(t)$ between limits $|f(t)| \leq f_{max}$. In this continuous optimal control problem, we would attempt to calculate the schedule of force application as a continuous function of time as illustrated in Fig. 3.24. With a genetic algorithm, since we must deal with finite-length structures, we first reduce the continuous problem to a finite number of parameters and then further reduce the finite parameters to string form through some coding process.

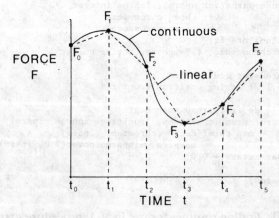

FIGURE 3.24   Discretized force control schedule.

The discretization of the continuum we require is more usually associated with topics like discrete control, interpolation, and finite elements. In the bicycle control problem, one way to discretize the continuous schedule into a finite parameter representation is by spacing force values f_i at regular intervals of time. We then assume some functional form, step function, linear interpolant, piecewise quadratic, or cubic spline, to fit through the points f_i. Figure 3.24 shows a linear interpolating function approximation to the continuous force schedule of the bicycle control problem.

CONSTRAINTS

Thus far, we have only discussed genetic algorithms for searching unconstrained objective functions. Many practical problems contain one or more constraints that must also be satisfied. In this section, we consider the incorporation of constraints into genetic algorithm search.

Constraints are usually classified as equality or inequality relations. Since equality constraints may be subsumed into a system model—the black box—we are really only concerned with inequality constraints. At first, it would appear that inequality constraints should pose no particular problem. A genetic algorithm generates a sequence of parameters to be tested using the system model, objective function, and the constraints. We simply run the model, evaluate the objective function, and check to see if any constraints are violated. If not, the parameter set is assigned the fitness value corresponding to the objective function evaluation. If constraints are violated, the solution is infeasible and thus has no fitness. This procedure is fine except that many practical problems are highly constrained; finding a feasible point is almost as difficult as finding the best. As a result, we usually want to get some information out of infeasible solutions, perhaps by degrading their fitness ranking in relation to the degree of constraint violation. This is what is done in a *penalty method*.

In a penalty method, a constrained problem in optimization is transformed to an unconstrained problem by associating a cost or penalty with all constraint violations. This cost is included in the objective function evaluation. Consider, for example, the original constrained problem in minimization form:

minimize $g(x)$

subject to $h_i(x) \geqslant 0$ $i = 1, 2, \ldots, n$

where x is an m vector

We transform this to the unconstrained form:

minimize $\dot{g}(x) + r \cdot \sum_{i=1}^{n} \Phi[h_i(x)]$

where Φ–penalty function,

r–penalty coefficient.

A number of alternatives exist for the penalty function Φ. In this book, we usually square the violation of the constraint, $\Phi[h_i(x)] = h_i^2(x)$, for all violated constraints i. Under certain conditions, the unconstrained solution converges to the constrained solution as the penalty coefficient r approaches infinity. As a practical matter, r values in genetic algorithms are often sized separately for each type of constraint so that moderate violations of the constraints yield a penalty that is some significant percentage of a nominal operating cost.

SUMMARY

This chapter has unveiled some of the genetic algorithm's mystery, through careful examination of the data structures, procedures, and details necessary to implement a practical, yet simple, genetic algorithm. Specifically, we have implemented a bare-bones genetic algorithm called the simple genetic algorithm (SGA), written in Pascal programming language for execution on commonly available microcomputers.

As might be expected, the primary data structure of the simple genetic algorithm is the string population. The SGA formulation uses two nonoverlapping populations to make birth and replacement as easy as possible. The populations themselves consist of an array of individuals that contain the bit strings, the decoded parameter, and the fitness function value along with other important auxiliary information.

The primary work of the SGA is performed in three routines, *select, crossover,* and *mutation.* Select performs simple stochastic selection with replacement, what we have been calling roulette wheel selection. Crossover and mutation perform their namesake operations as described in Chapter 1. Their action is coordinated by a procedure called *generation* that generates a new population at each successive generation.

After building SGA we have tested it in a small run on a simple function, $f(x) = c \cdot x^{10}$. While concrete conclusions are impossible on a single trial of a stochastic process, the GA does find near optimal results quickly after searching a small portion of the search space.

Various details of implementation have also been discussed. Objective-to-fitness transformations have been examined to convert normal objective function formulations, whether maximization or minimization formulations, to proper fitness function form. Additionally, fitness scaling has been suggested for maintaining more careful control over the allocation of trials to the best strings.

Some of the issues underlying the coding problem have been examined. The *principle of minimal alphabets* and the *principle of effective building blocks* have been laid down to help the GA user design more effective codings. A coding that has been useful in a number of problems has been presented in Pascal computer code form. This coding, the multiparameter, mapped, fixed-point coding, should be useful in many parameter optimization problems.

The need for discretization is not restricted to that imposed by codings. Many practical optimization problems require the specification of a control function or functions over a continuum. These optimization problems—more properly, optimal control problems—must first be reduced to finite parameter problems, which may in turn be discretized by the coding procedure discussed in this chapter. Discretization of this type is performed by selecting appropriate interpolation functions (often linear interpolation will suffice) and the parameters associated with the chosen interpolation form are then coded into a concatenated, finite-length bit string.

Last, we have recognized the need for special methods to adjoin inequality constraints to a problem. Genetic algorithms are naturally cast as an unconstrained search technique. After all, nature tries and tries again, only finding the constraints of its environment through the survival or death of its trials. Similarly, genetic algorithms must have fitness functions that reflect information about both the quality and the feasibility of solutions. Exterior penalty methods have been used successfully in a number of problems. With these methods, whenever a constraint is violated, the unconstrained objective function value is penalized by an amount related to a function of the constraint violation.

The examination of concrete code examples and a number of implementation issues has made GAs more accessible for our use in practical scientific, engineering, and business problems. In the next chapter, we look at a number of early and current applications of straightforward genetic algorithms.

■ PROBLEMS

3.1. Consider the fitness function $f(x) = x^n$ on the interval $x \in [0, 1]$. Calculate the expected population average of a randomly selected population of points. Calculate the probability of selecting a point $f > f_0$. Compare numerical values of the population average for $n = 2$ and $n = 10$. Compare probabilities of selecting one point $f > 0.9$ for the same two exponents.

3.2. A search space contains 2,097,152 points. A binary-coded genetic algorithm is compared to an octal-coded genetic algorithm. Calculate and compare the following quantities in the two cases, binary and octal:

a) Total number of schemata
b) Total number of search points
c) Number of schemata contained within single individual
d) Upper and lower bounds on number of schemata in population of size $n = 50$

3.3. A function of three variables, $f(x, y, z)$ is to be minimized. The x variable is known to vary between -20.0 and 125.0, the y variable is known to vary between 0 and $1.2(10^6)$, and the z variable is known to vary between -0.1 and

1.0. The desired precision for x, y, and z are 0.5, 10^4, and 0.001 respectively. Design a concatenated, mapped, fixed-point coding for this problem. What is the minimum number of bits required to obtain the desired precision? With the selected coding, determine the bit strings that represent each of the following points: $(-20, 0, -0.1)$, $(125.0, 1.2E6, 1.0)$, $(50, 100000, 0.597)$.

■ COMPUTER ASSIGNMENTS

A. Install the scaling routine of Fig. 3.21 in the simple genetic algorithm (SGA) code and reproduce the experiment on function $f(x) = cx^{10}$. Compare and contrast the results obtained with and without scaling installed.

B. Test the multiparameter, mapped, fixed-point coding routines of Fig. 3.23 on a three-parameter problem with parameter maximums, minimums, and substring lengths as follows:

$$\text{Max}_i = \quad 20, \ 100, \ 300$$

$$\text{Min}_i = \ -10, \ -5, \quad 0$$

$$\text{Length}_i = \quad 5, \ 10, \ 15$$

Test the coding routine on the all-0 string, the all-1 string, and the string 010101...0101. Check the computer calculation with a hand calculation. Also determine the precision of each of the subcodes within the coding. After testing, install the routines in the SGA code with appropriate initialization procedures.

C. Minimize the function $f(x, y, z) = x^2 + y^2 + z^2$. where x, y, and z are permitted to vary between -512 and 512. Use a 10-bit coding for each substring (this is De Jong's function $F1$).

D. Improve the efficiency of the selection procedure by implementing a binary search using cumulative selection probability distribution values.

E. Implement and test a routine to perform mutation as a mutation clock. (*Hint:* Use an exponential distribution and calculate the time until next mutation.)

F. Implement a coding routine to implement a floating-point code with specified mantissa and exponent.

G. Compare the performance of a binary-coded genetic algorithm to a nonbinary-coded genetic algorithm. Specifically, compare the performance of a binary-coded GA on the fitness function of this chapter $f(x) = x^{10}$ to an octal-coded GA on the same problem. Use a 30-bit code and a 10-position octal code {0, 1, 2, 3, 4, 5, 6, 7}. Compare and contrast the rate of convergence and ultimate convergence under both codings.

4 | Some Applications of Genetic Algorithms

To paraphrase a popular quip, "If GAs are so smart, why ain't they rich?" In fact, genetic algorithms *are* rich—rich in application across a large and growing number of disciplines. This chapter presents a cross section of genetic algorithm applications from old to new, from pure to applied, in fields as diverse as mathematics, medicine, engineering, and political science. Our aim is threefold. First, we seek historical perspective to better understand why the state of genetic algorithm art has arrived at its current position. Second, having dipped our toes into a puddle of computer code in the previous chapter, here we stroke our way past the applications of others to learn the practical side of the applications business. Last, by examining the diverse application of GAs, we continue to amass evidence in support of our earlier claims of genetic algorithm robustness: their diversity of application and the efficiency of operation are virtually unparalleled in the annals of blind search.

The survey of genetic algorithm applications starts with a review of early computer simulations of natural genetics and other signs of GA prehistory. After reviewing several early applications, from Bagley's pioneering dissertation to De Jong's pivotal work in pure function optimization, we investigate a potpourri of current applications drawn from engineering, medicine, and social science.

THE RISE OF GENETIC ALGORITHMS

Prior to the use of genetic algorithms for search in artificial systems, a number of biologists used digital computers to perform simulations of genetic systems (Barricelli, 1957, 1962; Fraser, 1960, 1962; Martin and Cockerham, 1960). Although these studies were aimed at understanding natural phenomena, Fraser's work was not too distant from the modern notion of a genetic algorithm. His work on epistasis considered a phenotype function as follows:

$$\text{Phenotype} = a + q \cdot a \mid a \mid + c \cdot a^3.$$

In this work a 15-bit string of 0's and 1's was decoded where five bits on a bit string decoded to the a parameter, five bits decoded to the q parameter, and five bits decoded to the c parameter. Fraser showed the interaction of the different parameters in the series of graphs recreated as Fig. 4.1. Selection in his simulations was performed by allowing genotypes (strings) with phenotype values (function values) between specified limits (-1 to $+1$) to be chosen as parents. Fraser simulated the evolution of future string generations and calculated the percentage of individuals with acceptable phenotypes with successive generations. The results of his computer simulations are shown in Fig. 4.2.

While these results look something like function optimization, there was no recognition in Fraser's writing that nature's search algorithm of choice might be useful in artificial settings. It remained for Holland and his students to apply geneticlike operators to artificial problems in adaptation. Holland laid the foundation for these applications with his writings on adaptive systems theory (Holland, 1962a–c). His goals were broad, as we see from the following early quotation (Holland, 1962c, p. 298):

> The study of adaptation involves the study of both the adaptive system and its environment. In general terms, it is a study of how systems can generate procedures enabling them to adjust efficiently to their environments. If adaptability is not to be arbitrarily restricted at the outset, the adapting system must be able to generate any method or procedure capable of an effective definition.

These are not the writings of a man simply looking for yet another method of solving this or that optimization problem. Holland's goal then as now was to develop the theory and procedures necessary for the creation of general programs and machines with unlimited capability to adapt to arbitrary environments. At the same time, Holland recognized the fundamental role of unnatural selection—an artificial survival of the fittest—in whatever programs and machines one might design (p. 300):

> Adaptation, then, is based upon differential selection of supervisory programs. That is, the more "successful" a supervisory program, in terms of the ability of its problem-solving programs to produce solutions, the more predominant it is to become (in numbers) in a population of supervisory programs.

Not only did Holland recognize the need for selection, he also unambiguously endorsed a populations approach to search rather than the single-structure-by-single-structure approach so prevalent in the literature. It is interesting to note that in these earliest adaptive systems writings, Holland only hinted at the im-

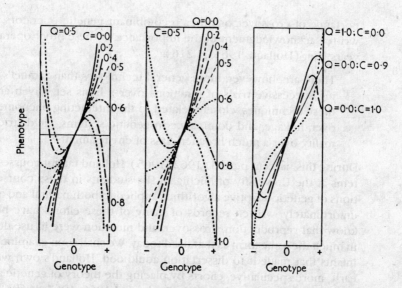

FIGURE 4.1 Sketch of Fraser's epistatic function (1962). Reprinted by permission from *Journal of Theoretical Biology*, vol. 2, 1962 by Academic Press London Ltd.

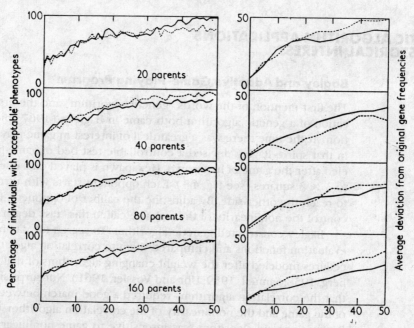

FIGURE 4.2 Results of genetic simulation on Fraser's epistatic function varying population size (1962). Reprinted by permission from *Journal of Theoretical Biology*, vol. 2, 1962 by Academic Press London Ltd.

portance of crossover or other recombinant genetic operators. The first direct written acknowledgment of the importance of these other operators came three years later (Holland, 1965, p. 216):

> There are, however, more general techniques than Samuel's for generating successive trials of functions over a basis set. Given any basis set, these techniques, closely related to the interacting phenomena of crossover, linkage, and dominance in genetic systems, yield strict near optimality over a much broader class of environments.

During this nascent period (1962–1965), Holland taught courses in adaptive systems at the University of Michigan. His students in these courses wrote simulations of genetic adaptive algorithms applied to both natural and artificial systems; unfortunately, written records of many of these efforts have been lost. We do know that reproduction, crossover, and mutation were in use during this period in much the same form as that used today. We shall soon examine those incubated infants that made it to dissertation adulthood. Holland's own work followed his early, more speculative, efforts by placing the theory of genetic adaptive systems on mathematical terra firma (Holland, circa 1966, 1967, 1969a, 1969c). The important theory of schemata was in place around the turn of the decade (Holland, 1968, 1971) with important results linking reproductive plans and the k-armed bandit problem following shortly thereafter (Holland, 1973a, 1975).

GENETIC ALGORITHM APPLICATIONS OF HISTORICAL INTEREST

Bagley and Adaptive Game-Playing Program

The first mention of the words "genetic algorithm" and the first published application of a genetic algorithm both came in Bagley's (1967) pioneering dissertation. At the time there was a great deal of interest in game-playing programs, and in that spirit, Bagley devised a controllable test bed of game-playing tasks modeled after the game of hexapawn. Hexapawn is played on a chessboard cut down to 3×3 squares (see Fig. 4.3). Each opponent starts with three pawns and tries to reach the other side. By adjusting the caliber of opponent, Bagley was able to control the nonlinearity of the task (he called this "task depth").

Bagley constructed genetic algorithms to search for parameter sets in game evaluation functions and compared them to correlation algorithms, learning procedures modeled after the weight-changing algorithms of that period (see Friedberg, 1958; Samuel, 1959; Uhr and Vossler, 1961). Not surprisingly, Bagley found that the correlation algorithms required a good match between the nonlinearity of the game and the nonlinearity of the correlation algorithm. On the other hand Bagley's genetic algorithm was insensitive to game nonlinearity and performed well over a range of environments (task depths).

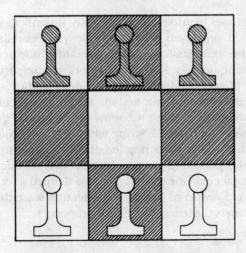

FIGURE 4.3   Sketch of hexapawn board.

Bagley's genetic algorithm was not unlike the genetic algorithms we use today. He constructed reproduction, crossover, and mutation operators similar to those described in the previous chapter; in addition, he used diploid string representations, dominance, and inversion. (The next chapter says more about these advanced operators.) Additionally, Bagley used nonbinary alphabets in coding strings. As we know from our previous study of schemata, there is good reason to use minimal alphabets. Bagley did not have access to Holland's theory of schemata, and as a result, his work could not be guided by it.

One area where Bagley's work foreshadows more modern research is in the area of reproduction and selection. Bagley was keenly aware of the need for appropriate selection rates at the beginning and the end of genetic algorithm runs. He introduced a fitness scaling mechanism to do two things: reduce the selection early in a run, thereby preventing domination of a population by a single super-individual, and increase the selection later in a run, thereby maintaining appropriate competition among highly fit and similar strings near population convergence. Similar procedures have been adopted by current researchers.

Bagley also introduced the first notion of genetic algorithm self-regulation in what he called *self-contained controls*. He suggested coding the crossover and mutation probabilities within the chromosomes themselves; he did not present any computer simulation results of experiments with this mechanism, however.

Rosenberg and Biological Cell Simulation

Working at the same time as Bagley, Rosenberg (1967) also investigated genetic algorithms in his early doctoral dissertation. Because he emphasized the biological and simulation aspects of his work, his contributions to the art of genetic algorithms are sometimes overlooked. In his study Rosenberg simulated a population of single-celled organisms with a simple yet rigorous biochemistry, a permeable membrane, and classical genetic structure (one gene, one enzyme). Despite his biological emphasis, Rosenberg's work was important to the subsequent development of genetic algorithms in artificial applications because of its resemblance to optimization and root-finding. We won't go into the details of his chemical kinetics models here; however, some of the genetic details are of interest. Rosenberg defined a finite-length string with a pair of chromosomes (diploid representation). In his studies the string length was limited to 20 genes, with a maximum of 16 alleles permitted per gene. He defined chemical concentrations x_j and desired chemical concentrations $\bar{x}_j$. He also defined a set of desired chemical concentrations as a *property*. Mating and selection were then performed according to the antifitness function (for the ith property):

$$f_i = \sum_j (x_j - \bar{x}_j)^2,$$

where the sum is taken over all chemicals in the ith property. Rosenberg calculated the inverse of the f_i quantities and performed mating and subsequent reproduction according to this inverse antifitness. In all of his simulations, he actually only considered a single property ($i = 1$), and as a result, passed up the chance to perform the first multiobjective genetic algorithm, a task later taken up by Schaffer (1984). His simulations were, however, the first application of genetic algorithms to a root-finding task; when properly viewed, searching for cells that minimize the antifitness function is equivalent to solving the highly nonlinear equation represented by the chromosome and cell biochemistry to obtain a particular property.

Like that of Bagley, Rosenberg's work preceded Holland's theory of schemata, and as a result he too adopted nonbinary alphabets. Like Bagley, Rosenberg was also concerned with inventing some means of keeping the selection process appropriately competitive. To do this, he adopted what he called the offspring generation function (OGF). He defined a quantity s that was related to the normalized antifitness of the offspring's parents, f_i/f. Using this s quantity, he reproduced the number of offspring according to the the OGF shown in Fig. 4.4.

Another interesting aspect of this work is its adaptive crossover scheme. Each gene contained so-called linkage factors x_i carried along with the allele values. In this implementation, integer linkage factors between 0 and 7 piggybacked each of the alleles and were reproduced during selection and crossed during crossover with their respective allele values. Instead of choosing the crossing site uniformly at random, Rosenberg selected a crossing site determined by the probability distribution defined over the linkage factors:

$$p_i = x_i / \Sigma x_j$$

Here the p_i represents the probability of a cross at site i. Rosenberg gave an example where tight linkage was important for discovering good results; indeed,

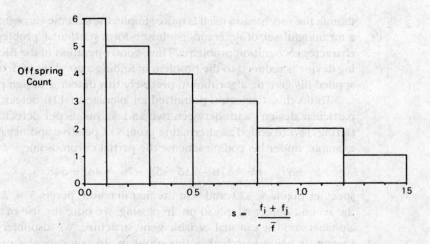

$$s = \frac{f_i + f_j}{\bar{f}}$$

FIGURE 4.4   Offspring generation function (OGF). After Rosenberg (1967).

the linkage factors adjusted to provide the tight linkage during the course of a simulation.

Cavicchio and Pattern Recognition

Following the groundbreaking efforts of Bagley and Rosenberg, other genetic algorithm applications were a few years in the making. In his 1970 study, "Adaptive Search Using Simulated Evolution," Cavicchio applied genetic algorithms to two problems of artificial search: a subroutine selection problem and a pattern recognition problem. Because of its size and connection to problems of current interest, we consider his pattern recognition problem in more detail.

Actually, Cavicchio did not tackle the pattern recognition problem directly. Rather, he applied a genetic algorithm to the design of a set of detectors for a pattern-recognizing machine of known architecture. To understand what is meant by the "design of a set of detectors," we need to have a better picture of the pattern-recognizing machine he used.

Cavicchio adopted the pattern-recognition scheme of Bledsoe and Browning (1959). In this early scheme an image is digitized on a 25 × 25 grid, forming 625 picture elements (pixels) where each pixel is a binary pixel, only capable of discriminating between two shades, light and dark (no gray shades). A set of specified feature detectors is chosen where each detector is itself a subset of the pixels. During a training phase, known images from named classes are presented to the recognition machine and lists of detector states are stored and associated with image class names. During the recognition phase, an unknown image is presented to the recognition device and a simple match score is calculated. A list of the ranked image class names is then constructed for the unknown image. Although the mechanism itself is quite simple, the scheme can work well only when a meaningful set of detectors is chosen for a particular problem (in this case a character recognition problem). Thus, good operation of the Bledsoe and Browning device is reduced to the problem of finding a good set of detectors. Cavicchio applied his genetic algorithm to precisely this detector design problem.

To do this, Cavicchio permitted an average of 110 detectors per device (a particular design) with between two and six pixels per detector. Chromosomes (strings) were coded as alternating groups of positive and negative integers. For example, under his coding scheme the partial chromosome

$$+5 \quad +372 \quad +9 \quad -518 \quad -213 \quad -35 \quad -76 \quad +44 \quad +348 \quad . \quad .$$

specifies pixels 5, 372, and 9 in the first detector, pixels 518, 213, 35, and 76 in the second detector, and so on. In passing, we note the use of a high-cardinality alphabet and the unusual variable gene structure. We also infer that a very large space was being searched in this problem. To compare this problem to binary-coded genetic algorithm problems, let's approximate the number of bits required to code this problem using a binary alphabet. Assuming an average of 110 detectors and four pixels per detector, this problem could be coded by a binary string of the following length:

$$l = 110 \cdot \log_2[\tbinom{625}{4}] = 3581.$$

This is still one of the largest problems ever attempted by any genetic algorithm.

In his genetic algorithm, Cavicchio permitted reproduction and crossover much as we use them today. He tried several selection (reproduction) operators and finally settled on one that rewarded highly fit individuals without permitting them to take over a high percentage of the available population slots. His simple crossover operator is similar to the one described in earlier chapters, except that cross sites are permitted to fall only between detector boundaries (between alternating groups of positive and negative numbers). Because of the variable gene structure and because of the high-cardinality alphabet, Cavicchio was forced to invent three mutation operators:

Mutation$_1$ Change a single pixel within a detector.
Mutation$_2$ Change all pixels within a detector.
Mutation$_3$ Change pixel associations between adjacent detectors.

He also permitted inversion, two-point crossover, and intrachromosomal duplication, but more will be said about these advanced operators in the next chapter.

One innovative mechanism adopted in this study was a so-called *preselection* scheme. Here, a good offspring replaced one of its parents in the hope of maintaining population diversity. Maintenance of diversity was a problem because of the small populations Cavicchio was forced to use (usually between 12 and 20). The preselection scheme seemed to help. A similar scheme was later adopted successfully by De Jong (1975) in an optimization study.

Cavicchio, like Bagley, was enamored of the idea of adapting the parameters of his adaptive algorithm; however, instead of coding the probabilities of cross-

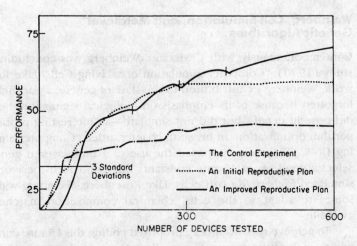

FIGURE 4.5 Comparison of three different adaptive schemes for image detector selection. From Cavicchio (1970).

over and mutation within the chromosome itself as Bagley suggested, Cavicchio used global rate of improvement data to adjust the operator parameters centrally. The scheme he adopted was very much like other weight-changing algorithms popular at that time, and we do not consider the details further.

Instead, it is important to pause and question the propriety of using centralized data in any adaptation algorithm borrowed from natural genetics. In a biological population, where are the wires, all-knowing intelligence, or deity necessary to twiddle parameters in a central fashion? Even if we admit the existence of central authority, what algorithm adjusts the control parameters of the central controller? Both of these questions are elegantly answered in biological systems by coding the control parameters within the chromosome itself. If we follow nature's lead and do the same thing in our artificial systems, in one fell swoop we eliminate the need for central control and avert the dilemma of infinite regress.

Despite the philosophical inconsistency of centralized control in genetics-based search, Cavicchio was able to show some advantage for central adaptation of the adaptation parameters as compared to simulations where the parameters were held constant. He compared the performance of his basic genetic algorithm (labeled "An Initial Reproductive Plan"), an improved scheme with the parameter adaptation mechanism and other bells and whistles (labeled "An Improved Reproductive Plan"), an adaptive scheme based on Klopf's (1965) method (labeled "The Control Experiment"), and a random search (labeled "3 Standard Deviations"). These results are summarized in Fig. 4.5. In this figure, the performance measure (maximum performance = 100) is plotted versus the number of devices sampled (number of detector combinations tried). Both genetic algorithms outperform the nongenetic adaptive scheme and the random search.

Weinberg, Cell Simulation, and Metalevel Genetic Algorithms

Contemporaneously with Cavicchio, Weinberg was concluding his dissertation study (1970), "Computer Simulation of a Living Cell." Like Rosenberg's earlier work, Weinberg's contribution to the state of genetic algorithm art is sometimes forgotten because of its emphasis on biological simulation; however, Weinberg did pose in detail—but did not simulate—an interesting problem of genetic algorithm optimization. In his sixth chapter, titled "Computer Simulation of Evolving DNA," Weinberg proposed the use of a multilayered genetic algorithm to select a good set of 15 rate constants that controlled the workings of different simulated *Escherichia coli* cells. Like Rosenberg, Weinberg wanted the chromosomes to adapt so the cells' chemical composition matched the chemicals available.

To achieve this, Weinberg proposed coding the 15 rate constants on a string where each of the constants was allowed to vary between 10^{-6} and 10^6. Crossover and inversion were enforced at parameter boundaries, and like other studies of the time, nonbinary coding required the design of a complex mutation operator (Weinberg called his operator *directed mutation*).

Like Bagley and Cavicchio, Weinberg could not resist the alluring siren song of GA parameter self-adaptation; however, Weinberg proposed doing this adaptation in a manner strikingly different from either the Bagley or Cavicchio schemes. Specifically, Weinberg suggested the use of a genetic algorithm to adapt the parameters of the lower level genetic algorithm. Weinberg called the upper level GA a nonadaptive genetic program, and he called the lower level GA an adaptive genetic program (its parameters are adapted). The relationships between the two genetic algorithms and the cell simulation are shown in the block diagram of Fig. 4.6. In the proposed scheme, a population of 10 strings coded to represent the crossover, inversion, and mutation probabilities would undergo selection, crossover, and mutation. Those parameters would be passed down to the nonadaptive genetic program, which in turn would generate and test populations (size 40) of rate constants to be used for subsequent cell simulation. Rate of improvement data would then be passed back up to the higher level GA to evaluate the population of GA parameters for subsequent high-level adaptation. Weinberg was aware that the need for centralized information in his scheme was equivalent to postulating the intervention of omniscient, omnipotent authority (1970, p. 101):

> We calculate the utility of an adaptive genetic-program indirectly, by using a god-like judge, the non-adaptive genetic program. The non-adaptive genetic program calculates the utility of an adaptive genetic-program by judging the population which has evolved under the direction of the adaptive genetic-program. It calculates a utility for the best string in the adaptive genetic-program's population. This is the utility awarded to that adaptive genetic-program. After each adaptive genetic-program has awarded a utility, the non-adaptive genetic-program directs the evolution of the population of adaptive genetic-programs.

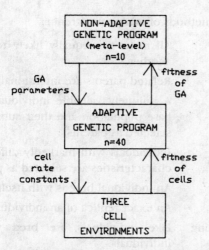

FIGURE 4.6 Schematic of multilevel genetic algorithm as suggested by Weinberg (1970).

As a biologist, Weinberg was probably bothered by the need for godlike intervention in his scheme. Although Weinberg described the simulation methods at great length, he did not present results from simulations of this system in his dissertation. The implementation of metalevel genetic algorithms would have to wait for the work of Mercer (1977) and Grefenstette (1986).

Hollstien and Function Optimization

The first dissertation to apply genetic algorithms to a pure problem (really a set of 14 problems) of mathematical optimization was Hollstien's (1971) work. The title of the dissertation, "Artificial Genetic Adaptation in Computer Control Systems," is something of a misnomer, implying the application of a genetic algorithm to digital feedback control of some engineering plant. Although Hollstien alluded to that possibility, the work was concerned with optimizing functions of two variables ($z = f(x,y)$) using dominance, crossover, mutation, and numerous breeding schemes based on traditional practices of animal husbandry and horticulture.

Hollstien investigated five different selection methods:

Progeny testing	Fitness of offspring controls subsequent breeding of parents.
Individual selection	Fitness of individual controls future use as parent.
Family selection	Fitness of family controls use of all family members as parents.
Within-family selection	Fitness of individuals within a family controls selection of parents for breeding within family.
Combined selection	Two or more of the other methods combine.

He considered eight methods of mating preference:

Random mating	All mates are equally likely to mate with one another.
Inbreeding	Related parents are intentionally mated.
Line breeding	A uniquely valuable individual is bred with a base population and their subsequent offspring selected as parents.
Outbreeding	Individuals with markedly different phenotypic characteristics are selected as parents.
Self-fertilization	An individual breeds with itself.
Clonal propagation	An exact replica of an individual is formed.
Positive assortive mating	Like individuals are bred with other like individuals.
Negative assortive mating	Unlike individuals are bred.

To test the effects of the different selection and mating schemes, Hollstien simulated different combinations of the 5 selection and 8 preference strategies on 14 functions of two variables. In all of Hollstien's computer runs, the strings were coded as 16-bit binary strings where two 8-bit parameters were decoded as either an unsigned binary integer or a Gray-coded integer. A table of 4-bit Gray codes is shown as Table 4.1, where we notice that adjacent integers differ by a single bit (a Hamming distance of 1). This adjacency property is a general char-

TABLE 4.1 Comparison of Binary-Coded and Gray-Coded Integers

Integer	Binary	Gray
0	0000	0000
1	0001	0001
2	0010	0011
3	0011	0010
4	0100	0110
5	0101	0111
6	0110	0101
7	0111	0100
8	1000	1100
9	1001	1101
10	1010	1111
11	1011	1110
12	1100	1010
13	1101	1011
14	1110	1001
15	1111	1000

acteristic of the Gray codes. Hollstien also discussed the possible use of hash codes (where one of the $(2^l)!$ coding permutations is generated and repeatedly used), but he did not give a practical demonstration. Regardless of the coding scheme used, Hollstien linearly mapped the resulting integer to the real interval $[0, 100]$.

In all genetic algorithm runs, Hollstien used populations of 16 strings. He tested various combinations of mating and breeding plans and finally settled on a recurrent inbreeding and crossbreeding plan as the most robust of the schemes he tried. He also claimed some benefit for using Gray codes rather than unsigned binary integers, and he attributed their relative success to the adjacency property and the small perturbation caused by many single mutations. In drawing conclusions from his work, he acknowledged the problems associated with using such a small population size ($n = 16$) and recommended larger population sizes for future studies.

Frantz and Positional Effect

Frantz (1972) took this advice and used larger population sizes ($n = 100$) and string lengths ($l = 25$) in his subsequent study of the effect of positional nonlinearities (epistasis) in genetic algorithm optimization. He constructed combined linear-nonlinear functions over binary haploid chromosomes and studied the position effects (linkage) of several functions where the chromosome ordering was changed to affect the length of particular building blocks. In his initial work, he used roulette wheel selection, simple crossover, and simple mutation to compare the effects of good and bad string orderings. He was able to demonstrate a correlation between tight linkage and rate of improvement. For the functions he considered, once the algorithms converged, however, there was no significant performance difference between simulations with good and bad orderings. This occurred because the functions he chose were insufficiently difficult to test the linkage hypothesis, a result of short string lengths and the weak nonlinearities he introduced through his nonlinear table look-up procedure. The problem here was not that the linkage hypothesis was incorrect; rather, Frantz's functions were simply not tough enough to provide the desired confirmation of theory. That he had difficulty designing difficult functions is not surprising in the light of what is now known about GA-deception. As was pointed out in Chapter 2, it is not sufficient to have long nonlinearities within a function-coding combination. Also needed are lower order building blocks that mislead. This theory and the mathematical tools required to design such problems were not available at the time of Frantz's investigation.

Frantz continued his study by investigating the addition of inversion, a reordering operator, to his genetic algorithm in an effort to search for better string permutations with the hope of creating better, more tightly linked building blocks. It should come as no surprise that Frantz's experiments with inversion were inconclusive (inversion is treated in the next chapter). To show a differential advantage for inversion requires a problem with a deceptive nonlinearity and his earlier experiments without inversion had already shown that this was not the case.

Frantz also used statistical analyses to show that certain allele combinations were being processed at levels significantly different from that expected at random. He also introduced two operators, a *partial complement* operator and a *multiple-point crossover* operator. The partial complement operator (which he called a *migration* operator) complemented roughly a third of the bits of selected individuals in the population. These individuals were called *immigrants* and were permitted to enter the subsequent generation. The partial complement operator was intended to maintain diversity in the population. Frantz found that this operator did add diversity, but this diversity was purchased at too high a cost: decreased performance. The multiple crossover operator he proposed permitted crossover sites to be selected by scanning right to left, successively switching sides with some specified probability. Although he proposed this operator, it was left to a later study by De Jong (1975) to show its strengths and weaknesses.

Bosworth, Foo, and Zeigler—Real Genes

The wave of genetic algorithm activity cresting around 1972 seemed to bifurcate along coding strategy lines. The minimalist camp seemed ready to buy into Holland's theory of schemata and the low-cardinality alphabets it recommended. The maximal alphabet camp seemed to prefer the comforting correspondence of one gene, one parameter regardless of the number of alternative alleles required for a particular gene. An extreme form of this latter philosophy was expounded in the work of Bosworth, Foo, and Zeigler (1972) (Also see Foo and Bosworth, 1972; Zeigler, Bosworth, and Bethke, 1973). In this study operators called reproduction, crossover, mutation, and inversion were applied to "strings" composed of between four and 40 real-type parameters. As with previous work in high-cardinality alphabets, a natural mutation operator was hard to come by, and as a result, five different mutation operators were used:

1. Fletcher-Reeves (FR) mutation
2. Uniform random mutation
3. Quadratic gaussian approximation mutation
4. Cubic gaussian approximation mutation
5. Zero mutation

Readers familiar with traditional optimization procedures will recognize the first "mutation" operator as a fairly sophisticated hill-climbing algorithm. In this so-called mutation operator, approximate gradient information (obtained from $2r$ other function evaluations where r is the number of real parameters) was used to determine the line of conjugate ascent, which was then explored using golden search (using still other function evaluations).

This is a far cry from the notion of simple mutation expounded in the first three chapters. More important, it is very distant from any reasonable biological precedent. If such an operator existed in nature, where would all those other function evaluations come from? Moreover, if such a search were used in a natural setting, could we ever be assured that derivative information would be meaningful in the fracted, discontinuous environments we would search? This is not to question the usefulness of these techniques. The use of reproduction, the parallel search from a population, and the use of sophisticated local search procedures may form powerful search techniques for some limited set of functions; however, in general the use of high-cardinality alphabets so severely reduces implicit parallelism that it is inappropriate to call these schemes genetic algorithms in the sense of Holland.

Box and Evolutionary Operation

This was not the first time that techniques have been called "genetic" or "evolutionary" when the actual resemblance to natural genetics was minimal. A very early effort along these lines was Box's (1957) scheme of *evolutionary operation.* This was less an algorithm and more a management technique to permit less technically minded industrial workers to execute a regular plan of experimentation about the current operating point. The aim was to use the experiments to improve some desirable process metric. To illustrate his scheme, Box gave an example of a process dependent on three variables: carbon treatment, air blowing, and rate of temperature rise. A hypercube was created around the current operating point (Fig. 4.7), and a systematic schedule of visiting the vertexes of the hypercube was undertaken. If significant improvement was found by visiting any of the neighboring points, a decision was made by the evolutionary operations committee to change the operating point, a new hypercube was created,

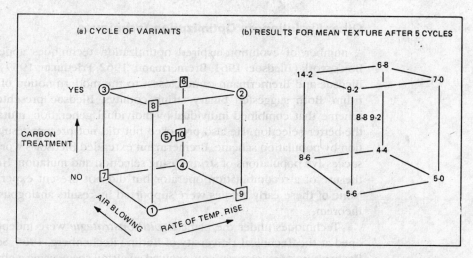

FIGURE 4.7 Use of a hypercube of points in Box's evolutionary operation scheme (Box, 1957). Reprinted by permission from *Journal of the Royal Statistical Society, C.*

and experimentation proceeded. Although the scheme sounds reasonable enough, and subsequent, more automated simplex schemes have proved useful in local search (Nelder and Mead, 1965; Spendley, Hext, and Himsworth, 1962), how is this scheme in any way evolutionary? Box (p. 83) put it this way:

> Living things advance by means of two mechanisms:
>
> (i) Genetic variability due to various agencies such as mutation.
> (ii) Natural selection.
>
> Chemical processes advance in a similar manner. Discovery of a new route for manufacture corresponds to a mutation. Adjustment of the process variables to their best levels, once the route is agreed, involves a process of natural selection in which unpromising combinations of the levels of process variables are neglected in favour of promising ones.

Although we can have little quarrel with his call for operators analogous to natural selection, under this definition, just about anything that changes a structure qualifies as a mutation. This is much too loose a definition, and we must be more careful that essential parts of the analogy are preserved. To some extent Box's use of a search hypercube is biological in that the search proceeds from a population of points (although nature does not restrict its search to some local neighborhood of the current creature, and biological populations are rarely so orderly or regular); however, the lack of a finite coding destroys the schema processing that underlies genetic search; the lack of a recombination operator prevents the innovative information exchange between pairs of structures we found so useful in earlier chapters. We must conclude, then, that the method of evolutionary operation, although a useful tool and an ancestor of other local search techniques, is not a genetic algorithm in the modern sense.

Other Evolutionary Optimization Techniques

A number of evolution-inspired optimization techniques appeared following Box's work (Bledsoe, 1961; Bremermann, 1962; Friedman, 1959). The studies of Bledsoe and Bremermann came closest to the modern notion of a genetic algorithm. Both suggested binary string codings. Bledsoe presented results of a scheme that combined individual-by-individual generation, mutation, and save-the-better selection. He also proposed but did not present results for a population-by-population scheme. Bremermann extended Bledsoe's work by generating successive populations of strings using selection and mutation. He also proposed the use of a recombination operator but did not present experimental results. None of these early studies were supported by results analogous to the schema theorem.

Techniques under the name *Evolutionstrategie* were independently developed at the Technical University of Berlin (Rechenberg, 1965; Schwefel, 1981). Rechenberg's first experiments evolved an airfoil shape using a physical apparatus that permitted local perturbation of airfoil geometry. Computer simulations of similar processes were performed following these early experiments. The use of real parameters limits the schema processing inherent in these methods. None-theless, the *Evolutionstrategie* has gained a devoted following in certain engi-neering and scientific circles, particularly in Germany (Rechenberg, 1986).

Fogel, Owens, and Walsh—Evolutionary Programming

Evolutionary operation and the techniques of evolutionary optimization were fol-lowed by the *evolutionary programming* techniques of Fogel, Owens, and Walsh (1966). The rejection of this work by the artificial intelligence community, more than any other single factor, was responsible for the widespread skepticism faced by more schema-friendly genetic algorithms of the late 1960s and mid-1970s.

In this work a variety of sequential symbol prediction tasks were performed by searching through a space of small finite-state machines. To better understand the task search space, consider a state diagram of a three-state machine as shown in Fig. 4.8. The Greek letters are output symbols, the 0 and 1 are input symbols, and the capital letters are states. For example, if the machine of Fig. 4.8 is in state A and the machine receives an input symbol of 1, a β is output and the machine remains in state A. On the other hand, if the machine is in state A and receives a 0 as input, a β is written and the machine moves to state B. A complete state transition description for this machine is contained in Table 4.2.

This type of machine was trained to predict repeating cycles of output sym-bols using the techniques of Fogel, Owens, and Walsh's evolutionary program-ming, which primarily consisted of two operators:

1. Selection
2. Mutation

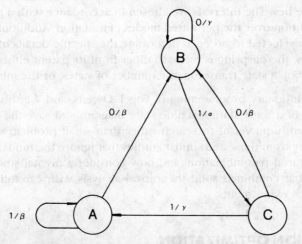

FIGURE 4.8 Schematic of finite-state machine transition diagram as learned in evolutionary programming (Fogel, Owens, and Walsh, 1966). Adapted by permis-sion of John Wiley & Sons, Inc. from *Artificial Intelligence Through Simulated Evolution* by L. J. Fogel, A. J. Owens, and M. J. Walsh, copyright © 1966 John Wiley & Sons, Inc.

TABLE 4.2   State Transition Table for Finite-State Machine (Fogel, Owens, and Walsh, 1967)

Present State	Input Symbol	Next State	OutputSymbol
C	0	B	β
B	1	C	α
C	1	A	γ
A	1	A	β
A	0	B	β
B	1	C	α

Adapted by permission of John Wiley & Sons, Inc. from *Artificial Intelligence Through Simulated Evolution* by L. J. Fogel, A. J. Owens, & M. J. Walsh. Copyright © 1966 John Wiley & Sons, Inc.

In its simplest form, their selection operator chose the better of two machines, the parent or the mutated offspring machine. Populations larger than size $n = 2$ were considered in their work; however, regardless of the number of parent machines saved, mutation operators were the only structure-modifying mechanism used in this work.

For Fogel, Owens, and Walsh, mutation was the single modification of the finite-state machine state diagram in the following sense (pp. 14–15):

> An offspring of this machine is then produced through mutation; that is, through a single modification of the parent machine in accordance with some mutation noise distribution. The mode of mutation is determined by the interval within which a number selected from a random number table lies. The intervals are chosen in accordance with a probability distribution over the permitted modes of mutation. Additional numbers are then selected in order to determine the specific details of the mutation. Thus, the offspring is made to differ from its parent either by an output symbol, a state transition, the number of states, or the initial state.

The evolutionary programming of Fogel Owens, and Walsh with its random alteration of a finite-state machine state diagram and save-the-best selection was insufficiently powerful to search other than small problem spaces quickly. We turn away from these and similar studies that ignore the fundamental importance of structured recombination, and now consider a pivotal study of genetic algorithms that combined solid theoretical analysis with carefully controlled computational experiments.

DE JONG AND FUNCTION OPTIMIZATION

The year 1975 was a particularly good one for genetic algorithms. Holland published his influential book, *Adaptation in Natural and Artificial Systems,* and in that same year De Jong completed his important and pivotal dissertation, "An

Analysis of the Behavior of a Class of Genetic Adaptive Systems." De Jong's study still stands as a milestone in the development of genetic algorithms because of its combination of Holland's theory of schemata and his own careful computational experiments. Because of its importance to the subsequent development of genetic algorithms and because of its carefully considered conclusions, we examine De Jong's study in somewhat greater detail than its predecessors.

Like Hollstien's (1971) earlier study, De Jong's work considered genetic algorithms in a function optimization setting although he was well aware of the potential for GAs in other domains: he was especially interested in their application in data structure design, algorithm design, and computer operating system adaptive control. Despite the attraction of these more esoteric concerns, De Jong recognized the importance of carefully controlled experimentation in an uncluttered problem domain. He thus stripped the genetic algorithm, the environment, and the performance criteria to bare essentials. It was these simplifications that permitted him to perform the baseline experiments that have served as the basis for all further GA studies and applications.

De Jong constructed a test environment of five problems in function minimization. He took care to include functions with the following characteristics:

Continuous/discontinuous
Convex/nonconvex
Unimodal/multimodal
Quadratic/nonquadratic
Low-dimensionality/high-dimensionality
Deterministic/stochastic

The functions and their coding characteristics are presented in Table 4.3. Two-dimensional, inverted sketches of the five functions are presented in Figs. 4.9–4.11.

To quantify the effectiveness of different genetic algorithms, De Jong devised two measures, one to gauge convergence and the other to gauge ongoing performance. He called these measures off-line (convergence) and on-line (ongoing) performance respectively. The names off-line and on-line refer to the difference in emphasis between off-line and on-line applications. In an off-line application, many function evaluations can be simulated and the best alternative so far saved and used after the achievement of some stopping criteria. An on-line application does not afford this luxury and function evaluations are achieved through real experimentation on line; as a result, a premium is placed on getting to acceptable performance quickly. As pointed out earlier, the usual emphasis on convergence is a major flaw in current thinking about search procedures.

In his study De Jong defined the on-line performance $x_e(s)$ of strategy s on environment e as follows:

$$x_e(s) = \frac{1}{T} \sum_{1}^{T} f_e(t),$$

where $f_e(t)$ is the objective function value for environment e on trial t. In words, the on-line performance is an average of all function evaluations up to and in-

TABLE 4.3   De Jong Five-Function Test Bed

Function Number	Function	Limits
1	$f_1(x_i) = \sum_1^3 x_i^2,$	$-5.12 \leq x_i \leq 5.12$
2	$f_2(x_i) = 100(x_1^2 - x_2)^2 + (1 - x_1)^2,$	$-2.048 \leq x_i \leq 2.048$
3	$f_3(x_i) = \sum_1^5 \text{integer}(x_i),$	$-5.12 \leq x_i \leq 5.12$
4	$f_4(x_i) = \sum_1^{30} i x_i^4 + \text{Gauss}(0,1),$	$-1.28 \leq x_i \leq 1.28$
5	$f_5(x_i) = 0.002 + \sum_{j=1}^{25} \dfrac{1}{j + \sum_{i=1}^{2}(x_i - a_{ij})^6},$	$-65.536 \leq x_i \leq 65.536$

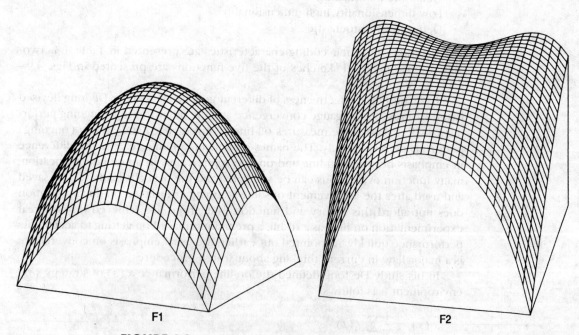

FIGURE 4.9   Inverted, two-dimensional versions of De Jong's (1975) test functions *F*1 and *F*2. Reprinted by permission.

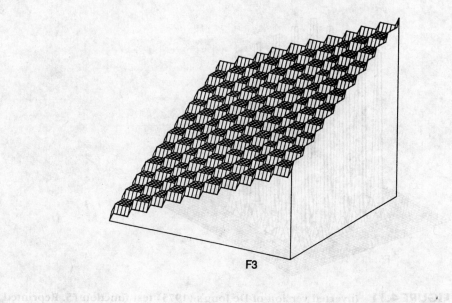

F3

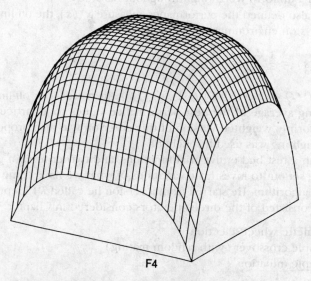

F4

FIGURE 4.10   Inverted, two-dimensional versions of De Jong's (1975) test functions *F*3 and *F*4. Reprinted by permission.

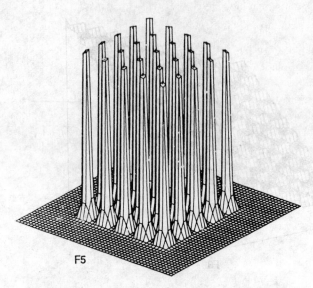

F5

FIGURE 4.11 **Inverted version of De Jong's (1975) test function _F_5. Reprinted by permission.**

cluding the current trial. De Jong actually presented a more general version of this criterion, which permitted nonuniform weighting of trials; however, he adopted a uniform weighting throughout his study.

He also defined the performance measure $x^*_e(s)$, the off-line performance of strategy s on environment e as follows:

$$x^*_e(s) = \frac{1}{T}\sum_1^T f^*_e(t),$$

where $f^*_e(t) = $ best $\{f_e(1), f_e(2),..., f_e(t)\}$. In words, the off-line performance is a running average of the best performance values to a particular time. Again, a nonuniformly weighted version of this criterion was also proposed, but uniform trial weighting was used throughout.

With a test bed of five trial functions, and two criteria of goodness defined, De Jong set out to investigate variations of what we have come to call the simple genetic algorithm. He started from a version he called $R1$ (reproductive plan 1), which consisted of the three operators considered in Chapter 3:

1. Roulette wheel selection
2. Simple crossover (with random mating)
3. Simple mutation

All operators were applied to successive populations of binary strings coded as mapped, concatenated unsigned binary integers.

De Jong was aware that the plan $R1$ was not just a single plan but rather a family of plans depending upon four parameters:

n = population size
p_c = crossover probability
p_m = mutation probability
G = generation gap

We are familiar with the first three of these from our work in the previous chapter. Generation gap G was introduced by De Jong to permit overlapping populations. It was defined between 0 and 1 as follows:

$G = 1$ nonoverlapping populations
$0 < G < 1$ overlapping populations

In the overlapping populations $n \cdot G$ individuals are selected for further genetic action. Resulting offspring are placed in the existing population by choosing $n \cdot G$ population slots uniformly at random (without replacement).

In his early studies De Jong considered the variation of each of the GA parameters first individually and then in limited combinations on the first trial function $F1$, a smooth, quadratic function of three variables. He later performed limited parametric studies on the entire five-function testbed.

Figures 4.12–4.14 show the results for population size experiments on function $F1$. As might be expected, larger populations lead to better ultimate off-line performance (convergence) because of the larger pool of diverse schemata available in a larger population. The inertia of a larger population also leads us to expect the poorer initial on-line performance shown in Fig. 4.14. On the other hand, smaller populations have the ability to change more rapidly and thus exhibit better initial on-line performance.

To combat premature allele loss, mutation rate increases are often suggested as a way to maintain sufficient diversity for continued improvement De Jong's studies have clearly demonstrated that this is no panacea, as is evident in Figures 4.15–4.17. In these runs (with $n = 50$, $p_c = 1.0$, $G = 1.0$) even though the increased mutation rate decreases the number of lost alleles, this decrease is bought at the expense of degraded off-line and on-line performance. As the mutation rate is increased to a value $p_m = 0.1$, the off-line performance of plan $R1$ more and more starts to resemble that of a simple random search. (Of course, a mutation rate $p_m = 0.5$ is a random search regardless of the p_c and n values.) Furthermore, the increases in mutation probability consistently degrade on-line performance.

De Jong also experimented with crossover probabilities and generation gap values. As a result of these studies he suggested a crossover probability $p_c = 0.6$ as a reasonable compromise between good on-line and off-line performance; later studies (Mercer, 1977; Grefenstette, 1986) have suggested that higher crossover rates ($p_c = 1.0$) are better when the stochastic errors of sampling are reduced through the use of more accurate selection procedures. The studies of generation

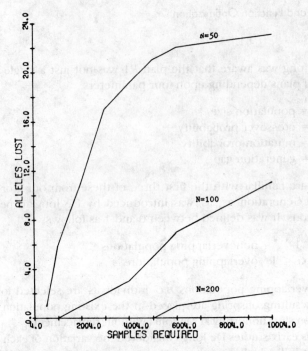

FIGURE 4.12 The effects of population size on allele loss for plan *R*1 on function *F*1 (De Jong, 1975). Reprinted by permission.

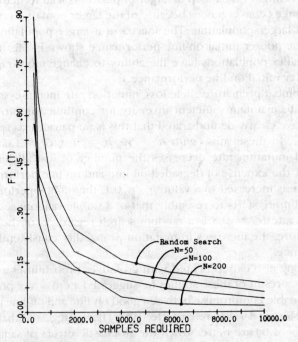

FIGURE 4.13 The effects of population size on off-line performance of plan *R*1 on function *F*1 (De Jong, 1975). Reprinted by permission.

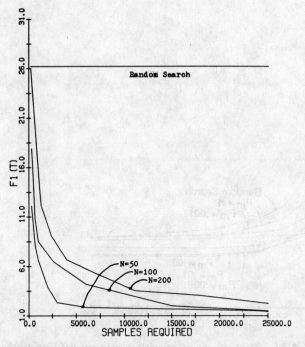

FIGURE 4.14 The effects of population size on on-line performance of plan *R*1 on function *F*1 (De Jong, 1975). Reprinted by permission.

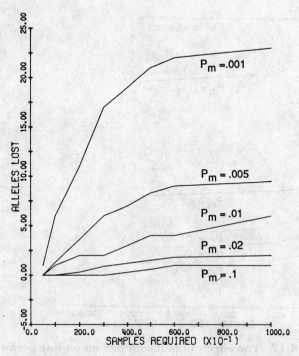

FIGURE 4.15 The effects of mutation rate on allele loss for plan *R*1 on function *F*1 (De Jong, 1975). Reprinted by permission.

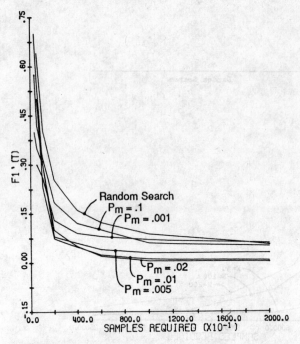

FIGURE 4.16 The effects of mutation rate on off-line performance of *R*1 on function *F*1 (De Jong, 1975). Reprinted by permission.

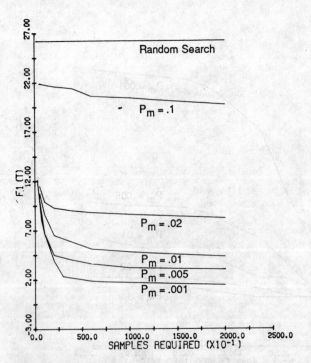

FIGURE 4.17 The effects of mutation rate on on-line performance of plan *R*1 on function *F*1 (De Jong, 1975). Reprinted by permission.

gap suggested that the nonoverlapping population model was best in most optimization studies, where off-line performance tends to be the overriding concern; however, De Jong's studies did show that on-line performance is not severely degraded by using smaller generation gap values. This fact is useful in machine learning where learning while performing well is important.

To improve performance of his baseline GA, De Jong investigated five variations of plan $R1$ as follows:

$R2$ Elitist model
$R3$ Expected value model
$R4$ Elitist expected value model
$R5$ Crowding factor model
$R6$ Generalized crossover model

In his *elitist model R2*, De Jong took special care to preserve his best structures (De Jong, 1975, p. 102):

Let $a^*(t)$ be the best individual generated up to time t. If, after generating $A(t + 1)$ in the usual fashion $a^*(t)$ is not in $A(t + 1)$, then include $a^*(t)$ to $A(t + 1)$ as the $(N + 1)$th member.

In his experiments with $R2$, De Jong found that on unimodal surfaces, the elitist plan significantly improved both on-line and off-line performance; however, on multimodal function $F5$, the elitist plan degraded both performance measures. As De Jong has pointed out, this suggests that elitism improves local search at the expense of global perspective.

To reduce the stochastic errors of roulette wheel selection, De Jong designed the *expected value model R3*. Recall that we wish to issue an exponentially increasing (or decreasing) number of copies to schemata if schema average fitness is above (or below) population average fitness. Under the base plan $R1$, we do this by calculating a probability of selection proportional to fitness and by drawing n individuals according to that probability distribution. As De Jong points out, this procedure leaves us open to two sources of error. First, since we cannot practically calculate actual schema average fitnesses, we are forced to estimate them through sequential finite sampling. Second, the selection scheme (roulette wheel selection) is itself a high-variance process with a fair amount of scatter between expected and actual numbers of copies. In $R3$ De Jong attempted to reduce the latter error. To do this, he calculated the expected number of offspring for each string $f/\bar{f}$ (assuming that the entire population n is reproduced each generation). Thereafter each time a string was selected for mating and crossover, its offspring count was decreased by 0.5 (in De Jong's study only one of the offspring was saved from crossover and mating, unlike the mechanism discussed in Chapter 3, where both offspring were saved). When an individual string was selected for reproduction without mating and crossover, its offspring count was decreased by 1.0. In either case an individual whose offspring count fell below zero was no longer available for selection. In this way the actual number of offspring was forced to be less than $f/\bar{f} + 1$ and was generally less than $f/\bar{f} + 0.5$.

Figure 4.18 compares the expected value plan $R3$ to plans $R2$ and $R1$ on function $F1$ on the basis of allele loss. Plan $R3$ loses far fewer alleles than the base or elitist plans. Figures 4.19 and 4.20 display De Jong's results comparing $R3$ to $R2$ and $R1$ on the basis of off-line and on-line performance respectively. $R3$ is clearly superior to the base plan $R1$ in on-line and off-line performance. Furthermore, although the elitist plan $R2$ is somewhat better than $R3$ on the low dimensional, unimodal function $F1$, plan $R3$ outperformed $R2$ and $R1$ in both on-line and off-line performance measures over the environment E (functions $F1$–$F5$). In limited additional experimentation with crossover probability p_c on plan $R3$, De Jong found that with the reduced stochastic error plan $R3$ could tolerate increasing sampling rates. Subsequent studies with other stochastic error-reducing sampling procedures (Booker, 1982; Brindle, 1981; Grefenstette, 1986) have confirmed this observation.

In plan $R4$, De Jong combined plans $R2$ and $R3$ to form an *elitist expected-value model*. The results he obtained were as one might expect: on unimodal functions ($F1$–$F4$) considerable improvement was observed, while on the difficult foxhole function $F5$, performance was degraded over the expected-value plan alone. Nonetheless, because of the improvement on the first four functions, the global robustness measures were superior.

De Jong was troubled by the degraded performance on the multimodal function $F5$; he took some naturally motivated steps to correct the difficulty in his reproductive plan $R5$. Following Holland (1975), De Jong reasoned that in nature, as like individuals begin to dominate a niche, increased competition for limited resources decreases life expectancy and birthrates. Less crowded niches experience less pressure and achieve life expectancy and birthrates much closer to their potential. To enforce such a crowding pressure in artificial genetic algorithms, De Jong forced newly generated offspring to replace similar, older adults in the hope of maintaining more diversity in the population.

To do this, De Jong adopted an overlapping population model and used generation gap values set at $G = 0.1$. He also defined a new parameter he called the crowding factor (CF). In this new plan $R5$, the *crowding model,* when an individual was born, one individual was selected to die. The dying individual was selected from a subset of CF members chosen from the full population at random. The dying individual was chosen as that individual that most closely resembled the new offspring using a simple bit-by-bit similarity count to measure resemblance. This procedure is not unlike Cavicchio's (1970) preselection scheme mentioned earlier.

Figure 4.21 shows that a crowding factor of CF = 2 gave nearly global optimal performance on function $F5$ over the interval of observation. The notion of crowding and niche has been exploited by others (Goldberg and Richardson 1987; Perry, 1984) in subsequent studies. These ideas are important in multimodal function optimization and machine learning, we shall pay careful attention to them in subsequent chapters.

The last model De Jong considered was his *generalized crossover model R6*. In this plan a parameter called the number of crossover points (CP) was defined.

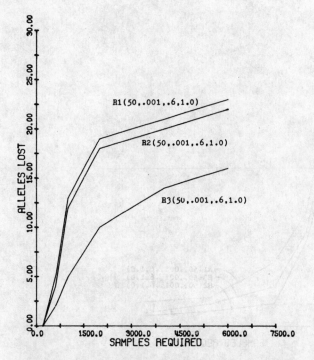

FIGURE 4.18 Comparison of allele loss of plans $R1$, $R2$, and $R3$ on function $F1$ (De Jong, 1975). Reprinted by permission.

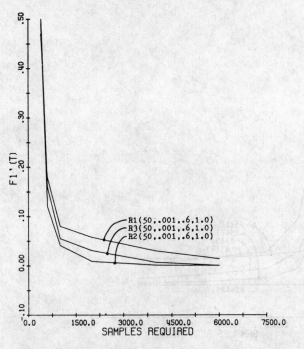

FIGURE 4.19 Comparison of off-line performance of plans $R1$, $R2$, and $R3$ on function $F1$ (De Jong, 1975). Reprinted by permission.

118

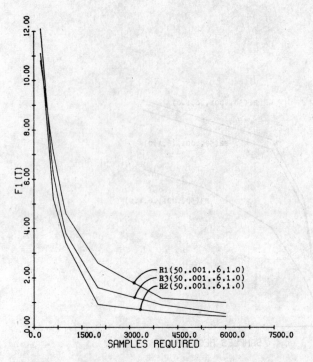

FIGURE 4.20 Comparison of on-line performance of plans *R*1, *R*2, and *R*3 on function *F*1 (De Jong, 1975). Reprinted by permission.

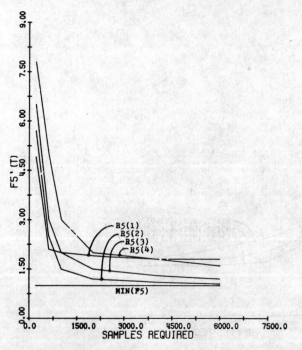

FIGURE 4.21 Effect of crowding factor on off-line performance, plan *R*5 on function *F*5 (De Jong, 1975). Reprinted by permission.

With CP set to 1, generalized crossover reduced to simple crossover. With even CP values, the string was treated as a ring with no beginning or end, and CP crossover points were selected around the circle uniformly at random. For example, with CP = 4 information was exchanged between the two strings (now visualized as rings), as shown in Fig. 4.22. With odd CP values a default crossing point was always assumed at position 0 (the string beginning), as illustrated in Fig. 4.23 with CP = 3.

This was not the first time more complex crossover operators had been defined. Earlier, Cavicchio (1970) defined a two-point crossover operator, and Frantz (1972) defined a generalized, single-parameter crossover operator in his study of positional nonlinearity. In De Jong's study, multiple-point crossover degraded off-line and on-line performance increasingly with increased number of cross points. De Jong explained this poor performance by calculating the survival of second-order schemata. A more intuitive explanation can be found by counting the number of unique operators involved. In the case of simple crossover, we have not just a single operator but a set of $l - 1$ (where l is the string length) operators. In the simple crossover models, we select among these $l - 1$ operators uniformly at random. With a two-point crossover operator (CP = 2) there are $\binom{l}{2}$ different ways of picking the two cross points. In general we have $\binom{l}{CP}$ operators for multiple-point crossover with parameter CP. As a result, when CP is increased, each operator is less likely to be picked during a particular cross, and less structure can be preserved. With more mixing and less structure, these more

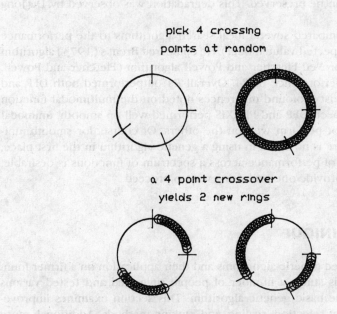

pick 4 crossing
points at random

a 4 point crossover
yields 2 new rings

FIGURE 4.22 Multiple-point crossover operator with even-numbered cross point (CP = 4).

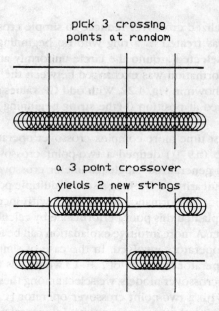

FIGURE 4.23 **Multiple-point crossover example with odd-numbered cross point (CP = 3).**

involved crossover operators become more like a random shuffle and fewer important schemata can be preserved. This degradation was observed by De Jong in his study.

De Jong also compared several local search algorithms to the performance of plan *R*4 (elitist expected-value model). He compared Brent's (1973) algorithm PRAXIS and the improved Fletcher and Powell algorithm (Fletcher and Powell, 1963) DFP to the performance of *R*4. Overall *R*4 outperformed both DFP and PRAXIS, with the most profound differences noted on the multimodal function *F*5. As we might expect, DFP and PRAXIS performed well on smooth, unimodal functions but did not perform well on the others. Of course, for smooth, unimodal functions there is no sense in using a genetic algorithm in the first place; however, if breadth of performance across a spectrum of functions is desirable, genetic algorithms provide one promising way to proceed.

IMPROVEMENTS IN BASIC TECHNIQUE

De Jong's work placed genetic algorithms and their application on a firmer foundation. Following his study, a number of people suggested and tested various improvements to the basic genetic algorithm. This section examines improvements in the areas of selection, scaling, and ranking methods. Additional, more advanced operators such as inversion, dominance, mating restriction, and niche are considered in Chapter 5.

Alternate Selection Schemes

After De Jong's success with expected value selection, several researchers investigated a number of selection alternatives, trying to reduce the stochastic errors associated with roulette wheel selection. Brindle's dissertation (1981) examined six schemes:

1. Deterministic sampling
2. Remainder stochastic sampling without replacement
3. Stochastic sampling without replacement
4. Remainder stochastic sampling with replacement
5. Stochastic sampling with replacement
6. Stochastic tournament (Wetzel ranking)

Stochastic sampling with replacement is a fancy name for our old friend, roulette wheel selection; stochastic sampling without replacement is another name for De Jong's expected-value model $R3$, described earlier. Deterministic sampling is a scheme where the probabilities of selection are calculated as usual, $pselect_i$ $= f_i/\Sigma f$. Then the expected number of individuals for each string e_i is calculated $e_i = pselect_i \cdot n$. Each string is allocated samples according to the integer part of the e_i values, and the population is sorted according to the fractional parts of the e_i values. The remainder of the strings needed to fill the population are drawn from the top of the sorted list.

Both remainder stochastic sampling methods (with and without replacement) start in a manner identical to deterministic sampling. Expected individual count values are calculated as before and integer parts are assigned. At this point the stochastic remainder schemes part company with their deterministic cousin. In stochastic remainder sampling with replacement, the fractional parts of the expected number values are used to calculate weights in a roulette wheel selection procedure that is then used to fill the remaining population slots. In stochastic remainder sampling without replacement, the fractional parts of the expected number values are treated as probabilities. One by one, weighted coin tosses (Bernoulli trials) are performed using the fractional parts as success probabilities. For example, a string with an expected number of copies equal to 1.5 would receive a single copy surely and another with probability 0.5. This process continues until the population is full.

The stochastic tournament procedure was suggested to Brindle by Wetzel (1983). In this method (which Brindle calls a ranking method), selection probabilities are calculated normally and successive pairs of individuals are drawn using roulette wheel selection. After drawing a pair, the string with higher fitness is declared the winner, inserted in the new population, and another pair is drawn. This process continues until the population is full.

Brindle tested each of these six procedures on a seven-function test bed of her own design. Subsequent investigation (K. A. De Jong and L. B. Booker, personal communication, 1985) has questioned Brindle's departure from standard test functions. A number of the functions in the Brindle test bed have numbers of peaks of the same order of magnitude to the number of points in her coding

(2^{30}). This resulted in what is referred to as an *aliasing* problem: insufficient sampling of equidistant points resulting in false periodicities and the inability to discriminate between different peaks through the exploitation of important similarities. Despite these difficulties, Brindle's study did confirm the fundamental inferiority of straight roulette wheel selection observed earlier by De Jong (1975). The performance differences among the other five mechanisms were small, and Brindle was unable to recommend one over the other although she did use the deterministic scheme in the remainder of her dissertation work.

Subsequent study of genetic search as part of Booker's (1982) investigation of machine learning demonstrated the superiority of stochastic remainder selection without replacement over De Jong's expected-value model (stochastic sampling without replacement). As a result of this work, the stochastic remainder selection procedure without replacement has become widely used in subsequent applications.

Because of its popularity, we examine one implementation in Fig. 4.24. In this program a dummy population *pop* is subjected to stochastic remainder selection through the introduction of two code modules: the procedure *preselect* and the function *select*. In *preselect* the integer and fractional counts are handled by assigning the index number of selected strings to the *choices* array. The *select* function then uses this *choices* array to choose one of the selected individuals at random. The integration of this piece of code into the SGA code of Chapter 3 and Appendix B is left as an exercise at the end of this chapter.

Scaling Mechanisms

Since De Jong's baseline study, scaling of objective function values has become a widely accepted practice. This is done to keep appropriate levels of competition throughout a simulation. Without scaling, early on there is a tendency for a few superindividuals to dominate the selection process. In this case objective function values must be scaled back to prevent takeover of the population by these superstrings. Later on, when the population is largely converged, competition among population members is less strong and the simulation tends to wander. In this case objective function values must be scaled up to accentuate differences between population members to continue to reward the best performers. Actually scaling mechanisms are nothing new, dating back to the earliest empirical studies of GAs by Bagley (1967) and Rosenberg (1967). A review of current scaling procedures is presented in Forrest (1985a). These methods include the following:

1. Linear scaling
2. Sigma (σ) truncation
3. Power law scaling

Linear scaling has already been discussed in Chapter 3. As the name implies, we simply calculate the scaled fitness f' from the raw fitness (objective function

```
type choicearray = array[1..maxpop] of integer;


var  choices:choicearray;              ( Array of choices )
     nremain:integer;


procedure preselect(popsize:integer; avg:real;
                     var pop:population; var choices:choicearray);
( Selection by stochastic remainder method )
var  j, jassign, k:integer;
     expected:real;
     winner:boolean;
     fraction:array[1..maxpop] of real;
begin
 j := 0; k := 0;
 repeat  ( Assign whole numbers )
   j := j + 1;
   expected := pop[j].fitness / avg;
   jassign  := trunc(expected);
   fraction[j] := expected - jassign;
   while (jassign > 0) do begin
     k := k + 1; jassign := jassign - 1;
     choices[k] := j
   end;
 until j = popsize;
 j := 0;
 while k < popsize do begin    ( Assign fractional parts )
   j := j + 1; if j > popsize then j := 1;
   if fraction[j] > 0.0 then begin
     winner := flip(fraction[j]); ( A winner if true )
     if winner then begin
       k := k + 1;
       choices[k] := j;
       fraction[j] := fraction[j] - 1.0;
     end;
   end;
 end;
end;


function select(var popsize,nremain:integer;
                var choices:choicearray; var pop:population):integer;
( select using remainder method )
var jpick:integer;
begin
 jpick := rnd(1,nremain);
 select  := choices[jpick];
 writeln('jpick=',jpick,' choices=',choices[jpick],' nremain=',nremain);
 choices[jpick] := choices[nremain];
 nremain := nremain - 1;
end;
```

FIGURE 4.24 Stochastic remainder selection procedure in Pascal. The procedures *preselect* and *select*.

value) using a linear equation of the form:

$$f' = af + b$$

In this equation the coefficients a and b are usually chosen to do two things: enforce equality of the raw and scaled average fitness values and cause maximum scaled fitness to be a specified multiple (usually two) of the average fitness. These two conditions ensure that average population members receive one offspring copy on average and the best receive the specified multiple number of copies. Caution must be exhibited in linear scaling to prevent negative scaled fitness values.

Linear scaling works well except when negative fitness calculation prevents its use. This is most usually a problem later in a run when most population members are highly fit, but a few lethals have a very low value. To circumvent this scaling problem, Forrest (1985a) suggested using population variance information to preprocess raw fitness values prior to scaling. In this procedure, which we call *sigma (σ) truncation* because of the use of population standard deviation information, a constant is subtracted from raw fitness values as follows:

$$f' = f - (\bar{f} - c \cdot \sigma).$$

In this equation the constant c is chosen as a reasonable multiple of the population standard deviation (between 1 and 3) and negative results ($f' < 0$) are arbitrarily set to 0. Following sigma truncation, fitness scaling can proceed as described without the danger of negative results.

Gillies (1985) suggested a power law form of scaling where the scaled fitness is taken as some specified power of the raw fitness f:

$$f' = f^k$$

In limited studies in a machine vision application, Gillies took $k = 1.005$; however, in general the k value is problem-dependent and may require change during a run to stretch or shrink the range as needed.

Ranking Procedures

The somewhat ad hoc nature of all these scaling procedures led Baker (1985) to consider a nonparametric procedure for selection. In this method the population is sorted according to objective function value. Individuals are then assigned an offspring count that is solely a function of their rank. Figure 4.25 shows one of the ways Baker allocated trials according to rank. He performed experiments comparing his ranking procedure to other selection schemes. His results were generally inconclusive, although ranking showed the same resistance to overselection and underselection demonstrated by normal selection schemes used in conjunction with scaling procedures. The method has been criticized because it essentially disassociates the fitness function from the underlying objective function; however, the direct link assumed between fitness and objective function is not grounded in theory and the ranking procedure does provide a consistent

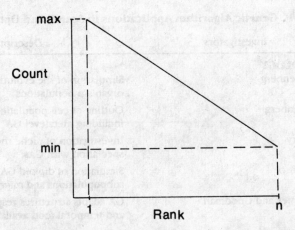

FIGURE 4.25 Count assignment mechanism in sorted selection scheme (Baker, 1985).

means of controlling offspring allocation. What is needed here are better theories of trial allocation so appropriate numbers of copies may be assigned to current population members without detailed knowledge of the underlying function or coding.

CURRENT APPLICATIONS OF GENETIC ALGORITHMS

Table 4.4 lists some of the early applications of genetic algorithms, the miscues and the benchmarks, along with some current applications. The remainder of the chapter samples a potpourri of current GA applications in science, engineering, business, and the social sciences. For the moment, we focus on applications that more or less use a version of the simple (three-operator) genetic algorithm. The next chapter opens our sights to experiments and experience with more complex operators and their application.

Optimization of Pipeline Systems

My own work has largely centered on engineering applications of genetic algorithms. After taking John Holland's courses in genetic algorithms at the University of Michigan, I embarked on Ph.D. studies where I applied GAs to optimization and machine learning problems in natural gas pipeline control (Goldberg, 1983).

In my first problem, I considered Wong and Larson's (1968) 10-compressor, 10-pipe, steady-state, serial pipeline problem. A schematic of that system is shown in Fig. 4.26. The problem is governed by nonlinear state transition equations that dictate the pressure drop through the pipelines and pressure rise across com-

TABLE 4.4   Genetic Algorithm Applications in Search and Optimization

Year	Investigators	Description
	BIOLOGY	
1967	Rosenberg	Simulation of the evolution of single-celled organism populations
1970	Weinberg	Outline of cell population simulation including metalevel GA
1984	Perry	Investigation of niche theory and speciation with GAs
1985	Grosso	Simulation of diploid GA with explicit subpopulations and migration
1987	Sannier and Goodman	GA adapts structures responding to spatia and temporal food availability
	COMPUTER SCIENCE	
1967	Bagley	Parameter search in hexapawn-like game evaluation function via GA
1979	Raghavan and Birchard	GA-based clustering algorithm
1982	Gerardy	Probabilistic automaton identification attempt via GA
1984	Gordon	Adaptive document description using GA
1985	Rendell	GA search for game evaluation function
1987	Raghavan and Agarwal	Adaptive document clustering using GAs
	ENGINEERING & OPERATIONS RESEARCH	
1981c	Goldberg	Mass-spring-dashpot system identification with simple GA
1982	Etter, Hicks, and Cho	Recursive adaptive filter design using a simple GA
1983	Goldberg	Steady-state and transient optimization of gas pipeline using GA
1985a	Davis	Bin-packing and graph-coloring problems via GA
1985b	Davis	Outline of job shop scheduling procedure via GA
1985	Davis and Smith	VLSI circuit layout via GA
1985	Fourman	VLSI layout compaction with GA
1985	Goldberg and Kuo	On-off, steady-state optimization of oil pump-pipeline system with GA
1986	Glover	Keyboard configuration design using a GA
1986	Goldberg and Samtani	Structural optimization (plane truss) via GA
1986	Goldberg and Smith	Blind knapsack problem with simple GA
1986	Minga	Aircraft landing strut weight optimization with GA

TABLE 4.4 (*Continued*)

Year	Investigators	Description
ENGINEERING & OPERATIONS RESEARCH		
1987	Davis and Coombs	Communications network link size optimization using GA plus advanced operators
1987	Davis and Ritter	Classroom scheduling via simulated annealing with metalevel GA
GENETIC ALGORITHMS		
1962c	Holland	Outline for adaptive systems with programs roving cellular computer
1968	Holland	Development of theory of schemata
1971	Hollstien	2-D function optimization with mating and selection rules
1972	Bosworth, Foo, and Zeigler	GA-like operators on real genes with sophisticated mutation
1972	Frantz	Investigation of positional nonlinearity and inversion
1973a	Holland	Optimal allocation of trials in a GA and the two-armed bandit problem
1973	Martin	Theoretical study of GA-like probabilistic algorithms
1975	De Jong	Baseline parametric study of simple GA in five-function test bed
1975	Holland	Publication of ANAS
1977	Mercer	GA controlled by metalevel GA
1981	Bethke	Application of Walsh functions to schema average analysis
1981	Brindle	Investigation of selection and dominance in GAs
1983	Pettit and Swigger	Cursory investigation of GAs in nonstationary search problems
1983	Wetzel	Traveling salesman problem (TSP) via GA
1984	Mauldin	Study of several heuristics to maintain diversity in simple GA
1985	Baker	Trial of ranking selection procedure on De Jong test bed
1985	Booker	Suggestion for partial match scores, sharing, and mating restriction
1985	Goldberg and Lingle	TSP using partially matched crossover (PMX) and o-schema analysis
1985	Grefenstette and Fitzpatrick	Test of simple genetic algorithm with noisy functions
1985	Schaffer	Multiobjective optimization using GAs with subpopulations

TABLE 4.4 (*Continued*)

Year	Investigators	Description
GENETIC ALGORITHMS		
1986a	Goldberg	Maximize marginal schema content for optimal population size estimate
1986	Grefenstette	GA controlled by metalevel GA
1987	Baker	Reduction of stochastic errors in selection procedures
1987	Bridges and Goldberg	Extended analysis of reproduction and crossover in l-bit GA
1987d	Goldberg	The minimal deceptive problem (MDP) under reproduction and crossover
1987	Goldberg and Richardson	Niche and species induction using sharing functions
1987	Goldberg and Segrest	Finite Markov chain analysis of reproduction and mutation
1987	Goldberg and Smith	Nonstationary function optimization using diploid GAs
1987	Oliver, Smith, and Holland	Simulation and analysis of permutation recombination operators
1987	Schaffer	Analysis of selection procedure effects on schema sampling
1987	Schaffer and Morishima	String-encoded adaptive crossover trial
1987	Whitley	Application of progeny testing to GA selection
HYBRID TECHNIQUES		
1985	Ackley	Connectionist algorithm with GA-like properties claimed
1985	Brady	Traveling salesman problem via genetic-like operators
1985	Grefenstette et al.	TSP via knowledge-augmented genetic operators
1987	Dolan and Dyer	Proposal to use GA to learn connectionist network topology
1987b	Grefenstette	Using nonpayoff, problem-specific information in genetic search
1987	Liepins, Hilliard, Palmer, and Morrow	Comparison of blind and greedy operators on combinatorial problems
1987	Shaefer	Globally modified adaptive representation technique (ARGOT)
1987	Sirag and Weisser	Simulated annealing-like control of genetic operator frequency in the TSP
1987a	Suh and Van Gucht	Knowledge-based genetic operators in the TSP

TABLE 4.4 (*Continued*)

Year	Investigators	Description
IMAGE PROCESSING & PATTERN RECOGNITION		
1970	Cavicchio	Selection of detectors for binary pattern recognition
1984	Fitzpatrick, Grefenstette, and Van Gucht	Image registration via GA to minimize image differences
1985	Englander	Selection of detectors for known image classification
1985	Gillies	Search for image feature detectors via GA
1987	Stadnyk	Explicit pattern class recognition using partial matching
PARALLEL GA IMPLEMENTATIONS		
1976	Bethke	Brief theoretical investigation of possible parallel GA implementations
1981	Grefenstette	Brief theoretical investigation of several parallel GA implementations
1987	Cohoon, Hegde, Martin, and Richards	Simulated parallel implementation of optimal linear arrangement
1987	Jog and Van Gucht	Combined knowledge-based and parallelized GA
1987	Pettey, Leuze, and Grefenstette	Parallel GA implementation on Intel hardware using De Jong test bed
1987b	Suh and Van Gucht	Localized selection in parallel GA search on the TSP
1987	Tanese	Parallel GA implemented on 64-NCUBE processor
PHYSICAL SCIENCES		
1985b	Shaefer	Nonlinear equation solving with GA for fitting potential surfaces
SOCIAL SCIENCES		
1979	Reynolds	GA-like adaptation in model of prehistoric hunter-gatherer behavior
1981	Smith and De Jong	Calibration of population migration model using GA search
1985a	Axelrod	Simulation of the evolution of behavioral norms with GA
1985b	Axelrod	Iterated prisoner's dilemma problem solution using GA

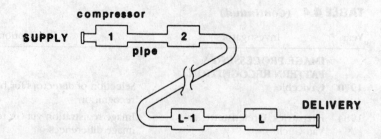

FIGURE 4.26   Serial gas pipeline schematic. From Goldberg (1983).

pressors. The difference in squared pressure varies as the square of the standard volumetric flow rate:

$$PS_{i+1}^2 - PD_i^2 = K_i Q_i \mid Q_i \mid$$

where PS = suction pressure, PD = discharge pressure, Q = standard volumetric flow rate, K = pipe resistance coefficient, and i = pipe-compressor index. The suction and discharge pressure, standard volumetric flow rate, and the power consumed by a compressor station are related by equations of the following form:

$$HP_i = Q_i [A_i (PD_i/PS_i)^{C_i} - B_i],$$

where HP = power consumed, and A, B, C = compressor station constants. Fuel for compression is removed directly from the pipeline flow stream itself at a known, constant rate according to the following equation:

$$Q_{i+1} = (1 - r_i) Q_i,$$

where r = fuel removal factor.

In this problem the objective is to minimize the power consumed subject to maximum and minimum pressure and pressure ratio constraints:

$$\min \Sigma HP_i$$

In my work constraints were adjoined to the problem using a quadratic, external penalty method as described in the previous chapter. Penalty coefficients were sized to give significant penalties with nominal constraint violations.

In their formulation Wong and Larson chose to use the squared pressure difference across each compressor station, $U_i = PD_i^2 - PS_i^2$, as their control variable in this problem even though station power or pressure ratio might have been a more physically appealing choice. For consistency, I adopted their selection and coded each of the station U_i variables as a four-bit, mapped, fixed-point integer subcode. To form the overall string, I concatenated the 10 subcodes together in station order, mapping each subcode between lower and upper limits of U_{min} = 0 psia^2 and U_{max} = 7.5(10^5) psia^2.

Results from three numerical experiments with this problem are shown in Figs. 4.27 and 4.28. In these experiments the following GA parameters were adopted and held constant:

$$n = 50 \quad \text{(population size)}$$
$$p_c = 1.0 \quad \text{(crossover probability)}$$
$$p_m = 0.001 \quad \text{(mutation probability)}$$

Selection is performed using stochastic remainder without replacement. Figures 4.27 and 4.28 show the generation best-of-generation and average results respectively. Figure 4.29 shows the pressure profile from the best of run 2 compared to the optimal profile obtained by Wong and Larson via dynamic programming (1968). In all three runs, near optimal results were obtained after examining an infinitesimal portion of the discretized search space.

To test the simple GA in another, very different pipeline problem, I coded Wong and Larson's single-pipe transient control problem. In this problem the objective is to minimize the energy of compression subject to maximum and minimum pressure and pressure ratio constraints. The details of the transient pipeline model I used are beyond the scope of this treatment. Suffice it to say that simplified partial differential equations of continuity and momentum were

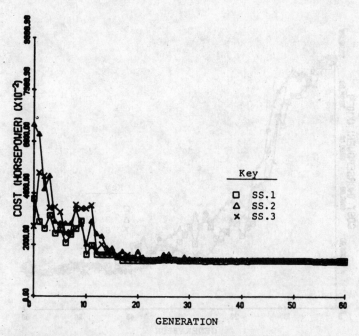

FIGURE 4.27 Serial gas pipeline best-of-generation results. From Goldberg (1983).

transformed to ordinary differential equations using the method of characteristics. These equations were then solved numerically on a regular space-time grid by a finite difference procedure. As in the steady-state problem, constraints were adjoined to the problem using a quadratic, external penalty method. Further details of the model, objective function, and constraints are contained in the original work (Goldberg, 1983). Here we concentrate on the coding and results obtained.

The time-continuous nature of the transient problem forced an additional level of discretization as compared to the steady problem. In the steady problem the compressor station control variables, the U_i, were simply coded as four-bit, mapped subcodes and strung together to form the overall system coding. In the transient problem, the control is a function, the schedule of input flow versus time at the upstream end of the pipe. To solve the problem via genetic algorithm, I discretized the continuous function by spacing flow rate values at 15 equidistant points. In between the points, the flow was assumed to vary linearly as shown in Fig. 4.30. This type of discretization is well developed in the literature of interpolation theory and finite element methods. Other interpolating functions (step function, higher degree polynomial, smooth spline, and others) could have been used, but the linear interpolant was sufficiently accurate for the intended purpose.

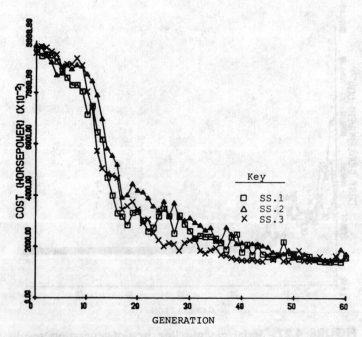

FIGURE 4.28 Serial gas pipeline generation average results. From Goldberg (1983).

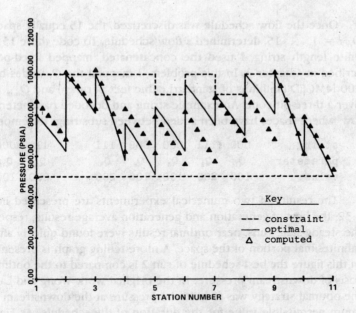

FIGURE 4.29 Serial gas pipeline pressure profile comparison, optimal versus genetic algorithm computation. From Goldberg (1983).

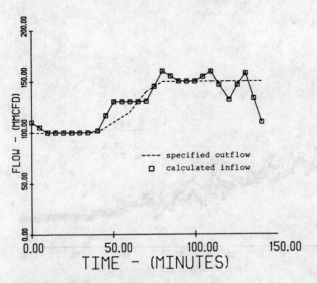

FIGURE 4.30 Transient gas pipeline control via genetic algorithm. Specified outflow (demand) and calculated inflow from first genetic algorithm run (TR.1). From Goldberg (1983).

Once the flow schedule was discretized, the 15 equally spaced flow values, $Q_i, i = 1, \ldots, 15$, determined a flow schedule. To code these 15 parameters as a finite length string, I used the concatenated, mapped fixed-point coding described in Chapter 3. In this problem, I mapped the Q_i values between $Q_{min} =$ 100 MMCFD (millions of standard cubic feet per day) and $Q_{max} = 200$ MMCFD over a three-bit code. An example string and decoded parameters are shown below, where spaces have been added between substrings for emphasis:

```
string:      000   111   000   000   111   ...   111   000
parameter    Q₁    Q₂    Q₃    Q₄    Q₅    ...   Q₁₄   Q₁₅
value:       100   200   100   100   200   ...   200   100
```

The results of two numerical experiments are presented in Figs. 4.31 and 4.32, the best-of-generation and generation average results, respectively. As with the steady-state runs, near optimal results were found quickly after searching an infinitesimal portion of the space. A more telling graph is presented in Fig. 4.33. In this figure the best schedule of run 2 is compared to the optimal result on the basis of downstream pressure. In the original work Wong and Larson found that the optimal strategy was to hold the pressure at the downstream end at the minimum permissible value for the duration of the schedule. As Fig. 4.33 suggests, the GA-calculated flow schedule caused the downstream pressure to follow this quite closely.

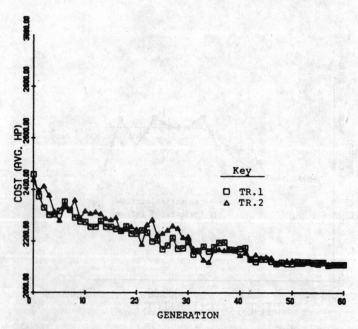

FIGURE 4.31 Transient gas pipeline control best-of-generation results. From Goldberg (1983).

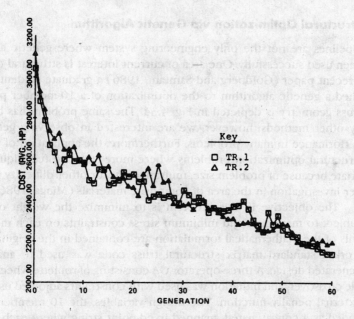

FIGURE 4.32 Transient gas pipeline control generation results. From Goldberg (1983).

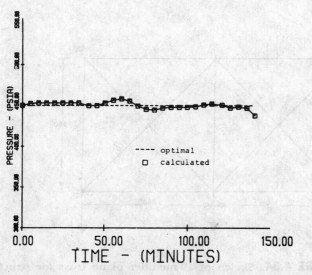

FIGURE 4.33 Transient gas pipeline control pressure time-history. Comparison of optimal versus genetic algorithm computations. From Goldberg (1983).

Structural Optimization via Genetic Algorithm

Pipelines are not the only engineering system where genetic algorithms have been used successfully. One area of current interest is structural optimization. In a recent paper (Goldberg and Samtani, 1986) a graduate student and I have applied a genetic algorithm to the optimization of a 10-member plane truss. The truss geometry is depicted in Fig. 4.34. The same problem has been optimized by other methods; however, we are interested in observing genetic algorithm performance in many problems. Furthermore, the application of GAs to tougher structural optimization problems where more standard techniques are inappropriate because of problem size, multimodality, or other difficulty is currently under investigation in the area of composite materials (Minga, 1986, 1987).

The objective in this problem is to minimize the weight of the structure subject to maximum and minimum stress constraints on each member. The details of the mathematical formulation are contained in the original paper. In our work a standard matrix structural truss code was used to analyze each GA-generated design. A three-operator GA consisting of roulette wheel selection, simple crossover, and mutation was used with constraints adjoined using a quadratic, external penalty function. The design variables, the 10 member areas A_i, were coded as a concatenated, mapped fixed-point string where each of the 10 four-bit area substrings was mapped linearly between $A_{min} = 0.1$ in^2 and $A_{max} = 10$ in^2. Results from the independent runs of the GA are presented in Figs. 4.35 and 4.36, the best-of-generation and generation average results, respectively. Convergence was not dissimilar from that observed in other studies.

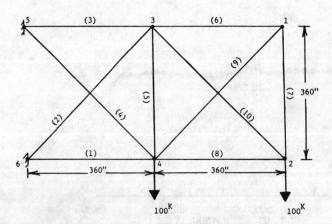

FIGURE 4.34 Sketch of 10-member plane truss for structural optimization (Goldberg and Samtani, 1986) Reprinted by permission from 9th Conference on Electronic Computation ASCE, February, 1986.

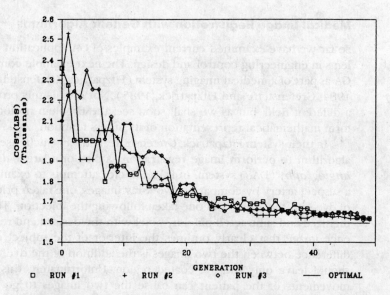

FIGURE 4.35 Structural optimization best-of-generation results (Goldberg and Samtani, 1986). Reprinted by permission from 9th Conference on Electronic Computation ASCE, February, 1986.

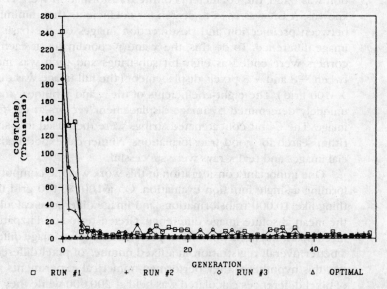

FIGURE 4.36 Structural optimization generation average results (Goldberg and Samtani, 1986). Reprinted by permission from 9th Conference on Electronic Computation ASCE, February, 1986.

Medical Image Registration with Genetic Algorithms

So far we have examined current examples of GA application drawn from problems in engineering control and design. The next example considers the use of a GA as part of a medical imaging system (Fitzpatrick, Grefenstette, and Van Gucht, 1984; Grefenstette and Fitzpatrick, 1985). Not only is this problem drawn from a different field, but as we shall soon see, the problem no longer has a closed-form mathematical representation of its fitness function.

In their system Fitzpatrick, Grefenstette, and Van Gucht used a simple genetic algorithm to perform image registration as part of a larger *digital subtraction angiography* (DAS) system. In DAS a doctor attempts to examine the interior of a suspect artery by comparing two x-ray images, one taken prior to the injection of dye into the artery and one taken following the injection. The two images are digitized and subtracted pixel by pixel with the desired end result being a difference image that clearly outlines the interior of the subject artery. If the only difference between the two images is the addition of the dye, image subtraction should leave only the dye-coated region. Unfortunately, this is a big if. Slight movements of the patient can cause the two images to go out of alignment, thereby disturbing the difference image. As a result, the images must be aligned or *registered* prior to calculation of the difference image.

This was where Fitzpatrick et al. used a genetic algorithm. In their procedure, the preinjection image was transformed by a bilinear mapping ($x'(x, y) = a_0 + a_1x + a_2y + a_3xy$ and $y'(x, y) = b_0 + b_1x + b_2y + b_3xy$) to a transformed image, as shown in Fig. 4.37. Although the mathematical form of the transformation was fixed, the coefficients of the transformation were considered to be unknowns. A GA was used to search for coefficients that minimized the difference between preinjection and postinjection images on the basis of mean absolute image difference. To do this, the x and y coordinates at each of the four image corners were coded as eight-bit substrings and each was mapped linearly between -8 and $+8$ pixels displacement (the full image was discretized on a 100 $\times$ 100 grid). The eight coefficients of the x and y bilinear mappings were then uniquely determined by image displacement vectors at the four corners of the image. The 64-bit concatenated strings were then used in a simple genetic algorithm search for good transformations. Numerical experiments with both artificial images and real x-rays were successful.

One important consideration in this work was the computational cost of performing a single function evaluation. On a 100 $\times$ 100 grid this requires something like 10,000 transformations and image difference calculations to calculate the mean absolute image difference. Grefenstette and Fitzpatrick (1985) recognized that it might be possible to perform a sampled image difference and achieve a better overall registration in a fixed number of pixel difference operations. To test this hypothesis, they performed numerical experiments where the number of pixel differences calculated was held at 200,000 while they varied the number of pixel samples per evaluation. The results of these experiments are shown in Fig. 4.38. This remarkable graph shows that the optimal number of pixels to sam-

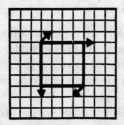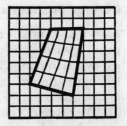

Before transformation   **After transformation**

FIGURE 4.37 **Image registration before and after image transformation. Vectors show image corner displacement (Grefenstette and Fitzpatrick, 1985). Reprinted by permission.**

ple was something like 10 (out of 10,000) for a fixed level of pixel difference computation. This work seems to imply that in some sense GAs prefer a noisy and crude function evaluation, if this in turn permits resources to be used for exploring (even approximately) other points in the search space. This result is not unexpected, because as the theory predicts, GAs can tolerate extremely noisy function evaluation because it is the schemata, not the individual strings, which are being sampled, propagated, and reevaluated in future generations. This tolerance of fuzzy function evaluation can pay handsome dividends in problems where there is a choice between expensive and accurate computation or quick and dirty guesstimation.

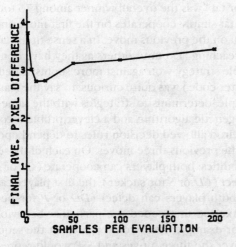

FIGURE 4.38 **Performance versus samples per evaluation in GA image registration (Grefenstette and Fitzpatrick, 1985). Reprinted by permission.**

Iterated Prisoner's Dilemma Problem

For our last current example of GA search we consider a problem drawn from political science and game theory, the iterated prisoner's dilemma problem studied by Axelrod (1985b, 1987) and programmed by Forrest (1985a). This problem moves toward the machine learning problems and systems to be considered in Chapters 6 and 7.

The prisoner's dilemma is a classic, some might say the archtypical, problem of conflict and cooperation. In its simplest form, each of two players has a choice of cooperating with the other or defecting. Depending on the two players' decisions, each receives payoff according to a payoff matrix similar to the one shown in Fig. 4.39. When both players cooperate they are both rewarded at an equal, intermediate level (the reward, R). When only one player defects, he receives the highest level payoff (the temptation, T) while the other player gets the sucker's just deserts (the sucker, S). When both players defect they each receive an intermediate penalty (the penalty, P). The prisoner's dilemma has often been cited as a simple yet realistic model of the inherent difficulty of achieving cooperative behavior when rewards are available for the successful miscreant. The problem is called the prisoner's dilemma because it is an abstraction of the situation felt by a prisoner who can either cut a deal with the prosecutor and thereby rat on his partner in crime (defect) or keep silent and thereby tell nothing of the misdeed (cooperate).

The problem is made more interesting by playing it repeatedly with the same player or group of players, thereby permitting partial time histories of behavior to guide future cooperation-defection decisions. This so-called iterated prisoner's dilemma has drawn interest from game theorists for a number of years. Computer tournaments (Axelrod, 1985b) have pitted different computer procedures against one another in two recent round robin contests. In both contests, a very simple strategy called "tit for tat" was the overall winner among 76 total entrants. As the name implies, tit for tat simply cooperates on the first move and then does whatever its opponent did on the previous move. In a sense tit for tat turns the golden rule inside out by preaching "Do unto others as they have done unto you."

That such a simple strategy won against more sophisticated opponents (with more lines of computer code) was quite curious, to say the least, and Axelrod set out to find other simple, deterministic strategies with the same or greater power. To do this he used a genetic algorithm and a clever problem coding to search for better strategies. Axelrod allowed decision rules to depend upon the behavior of both parties during the previous three moves. On each of those moves there are, of course, four possibilities: both players can cooperate (*CC* or *R* for reward), the other player can defect (*CD* or *S* for sucker), the first player can defect (*DC* or *T* for temptation), or both players can defect (*DD* or *P* for penalty). To code a particular strategy, Axelrod first coded the particular behavioral sequence as a three-letter string. For example, *RRR* would represent the sequence where both parties cooperated over the three moves and *SSP* would represent the sequence where the first player was played for a sucker twice and finally defected. The

FIGURE 4.39   A typical payoff matrix in the prisoner's dilemma problem.

three-letter sequence was then used to generate a number between 0 and 63 by treating the code as an integer base 4 where the behavioral alphabet is decoded in the following way: $CC = R = 0, DC = T = 1, CD = S = 2, DD = P = 3$. In this way, for example, three mutual defections (PPP) would decode to a 63. Using this coding, Axelrod then defined a particular strategy (over the past three moves) as a 64-bit binary string of C's (cooperate) and D's (defect) where the ith C or D corresponds to the ith behavioral sequence. Using this scheme, for example, a D in position 0 would be decoded as a rule of the form RRR $\rightarrow$ D and a C in the third position would be decoded as a rule of the form RRP $\rightarrow$ C.

Actually, the situation is somewhat more complex than stated. Since the set of rules generated by a 64-bit string depends upon the past three plays, behavior at the game's beginning is indeterminate. To get around this problem, Axelrod added six bits (six C's and D's) to the coding to specify a strategy's *premises* or assumptions about pregame behavior. The six bits were used sequentially to simply specify the assumed behavior of both players prior to the game beginning. In this way the normal rules could be used in conjunction with the premises to specify opening game as well as middle game behavior. (In an earlier version Axelrod assumed initial mutual cooperation, but he found that early game behavior was very important to developing strategies that could beat tit for tat.) Together, each of the 70-bit strings thus represented a particular strategy with 64 bits for the rules and six bits for the premises.

Having coded the problem, Axelrod set about finding better strategies for playing this game. To give each strategy a representative test, Axelrod set up an environment of eight opponents taken from his computer tournaments. Together these eight opponents represented 98 percent of the behavior observed in the computer tournament. Each of the string strategies in a population of size 20 played each of the eight opponents in a game of 151 moves. A fitness measure was calculated by taking a weighted average of the point scores against each of the eight opponents where the weights were chosen to closely match tournament conditions. From a random start, the genetic algorithm discovered strategies that beat the overall performance of tit for tat. In Axelrod's own words (1985b, p. 13):

> This is a remarkable achievement because to be able to get this added effectiveness, a rule must be able to do three things. First, it must be able to discriminate between one representative and another based upon only the behavior the other player shows spontaneously or is provoked into showing. Second, it must be able to adjust its own behavior to exploit a representative that is identified as an exploitable player. Third, and perhaps most difficult, it must be able to achieve this discrimination and exploitation without getting into too much trouble with the other representatives. This is something that none of the rules originally submitted to the tournament were able to do.

> These very effective rules evolved by breaking the most important device developed in the computer tournament, namely to be "nice," that is never to be the first to defect. These highly effective rules always defect on the very first move, and sometimes on the second move as well, and use the choices of the other player to discriminate what should be done next. The highly effective rules then had responses that allowed them to "apologize" and get to mutual cooperation with most of the unexploitable representatives, and they had different responses which allowed them to exploit a representative that was exploitable.

Perhaps we should wonder if policymakers in Western capitals are listening to these results. Perhaps more to the point, we should observe that a genetic algorithm was able to explore a large, discontinuous, and nondeterministic space very quickly. Furthermore, we should stand back and look at this problem more abstractly. Even though this problem is cast as one of optimization, it is really a problem in machine learning because the structures we are modifying are rules of behavior. Chapter 6 examines other ways of using genetic algorithms to learn rules of behavior in complex problem domains.

SUMMARY

In this chapter we have explored the rise of genetic algorithms and their establishment as a viable methodology in search and optimization problems. The chapter has detailed the immediate prehistory of general algorithms, Holland's early theoretical developments, early applications in game-playing, biological simulation, and function optimization, as well as more recent applications.

Pre-GA history was populated by a number of digital computer simulations of natural genetic systems. Although some of these had the flavor of function optimization, the spark of insight that transferred nature's example to artificial systems waited for Holland's early theoretical developments; these were closely followed by the first practical GA implementations by Bagley and Rosenberg.

These and other early genetic algorithms were characterized by a busy complexity and the proliferation of intricate operators. Early studies were varied in their coverage, however, including such diverse concerns as adaptive game-playing, biological simulation, pattern recognition, and function optimization. In a word, we might characterize this time as the shotgun era of GAs: simulations were loaded up with operators and complex mechanisms in quest of the holy grail of rapid search. Careful experiments designed to isolate the importance of individual mechanisms were rarely performed.

In some sense, however, the theoretical and computational tools were not yet available to those pioneers. Holland's development of the theory of schemata around the turn of the decade for the first time identified the fundamental importance of structured recombination to the achievement of implicit parallelism. Until that time researchers were not aware of what their genetic algorithms were processing, and new operators were designed without concern for their effect on high-performance building blocks. The development of this theory quickly led to more carefully controlled experiments in function optimization, starting with Hollstien's dissertation and culminating in De Jong's pivotal work. De Jong's dissertation stripped away much of the complexity of earlier genetic algorithms and was able to document the relative importance of reproduction and crossover. He was also able to show the secondary role of mutation in artificial genetic search.

Following De Jong's study, applications of genetic algorithms proliferated. Here, we have surveyed a smattering of these applications drawn from fields as diverse as engineering, medicine, and political science. Although there is still much to learn about the theory and application of genetic algorithms, the diversity and effectiveness of genetic algorithms in many problem areas is cause for optimism. The next chapter examines some of the advances in technique that should continue to lead to improved GA performance.

■ PROBLEMS

4.1. In Cavicchio's pattern recognition detector selection problem, design a binary coding that permits 110 detectors, six pixels per detector for the 25×25 pixel array. Compare the length of this coding to Cavicchio's average length and the minimum binary length calculated in the text. Also compare the number of schemata available in both Cavicchio's and the binary codings.

4.2. Estimate the survival probability of a schema of defining length δ under De Jong's multiple-point crossover operator with CP = 1, 2, 3, . . . on a structure of length l.

4.3. In Rosenberg's adaptive crossover scheme, assume you have a structure of length $l = 10$ and nine crossing factors $x_j = 1, 5, 6, 3, 2, 6, 7, 4, 5$. Determine the probability of a cross at site 4. Compare estimates of the survival probability of the schema ***011**** under adaptive crossover and simple crossover.

4.4. A large population of points is uniformly distributed over the interval $0 \leq x \leq 2$. With a raw fitness function $f(x) = x^2$, calculate the average expected raw fitness. If power law scaling $f' = f^k$, assuming $k = 1.005$, is used to scale the raw fitness, calculate the average expected scaled fitness. Calculate the expected number of copies under the usual reproduction of the original raw average point before and after scaling.

4.5. In a ranking method, assume the median population member is assigned one copy. If the highest ranking population is assigned MAX copies, calculate a formula relating the population size and MAX to the number of copies received by the lowest ranking population member, MIN. Assume a straight line variation in copy allocation. What restrictions (if any) exist on the values of MAX and MIN?

4.6. In the serial gas pipeline problem (Goldberg, 1983) with the 10 U_i values $U_i = 0, 7.5(10^5), 2(10^5), 1(10^5), 0, 0, 7.5(10^5), 5(10^5), 0, 7.5(10^5)$, construct the 40-bit, mapped binary, concatenated string where the U_i map from $U_{min} = 0$ to $U_{max} = 7.5(10^5)$ psia^2.

4.7. In the transient gas pipeline problem (Goldberg, 1983) with the 15 three-bit Q_i values, construct a string representation of a sine wave with mean 150 MMCFD and amplitude 50 MMCFD and a period of 140 minutes. The Q_i map from $Q_{min} = 100$ to $Q_{max} = 200$ MMCFD and they are spaced at 10-minute intervals starting at time 0.

4.8. In Grefenstette and Fitzpatrick's image registration problem for digital angiography subtraction, the postinjection image (100×100 pixels) is mapped by bilinear transformations so the transformed coordinates are related to original coordinates by mappings of the following form:

$$x' = a_0 + a_1 x + a_2 y + a_3 xy \text{ and}$$
$$y' = b_0 + b_1 x + b_2 y + b_3 xy.$$

Transformations are coded as x and y displacements of the four corners of the image (in pixel units). If a string indicates a displacement of the lower right-hand corner of the image by $+3$ units in the x direction and displacement of the upper right-hand corner of the image by $+5$ units in the x direction and $+8$ units in the y direction, and there are no other displacements, calculate a set of a_i and b_i for the bilinear transformations. Assume that the origin is at the lower left corner of the image prior to transformation.

4.9. Derive a relationship between De Jong's on-line performance measure $x_e(t)$ and population average fitness $f_{avg}(t)$.

4.10. In the iterated prisoner's dilemma problem, suppose the defection-cooperation decision depends upon the last five moves. Design a coding for the rule sets that implements rules analogous to Axelrod's 70-bit coding for rules over the past three moves.

■ COMPUTER ASSIGNMENTS

A.   Integrate *select2,* stochastic remainder selection without replacement into the simple genetic algorithm SGA.

B.   Develop a ranking procedure that gives one copy to the population mean, MAX copies to the population best, with linear variation of copies assumed everywhere else. Use stochastic remainder selection after ranking and assignment.

C.   Develop a multiple-point crossover procedure similar to De Jong's with parameter CP (number of crossover points).

D.   Develop a statistical routine to track population fitness standard deviation and then create a routine for sigma (σ) truncation.

E.   Develop a variation of the simple genetic algorithm that uses overlapping populations and generation gap *G.* Implement a crowding operator similar to De Jong's. Test the procedure on a multimodal function like *F*5 and contrast the results to those using a GA without crowding.

F.   Compare and contrast alternative selection methods.

G.   Compare and contrast alternative scaling schemes.

H.   Compare and contrast alternative ranking procedures.

5 | Advanced Operators and Techniques in Genetic Search

The first few chapters of this book were confined to simple genetic algorithms—GAs guided largely by the machinations of three operators: reproduction, crossover, and mutation. With this focus, we have been able to see, both theoretically and empirically, the central role of unnatural selection and randomized, structured recombination in artificial genetic search. In our zeal to keep things simple, we have, however, neglected several interesting natural operators and phenomena. In this chapter we abstract and consider the role of these mechanisms as we attempt to improve upon the robustness of simple GAs. The efforts and coverage are limited by those things that have already been tried and by the current state of knowledge concerning natural genetic mechanisms. Despite these limitations, the abstraction, analysis, and implementation of advanced operators and techniques are the most fruitful avenues for further improvement of genetic algorithms.

We consider low-level operators such as dominance, inversion, intrachromosomal duplication, deletion, translocation, and segregation. We induce niche exploitation and speciation through higher level, population-oriented operators such as migration, marriage restriction, and sharing functions. We consider related work in multicriteria optimization. We also examine knowledge-augmented genetic operators and other methods of using problem-dependent, nonpayoff information. Finally, we catalog some current efforts aimed at using GAs on emerging parallel computers.

DOMINANCE, DIPLOIDY, AND ABEYANCE

Readers with some training in natural genetics have probably been puzzled why the discussion so far has ignored diploidy (pairs of chromosomes) and dominance (an important genotype-to-phenotype-mapping). After all, don't most elementary genetics textbooks start with a discussion of Mendel's pea plants and some mention of dominance? We have postponed this exercise intentionally to stress the fundamental importance of selection and structured, randomized recombination. Nonetheless, the existence of so many successful diploid and polyploid organisms begs us to question whether diploidy and dominance can be put to good use in artificial genetic search. This section reviews the diploid genotype and dominance operators to explain their roles in shielding alternate solutions from excessive selection.

So far we have considered only the simplest genotype found in nature, the haploid or single-stranded chromosome. In this simple model, a single-stranded string contains all the information relevant to the problem we are considering. While nature contains many haploid organisms, most of these tend to be relatively uncomplicated life forms. It seems that when nature wanted to build more complex plant and animal life it had to rely on a more complex underlying chromosomal structure, the diploid or double-stranded chromosome. In the diploid form a genotype carries one or more pairs of chromosomes (called homologous chromosomes), each containing information for the same functions. At first this redundancy seems unnecessary and confusing. Why keep pairs of genes that decode to the same function? Furthermore, when the pair of genes decode to different function values, how does nature decide which allele to pay attention to? To answer these questions, let's consider a diploid chromosomal structure where different letters represent different alleles (different gene function values):

```
AbCDe
aBCde
```

Each position (locus) of a letter represents one allele; the capital form and the lowercase form represent the alternative alleles at that position. In nature each allele might represent a different phenotypic characteristic (or have some nonlinear or epistatic effect on one or more phenotypic characteristics). For example, the B allele might be the brown-eyed gene and the b allele might be the blue-eyed gene. Although this scheme of thinking is not much changed from the haploid (single-stranded) case we have already considered, one difference is clear. Because we now have a pair of genes describing each function, something must decide which of the two values to choose because, for example, the phenotype cannot have both brown and blue eyes at the same time (unless we consider, as nature sometimes does, the possibility of intermediate forms, but we shall not concern ourselves with that possibility here).

The primary mechanism for eliminating this conflict of redundancy is through a genetic operator that geneticists have called *dominance*. At a locus, it has been observed that one allele (the dominant allele) takes precedence over (dominates) the other alternative alleles (the recessives) at that locus. More specifically, an allele is dominant if it is *expressed* (it shows up in the phenotype) when paired with some other allele. In the preceding example, if we assume that all capital letters are *dominant* and all lowercase letters are *recessive*, the phenotype expressed by the example chromosome pair may be written:

$$\begin{matrix} AbCDe \\ aBCde \end{matrix} \rightarrow ABCDe$$

At each locus we see that the dominant gene is always expressed and that the recessive gene is only expressed when it shows up in the company of another recessive. In the geneticist's parlance we say that the dominant gene is expressed when *heterozygous* (mixed, $Aa \rightarrow A$) or *homozygous* (pure, $CC \rightarrow C$) and the recessive allele is expressed only when homozygous ($ee \rightarrow e$).

The mechanics of diploidy and dominance seem relatively clear. On a more abstract level, we can think of dominance as a genotype-to-phenotype or a genotype reduction mapping. Yet, if we continue to ponder the nature and action of diploidy and dominance, we find them really quite bizarre. Why does nature double the amount of information carried within the genotype and then turn around and cut by half the quantity of information it uses? On the surface this seems wasteful and unnecessarily tedious; yet nature is no spendthrift, nor is she given to whimsy or caprice. There must be good reason for the added redundancy of the diploid genotype and for the masking or shielding of the dominance operator.

Diploidy and dominance have long been the object of genetic study, and numerous theories and explanations of their role have been put forth. The theories that make the most sense in the context of artificial genetic search hypothesize that diploidy provides a mechanism for remembering alleles and allele combinations that were previously useful and that dominance provides an operator to shield those remembered alleles from harmful selection in a currently hostile environment. In a natural context, we can understand the need for such a distributed, long-term memory and for a means of protecting that memory against rapid destruction. Over the course of the evolution of life on earth, the planet has undergone many changes in environmental conditions. From hot to cold and back to moderate temperatures, from dark to light to somewhere in between, there have been many dramatic and rapid shifts. The most effective organisms have been those able to adapt most rapidly to the changing conditions. Animals and plants with diploid or polyploid structure have been the most capable of surviving, because their genetic constitution did not easily forget the lessons learned prior to previous environmental shifts. The redundant memory of diploidy permits multiple solutions (to the same problem) to be carried along with only one particular solution expressed. In this way old lessons are not lost forever, and dominance and dominance change permit the old lessons to be remembered and tested occasionally.

A favorite natural example of the long-term memory induced by diploidy and dominance can be found in the shifts in population balance of the peppered moth in Great Britain during the Industrial Revolution. The wild form (and originally the dominant form) of this lepidopteran had white wings with small black specks. Prior to the Industrial Revolution, this coloration was effective camouflage against birds and other beasts of prey in the moth's natural habitat, lichen-covered trees. In the middle of the nineteenth century, black forms were caught in the neighborhood of industrial towns. Careful experiments by Kettlewell (Berry, 1965) showed that the speckled version was advantageous in the pristine setting, while the melanic (dark) form was advantageous in the industrial environment where pollution had killed off the lichen covering the tree trunks. It turned out that the melanic forms were controlled by a single dominant gene, indicating that a shift in dominance had occurred. When the balance shifted toward the darkened form, the darkened form became dominant and the speckled form was held in abeyance. Note that the melanic form was not a new invention; this was no case of fortuitous mutation magically concocting the needed form. Instead, the black form had been invented earlier, perhaps in response to forests where lichen was naturally suppressed. When the by-products of industry caused the lichen to disappear, the melanic form was sampled more frequently and then evolved to be the dominant form. With this alternative solution held in the background, the peppered moth was easily able to adapt rapidly to the selective pressures of its changing environment.

In this example we see how diploidy and dominance permit alternate solutions to be held in abeyance—shielded against overselection. We also see how dominance is no absolute state of affairs. Biologists have hypothesized and proven that dominance itself evolves. In other words the dominance or nondominance of a particular allele is itself under genic control. Fisher's work on the evolution of dominance (1958) may be referenced for further biological detail. Here we examine some of the diploidy-dominance schemes used in artificial genetic search to see how they handle the representation of the structure, the dominance operator, and the evolution of dominance.

Diploidy and Dominance in GAs, a Historical Perspective

Some of the earliest examples of practical genetic algorithm application contained diploid genotypes and dominance mechanisms. In Bagley's dissertation, a diploid chromosome pair mapped to a particular phenotype using a variable dominance map coded as part of the chromosome itself (Bagley, 1967, p. 136):

> Each active locus contains, besides the information which identifies the parameter to which it is associated and the particular parameter value, a dominance value. At each locus the algorithm simply selects the allele having the highest dominance value. Unlike the biological case where partial dominance may be permissible (resulting, for example, in speckled eyes), our interpretation demands that only one of the alleles of the homologous loci be chosen. The decision process in the case of ties (equal dominance values) involves position effects and is somewhat

complicated so that it will be necessary to outline the process in some detail.

One of the chromosomes is arbitrarily selected to be the "key" chromosome and its sites are examined in turn proceeding from left to right. Each time an active locus is discovered, the contents of its homologous locus are retrieved from the other chromosome. The dominance values are compared and the allele which is associated with the highest dominance value is selected. If the dominance values are identical, the dominance follows the key chromosome. That is, the nearest active site on the key chromosome to the left of site [sic] under examination is checked. If the locus at that site was dominant, the present locus on the key chromosome is set to be dominant, otherwise the homolog dominates. If the locus under examination happens to occupy the initial active site on the key chromosome, the key locus dominates.

The introduction of a dominance value for each gene allowed this scheme to adapt with succeeding generations. Unfortunately, Bagley found that the dominance values tended to fixate quite early in simulations, thereby leaving dominance determination in the hands of his somewhat complicated and arbitrary tie-breaking scheme. To make matters worse, Bagley prohibited his mutation operator from processing dominance values, thereby further aggravating this premature convergence of dominance values. Additionally, Bagley did not compare haploid and diploid schemes, and in all of his cases the environment was held stationary. In the end the convergence of dominance values at all positions led to an arbitrary, random-choice dominance mechanism and inconclusive results.

Rosenberg's (1967) biologically oriented study contained a diploid chromosome model; however, since biochemical interactions were modeled in some detail, dominance was not considered as a separate effect. Instead, any dominance effect in this study was the result of the presence or absence of a particular enzyme. The enzyme could then inhibit or facilitate a biochemical reaction, thus controlling some phenotypic outcome.

Hollstien's study (1971) included diploidy and an evolving dominance mechanism. In fact Hollstien described two simple, evolving dominance mechanisms and then put the simplest to use in his study of function optimization. In the first scheme, each binary gene was described by two genes, a modifier gene and a functional gene. The functional gene took on the normal 0 or 1 values and was decoded to some parameter in the normal manner. The modifier gene took on values of M or m. In this scheme 0 alleles were dominant when there was at least one M allele present at one of the homologous modifier loci. This resulted in a dominance expression map like the one displayed in Fig. 5.1. Hollstien recognized that this two-locus evolving dominance scheme could be replaced by a simpler one-locus scheme by introducing a third allele at each locus. In this triallelic scheme, Hollstien drew alleles from the 3-alphabet $\{0, 1, 2\}$. In his scheme the 2 played the role of a dominant "1" and the 1 played the role of recessive "1." The dominance expression map he used is displayed in Fig. 5.2. The action of this

	0 M	0 m	1 M	1 m
0 M	0	0	0	0
0 m	0	0	0	1
1 M	0	0	1	1
1 m	0	1	1	1

FIGURE 5.1 Two-locus dominance map. After Hollstien (1971).

mapping may be summarized by saying that both 2 and 1 map to "1," but 2 dominates 0 and 0 dominates 1. Holland (1975) later discussed and analyzed the steady-state performance of the same triallelic scheme, although he introduced the clearer symbology $\{0, 1_o, 1\}$ for Hollstien's $\{0, 1, 2\}$.

The Hollstien-Holland triallelic scheme is the clearest, simplest scheme suggested for artificial genetic search thus far, combining both dominance map and allele information at a single position. With this scheme the more effective allele becomes dominant, thereby shielding the recessive. Minimum excess storage is required (half a bit extra per locus) and furthermore, dominance shift can easily be handled as a mutationlike operator, mapping a 2 to a 1 (a 1 to a 1_o using Holland's notation) and vice versa. Despite the clarity of the scheme, Hollstien's results with diploidy and dominance were mixed. Although his Breed Type III simulations maintained better population diversity (as measured by population variance) than did his haploid simulations, there was no significant overall improvement in average or ultimate performance. This seems surprising until we recognize that his test bed contained only stationary functions. If the purpose of dominance-diploidy is shielding or abeyance, we should only expect significant performance differences between haploid and diploid genetic algorithms when

	0	1	2
0	0	0	1
1	0	1	1
2	1	1	1

FIGURE 5.2 Single-locus, triallelic dominance map. After Hollstien (1971).

the environment changes with time. It is surprising in this light that such shifts were not studied in conjunction with this operator.

Brindle (1981) performed experiments with a number of dominance schemes in a function optimization setting. Unfortunately, the test functions and codings she used have been questioned. Furthermore, she ignored previous work in artificial dominance and diploidy, and a number of schemes she developed were without theoretical basis or biological precedent.

She considered a total of six schemes:

1. Random, fixed, global dominance
2. Variable, global dominance
3. Deterministic, variable, global dominance
4. Choose a random chromosome.
5. Dominance of the better chromosome
6. Haploid controls diploid adaptive dominance.

In the random, fixed, global dominance scheme, dominance of binary alleles is determined for all loci, for all time at the beginning of a run. A single dominance map is recorded by flipping an unbiased coin at each locus. Thereafter, the dominant allele is expressed whether carried singly (heterozygous) or in pairs (homozygous), and the recessive allele is expressed only when carried in pairs (homozygous).

The variable global dominance map is a scheme where the probability of dominance of a 0 or a 1 at a particular locus is calculated as the proportion of 0's or 1's in the current generation. After calculating the proportion of 0's and 1's at each locus, the expression of alleles at each locus is performed as determined by successive Bernoulli trials for heterozygous loci.

In the deterministic, variable, global dominance scheme the proportion of 0's and 1's is again calculated at each of the loci; however, with this mechanism, the majority rules, and the allele with the greatest proportion is declared to be the winner (the dominant allele).

In Brindle's scheme of dominance of the random chromosome, a chromosome is selected at the flip of an unbiased coin and all its alleles are assumed to be dominant. This is, of course, equivalent to selecting and using one of a homologous pair of chromosomes at random (nothing the recessive chromosome carries can change the outcome of the mapping).

The scheme of dominance of the better chromosome evaluates the fitness of both chromosomes and chooses the better chromosome as dominant.

In the scheme in which the haploid controls the diploid, a third chromosome (haploid) carries an adaptive dominance map to determine the expression of the normal diploid pair (Brindle, 1981, p. 115):

> The construction of a map which benefits an organism in this manner may best be achieved by allowing the genetic algorithm to develop dominance maps dynamically. Each individual in the population carries a third chromosome which acts during evaluation as the dominance map for that individual. During the reproductive cycle, this chromosome be-

haves like a haploid organism, recombining with the dominance chromosome of the second parent during mating. It mutates with the same frequency as the homologous chromosomes. . . . Good dominance maps should develop in parallel with good organisms.

This scheme is the most natural of the schemes she adopted. Like Hollstien's (1971) and Bagley's (1967) earlier schemes, this method uses an adaptive dominance map; however, Brindle completely separated the dominance map (the modifying genes) from the normal chromosome (the functional genes). From a biological viewpoint this seems strange. Genotypes in nature are not half diploid, half haploid. Furthermore, it seems that a modifying gene should be fairly tightly linked to its corresponding functional gene to create a rarely disrupted (by the action of crossover) building block. The separation Brindle imposes effectively destroys linkage between the dominance map and the functional genes.

There are objections to her other schemes as well. Two of the schemes require global information to guide dominance decisions at a local level. Earlier we questioned the use of metalevel genetic algorithms because they required global information. We should have the same objection to using global information in local dominance decisions. Once again we must ask where this global information comes from in nature. This may seem like GA purism but it is not a case of sticking to natural analogy for its own sake. The primary beauty of both natural and artificial genetic search is their global performance through local action. Once we insert this or that global operator, we destroy this attractive feature. This is no small matter if we are ultimately concerned with efficient implementation of these methods on parallel computer architectures.

In her dissertation Brindle simulated and compared the six schemes, but because the test bed was inappropriate and because she only considered stationary functions, diploidy and dominance were not well tested by this study.

More recent studies (Goldberg and Smith, 1987; R. E. Smith, 1987, 1988) have focused on the role of dominance and diploidy as abeyance structures and mechanisms. Smith and I have compared the performance of a haploid GA, a diploid GA with fixed dominance map (1's dominate 0's) and a diploid GA with Hollstien-Holland triallelic dominance map on a blind, nonstationary knapsack problem. In the normal knapsack problem, the objective is to maximize the total value of objects placed in a sack subject to one or more maximum weight constraints. Mathematically, the problem may be written succinctly as follows:

$$\max \Sigma v_i x_i \quad \text{where } x_i \in \{0, 1\}$$
$$\text{subject to } \Sigma w_i x_i \le W.$$

In a blind knapsack problem, the algorithm, of course, has no knowledge of problem structure, values v_i, or weights w_i. In this case the problem was complicated by making the weight constraint a periodic function of time such that $W(t) \in \{W_0, W_1\}$ and every T_{period} generations the weight shifts to the other value. Figures 5.3–5.6 compare a haploid GA to a simple diploid GA. The haploid GA is

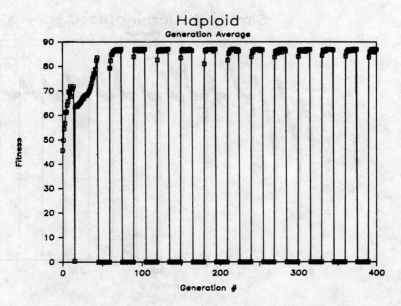

FIGURE 5.3 Nonstationary knapsack problem, haploid run population average results (Goldberg and Smith, 1987).

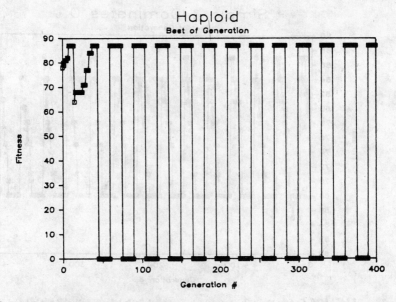

FIGURE 5.4 Nonstationary knapsack problem, haploid run best-of-generation results (Goldberg and Smith, 1987).

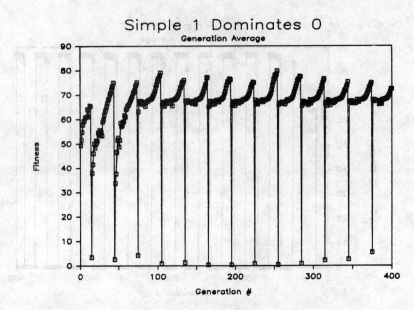

FIGURE 5.5 Nonstationary knapsack problem, simple diploid run (1 dominates 0) population average results (Goldberg and Smith, 1987).

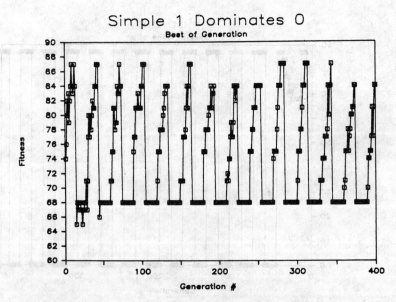

FIGURE 5.6 Nonstationary knapsack problem, simple diploid run (1 dominates 0) best-of-generation results (Goldberg and Smith, 1987).

unable to track the oscillation, while the simple diploid scheme is able to switch to some extent. Experiments with the Hollstien-Holland triallelic scheme were also performed. These results are a significant improvement over the original fixed dominance map, as should be expected. Figures 5.7 and 5.8 show generation average and generation best results for the same nonstationary, blind knapsack problem. Because the triallelic scheme permits evolution of dominance at each locus, the population is able to adapt more quickly and more fully than is possible in cases with either a fixed dominance map or haploid structure.

An Analysis of Dominance and Diploidy in GA Search

The empirical evidence supporting diploid structures and dominance operators in GA search is starting to gel. Where once diploidy and dominance were looked to as a magic elixir to cure all GA ills, the focus is now on their important role in shielding once successful schemata from overzealous extinction. Current investigations have started to examine dominance and diploidy in nonstationary problems, and future work should confirm this role. As the empirical evidence has started to appear, so has the theoretical case for diploidy and dominance become much clearer. This section examines how the combined action of diploidy and dominance prolongs the life of currently weak, but once useful, alternatives. We also see how diploidy and dominance permit a lower background mutation rate to maintain a certain level of diversity.

To understand the effect of diploidy and dominance, we first consider how they change our expectation of schemata growth or decay. Referring to Chapter 2, the number of schemata H contained in the next population (written as $m(H, t + 1)$) is related to the number in the current population ($m(H, t)$) by the following equation:

$$m(H, t + 1) \geq m(H, t)\frac{f(H)}{\bar{f}}\left[1 - p_c \frac{\delta(H)}{l - 1} - o(H)\,p_m \right].$$

In this equation, p_c and p_m are the crossover and mutation probabilities respectively, $f(H)$ is the schema average fitness, f is the population average fitness, $\delta(H)$ is the defining length of the schema (distance between outermost fixed positions), and $o(H)$ is the schema order (number of defined positions). With the addition of dominance and diploidy, this equation is still an accurate description of the growth or decay of schemata if we recognize the effect of dominance and allele expression on the schema average fitness, $f(H)$. This difference becomes most striking if we separate the physical schema H from the expressed schema H_e. In other words, a real or physical schema H may or may not be expressed, depending upon its state of dominance and its current homologous partner. This requires the following modification to the schema growth equation:

$$m(H, t + 1) \geq m(H, t)\frac{f(H_e)}{\bar{f}}\left[1 - p_c \frac{\delta(H)}{l - 1} - o(H)\,p_m \right].$$

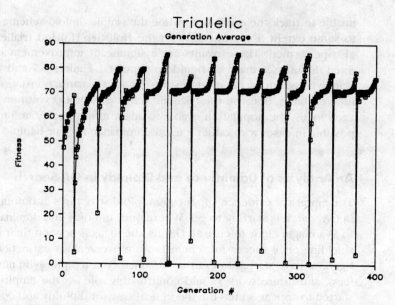

FIGURE 5.7   Nonstationary knapsack problem, triallelic diploid run population average results (Goldberg and Smith, 1987).

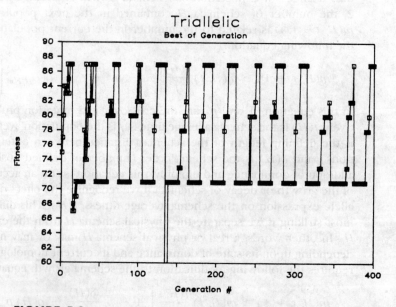

FIGURE 5.8   Nonstationary knapsack problem, triallelic diploid run, best-of-generation results (Goldberg and Smith, 1987).

Everything remains the same, except the average fitness of the schema H, $f(H)$, is replaced by the average fitness of the expressed schema H_e, $f(H_e)$. In the case of a fully dominant schema H, the average fitness of the physical schema always equals the expected average fitness of the expressed schema H_e:

$$f(H) = f(H_e).$$

In the case of a dominated schema H, the hope is, of course, that the average fitness of the expressed schema is greater than or equal to the average fitness of the physical schema:

$$f(H_e) \geq f(H).$$

This situation is most likely to occur when the dominance map is permitted to evolve as was suggested earlier. If this situation does arise, then the currently deleterious, dominated schema will not be selected out of the population as rapidly as in the corresponding haploid situation. This is how dominance and diploidy shield currently out-of-favor schemata.

To make this argument more quantitative, let's consider a simple case where only two alternative, competing schemata may be expressed, one dominant and the other recessive. Physically this represents two alleles at a single locus or two multilocus schemata that have come to dominate a particular set of loci. In either case the dominant alternative is assumed to be expressed whether heterozygous or homozygous and that the recessive alternative is expressed only when homozygous. Rearrangement of the schema growth equation permits us to calculate the proportion of recessive alleles, P', in successive generations, t. If we assume that there are only two alternatives, the dominant form having a constant expected fitness value of f_d and the recessive f_r, the proportion of recessives expected in the next generation may be calculated (Goldberg and Smith, 1987) as follows:

$$P^{t+1} = P^t K \left[\frac{P^t + r(1 - P^t)}{(1 - r)P^t \cdot P^t + r} \right].$$

where $r = f_d/f_r$, and K = crossover-mutation loss constant.

A similar equation may be derived for the haploid case where the deleterious alternative (the recessive) is always expressed when present in a haploid structure:

$$P^{t+1} = P^t \frac{K}{P^t + r(1 - P^t)}$$

Proportion ratio $(P(t + 1)/P(t))$ versus proportion $P(t)$ is plotted for haploid and diploid cases in Fig. 5.9. The most important conclusion we can draw from this graph is that for a comparable proportion of alleles the haploid case always destroys more (always has a smaller proportion ratio) than the corresponding diploid case. Of course, this does not imply that the diploid case has a low online performance measure. In fact, the sampling rate remains low (proportional

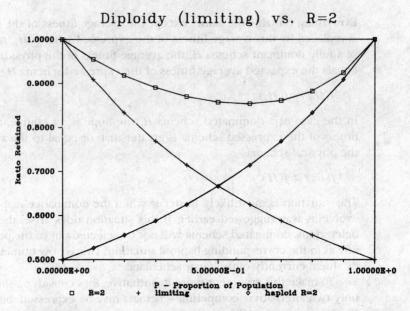

FIGURE 5.9 Retention ratio P^{t+1}/P^t versus proportion P^t for haploid ($r = 2$), diploid ($r = 2$), and limiting diploid ($r = \infty$). From Goldberg and Smith (1987).

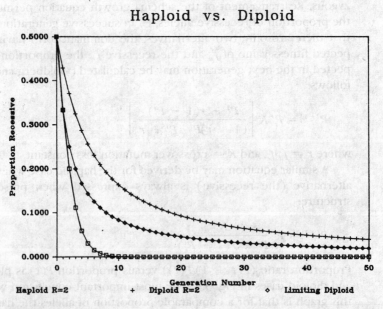

FIGURE 5.10 Proportion P versus generation t for haploid ($r = 2$), diploid ($r = 2$), and limiting diploid ($r = \infty$). From Goldberg and Smith (1987).

to P^2) for the poor (recessive) alleles in the diploid case. In this way once successful solutions are saved to fight another day without excessive sampling, without excessive selection. Similar conclusions may be drawn by examining recessive proportion time histories as shown in Fig. 5.10. Analogous results are presented for the triallelic scheme in Smith (1988).

The previous analysis clearly demonstrates the long-term memory induced by diploidy and dominance. Because of this effect, under diploidy and dominance we expect that mutation should play an even smaller role in the operation of the GA. Holland (1975) has presented an analysis of the steady-state mutation requirements of diploid structures as compared to haploid structures.

For a haploid structure under selection and mutation it may be shown that the proportion of recessive alleles in the next generation P^{t+1} is related to the proportion in the current generation, P^t, by the following equation:

$$P^{t+1} = (1 - \varepsilon)P^t + p_m(1 - P^t) - p_m P^t.$$

Here we have the sum of three terms, the proportion due to selection, the source of alleles from mutation, and the loss of alleles from mutation. The $\varepsilon(t)$ factor is the proportion lost due to selection and other operator losses. At steady state, $P^{t+1} = P^t = P_{ss}$. Solving for P_{ss}, we obtain the following equation:

$$P_{ss} = \frac{p_m}{2p_m + \varepsilon}.$$

This equation suggests that the final steady-state proportion of alleles is directly proportional to the mutation rate (with large ε and small p_m).

For a diploid structure under selection and mutation it may be shown that the proportion of recessive alleles in the next generation is related to the number in the current generation by the following equation:

$$P^{t+1} = (1 - 2\varepsilon P^t)P^t + 2p_m(1 - 2P^t).$$

At steady state we obtain a relationship between the required mutation rate and the steady proportion of recessive alleles:

$$p_m = \varepsilon \cdot P_{ss}^2/(1 - 2P_{ss}).$$

For small steady-state proportions of recessive alleles, $P_{ss} \ll 1$, this equation suggests that the mutation rate required to keep a certain proportion of recessive alleles available is proportional to the square of the proportion. Of course, the presence of the same proportion of alleles in the diploidy case does not mean that they will be sampled as frequently. Although the same proportion is in existence, they are sampled much less frequently (as the square of the proportion). This underlines the need for occasional dominance changes so stored alleles can be sampled in the current context.

Computer Implementation of Triallelic Diploidy and Dominance

Only minor modifications are required in our simple genetic algorithm (SGA) code to implement the Holland-Hollstien triallelic dominance-diploidy scheme. The data structures of SGA must change to accommodate the homologous pairs of chromosomes and the three alleles per locus. A modified data declaration for the SGA with dominance (SGADOM) is shown in Fig. 5.11. In this declaration we notice that the *allele* type is now defined over the integer subrange $-1 \ldots 1$ (it was previously defined as a boolean type). With this subrange we intend for a -1 to map to a recessive 1 (a 1_o in Holland notation), a 0 to map to a 0, and a 1 to map to a dominant 1 (a 1 in Holland notation). The dominance expression map under this coding may be expressed by the greater than or equal to ($\geq$) relation. This fact is used in the function *mapdominance* displayed in Fig. 5.12. Dominance expression for a pair of homologous chromosomes is carried out through locus-by-locus calls to *mapdominance* in the procedure *dominance* also displayed in Fig. 5.13.

The details of offspring production under diploidy and dominance are somewhat different from those in the haploid case. In the procedure *gametogenesis*, a homologous pair of chromosomes generates a pair of gametes which in turn are fertilized by a second pair of gametes within the procedure *fertilization*. This process flies in the face of biological reality to some extent; however, it does pay attention to the important details, and the differences that do exist are there to

```
const maxpop       = 100;
      maxstring    = 30;
      version      = 'v1.0';

type  allele       = -1..1; { triallelic scheme (-1, 0, 1) }
      chromosome   = array[1..maxstring] of allele; { trits }
      chrompack    = array[1..maxploidy] of chromosome;
      parentid     = record xsite, parent:integer end;
      idpack       = array[1..maxploidy] of parentid;
      individual   = record
                       chrom:chrompack;   { pack of chroms  }
                       echrom:chromosome; { expressed chrom }
                       x, objective, fitness:real;
                       parents:idpack; { parent info }
                     end;
      population   = array[1..maxpop] of individual;

var   oldpop, newpop:population;              { non-overlapping }
      popsize, lchrom, gen, maxgen:integer;   { integer globals }
      pcross, pmutation, sumfitness:real;     { Real globals    }
      nmutation, ncross:integer;              { Integer stats   }
      avg, max, min:real;                     { Real stats      }
```

FIGURE 5.11 Triallelic dominance in Pascal (SGADOM): constant, type, and data declarations.

```pascal
function mapdominance(allele1,allele2:allele):allele;
{ dominance map using > relation among (-1,0,1) }
begin
 if (allele1 >= allele2) then mapdominance := abs(allele1)
  else mapdominance := abs(allele2)
end;

procedure dominance(var lchrom:integer;
                    var homologous:chrompack;
                    var expressed:chromosome );
{ express dominance - homologous pair --> single chrom }
var j:integer;
begin
  for j:=1 to lchrom do
    expressed[j]:=mapdominance(homologous[1,j],homologous[2,j])
end;
```

FIGURE 5.12 Triallelic dominance in Pascal (SGADOM), function *mapdominance* and procedure *dominance*.

```pascal
procedure gametogenesis(var ancestor,gamete:individual;
                        var lchrom, nmutation, ncross,
                            jparent:integer;
                        var pmutation, pcross:real);
{ Create a pair of gametes from a single parent }
var j,jcross:integer;
begin
 { handle crossover and mutation }
 crossover(ancestor.chrom[1], ancestor.chrom[2],
           gamete.chrom[1], gamete.chrom[2],
           lchrom, ncross, nmutation, jcross,
           pcross, pmutation);
 { set parent and crossing pointers }
 for j := 1 to maxploidy do with gamete do begin
   chromid[j].parent := jparent;
   chromid[j].xsite  := jcross;
  end;
end;

procedure fertilization(var chrom1, chrom2:chromosome;
                        var parent1, parent2:parentid;
                        var newindividual:individual);
begin with newindividual do begin
 chrom[1] := chrom1;
 chrom[2] := chrom2;
 chromid[1] := parent1;
 chromid[2] := parent2;
end; end;
```

FIGURE 5.13 Triallelic dominance in Pascal (SGADOM), procedures *gametogenesis* and *fertilization*.

minimize the deleterious effects caused by small finite populations often used in
artificial genetic search.

The creation of a new generation is controlled by the procedure *generation,*
as shown in Fig. 5.14. This procedure differs from the original version contained
in SGA as it accommodates the procedures *gametogenesis* and *fertilization.* As
in the earlier version, pairs of mates are first selected using the function *select.*
Thereafter *gametogenesis* is called twice, once for each mate. The procedure

```
function other(j1:integer):integer;
begin if (j1=1) then other := 2 else other := 1 end;

procedure generation;
{ Create a new generation through select, crossover, and mutation }
var j, j1, j2, mate1, mate2, jcross:integer;
    gamete1, gamete2:individual;
begin
 j := 1;
 repeat    { select, generate gametetes until newpop is filled }
  { pick 2 mates }
  mate1 := 2; {select(popsize, sumfitness, oldpop);  pick pair of mates }
  mate2 := 1; {select(popsize, sumfitness, oldpop); }
  { make 4 gametes to make 2 zygotes }
  gametogenesis(oldpop[mate1], gamete1,
                lchrom, nmutation, ncross, mate1,
                pmutation, pcross);
  gametogenesis(oldpop[mate2], gamete2,
                lchrom, nmutation, ncross, mate2,
                pmutation, pcross);
  { flip honest coin to decide arrangement }
  if flip(0.5) then begin j1 := 1; j2 := 1 end
    else begin j1 := 1; j2 := 2 end;
  { fertilize without replacment }
  fertilization(gamete1.chrom[j1], gamete2.chrom[j2],
                gamete1.chromid[j1], gamete2.chromid[j2],
                newpop[j]);
  j1 := other(j1); j2 := other(j2);
  fertilization(gamete1.chrom[j1], gamete2.chrom[j2],
                gamete1.chromid[j1], gamete2.chromid[j2],
                newpop[j+1]);
  { express, decode, and evaluate objective function }
  with newpop[j  ] do begin
    dominance(lchrom, chrom, echrom);
    x := decode(echrom, lchrom);
    objective := objfunc(x);
  end;
  with newpop[j+1] do begin
    dominance(lchrom, chrom, echrom);
    x := decode(echrom, lchrom);
    objective := objfunc(x);
  end;
  { Increment population index }
  j := j + 2;
 until j>popsize
end;
```

FIGURE 5.14 Triallelic dominance in Pascal (SGADOM), modified procedure
generation to include triallelic dominance and diploidy.

fertilization takes the two sets of gamete pairs and trades them off (without replacement) to form two offspring. An unbiased coin is flipped to decide which gamete fertilizes which and the designated exchange takes place. The objective function evaluation occurs following fertilization, with lineage data and cross site information stored for detailed reporting.

In addition to the aforementioned changes, minor modifications are also required in the mutation operator, initialization code, and reporting code. The *mutation* function has been changed to reflect the presence of three alleles. To get an expected 50–50 split of expressed 1's and 0's in the initial population, recessive ones, zeroes, and dominant ones should be randomly chosen with probabilities 0.25, 0.50, and 0.25 respectively. The reporting procedure *writechrom* has also been rewritten to report the three alleles correctly. A percent sign (%) has been used to represent the recessive one, 1_o. The changes in *writechrom* and *mutation* are shown in Fig. 5.15.

```
function mutation(alleleval:allele; pmutation:real;
                  var nmutation:integer):allele;
{ Mutate an allele w/ pmutation, count number of mutations }
var mutate:boolean; temp:allele;
begin
 mutate := flip(pmutation);    { Flip the biased coin }
 if mutate then begin
   nmutation := nmutation + 1;
   temp := alleleval + rnd(1,2);  { Add one or two }
   case temp of
     -1: mutation := temp;
      0: mutation := temp;
      1: mutation := temp;
      2: mutation := -1;
      3: mutation := 0;
     end {case}
 end else
   mutation := alleleval;      { No change }
end;


procedure writechrom(var out:text; chrom:chromosome; lchrom:integer);
{ Write a chromosome as a string of 1's (true's) and 0's (false's) }
var j:integer; ch:char;
begin
 for j := lchrom downto 1 do
  begin
   case chrom[j] of
     -1: ch := '%';
      0: ch := '0';
      1: ch := '1';
   end;
   write(out,ch);
  end;
end;
```

FIGURE 5.15 Triallelic dominance in Pascal (SGADOM), modified function *mutation* and procedure *writechrom* to include triallelic dominance and diploidy.

INVERSION AND OTHER REORDERING OPERATORS

One article of faith that has carried us through earlier arguments related to genetic algorithm power has been that short defining length, low-order, high-
performance schemata (we have called these building blocks) combine with
other such building blocks to form strings with above-average performance; however, the different application examples we have seen make us realize that many
of the coding decisions we make seem arbitrary. In this light, how do we know
that the schemata contained in a given coding in a given problem will lead to the
desired improvement? The bald truth is that we don't know. We cannot be sure
that an arbitrary coding leads to improvement using a simple genetic algorithm
in an arbitrary problem. At first this may seem disconcerting until we recognize
that nature is herself unsure of her codings and has devised operators to search
for better codings at the same time she searches for better sets of allele values.
In this section we examine these reordering operators to see if the same mechanisms can be used effectively in artificial genetic search.

The primary natural mechanism responsible for recoding a problem is the
inversion operator. Under inversion two points are chosen along the length of
the chromosome, the chromosome is cut at those points, and the end points of
the cut section switch places. At first this operator seems a bit strange if we view
it in the context of our simple artificial string chromosomes. For example, consider the following eight-position string where two inversion sites are chosen at
random (perhaps sites 2 and 6 as marked by the ^ characters):

```
1 0 1 1 1 0 1 1
  ^       ^
```

If we were to use the inversion operator blindly, we would obtain the following
string:

```
1 0 0 1 1 1 1 1
```

It is not at all clear how the inversion operator is helping us search for a new
representation. In fact, it looks as though it is just partially shuffling the alleles
within a string. The problem here is our simple representation. We have, since
the first chapter, assumed that an allele's meaning is linked to its locus, its position. In nature genes can be shuffled on a string and still be responsible for the
production of the same enzyme. In other words, in nature an allele's meaning is
position-independent. To provide the same flexibility in our representation, let's
name our alleles using integers between 1 and 8 and see what happens when we
apply the inversion operator under the extended representation:

```
1 2 3 4 5 6 7 8
1 0 1 1 1 0 1 1
  ^       ^
```

Now when we do the same inversion, we carry along the allele name information as well:

```
1 2 6 5 4 3 7 8
1 0 0 1 1 1 1 1
```

Using this extended representation, the bit values retain their intended meaning regardless of their position. In biological terms, this extended representation separates gene from locus. An interesting consequence of doing this is that a single inversion operator acting alone has no immediate effect on string fitness. After all, since the alleles are now named, switching their position on the string has no effect on the way the string is decoded, and thus the fitness of the string remains unaffected.

While it is now clear how the extended representation permits inversion to act without jumbling allele meanings, it is not yet clear what positive contribution the inversion operator and the extended representation make to genetic search. After all, we have just reasoned that a single inversion has no direct effect on string fitness, so why does nature (and why should we) bother with this occasional game of allelic musical chairs? We will consider the theory behind the inversion operator in some detail later in this chapter; at this point, we simply acknowledge how inversion might be useful in searching for good string arrangements at the same time other genetic operators are searching for good allele sets. If the current population contains bad orderings (where alleles with highly epistatic or nonlinear interaction are spaced at great distances on the chromosome), crossover will destroy important allele packets with high probability. On the other hand, if a reordering operator can rearrange allele placement, then there is some chance we can obtain good allele orderings that will subsequently permit more efficient propagation of building blocks.

In a moment we will examine this argument more rigorously. In the next section, we review past research into reordering operators in artificial genetic search.

Reordering Operators in GAs, a Historical Perspective

Bagley's (1967) computer simulations contained an inversion operator. He implemented the simple inversion operator and extended string representation discussed above. One of the decisions he faced was how to treat crosses between nonhomologous pairs of strings. To see why this is important, consider a simple cross between two strings, A and B:

$$
\begin{aligned}
A = \quad & \begin{array}{cccc|cccc} 1 & 2 & 3 & 4 & 5 & 6 & 7 & 8 \\ 1 & 0 & 1 & 1 & 1 & 0 & 1 & 1 \end{array} \\
\\
B = \quad & \begin{array}{cccc|cccc} 1 & 2 & 6 & 5 & 4 & 3 & 7 & 8 \\ 1 & 0 & 0 & 1 & 1 & 1 & 1 & 1 \end{array}
\end{aligned}
$$

If we naively cross the strings using simple crossover, perhaps at cross site four (marked by the | character), we obtain the two offspring strings as follows·

$$A' = \begin{array}{cccc|cccc} 1 & 2 & 3 & 4 & 4 & 3 & 7 & 8 \\ 1 & 0 & 1 & 1 & 1 & 1 & 1 & 1 \end{array}$$

$$B' = \begin{array}{cccc|cccc} 1 & 2 & 6 & 5 & 5 & 6 & 7 & 8 \\ 1 & 0 & 0 & 1 & 1 & 0 & 1 & 1 \end{array}$$

We notice immediately that neither of the offspring strings contains a full gene complement, and in general this problem is the primary argument against permitting simple crosses between arbitrarily ordered strings. Bagley adopted a straightforward measure to eliminate this difficulty: he prohibited crosses between nonhomologous strings. Unfortunately, his results under these conditions were disappointing (Bagley, 1967, p. 168):

> The inversion results ... were some what [*sic*] disappointing. The most obvious effect of inversion is a large increase in the length of the runs. Recall that one of the consequences of inversion is a decrease in the effective crossover rate since crossover is inhibited between parts of chromosomes which are not locus homologous. As we have seen, a lower crossover rate has an adverse effect on the simulation and it is this effect that was predominant in our results. The desirable consequence of inversion, which is the appearance in the population of gametes whose geographical gene linkages reflect combinations ... , was not observed.

Bagley went on to attribute the lack of success with inversion to his problem environment (a game-playing task). He concluded that the problem was insufficiently difficult (epistatic) to give inversion a good trial. Put another way, the simple genetic algorithm worked too well without inversion for the inversion-augmented GA to show either better rate of convergence or better ultimate convergence. This problem (that the simple GA works too well) has reared its not-too-ugly head more than once since Bagley's study and has made it difficult to show linkage effects in artificial genetic search. There were, however, other reasons Bagley was unable to show an advantage for inversion. Recall that Bagley allowed only homologous substrings to exchange during crossover. This essentially prevents crosses between many pairs of population members. A more liberal policy has been adopted by nature; other less restrictive policies have also been used by later GA researchers interested in inversion.

Cavicchio's (1970) study of genetic search in a pattern recognition detector design task used an inversion operator with unrestricted inversion and subsequent crossing; however, recall from Chapter 4 that Cavicchio's genes consisted of pixel identification numbers grouped in detector clusters. With this representation, any inversion can be performed, always generating a viable chromosome. Furthermore, subsequent crossing of pairs of strings at any point generate meaningful new strings regardless of string ordering. Although these good properties resulted from the problem-dependent coding he used, Cavicchio's results were encouraging. In one set of experiments, relatively high values of crossover and inversion resulted in a good rate of convergence and a high level of ultimate performance.

Frantz's (1972) study of epistasis in artificial genetic search was not as successful in demonstrating the usefulness of inversion. He attempted several variations on inversion operators and mating rules in functions with differing degrees of controlled nonlinearity. He tried two variations on inversion:

1. Linear inversion
2. Linear + end inversion

Linear inversion is simply Frantz's name for the simple two-point inversion operator described earlier. Linear + end inversion performed linear inversion with a specified probability (0.75). If linear inversion was not performed, end inversion would be performed with equal probability (0.125) at either the left or right end of the string: under end version the left or right end of the string was picked as one inversion point and a second inversion point was picked uniformly at random from points no farther away than one-half the string length. Linear + end inversion was Frantz's attempt to minimize the tendency for linear inversion to disrupt alleles located near the center of the string disproportionately to those alleles located near the ends.

Frantz applied either of his inversion operators in one of two modes:

1. Continuous inversion
2. Mass inversion

In his continuous inversion mode, inversion was applied with specified inversion probability, p_i, to each new individual as the individual was created. In mass inversion mode, no inversion took place until a new population was created; thereafter, one-half the population underwent identical inversion (using the same two inversion points). Mass inversion was designed to eliminate the proliferation of noninteracting subpopulations that accompanies strict-homologue mating.

Frantz tried four mating rules to prevent the usual problem with naive crosses between homologous pairs of strings:

1. Strict homology mating
2. Viability mating
3. Any-pattern mating
4. Best-pattern mating

Strict homology mating is the same form adopted by Bagley where only homologous strings are permitted to mate. Viability mating permits an attempted cross between nonhomologous strings; however, if the resulting "offstrings" do not have a full gene complement, they are not inserted into the new population. In any-pattern mating, two mates are randomly selected and one or the other is chosen to be the prime ordering. The other string is mapped to the prime ordering and a simple cross is made. The mapping operation thereby guarantees the viability of the cross. Best-pattern mating is the same as any-pattern mating except the better of the two strings is chosen to determine the prime ordering.

Despite the number and variety of options attempted, Frantz was unable to demonstrate clear position effect. Furthermore, he was unable to show clear advantage for inversion in any form, mode, or mating combination. The underlying problem here was the problem environment adopted. Frantz used a linear combination of bitwise linear and nonlinear functions each combining between six and seven alleles on a length $l = 25$ string. The nonlinear functions used a table lookup of the 2^6 or 2^7 alternatives among the six or seven alleles in the group. Unfortunately, the functions he chose were insufficiently difficult to require inversion. As Bethke (1981) has pointed out, not only must a GA-hard function be epistatic, the epistasis must be misleading. In other words short, high-performance schemata must point toward poor areas of the space. This was not the case in Frantz's study, so the simple genetic algorithm without inversion was able to find good solutions quickly.

After Frantz's study, other investigations of inversion and reordering operators were a long time coming. Holland (1975) makes brief mention of inversion, presenting modifications to the schema theorem to include the approximate effect of simple inversion. Thereafter not much mention is made of reordering operators until the 1985 International Conference on Genetic Algorithms and Their Application. At that conference, several authors (Davis, 1985b; Goldberg and Lingle, 1985; Smith, 1985) described the construction of reordering operators that combine features of inversion and crossover into a single operator. While derived independently, these operators are similar. We will consider each of these three operators: *partially matched crossover* (PMX), *order crossover* (OX), and *cycle crossover* (CX).

PMX arose in considering ways to tackle a blind traveling salesman problem. In the traveling salesman problem (TSP), a hypothetical salesman must make a complete tour of a given set of cities in the order that minimizes his total distance traveled. In the blind traveling salesman problem, the salesman has the same objective with the added restriction that he is unaware of the distance he travels until he actually traverses a complete tour. The traveling salesman problem by itself is difficult enough (it is a member of a class of problems believed to be unsolvable in polynomial time) without imposition of the blindness restriction. In considering ways to code the blind traveling salesman problem, it is difficult to conceive of codings where building blocks are acted upon reasonably. In some ways it seems natural to code ordering problems like the TSP in permutation form. For example, in an eight-city problem where each city is visited in ascending order, the tour can be represented as follows:

1 2 3 4 5 6 7 8

The permutation representation of cities visited in reverse order would be represented as the following permutation:

8 7 6 5 4 3 2 1

Although the permutation representation seems natural enough, how does it fit into the representation schemes of early simple genetic algorithm application?

In a previous discussion we took great pains to separate an allele's locus from its meaning. Mathematically we might say that a fitness f should only depend on allele value v, $f = f(v)$ only; however, in many problems it may be useful to allow fitness to depend on string arrangement: fitness f can depend on some combination of allele value v and ordering o, $f = f(v, o)$.

In the traveling salesman problem with permutation representation we have gone to the other extreme. We have a problem where fitness depends only on the ordering information, $f = f(o)$ only. We can imagine augmented TSPs where the salesman must make decisions as he makes his rounds and those decisions could easily be appended to the ordering information to create a mixed ordering-value problem $f = f(o, v)$:

```
1 2 3 4 5 6 7 8
0 0 0 0 0 0 0 0
```

In the example, the ascending, ordinal tour carries along allele information (a zero) for each city. In this way we recognize that in general there is a spectrum of possible coding methods that more or less depend on ordering and value.

Once we allow this possibility, we need to search for an operator analogous to crossover, which permits the exchange of important ordering similarities between pairs of parents to form offspring. Recall that the power of genetic search lies in the combined effect of selection and structured, randomized recombination: mutation is simply an insurance policy against the irreversible loss of genetic material. Under an ordering representation, inversion, like mutation, is a unary operator. If we are to create operators with the power of crossover, they must (like crossover) be binary operators and they must combine ordering building blocks from above-average parents in a sensible way. Goldberg and Lingle (1985) have suggested such an operator in the partially matched crossover (PMX) operator.

Under PMX, two strings (permutations and their associated alleles) are aligned, and two crossing sites are picked uniformly at random along the strings. These two points define a *matching section* that is used to effect a cross through position-by-position exchange operations.

To see this, consider two strings:

```
A = 9 8 4 | 5 6  7 | 1 3 2 10
B = 8 7 1 | 2 3 10 | 9 5 4  6
```

PMX proceeds by positionwise exchanges. First, mapping string B to string A, the 5 and the 2, the 3 and the 6, and the 10 and the 7 exchange places. Similarly mapping string A to string B, the 5 and the 2, the 6 and the 3, and the 7 and the 10 exchange places. Following PMX we are left with two offspring, A′ and B′:

```
A′ = 9  8 4 | 2 3 10 | 1 6 5 7
B′ = 8 10 1 | 5 6  7 | 9 2 4 3
```

where each string contains ordering information partially determined by each of its parents.

Figure 5.16 displays a set of Pascal routines that implement PMX. These routines have been used to obtain the results on Karg and Thompson's (1964) 10- and 33-city problems displayed in Figs. 5.17 and 5.18. Figure 5.17 displays best-of-generation tour length versus generation number on two independent runs of

```
function find_city(city_name,n_city:city; var tour:tourarray):city;
var j1:integer;
begin
 j1:=0;
 repeat
  j1:=j1+1;
 until ( (j1>n_city) or (tour[j1]=city_name) );
 find_city:=j1;
end;

procedure swap_city(city_pos1,city_pos2:integer; var tour:tourarray);
var temp:city;
begin
 temp:=tour[city_pos1];
 tour[city_pos1]:=tour[city_pos2];
 tour[city_pos2]:=temp;
end;

procedure tour_norm(city_name,n_city:city; var tour:tourarray);
var temp_tour:tourarray;
    j1,j2:city;
begin
 j1 := find_city(city_name,n_city,tour);
 if (j1 <> 1) then begin (* normalization *)
    for j2 := 1 to n_city do begin
       temp_tour[j2]:=tour[j1];
       j1:=j1+1; if (j1>n_city) then j1:=1;
      end;
     tour:=temp_tour;
    end
end;

procedure cross_tour(n_city,lo_cross,hi_cross:city;
                     var tour1_old,tour2_old,tour1_new,tour2_new:tourarray);
var j1,hi_test:integer;
begin
 if traceison then writeln('lo_cross,hi_cross=',lo_cross,' ',hi_cross);
 hi_test := hi_cross + 1; if (hi_test>n_city) then hi_test:=1;
 tour1_new := tour1_old;
 tour2_new := tour2_old;
 if ( (lo_cross <> hi_cross) and (lo_cross <> hi_test) ) then begin
   j1 := lo_cross;
   while (j1<>hi_test) do begin (* mapped crossover on both tours *)
    swap_city(j1,find_city(tour1_old[j1],n_city,tour2_new),tour2_new);
    swap_city(j1,find_city(tour2_old[j1],n_city,tour1_new),tour1_new);
    j1:=j1+1; if (j1>n_city) then j1:= 1;
   end;
  end;
end;
```

FIGURE 5.16 Partially matched crossover (PMX) operator in Pascal. Procedure *cross_tour* implements PMX. Function *find_city* and procedure *swap_city* are used by procedure *cross_tour*. From Goldberg and Lingle (1985).

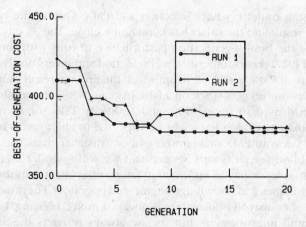

FIGURE 5.17 Partially matched crossover (PMX) operator in 10-city blind traveling salesman problem. Run 1 converges to optimal results. Population size $n = 200$ with $p_c = 0.6$. From Goldberg and Lingle (1985).

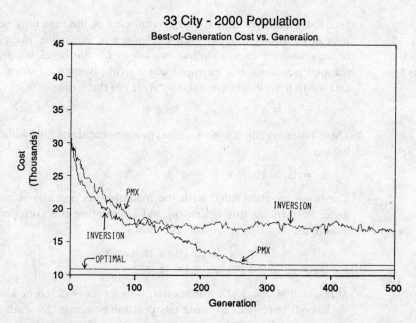

FIGURE 5.18 Partially matched crossover (PMX) operator in 33-city blind traveling salesman problem.

a GA using roulette wheel selection and PMX. One of the runs has found the optimal result and the other has come quite close. The 33-city results (Fig. 5.18) compare the best-of-generation performance of runs with roulette wheel selection and PMX versus roulette wheel selection and inversion. The binary exchange capability of PMX permits it to approach the optimal result quite closely, whereas the inversion run gets stuck on a false plateau. While the results are encouraging, in a world used to seeing 500- and 1000-city TSPs solved to optimality, such approximate performance might be expected to elicit yawns until we remember that the GA with PMX makes no use of city distance data. The restriction of pure GAs to blind search is very severe, and we will consider methods that are permitted to use nonpayoff information later in the chapter in the discussion of hybrid techniques and knowledge-augmented operators. For now, we recognize that the use of nonpayoff information is always a mixed blessing. Using it may permit more rapid improvement, but its use always restricts the applicability of the search.

Operators similar to PMX have also been devised (Davis, 1985a,b; Davis and Smith, 1985; Oliver, Smith, and Holland, 1987; Smith, 1985) and applied to problems with permutation representation. We examine the mechanics of two such operators: order crossover (OX) and cycle crossover (CX).

The order crossover operator starts off in a manner similar to PMX. Starting with the example strings A and B used to illustrate PMX, we select a matching section (for comparison, we choose the matching section of the PMX example):

```
A = 9 8 4 | 5 6 7 | 1 3 2 10
B = 8 7 1 | 2 3 10 | 9 5 4  6
```

Like PMX, each string maps to constituents of the matching section of its mate. Instead of using point-by-point exchanges to effect the mapping as PMX does, order crossover uses a sliding motion to fill the holes left by transferring the mapped positions. For example when string B maps to string A, the cities 5, 6, and 7 will leave holes (marked by an H) in the string:

```
B = 8 H 1 | 2 3 10 | 9 H 4 H
```

These holes are filled with a sliding motion that starts following the second crossing site:

```
B = 2 3 10 H H H 9 4 8 1
```

The holes are then filled with the matching section city names taken from the mate. Performing this operation and completing the complementary cross we obtain the offspring A' and B' as follows:

```
A' = 5 6 7 | 2 3 10 | 1 9 8 4
B' = 2 3 10 | 5 6 7 | 9 4 8 1
```

Although PMX and OX are similar, they process different kinds of similarities. PMX tends to respect absolute city position, whereas OX tends to respect relative city position. We will have more to say about this in the next section. Before that we examine the last of these permutation operators, cycle crossover.

The cycle crossover operator is a cross of a different color. Cycle crossover performs recombination under the constraint that each city name come from one parent or the other. To see how this is done we start with example tours C and D below:

```
C = 9 8 2 1 7 4 5 10 6  3
D = 1 2 3 4 5 6 7  8 9 10
```

Instead of choosing crossing sites, we start at the left and choose a city from the first parent:

```
C' = 9 - - - - - - - - -
```

Since we want every city to be taken from one of the two parents, the choice of city 9 from string C means that we must now get city 1 from string C because of the 1 in position of string D.

```
C' = 9 - - 1 - - - - - -
```

This selection in turn requires that we select city 4 from string C. This process continues until we are left with the following pattern:

```
C' = 9 - - 1 - 4 - - 6 -
```

The selection of a 6 means that we should now choose a 9 from string C; however, this is not possible; a 9 having been selected as the first city. That we eventually return to the city of origin completes a *cycle*, thus giving the operator its name. Following the completion of the first cycle, the remaining cities are filled from the other string. Completing the example and performing the complementary cross yields the following children tours:

```
C' = 9 2 3 1 5 4 7  8 6 10
D' = 1 8 2 4 7 6 5 10 9  3
```

Further theoretical and empirical results comparing PMX, OX, CX are presented in Oliver, Smith, and Holland (1987).

Theory of Reordering Operators

Until recently there has been a paucity of theory related to reordering operators. Frantz (1972) calculated several quantities of interest in his study of inversion. He calculated the probability distribution of orderings of a given specificity and defining length. He also determined the probability of movement of a gene located at a particular locus. The probability that a randomly ordered permutation with o alleles of interest has a defining length exactly equal to δ is given by the following expression:

$$P\{D = \delta\} = \frac{(l - \delta + 1)\binom{\delta - 2}{o - 2}}{\binom{l}{\delta}}$$

He also calculated the corresponding cumulative distribution:

$$P\{D \leq \delta\} = \frac{\binom{\delta}{o}\left(\dfrac{l\delta - o\delta + \delta}{l}\right)}{\binom{l}{o}}$$

Frantz calculated the probability of gene movement under inversion for a gene at locus k on a string of length l as follows:

$$P\{\text{gene moved}\} = \frac{2[k(l + 1) - k^2 + 1)]}{l^2}.$$

For long string lengths the expression reduces to

$$P\{\text{moved}\} = 2(x - x^2),$$

where x is the nondimensionalized locus $x = k/l$. This asymptotic expression has a maximum of $P = 0.5$ at $x = 0.5$.

This imbalance in movement probability caused Frantz to devise his linear + end inversion operator discussed earlier. There are other ways of reducing these end effects. One way (with precedence in nature) is to treat the chromosome as a ring. With no beginning and no end, each locus is equally likely to be moved under a single inversion. An analogous situation in Chapter 4 involved a two-point, ring crossover operator. Another possibility is simply to leave the operator alone and live with its locus dependency. It is possible that the end effect might be useful in both natural and artificial genetic search by acting as a probabilistic shield for useful groupings of genes. If this is the case, successful groupings of genes could migrate toward the string ends, thereby using this *inversion shadow* to retard further disruption. On the other hand unsettled groupings of genes might seek out the string center, thereby guaranteeing themselves a high probability of movement.

Frantz's concern with the locus-dependence of movement probability on the one hand seems quite reasonable. Perhaps it is important to smooth out this probability, or perhaps, as we have just pointed out, the locus dependence is an exploitable side effect of the operator. If we are only concerned with finding tightly linked building blocks, the absolute locus does not seem like the most relevant variable of interest. Rather, maintenance or consistency in relative locus seems like a more reasonable measure of operator disruptive potential. Holland (1975) recognized this fact in his calculation of the probability of schema disruption due to inversion:

$$P\{\text{disruption}\} = 2p_i \frac{\delta(H)}{l - 1}\left[1 - \frac{\delta(H)}{l - 1}\right].$$

The second-order term arises because the length of a schema is not increased when both inversion points fall within a schema as illustrated below.

```
Disruptive Inversion
! ! 3 ! 2 6 ! ! ! !      ! 3 ! ! 2 6 ! ! ! !
* * 0 * 0 1 * * * *   →  * 0 * * 0 1 * * * *
 ^    ^
```

```
Nondisruptive Inversion
! ! 3 ! 2 6 ! ! ! !       ! ! 3 2 ! 6 ! ! ! !
* * 0 * 0 1 * * * *   →   * * 0 0 * 1 * * * *
     ^   ^
```

The notation here is a little different from anything defined so far in this book. The allelic "don't care" symbols (*) retain their usual meaning; however, the exclamation points (!) are used to indicate any of the possible orderings over the remaining unmentioned genes. Holland did not use this notation or define an ordering schema or template in his original work; however, he did allow for the possible modification of an allelic schema's defining length under inversion.

A start toward a more comprehensive allelic-ordering theory of schemata began when I defined *ordering schemata* in connection with PMX (Goldberg and Lingle, 1985). This study defined the space of all ordering similarities using the ordering don't care symbol, the exclamation point (!), as illustrated above. In the same way that *'s define all possible allele similarities (the allelic schemata or *a*-schemata), the ordering schema (we call them *o*-schemata) define all possible similarities. For example, the *o*-schema

$$! \ ! \ 2 \ 3 \ ! \ ! \ ! \ ! \ ! \ !$$

defines the subset of all orderings that have gene 2 and 3 in positions 3 and 4 respectively. A particular *o*-schema of order (specificity) *o* describes that subset of $(l - o)!$ orderings over the $l - o$ unspecified positions. For example, in the *o*-schema above there are $(10 - 2)! = 8!$ orderings of the symbols $\{1, 4, 5, 6, 7, 8, 9, 10\}$ in the eight unspecified positions. Straightforward counting arguments enable us to count the number of *o*-schemata. Since there are $\binom{l}{o}$ ways to choose *o* fixed positions among *l* slots and since there are $\binom{l}{o}o!$ ways to order *l* symbols in $l - o$ slots, the total number of *o*-schemata, n_{os}, may be calculated as follows:

$$n_{os} = \sum_{j=0}^{l} \frac{l!}{(l-j)!j!} \cdot \frac{l!}{(l-j)!}$$

Straightforward arguments show how a particular string is itself a representative of 2^l schemata and that a population of *n* strings contains representatives of between 2^l and $n \cdot 2^l$ such *o*-schemata.

The previous definition of an *o*-schema is only one of a family of possible definitions. If we want the relative position of an allele to matter instead of its absolute position, we should define a relative *o*-schema (an *o*-schema, type *r*).

Using the notation $r^l(\ \ )$ to generate absolute schemata of length l, the symbols $r^{10}(3\ !\ !\ 2\ 8)$ would generate the following absolute o-schemata (o-schemata, type a):

```
3 ! ! 2 8 ! ! ! ! !
! 3 ! ! 2 8 ! ! ! !
! ! 3 ! ! 2 8 ! ! !
! ! ! 3 ! ! 2 8 ! !
! ! ! ! 3 ! ! 2 8 !
! ! ! ! ! 3 ! ! 2 8
```

In addition, if we treat the string as a circular structure with no beginning and no end, the same type r, o-schema picks up the following absolute o-schemata in the bargain:

```
8 ! ! ! ! ! ! 3 ! ! 2
2 8 ! ! ! ! ! ! 3 ! !
! 2 8 ! ! ! ! ! ! 3 !
! ! 2 8 ! ! ! ! ! ! 3
```

This idea of sliding the gene identifiers about leads us to consider a third type of o-schema. So far we have considered o-schemata where the absolute position of different genes has mattered (o-schemata, type a) and where the relative position of different genes has mattered (o-schemata, type r). Now consider a certain set of genes with a specified defining length and permit the entire packet to slide about (in the sense of an o-schema, type r); as long as it has the specified defining length, we may define a new type of o-schema that may be useful in characterizing certain problems. Let us call this new entity a relative o-schema with sliding (in shorthand, an o-schema type rs). To describe o-schemata type rs, we introduce the functional notation $rs_\delta^l(\ \ )$ to generate type r, o-schemata of defining length δ and total length l. The argument of this function is an ordered list of numbers used to generate a set of o-schemata type r. For example the o-schema $rs_4^{10}(2\ 3\ 8)$ expands to the following set of o-schemata type r:

```
r^10(2 3 ! ! 8)
r^10(2 ! 3 ! 8)
r^10(2 ! ! 3 8)
```

These type r, o-schemata may themselves be expanded to absolute o-schemata.

In some problems it may not even be necessary to maintain relative order among the numbered objects. For these we define one last extension of the notation which permits exchanges in order: a relative, sliding o-schema with exchange (type rse). Thus the notation $rse_\delta^l(\ \ )$ expands an unordered list of numbers into a set of o-schemata type rs. For example, the type rse o-schema $rse_4^{10}(2\ 3\ 8)$ expands to the set of 6 o-schemata type rs defined by the six permutations of the numbers 2, 3, and 8. These may in turn be expanded to type r and type a o-schemata.

The consideration of both o-schemata and a-schemata adds considerable perspective to the study of genetic algorithm performance under combined allelic and reordering operations. This perspective is enhanced if we recognize that the schema theorem operates on both o-schemata, a-schemata, and their combinations. We must be careful to match the operator survival probabilities to the type of schema we are discussing. For example, in Goldberg and Lingle (1985) the survival probability is calculated for a pure o-schema, type a (absolute) under the PMX operator. Holland's (1975) calculation of inversion "schema" disruption probability is for an o-schema, type rse (relative with sliding and exchange). Extended schema analyses like those performed on the minimum deceptive problem (MDP) in Chapter 2 should help shed additional theoretical light on the combined workings of o-schemata and a-schemata in particular problems.

OTHER MICRO-OPERATORS

A number of other low-level operators have been suggested for use in genetic adaptive search. Although these add marginal power to genetic algorithms as compared to the addition of abeyance (dominance) and reordering operators, we briefly review some of the other operators suggested for use in GA search: segregation, translocation, intrachromosomal duplication, deletion, sexual differentiation.

Segregation, Translocation, and Multiple Chromosome Structures

So far, we have examined genotypes with a single chromosome (haploid) or a single chromosome pair (diploid). In nature many organisms carry genotypes with multiple chromosomes. For example, the human carries 23 pairs of diploid chromosomes. Adopting a similar structure in artificial genetic search requires extending the representation once more and permitting a genotype to be a list of k string pairs (assuming diploidy). But why should we want to make the representation more complex in this way? Holland (1975) has suggested that multiple-chromosome genotypes might be useful in extending the power of genetic algorithms when used in conjunction with two operators: segregation and translocation.

To see how segregation works, we simply imagine the process of gamete formation when we have more than one chromosome pair in the genotype. Crossover occurs as before; however, when we go to form a gamete we randomly select one of each of the haploid chromosomes. This random selection process, known as *segregation,* effectively disrupts any linkage that might exist between genes on different chromosomes. Of course, genes located on the same chromosome still are linked more or less tightly depending upon the distance separating them. Segregation is a useful operator if relatively independent genes happen to have located themselves on different chromosomes. In this way, with linkage effectively destroyed, poor alleles cannot piggyback their way to survival on the strength of highly fit, unrelated alleles.

There is an article of faith in this last assertion. If segregation can exploit the proper organization of the chromosome, how does the chromosome become organized in an appropriate manner? Holland has suggested that this is where the *translocation* operator steps in. Translocation may be viewed as an interchromosomal crossover operator. To implement such an operator in an artificial setting, we need to tag alleles with their gene name so we can identify their intended meaning when they are shuffled from chromosome to chromosome by the translocation operator. In nature, it is possible to produce genotypes without the full gene complement following a translocation. This can and probably should be avoided in artificial genetic search.

There has not been much experimentation with these operators in artificial genetic search. Hollstien (1971) used a segregationlike operator in studying single diploid chromosome genotypes. He assumed segregation to be a random shuffle of alleles between parental strings during meiosis. The experiments he performed were limited in scope and he drew no general conclusions about this form of the operator. Later studies of genetic algorithms in machine learning applications have required extended genotypes and operators (see Schaffer, 1984; Smith, 1980) similar to segregation and translocation.

Duplication and Deletion

Duplication and *deletion* are a pair of low-level operators suggested for artificial GA search. Intrachromosomal duplication acts by duplicating a particular gene and placing it along with its progenitor on the chromosome. Deletion acts by removing a duplicate gene from the chromosome. Holland (1975) has suggested that these operators can be effective methods to adaptively control the mutation rate. If the background mutation rate remains constant and duplication causes k copies of a particular gene, the effective mutation probability (the probability that at least one of the k copies undergoes a mutation) for this gene is multiplied by k. Conversely, when a deletion occurs, the effective mutation rate is decreased. Notice, of course, that once a mutation occurs in one of the new genes under this scheme, we must decide which of the alternatives is expressed. We faced the same situation when we talked about dominance and diploidy. In fact we may view the multiple copies as inducing an *intrachromosomal dominance* as opposed to the more usual interchromosomal dominance that comes about in diploidy. Holland has suggested the use of a dominancelike arbitration scheme to make the necessary choice among competing alternatives, although there have been no published studies of such mechanisms to date.

We might wonder if intrachromosomal duplication and deletion serve only the function of inducing an adaptive mutation rate. Perhaps this is part of the story; however, we have already seen one example where duplication was used in a GA for a more fundamental purpose. Recall from Chapter 4 how Cavicchio (1970) used intrachromosomal duplication to generate new image feature detectors. Each of his genes specified a set of pixels as part of a single detector. In this problem intrachromosomal duplication causes no arbitration problems, and subsequent mutations or crosses involving the new detector may create a better, more appropriate detector. In some respects genes in nature are like Cavicchio's "messy codings," and perhaps there is some benefit in considering codings that permit redundancy, variable lengths, and underspecification.

Sexual Determination and Differentiation

It is odd, at least curious. in a book where we model algorithms after natural examples of reproduction and genetics that we have not yet discussed sex. It is not for lack of interest, nor is it because sex is an unimportant mechanism with negligible side effects. In this section we examine the mechanisms of sex determination and examine how these may be useful in genetic algorithm search.

Nature doesn't work as simply as we have assumed. In our simpleminded mating schemes, we have permitted any individual to mate with any other, and we have always divided the resulting genetic products in a manner that has ensured a viable genotype. In nature many organisms may be of two (or more) distinct sexes, and in some way the two must come together to propagate the species. The details of sex determination are handled differently in different species; however, the human example is sufficiently representative for us to use as a model.

One of the 23 pairs of human chromosomes determines sex. Females have two homologous sex chromosomes (X chromosomes), and males have two dissimilar sex chromosomes (one X chromosome and one Y chromosome). During gametogenesis males form sperm, which carry either X or Y chromosomes (in equal proportions); whereas females produce eggs, which carry only X chromosomes. When fertilization occurs, the certainty of X-chromosome production by the female combined with the coin-toss uncertainty of X or Y-chromosome production by the male leads to an expected (and observed) 1:1 sex ratio of males and females.

Although the mechanics of sex determination in humans is straightforward, nature tosses in interesting complications. A number of factors unrelated to gender can piggyback on the sex chromosomes. These so-called sex-linked factors are most frequently identified with the X chromosome. Additionally, although in most organisms the loci found in the X chromosome are not found in the Y chromosome, there are organisms where portions of the Y chromosome are homologous to a portion of the X chromosome. When this occurs, crossing over between these homologous X and Y chromosomes can display incomplete sex linkage as compared to organisms where the lack of homology inhibits crossing over.

All this is very interesting. Yet, we are not about to give up our pragmatic viewpoint in exchange for a few arcane details of reproduction. More to the point, what can sexual determination and differentiation do for us in artificial genetic search? Unfortunately, there have been no published theoretical or empirical studies of sex determination and differentiation in the literature of genetic algorithms. Nonetheless, some straightforward reasoning can lead to a plausible explanation of their utility. Clearly, the establishment of sex difference effectively divides a species into two (or more) cooperative groups. This bifurcation allows males and females to specialize somewhat, thereby covering the range of behaviors necessary for survival more broadly than would be possible with a single competing population.

To show this quantitatively, we consider an idealized function demonstrating the benefit of cooperation and specialization implied by natural sexual difference. Suppose an individual has a choice between hunting for food or nurturing his or her offspring. Letting h be the proportion of time spent hunting and n be the proportion of time spent nurturing, we may postulate that the offspring survival probability s is proportional to the product of the hunting and nurturing proportions:

$$s(n, h) = nh.$$

An individual must make a choice between allocating his or her time to the nurturing and hunting activities, and if we further assume that there is a loss of time available for either activity proportional to the product of the activity proportions (a jack-of-all-trades loss), we obtain an equation relating the time spent hunting and nurturing as follows:

$$n + h + anh = 1.$$

where a is the loss coefficient for not specializing. Maximizing the survival s using elementary methods, we obtain the optimum level of nurturing n^* and hunting h^* for a single individual as follows:

$$n^* = h^* = \frac{-1 + \sqrt{1 + a}}{a},$$

which approaches the limit $n^* = h^* = 0.5$ for the case where the loss coefficient $a = 0$. In words, an individual can do no better than compromise between the two necessary activities; excess time expended on either activity is penalized by lower rates of survival for offspring. This is shown graphically in Fig. 5.19, which depicts the variation of survival s as a function of nurturing n for two cases $a = 1.9$ and $a = 0.0$.

Permitting two individuals to cooperate and act as a hunting-nurturing unit produces a similar model of offspring survival. Assuming hunting and nurturing proportions for individuals 1 and 2, h_1, n_1, h_2, and n_2, we obtain the survival proportion s as follows:

$$s(n_1, h_1, n_2, h_2) = \tfrac{1}{2}(n_1 + n_2)(h_1 + h_2),$$

where the factor of one-half permits direct comparison to the single individual probability (there are now twice as many mouths to feed and nurture). The two individuals' time proportions are governed by the following equations:

$$n_i + h_i + an_ih_i = 1, \qquad i = 1, 2.$$

Maximizing the survival s with respect to the hunting and nurturing proportions,

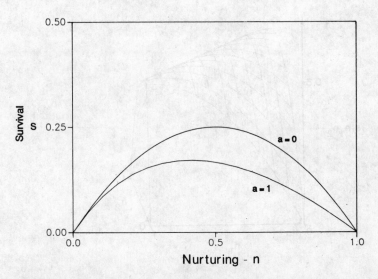

FIGURE 5.19 A single individual must compromise between nurturing and hunting to maximize survival. The jack-of-all-trades loss ($a > 0$) further impairs the individual's ability to achieve high survival.

we obtain two cases. With no jack-of-all-trades loss, the survival probability is a maximum along the line defined by the equation

$$n_1^* + n_2^* = 1,$$

as depicted in Fig. 5.20a, a graph of survival versus the nurturing proportions. Without jack-of-all-trades loss there is incentive to cooperate (survival has risen from 0.25 (individual) to 0.5 (cooperative pair)), but there is no incentive for specialization; either individual may nurture or hunt as long as total nurturing and hunting sum to one.

With some jack-of-all-trades loss ($a > 0$), the situation is quite different, as is depicted in Fig. 5.20b. The optimal behavior now requires specialization. Maximal survival is obtained when $(n_1, n_2) = (1, 0)$ or $(0, 1)$. The survival at these optima still shows the increment over the uncooperative individual and the jack-of-all-trades loss is minimized.

Although the foregoing modes are idealized, they demonstrate the essential cooperation and specialization served by sexual differentiation. Future trials of sex in artificial genetic search are likely to show an advantage for sex operators in problems that likewise require this combination of cooperation and specialization.

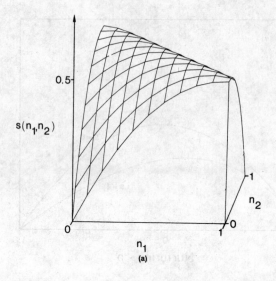

$s(n_1, n_2)$

n_2

n_1

(a)

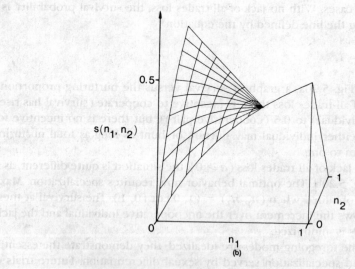

$s(n_1, n_2)$

n_2

n_1

(b)

FIGURE 5.20 Cooperation between individuals enhances survival; however, without jack-of-all-trades loss, there is no motivation for specialization as shown in (a). With a jack-of-all-trades loss, maximum survival is achieved with maximal specialization as shown in (b).

NICHE AND SPECIATION

The specialization permitted by sexual differentiation is carried further in nature through speciation and niche exploitation. Intuitively we may view a niche as an organism's job or role in an environment, and we can think of a species as a class of organism with common characteristics. This separation of the environment and the organisms exploiting that environment into different subsets is so common in nature that we scarcely give it a second thought. In this light, it is curious that we have not observed stable subpopulations of strings (species) serving different subdomains of a function (niches) in most of our examples thus far. This section shows how the inducement of niche and species can help GA search, presents the relevant theory, and demonstrates how we might cause nichelike and specieslike behavior in genetic algorithms.

To understand why we might like to encourage the formation of niche and species in GAs, let's consider the action of a simple genetic algorithm on the simple function shown in Fig. 5.21a. If we start from an initial population chosen uniformly at random, we obtain a relatively even spread of points across the function domain. As reproduction, crossover, and mutation proceed, the population climbs the hills, ultimately distributing most of the strings near the top of one hill among the five. This ultimate convergence on one peak or another without differential advantage is caused by genetic drift—stochastic errors in sampling

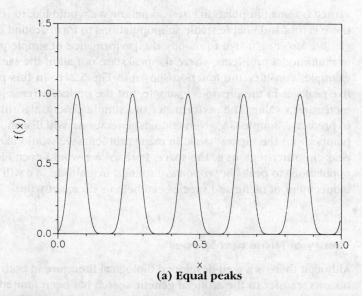

(a) Equal peaks

FIGURE 5.21 Sample functions where stable, relatively noncompetitive subpopulations might be useful. In (a) we would like subpopulations to be roughly equal in size. In (b) we would like subpopulation sizes to decrease with decreasing peak size (see p. 186).

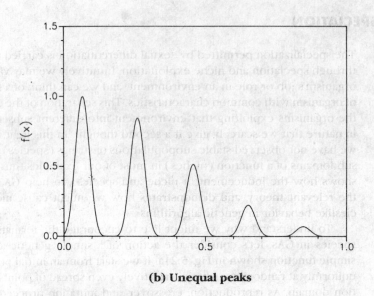

(b) Unequal peaks

FIGURE 5.21   (*Continued*)

caused by small population sizes. Somehow we would like to reduce the effect of these errors and enable stable subpopulations to form around each peak.

We also might like to modify the performance of simple genetic algorithms in multimodal problems where the peaks are not all of the same magnitude. For example, consider the function shown in Fig. 5.21b. In this problem there are five peaks as in the previous example, but the peaks decrease in magnitude with increasing x value. The performance of a simple genetic algorithm is easy enough to predict. A simple GA, given enough generations, will distribute almost all of its points about the highest peak. In many problems we would like to identify other peaks in other regions of the space. Perhaps we would even like to allocate sub-populations to peaks in *proportion* to their magnitude. We will soon see how the inducement of niche and species can help us do exactly this.

Theory of Niche and Species

Although there is a well-developed biological literature in both niche and specia-tion, its transfer to the artificial genetic search has been limited. Like many other concepts and operators, the first theories directly applicable to artificial genetic search are attributed to Holland (1975). To illustrate niche and species, Holland introduced a modification of the two-armed bandit problem with distributed pay-off and sharing. Let's examine his argument with a concrete formulation of the same problem.

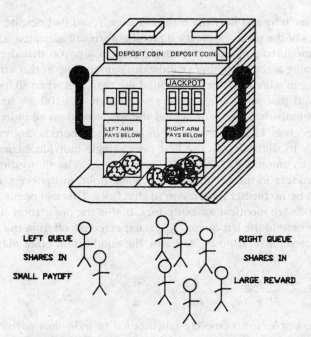

FIGURE 5.22 Schematic of a two-armed bandit with sharing among individuals in two queues.

Imagine a two-armed bandit as depicted in Fig. 5.22. As in the two-armed bandit problem discussed in Chapter 2, there are two arms, a left arm and a right arm, and different payoffs associated with each arm. Suppose the expected payoff associated with the right arm is $75 and the expected payoff associated with the left arm is $25; as in the original problem, we are unaware initially which arm pays the higher amount. Let's further suppose that we have a population of 100 players and that each player receives the full payoff amount from the arm he chooses on a particular play. If we leave matters alone at this point and allow the players to play either arm, we connect directly with the original two-armed bandit problem discussed in Chapter 2. If the players reproduce according to fitness (under reproduction), more and more population members should line up behind the best (right) arm until the population converges substantially to that arm.

So far we have no reason to expect any nichelike behavior: all trials eventually go to the observed best arm. It is at this point that we introduce the important modification to the game that permits stable subpopulations to serve both arms. Instead of allowing a full share of payoff for each individual, individuals who choose a particular arm are now forced to *share* the wealth derived from a given arm on a given play. At first glance this change appears to be quite minor. In fact this single modification causes a strikingly and surprisingly different outcome in the modified two-armed bandit.

To see why and how the results change, recall that despite the slightly different rules of the game, population members are still allocated according to payoff.
In the modified game an individual receives a payoff that depends on the arm
payoff value and the number of individuals queued up at that arm. In the concrete
example, an individual lined up behind the right arm when all individuals are lined
up behind that same arm receives an amount \$75/100 = \$0.75. On the other
hand an individual lined up behind the left arm when all individuals are queued
there receives \$25/100 = \$0.25. In both cases there is motivation for some individuals to shift lines. In the first case a single individual changing lines stands
to gain an amount \$25.00 − \$0.75 = \$24.25. The motivation to shift lines is
even stronger in the second case. At some point in between, we should expect
there to be no further motivation to shift lines. This will occur when the individual payoffs are identical for both lines. If M is the population size and m_{left} is the
number behind the left queue, f_{right} is expected payoff from the right arm, and f_{left}
is expected payoff from the left arm, the equilibrium point may be calculated as
follows:

$$\frac{f_{right}}{m_{right}} = \frac{f_{right}}{M - m_{left}} = \frac{f_{left}}{m_{left}}.$$

In the example, this complete equalization of individual payoff occurs when 75
players select the right arm and 25 players select the left arm, because \$75/75 =
\$25/25 = \$1.

Directly extending this problem to the k-armed case does not change the
fundamental conclusions. The incorporation of forced sharing causes the formation of stable subpopulations (species) behind different arms (niches) in the
problem. Furthermore, the number of individuals devoted to each niche is proportional to the expected niche payoff. This is exactly the type of solution we
had hoped for when we considered the multimodal problems of Fig. 5.21. Of
course the extension of the sharing concept to real genetic algorithm search is
more difficult than the single idealized case implies. In a real genetic algorithm
there are many arms and deciding who should share and how much should be
shared becomes a nontrivial question. The next section presents the efforts to
induce niche formation through sharing or sharinglike mechanisms. Before examining what has been attempted, we must examine one further theoretical issue
in connection with speciation.

Once we recognize the importance of sharing to niche formation, we have
most of the necessary theory to understand its workings in artificial genetic
search; however, one other observation of nature may help us do a better job. In
our simple genetic algorithm work so far we have caused mating to occur at
random. This is contrary to most biological example. For instance, people do not
attempt to mate with cats, and frogs do not attempt to mate with scientists (although the latter possibility might result in a researcher who jumps to conclusions). The observation that species are unlikely to mate with organisms
dissimilar to themselves begs us to question why this might occur. Put another
way, what is the selective advantage of the rule that like mates like (positive

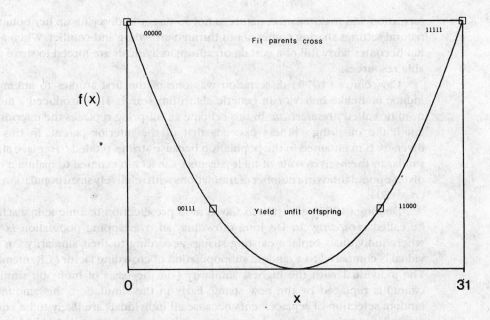

FIGURE 5.23 Simple bimodal function illustrating need for mating restriction. Crosses between dissimilar near-optima almost always cause lethals.

assortive mating) that seems to govern the mating behavior of many species? A simple example drawn from function optimization may again help illuminate the key ideas. Suppose we have a function as shown in Fig. 5.23 with peaks at the extremes of a one-dimensional space. Using a normal binary fraction to code strings in this space, individuals located near the leftmost peak tend to have many zeros in them, whereas individuals located at the rightmost peak tend to have many ones in them (the leftmost optimum is the string 00000, whereas the rightmost optimum is the string 11111). When a population of strings is repeatedly reproduced, mated, and crossed, the resultant offspring tend to be strings like 00111 or 11000 (a relatively useless—in this problem—blend of 1's and 0's). Interspecies mating in this manner tends to generate low-performance offspring (lethals). If, on the other hand, some pressure can be maintained to cause similar individuals to mate with one another, the generation of fruitless offspring can be reduced. This highlights the need for methods of encouraging more fruitful mating patterns.

Niche Methods for Genetic Search

A number of methods have been implemented to induce niche formation in genetic algorithms. In some of these techniques the sharing comes about indirectly. Although the shared two-armed bandit problem is a simple abstraction of niche formation and maintenance, nature is not so direct in divvying up her bounty. In natural settings sharing comes about through crowding and conflict. When a habitat becomes fairly full of a certain organism, individuals are forced to share available resources.

Cavicchio's (1970) dissertation was one of the first studies to attempt to induce nichelike behavior in genetic algorithm search. He introduced a mechanism he called *preselection*. In this scheme an offspring replaces the inferior parent if the offspring's fitness exceeds that of the inferior parent. In this way diversity is maintained in the population because strings tended to replace strings similar to themselves (one of their parents). Cavicchio claimed to maintain more diverse populations in a number of simulations with relatively small population sizes ($n = 20$).

De Jong (1975) generalized Cavicchio's preselection technique in a scheme he called *crowding*. In De Jong crowding, an overlapping population is used where individuals replace existing strings according to their similarity. An individual is compared to a random subpopulation of crowding factor (CF) members. The individual with the highest similarity (on the basis of bit-by-bit similarity count) is replaced by the new string. Early in the simulation, this amounts to random selection of replacements because all individuals are likely to be equally dissimilar. As the simulation progresses and more and more individuals in the population are similar to one another (one or more species has gotten a substantial foothold in the population), the replacement of individuals by similar individuals tends to maintain diversity within the population and reserve room for two or more species. De Jong had success with the crowding scheme on multimodal functions when he used crowding factors CF = 2 and CF = 3. De Jong-like crowding has subsequently been used in a machine learning application (Goldberg, 1983).

Note that neither Cavicchio's preselection scheme nor De Jong's crowding scheme appears to use the sharing analogy discussed earlier; however, both schemes induce a form of implicit sharing in the following sense. Without crowding or preselection, an individual in a nonoverlapping population is replaced by uniform random selection. If the individual is replaced faster than this rate (as is the case under crowding or preselection when a species gains a foothold), he loses payoff (offspring) because he does not reach his full reproductive potential. Put another way, even though crowding and preselection focus on the replacement side of the equation, by forcing early retirement of too-numerous species members they cause a lower offspring count, thereby making room for others.

The most direct exploration of biological niche theory in the context of genetic algorithms occurred in Perry's (1984) dissertation. In this work Perry defines a genotype-to-phenotype mapping, a multiple-resource environment, and a special entity called an *external schema*. External schemata are special similarity templates defined by the simulation designer to characterize species membership. Unfortunately the required intervention of an outside agent limits the practical use of this technique in artificial genetic search. Nonetheless the reader interested in the connections between biological niche theory and GAs should be interested in this work.

Grosso (1985) also maintained a biological orientation in his study of explicit subpopulation formation and migration operators. Since multiplicative, heterotic (heterozygote better than homozygote) objective functions were used in this study, the results are not directly applicable to most artificial genetic search; however, Grosso was able to show the advantage of intermediate migration rate values over either isolated subpopulations (no migration) and panmictic (completely mixed) subpopulations. This study suggests that the imposition of a geography on genetic search may also be a useful way of assisting the formation of diverse subpopulations. Further studies are needed to determine how to do this in typical artificial search problems.

A practical scheme that directly uses the sharing metaphor to induce niche and species is detailed by Goldberg and Richardson (1987). In this scheme, a *sharing function* is defined to determine the neighborhood and degree of sharing for each string in the population. To see how this works, consider the simple one-dimensional test functions presented earlier in Fig. 5.21 and the simple sharing function shown in Fig. 5.24. For a given individual the degree of sharing is determined by summing the sharing function values contributed by all other strings in the population. Strings close to an individual require a high degree of sharing (close to one), and strings far from the individual require a very small degree of sharing (close to zero). Since an individual is very close (as close as possible) to itself, its sharing function value is one (as is any other string identical to that individual). After accumulating the total number of shares in this manner,

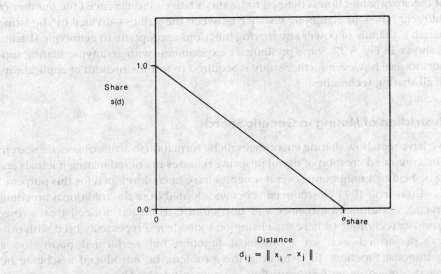

FIGURE 5.24 Triangular sharing function. After Goldberg and Richardson (1987).

an individual's derated fitness is calculated by taking the potential fitness (the unshared value) and dividing through by the accumulated number of shares:

$$f_s(x_i) = \frac{f(x_i)}{\sum_{j=1}^{n} s(d(x_i, x_j))}$$

Thus, when many individuals are in the same neighborhood they contribute to one another's share count, thereby derating one another's fitness values. As a result this mechanism limits the uncontrolled growth of particular species within a population.

To see this mechanism in action, we examine its performance on the one-dimensional objective function shown in Fig. 5.21a. Using the triangular sharing function of Fig. 5.24, an even distribution of points is found at each peak after 100 generations, as shown in Fig. 5.25a. This is the expected result as the peaks in this test function are equally high. By contrast, a simple GA with no sharing loses points due to genetic drift, as shown in Fig. 5.25b.

In another problem, stable subpopulations of appropriate size (proportional to peak fitness) form at successively smaller peaks, as shown in Fig. 5.26a. By contrast, with no sharing (Fig. 5.26b), a simple genetic algorithm quickly allocates all trials to the highest peak.

The scheme as proposed is not entirely problem-independent. Richardson and I suggested multidimensional extensions of the sharing function to permit its use in multidimensional optimization problems (Goldberg and Richardson, 1987). We have also suggested a more interesting (and perhaps more general) approach to sharing based upon comparisons at the genotypic (string) level instead of the phenotypic (parameter set) level. In genotypic sharing, the argument of the sharing function is defined to be the relative bit difference (the number of different bits—the Hamming distance between the strings—divided by the string length). A family of power law sharing functions appropriate to genotypic sharing is shown in Fig. 5.27. Some preliminary experiments with genotypic sharing support its use; however, further study is required to test the breadth of applicability of all sharing techniques.

Restriction of Mating in Genetic Search

We have seen how sharing encourages niche formation in artificial genetic search. The continued creation of useful offspring requires restricted mating if lethals are to be held to a minimum. Several schemes have been developed for this purpose.

Hollstien (1971) introduced schemes adopted from the traditional breeding practices of animal husbandry and horticulture. Hollstien noticed that a *line-breeding* technique (where the champion individual is repeatedly bred with others) performed well on a unimodal function but performed poorly on a multimodal function. To overcome this problem, he introduced a scheme he called *inbreeding with intermittent crossbreeding*. Here he required close individuals to mate with one another as long as the family average fitness continued

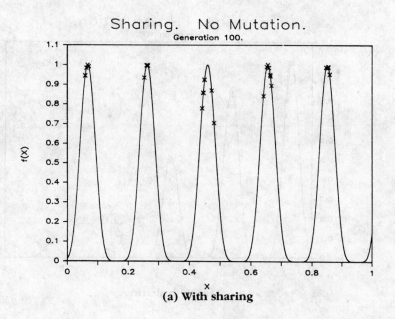

(a) With sharing

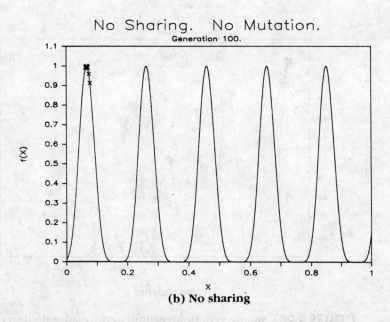

(b) No sharing

FIGURE 5.25 Simple genetic algorithm performance on equal peaks with (a) and without (b) sharing. Population distribution at generation 100. From Goldberg and Richardson (1987).

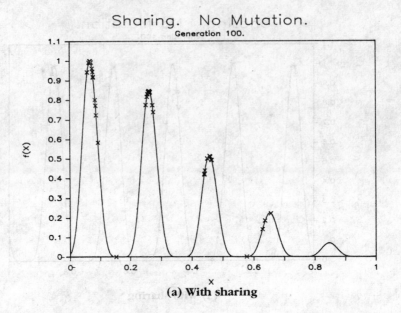

(a) With sharing

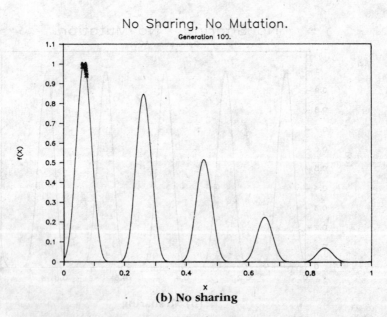

(b) No sharing

FIGURE 5.26 Simple genetic algorithm performance on decreasing peaks with (a) and without (b) sharing. Population distribution at generation 100. From Goldberg and Richardson (1987).

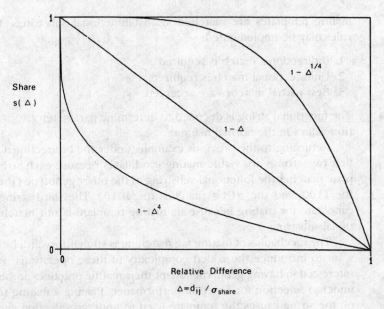

FIGURE 5.27   Power law sharing functions where share is a function of relative string difference (Goldberg and Richardson, 1987).

to rise. When this did not occur, crossbreeding between different families was tried. This mating scheme showed marked improvement over his linebreeding technique.

Booker (1982, 1985) also mentioned the need for restrictive mating to reduce the formation of lethals. In both of these studies he also discussed the need for sharing to encourage niche and species formation, but since the sharing technique he suggested was restricted to a machine learning application (a classifier system), we will postpone consideration of that part of his work until a later chapter. Instead, let us consider his call for *mating templates* to adaptively restrict mating between dissimilar species.

Booker called for an explicit match between a mating template and the functional portion (the decoded part) of a string. To illustrate this, let's create some augmented strings containing both templates and functional substrings:

```
<Template>:<Functional>
    #10#:1010
    #01#:1100
    #00#:0000
```

In these strings the mating template (the substring to the left of the colon) is constructed over a three-letter alphabet {0, 1, #}. In this alphabet, a 0 (in the template) matches a 0 (in the functional substring), a 1 matches a 1, and a # matches either a 0 or a 1. To determine whether strings are permitted to mate, mating templates are matched against functional substrings. Different mating rules may be implemented:

1. Bidirectional match is required.
2. Unidirectional match is required.
3. Best partial matches are accepted.

The functional string is decoded to determine parameter values and fitness function values in the normal manner.

Returning to the previous example, under the bidirectional mating rule, the first two strings are viable mating candidates because each string's mating template matches the functional substring of the other genotype (the #10# matches the 1100, and the #01# matches the 1010). The third string is not a viable candidate for mating because its mating template is not matched by any functional substring.

The mechanics of mating tag matching is straightforward, but why should we want to introduce the added complexity of these operations? Primarily, we are interested in having genotypes adapt their mating practices at the same time they undergo selection for function performance. Placing a mating template directly on the string causes the template itself to undergo selection and genetic operations (crossover, mutation, and others). Thus population members evolve a preference for mates that help them produce better offspring. This kind of second-order effect seems counterintuitive at first; however, we have already discussed similar second-order adaptation when we reviewed the possibility of having the genome control genetic algorithm parameters such as crossover and mutation probabilities (Bowen, 1986). In the present case, since mating tags do not directly affect fitness themselves (they do not alter the problem parameters), we are really discussing a rate effect: preference for good mates increases the probability of subsequent improvement (decreases the probability of subsequent destructive loss), and we expect an increase in the rate of improvement over a genetic search without adaptive, restrictive mating.

A number of additions and modifications have already been suggested to improve the basic mating template scheme. One objection to the Booker scheme is the need to carry a mating template of the same length as the functional substring. Since mating restriction is at best a second-order operator, it is doubtful that an investment of more than twice the storage (not to mention the added computational expense of full-string matching) would be a worthwhile investment of computer resources. To answer this objection, Holland (personal communication, 1985) has suggested a three-part string with a short mating template, a short mating tag, and a full-length, functional substring. In this scheme the short mating templates are matched to the short mating tags and the functional strings are left out of the mating ritual. A sample pair of three-part chromosomes is shown below:

```
temp  tag   functional
#10#:1010:10010011101010
#0##:1100:11111000010010
```

Note that the first string's template matches the second string's tag and vice versa.

There are many variations on these mating restriction schemes. Whether a double- or single-sided match is required is open to debate, and Booker (1982, 1985) has gone so far as to suggest various partial match scores when no complete matches occur. While these schemes and their permutations seem plausible, little simulation or theory has been presented to support these ideas. As a result, mating tags and templates remain a fertile avenue for future research.

MULTIOBJECTIVE OPTIMIZATION

All of the optimization and search problems presented thus far reduce to a single criterion. This criterion (represented by the objective function) has been transformed to fitness function form, and we have thereafter proceeded with our reproductive plans and genetic operators. This approach works well in many problems, but there are times when several criteria are present simultaneously and it is not possible (or wise) to combine these into a single number. When this is the case, the problem is said to be a *multiobjective* or *multicriteria* optimization problem. These problems have long attracted the attention of researchers using traditional techniques of optimization and search. More recently (Schaffer, 1984), genetic algorithms have been applied to the search for multicriteria optima.

In single-criterion optimization, the notion of optimality scarcely needs any explanation. We simply seek the best (highest or lowest) value of the assumedly well-defined objective (utility or cost) function. In multiobjective (or vector-valued) optimization the notion of optimality is not at all obvious. If we refuse beforehand to interrelate the relative values of the different criteria—if we refuse to compare apples to oranges—then we must come up with a different definition of optimality, one that respects the integrity of each of our separate criteria. The concept of *Pareto optimality* helps us do this in a rational way. This notion is best illustrated with a simple example.

Suppose a widget manufacturer wishes to minimize both on-the-job accidents and widget cost. Both of these criteria are important to the successful operation of the widget plant, and furthermore, it is hard to estimate the dollar cost of an accident. Thus the case is a good candidate for multicriteria optimization. Suppose further that we have five possible ways of running the plant (scenarios A, B, C, D, and E), which result in the following widget cost and accident count values:

$A = (2, 10)$ (widget cost, accident count)
$B = (4, 6)$
$C = (8, 4)$
$D = (9, 5)$
$E = (7, 8)$

These data are plotted in Fig. 5.28, a graph of accident count versus widget cost. The figure makes little sense at first glance: it is just a scatter plot of five points.

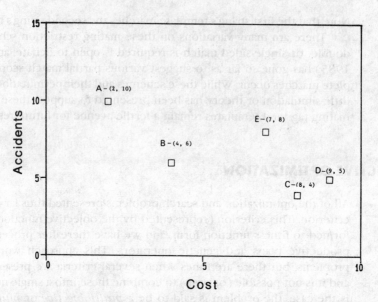

FIGURE 5.28   Illustration of multiobjective optimization. Five scenarios compared on the basis of accidents and widget cost. The scenarios A, B, and C are said to be nondominated.

Scanning the graph further reveals that the best points are lower on the page and to the left. In particular, scenarios A, B, and C seem like good possible choices: even though none of the three points is best along both dimensions, we can see that there are trade-offs from one of these three scenarios to another; there is gain along one dimension and loss along others. In optimization terminology we say these three points are *nondominated* because there are no points better than these on all criteria. On the other hand scenarios D and E seem to be poor choices. This is the case because both scenarios are *dominated* by another point. Scenario E (7,8) is dominated by B (4,6), because $4 < 7$ and $6 < 8$. And scenario D (9,5) is dominated by C (8,4), because $8 < 9$ and $5 < 9$. Thus, in this problem (and in other multicriteria problems) instead of obtaining a single answer, we obtain a set of answers that are not dominated by any others, the Pareto optimal (P-optimal) set. In the particular case the P-optimal set is {A, B, C}. As a practical matter, the concept of Pareto optimality does not help us to select a single alternative from the P-optimal set. The decision maker must ultimately make a value judgment among the alternatives to arrive at a particular decision.

To make the conditions of Pareto optimality mathematically more rigorous, we state that a vector $\mathbf{x}$ is partially less than $\mathbf{y}$, symbolically $\mathbf{x} <_p \mathbf{y}$, when the following conditions hold:

$$(\mathbf{x} <_p \mathbf{y}) \Leftrightarrow (\forall_i)(x_i \leq y_i) \wedge (\exists i)(x_i < y_i).$$

Under these circumstances we say that point $\mathbf{x}$ *dominates* point $\mathbf{y}$. If a point is not dominated by any other, we say that it is *nondominated* or *noninferior.* We use these basic definitions to investigate genetic algorithm search applied to multicriteria problems.

The notion of genetic search in a multicriteria problem dates back to the early days of GA experimentation. Rosenberg's (1967) study contained a suggestion that would have led to multicriteria optimization if he had carried it out as presented. He suggested using multiple *properties* (nearness to some specified chemical composition) in his simulation of the genetics and chemistry of a population of single-celled organisms. His actual implementation contained only a single property, and as a result it can only be considered a hint of things to come.

A practical scheme was developed 17 years later by Schaffer (1984) in his Vector Evaluated Genetic Algorithm (VEGA) program. Schaffer extended Grefenstette's GENESIS program (1984a,b) to include multicriteria functions. He created equally sized subpopulations for selection along each of the criteria components in the evaluation vector. In this scheme selection was performed independently for each criterion; however, mating and crossover were performed across subpopulation boundaries. Although this scheme was simple to implement, Schaffer was aware that the independent selection of champions in each criterion held the potential for bias against middling individuals (points like point B that are good but not excellent along any criterion). He developed several heuristics, including a wealth redistribution scheme and a crossbreeding plan, to try to overcome this difficulty, but he ended up settling for the bare independent selection scheme in the remainder of his study.

Schaffer tried VEGA on seven functions. De Jong's function $F1$ was used to validate the code. Two simple functions were drawn from the multiobjective optimization literature (Vincent and Grantham, 1981), and four functions were system identification problems drawn from the control engineering literature with control objects ranging from second- to seventh-order systems. To see VEGA's typical performance, let's look at Schaffer's second function, the function $F2$.

This function is a two-valued function of a single parameter. We use the notation F_{21} for the first value, F_{22} for the second value, and t for the single, independent parameter:

$$F_{21}(t) = t^2.$$
$$F_{22}(t) = (t - 2)^2.$$

These may be mapped to a Pareto plane as shown in Fig. 5.29, where the Pareto front of nondominated points is highlighted. All other points are dominated by these and VEGA should be able to sort out the good points. Figure 5.30 shows the results of a VEGA run at generation 0 and at generation 3. VEGA has identified the front; however, there has been some tendency to ignore the middling points.

This problem of bias against middling points is a serious one. During a given generation there should be no bias against any locally nondominated individuals. If we accept the rationale of Pareto optimality, these individuals all should have

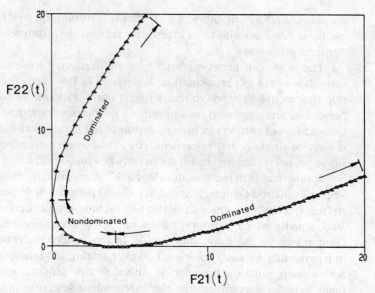

FIGURE 5.29 **Sketch of Schaffer's second problem (*F*2) in the solution plane. Pareto or nondominated front is marked.**

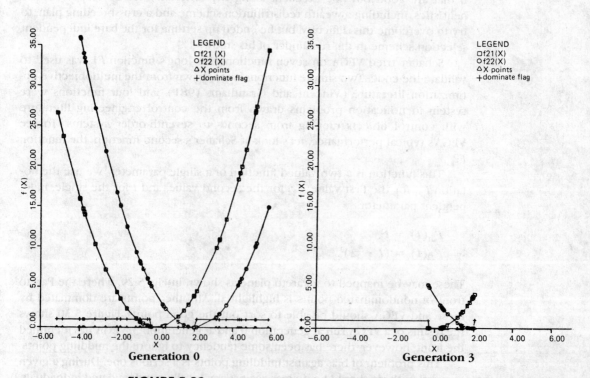

FIGURE 5.30 **Vector Evaluated Genetic Algorithm (VEGA) computation results on Schaffer's second problem (*F*2). Comparison of generation 0 versus generation 3 (Schaffer, 1984). Reprinted by permission.**

the same reproductive potential. One way to achieve equal reproductive potential for all points at the same level is through a nondominated sorting procedure. This procedure is similar to single-criterion ranking selection procedures (Baker, 1985); however, the population is ranked on the basis of nondomination. All nondominated individuals in the current population are identified and flagged. These are placed at the top of the list and assigned a rank of 1. These points are then removed from contention and the next set of nondominated individuals is identified and assigned rank 2. This process continues until the entire population is ranked. Thereafter, reproduction count values or selection probabilities may be assigned according to rank. To maintain appropriate diversity, this procedure should be used in conjunction with the techniques of niche formation and speciation. Niche and speciation methods may be especially useful for stabilizing the multiple subpopulations that arise along the Pareto-optimal front, thereby preventing excessive competition among distant population members.

KNOWLEDGE-BASED TECHNIQUES

For the better part of five chapters this text has hammered away at the idea that genetic algorithms work because of the combined effect of reproduction and crossover. Recall the fuzzy reasoning of Chapter 1, where the exchange of fit building blocks under reproduction and crossover was likened to human processes of innovative thought. A parallel was drawn between the exchange of building blocks (highly fit, short-defining-length schemata or similarity templates) to form new strings and the exchange of *notions* to form *ideas*. At the time, the argument was appealing because, no doubt, we humans do combine high-performance notions to speculate on new ideas. In another sense, however, the view of random crossover as *the* means of human innovation seems much too simplistic. When trying to think new thoughts, humans are certainly more deliberate about selecting the notions they cross to form their new ideas. People bring to bear a healthy dose of knowledge, deciding which notions might plausibly go together and evaluating (without direct experiment or sampling) whether the resulting combination makes any sense in the current context. In other words the operators of human innovative thought are (at least at times) directed by knowledge. By contrast, in their purest form, genetic algorithms are blind search procedures: they exploit only the coding and the objective function value to determine plausible trials in the next generation. This is both a blessing and a curse. On the one hand, their indifference toward problem-specific information in large part gives genetic algorithms their broad competence (a procedure that works well without knowledge peculiar to a specific problem has a better chance of transferring to another domain). On the other hand, not using all the knowledge available in a particular problem puts genetic algorithms at a competitive disadvantage with methods that do make use of that information.

This section discusses several ways to combine problem-specific information with genetic algorithms. We examine hybrid techniques, knowledge-directed operators, and approximate function evaluation methods.

Hybrid Schemes

When problem-specific information exists, it may be advantageous to consider a GA hybrid. Genetic algorithms may be crossed with various problem-specific search techniques to form a hybrid that exploits the global perspective of the GA and the convergence of the problem-specific technique. A number of authors have suggested such hybridization (Bethke, 1981; Bosworth, Foo, and Zeigler, 1972; Goldberg, 1983); however, there has not been much published work describing the results of GA-hybrid study. Nonetheless, the idea is simple, has merit, and may be used to improve ultimate genetic search performance.

Local optimization of a continuous function of one or more variables is a well-developed art form, and numerous gradient and gradient-less techniques are available for finding local optima in these problems (Avriel, 1976). To develop a GA hybrid for a calculus-friendly function, we simply cross our favorite local search technique with a genetic algorithm. In a sense, the genetic algorithm finds the hills and the hill-climber goes and climbs them.

Even without a calculus-friendly function, we can still use hybrid techniques. Greedy algorithms (Lawler, 1976; Syslo, Deo, and Kowalik, 1983) in combinatorial optimization are a form of local search, and many popular problems have well-developed heuristic search schemes. The problem-specific nature of local search techniques requires that we develop a different hybrid technique for each different problem or class of problems. We cannot get away from the question of efficiency versus breadth. If we want to use problem-specific knowledge, we must be willing to sacrifice some generality; however, the use of GA-hybrid techniques allows us to do this in a fairly modular fashion.

There are a number of ways to hybridize GAs and still maintain a fairly modular program structure. A batch approach is illustrated in Fig. 5.31. In this way we simply allow the genetic algorithm to run to substantial convergence and then we permit the local optimization procedure to take over, perhaps searching from the top 5% or 10% of points in the last generation. If this approach is adopted, the niche and speciation techniques of the previous section may be useful in maintaining diversity within the genetic algorithm population, thereby allowing stable subpopulations to form at different peaks in the function domain.

A parallel approach to hybrid implementation is depicted in Fig. 5.32. Here we envision the availability of numerous parallel processors of sufficient processing capability so function evaluations may be carried out simultaneously for different strings within a generation. In this way the parallel processors can be used to evaluate string fitness values. They can also be used to perform occasional iterations of the local search scheme to attempt to improve the current string. (More will be said about parallel hardware and genetic algorithms in a later section.)

A more canonical method of local search that can be hybridized with genetic algorithms is *G-bit improvement* (gradientlike-bitwise improvement). In Goldberg (1983) I pointed out the similarity between changing single bits and gradient information. This similarity can be used in G-bit improvement to obtain a

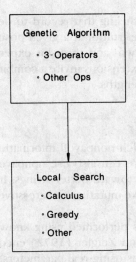

FIGURE 5.31   **Schematic of genetic algorithm hybrid using a batch scheme. GA sorts out peaks and local search climbs hills.**

more general local search procedure that can be used regardless of coding or problem structure. G-bit improvement includes the following steps:

1. Select one or more of the best strings from the current population.
2. Sweep bit by bit, performing successive one-bit changes to the subject string or strings, retaining the better of the last two alternatives.
3. At the end of the sweep, insert the best structure (or *k*-best structures) into the population and continue the normal genetic search.

It can be shown that G-bit improvement converges to the best solution of a deterministic, bitwise-linear function. The method is enhanced by keeping an ex-

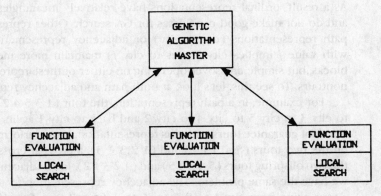

FIGURE 5.32   **Genetic algorithm hybrid using a parallel implementation.**

plicit record of successful bits and by using that record to determine whether further experimentation is likely to be fruitful at a given position. The method can also be extended to include all two- and three-bit experiments; however, caution should be exercised as these extensions invite a combinatorial explosion in problems with even modest string lengths.

Knowledge-Augmented Operators

Hybrid techniques are one way in which nonpayoff information can be used to speed up genetic algorithm search. We can also use nonpayoff information to guide genetic operators more directly toward better strings. In a sense, we can augment random choice in operators like mutation and crossover by using knowledge specific to a particular problem.

The earliest work in this area was performed using knowledge-augmented mutation operators. Bosworth, Foo, and Zeigler (1972) encoded multidimensional parameter optimization problems using real parameters. They performed crossover (at parameter boundaries) and developed several mutation operators incorporating nonpayoff information. They used Fletcher-Reeves (a conjugate gradient method) and golden search together as a mutation operator. This approach is not unlike the hybrid schemes suggested in the previous section.

The use of knowledge-augmented operators has not been restricted to mutation. Knowledge-augmented crossover has been tried in the traveling salesman problem (TSP). Grefenstette, Gopal, Rosmaita, and Van Gucht (1985) developed a greedy, heuristic crossover operator for the TSP. Let's look at the representation they selected and the operator they devised.

Before proceeding they examined a number of different representations for the TSP, including an ordinal representation, a path representation, and an adjacency representation. In the ordinal representation, an ordered stack of remaining city names is maintained, and the tour representation is simply the current ordinal number (in that stack) of the city to be visited next. The good news concerning an ordinal representation is that it preserves tours under crossover. The bad news is that small changes in the coding can induce massive reordering of a tour. As a result, ordinal representations have relatively meaningless building blocks and do not make good candidates for GA search. Other representations such as path representations (city-to-city) or adjacency representations (ith location with value j implies city i goes to city j) maintain more meaningful building blocks, but simple crossover operating on either of these representations creates nontours. To see this, let's look at both path and adjacency representations.

For example, in a path representation, the tour (1 3 5 4 2) goes from city 1 to city 3 to city 5 to city 4 to city 2 and back to city 1 again. Crossover clearly does not guarantee tours with this representation. If we perform simple crossover on the two tours (5 4 3 1 2) and (1 2 3 4 5), a cross at crossover site 3 yields the two offspring tours (5 4 3 4 5) and (1 2 3 1 2). In an adjacency representation, we have the same problem. The adjacency representation (5 4 1 3 2) describes a tour going from city 1 to 5, from 5 to 2, from 2 to 4, from 4 to 3, and from 3 back to 1. A cross of the two adjacency tours (5 4 1 3 2) and (2 3 4 5 1) at site 3 yields the two nontours (5 4 1 5 1) and (2 3 4 3 2).

Recognizing this problem, Grefenstette et al. used an adjacency representation and a heuristic crossover (a greedy crossover) that constructs an offspring by choosing the better of two parental edges (Grefenstette et al., 1985, p. 164):

> This operator constructs an offspring from two parent tours as follows: Pick a random city as a starting point for the child's tour. Compare the two edges leaving the starting city in the parents and choose the shorter edge. Continue to extend the partial tour by choosing the shorter of the two edges in the parents which extend the tour. If the shorter parental edge would introduce a cycle into the partial tour then extend the tour by a random edge. Continue until a complete tour is generated.

Using this operator with reproduction, good results were obtained on problems of up to 200 cities with near optimal answers and computational effort on the order of results obtained by simulated annealing procedures (Bonomi and Lutton, 1984; Kirkpatrick, Gelatt, and Vecchi, 1983). Figures 5.33 and 5.34 compare a representative tour of the initial population to the best tour of a later generation in a 200-city problem. This work is not directly comparable to the purer approaches discussed earlier in this chapter under reordering operators. The greedy

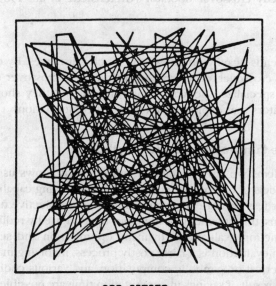

200 CITIES
DISTANCE = 1475.68
INITIAL POPULATION

FIGURE 5.33   Representative initial tour in 200-city traveling salesman problem (Grefenstette et al., 1985). Reprinted by permission.

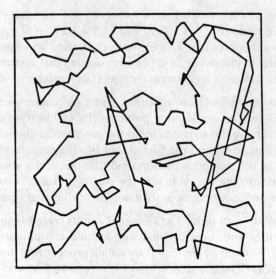

200 CITIES
DISTANCE = 203.46
GENERATION 493   24596 TRIALS

FIGURE 5.34 200-city traveling salesman problem, best tour of last generation 493 using greedy crossover operator (Grefenstette et al., 1985). Reprinted by permission.

crossover depends heavily on knowledge of city distances. By contrast, the partially matched crossover, order crossover, and cycle crossover operators do not depend upon specialized nonpayoff information, and they should not be compared to operators that exploit problem-specific information.

Approximate Function Evaluation Methods

In many problems we have specific knowledge that allows us to construct approximate models of our problem. In turn, this modeling capability allows us to create more or less accurate approximations to our objective function. With genetic algorithms, this knowledge can be put to good use by reducing the number of full-cost function evaluations. In many optimization and search problems a single function evaluation is a fairly costly process, involving many layers of subroutines, numerical or symbolic computation, and various coding and decoding functions. As a result, if savings in computation time are possible through approximate, perhaps erroneous, function evaluation, they may be worth pursuing so more evaluations can be perrormed in the same time. This observation is relevant to genetic algorithms, as we expect GAs to behave robustly under error and noise because of their population sampling approach.

We have already examined one approximate function evaluation technique in the image registration work performed by Grefenstette and Fitzpatrick (1985).

Recall that the function evaluation in that problem was an accumulated pixel-by-pixel difference taken between two images, one of an artery before dye injection and one after dye injection. The GA searched for parameters of an affine transformation that minimized the pixel-by-pixel image difference. In the pilot study the full function evaluation was fairly expensive as the image consisted of $100 \times 100 = 10,000$ pixels. After a number of experiments, Grefenstette and Fitzpatrick found that a function evaluation based on a random sample of only 10 (of 10,000) pixels yielded the best solution in a fixed number of pixel samples (200,000). This idea can be applied directly to other sampled function evaluations. We can also use the general idea of approximate function evaluation in problems with a traditional mathematical structure.

In many optimization problems we have some fairly detailed knowledge of the mathematical form of both a system model and the objective function. This information is useful for creating approximate, relatively inexpensive models of the system. Suppose we have the following idealized objective function:

$$\max f(\boldsymbol{s}, \boldsymbol{d})$$

where $\boldsymbol{s}$ is an n-vector of state variables and $\boldsymbol{d}$ is an m-vector of decision variables. Suppose further that we have a mathematical model of the system given by the following vector equation:

$$g(\boldsymbol{s}, \boldsymbol{d}) = 0, \qquad \boldsymbol{g} \text{ an } n\text{-vector.}$$

In solving these equations by traditional means, usually the model equations must undergo processing where the state variable is guessed, the nonlinear model is linearized, and new state variables are calculated. After a solution has been obtained in this manner, it is a simple matter to obtain a linearized sensitivity analysis about the current solution:

$$\Delta \boldsymbol{s} = - \left[\frac{\partial \boldsymbol{g}}{\partial \boldsymbol{s}} \right]^{-1} \left[\frac{\partial \boldsymbol{g}}{\partial \boldsymbol{d}} \right] \Delta \boldsymbol{d}.$$

Thus it becomes possible to update the state variables in a linear sense for subsequent changes in the decision variables. This provides the opportunity to perform a linearized update of the function evaluation as given by the following equation:

$$\Delta f = \frac{\partial f}{\partial \boldsymbol{s}} \Delta \boldsymbol{s} + \frac{\partial f}{\partial \boldsymbol{d}} \Delta \boldsymbol{d}.$$

We may also use the exact objective function in conjunction with the approximate state variables. However we decide to approximate an offspring's fitness, we must recognize that an offspring has two parents and we should systematically use both parents' model information in the child's approximate evaluation. There is more than one way of doing this:

a) Use the closest parent.
b) Use the weighted average of parents.
c) Use the most recently evaluated parent.

Thereafter the parents may pass on Jacobian matrixes to their offspring to propagate an approximate model as well as an approximate fitness value. If desired, approximate techniques of Jacobian updating may be used to try to extend the useful life of the linear model. Other possibilities exist for using population data to obtain a better approximate model than that obtained from the parents alone. These techniques have not been adopted in practice; however, they should provide a way of making genetic search more cost-competitive when linearized model information is available as a result of the normal modeling process.

GENETIC ALGORITHMS AND PARALLEL PROCESSORS

In a world where serial algorithms are usually made parallel through countless tricks and contortions, it is no small irony that genetic algorithms (highly parallel algorithms) are made serial through equally unnatural tricks and turns. Thus it is surprising that until recently very little work has been performed in mapping genetic algorithms to existing and proposed parallel hardware. In this section, we examine the implementation of genetic algorithms on parallel architectures.

Holland's earliest speculative work (1962c) recognized the parallel nature of the reproductive paradigm and the inherent efficiency of parallel processing. He even went so far as to discuss the mapping of reproductive plans to a type of cellular computer called an *iterative circuit computer* (1959, 1960).

Other early genetic algorithm researchers paid little attention to the combined possibilities of genetic algorithms and parallel computer architectures. Bethke (1976) calculated several complexity estimates for a particular mapping of genetic algorithms to a parallel machine. He concluded that population average fitness calculation was the primary serial bottleneck in genetic algorithm implementations of that time. He did not, however, simulate or implement a parallel genetic algorithm.

Grefenstette (1981) examined several parallel implementations of genetic algorithms. Specifically he outlined four prototypes:

a) Synchronous master-slave
b) Semisynchronous master-slave
c) Distributed, asynchronous concurrent
d) Network

The *master-slave* prototype already has been depicted in Fig. 5.32. In it we take a single master process that coordinates k slave processes. The master process controls selection, mating, and the performance of genetic operators. The slaves simply perform function evaluations. The scheme is straightforward and relatively easy to implement; however, it suffers from two major drawbacks. First, a fair amount of time is wasted if there is much variance in the time of function evaluation. Second, the algorithm is not very reliable, since it depends on the health of the master process. If the master goes down, the system halts.

The first drawback is answered by Grefenstette's second prototype, the *semisynchronous master-slave*. This prototype relaxes the requirement for synchrous operation by inserting and selecting members on the fly as slaves complete their work. This prototype operates much like De Jong's overlapping population model with low generation gap *G* value (see Chapter 4). Like the first prototype, the semisynchronous master-slave prototype is unreliable because of its dependence on a single process.

In the *asynchronous, concurrent* genetic algorithm (depicted in Fig. 5.35), *k* identical processors perform both genetic operations and function evaluations independently of one another, accessing a common shared memory. The shared memory requires that the processes avoid simultaneous hits on identical memory locations; otherwise, there are no further timing requirements for this configuration. This scheme is slightly less straightforward to implement than either of the master-slave prototypes, but the reliability of the system is much improved. As long as one of the concurrent processes and some of the shared memory continue to function, some useful processing is performed.

The *network* prototype is depicted in Fig. 5.36. In this scheme, *k* independent simple genetic algorithms run with independent memories, independent genetic operations, and independent function evaluations. The *k* processes work normally, with the exception that the best individuals discovered in a generation are broadcast to the other subpopulations over a communications network. With the relatively intermittent need for communication, link bandwidth is reduced as compared to the other schemes. Reliability of this scheme is high because of the autonomy of the independent processes.

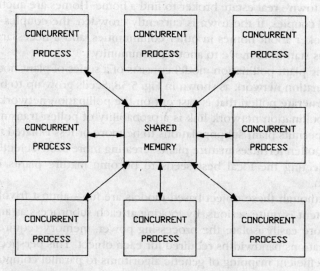

FIGURE 5.35 **Schematic of an asynchronous concurrent genetic algorithm.**

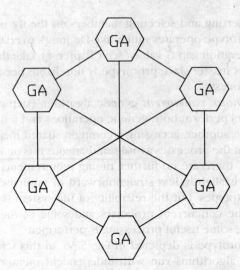

FIGURE 5.36   Schematic of a network genetic algorithm.

More recently, I have suggested an object-based design procedure for parallel genetic algorithms. Here we consider two design models: a *community* model and a *plant pollination* model. The community model is depicted in Fig. 5.37. Here the genetic algorithm is mapped to a set of interconnected communities. The communities consist of a set of homes connected to the centralized, interconnected towns. Parents give birth to offspring in their homes and perform function evaluations there. The children are sent on to a centralized singles bar (in town) where they meet up with prospective mates. After mating, the couples go to the town's real estate broker to find a home. Homes are auctioned off to competing couples. If the town is currently crowded, the couples may also consult the broker about homes in other communities, and if necessary they may go to the bus station to move to another community.

The plant pollination model consists of a series of plant nodes connected by a pollination network as shown in Fig. 5.38. Seeds grow up to become full plants that generate pollen that is cast out on the pollination network. Associated with each pollination network link is a probability of pollen transmission. This capability permits plant subpopulations to be more or less isolated from one another. Plant pollen fertilizes mature plants, creating more seed. Selection occurs locally by selecting the local best seeds to become mature plants in a probabilistic fashion.

Although these object-based models are fun—almost frivolous—to imagine, the intent is quite serious. By looking at each subprocess as an object or entity, we more easily isolate the processing power, memory requirements, and communications bandwidths required for each object. This perspective should allow more efficient mapping of genetic algorithms to parallel computers.

A number of parallel-simulation activity or implementations have recently been reported (Pettey et al., 1987; Tanese, 1987; and Cohoon, Hegde, Martin, and Richards, 1987). As well, genetic algorithms continue to flourish on serial machines, as parallel hardware and techniques become more widespread and more readily...

In this chapter we have examined... the advanced operators and GA implementations available to improve... such topics... operators that examine the... advanced operators... micro-operators... and macro-synchronic-level... which are oriented... to the... community-based and... continue up... etc.

Dominance and diploidy have been... there is a method of implementing a form... correlation mechanism...... and sometimes they show that dominance and diploidy are useful in nonstationary functions, especially cyclical functions.

The importance of... operators... something... rendering... and their their... They help in guarantees that... the... features... structure more information is carried along with the other... chromosomes... such as inversion and multi- operations... we partially resolve... the... order crossover and cycle crossover have been examined... Although... the... problem of... ordering... has been coupled to be a... for... number of... combinations... including... some... a new... taxonomy of... operators (ordering operators)... including... adaptive... relative... guide... and... changing... schema...

Higher-level people... priority... operators... something... you... can... contain in a... been discussed. These cognitive extensions of the... develop... in... many... multiple... chromosomes. Duplication and deletion also cause us to... logical segmentation of appropriate representation; they force us to consider whole... chromosome... representation... upon... the role and... process of... natural differentiation... between... or... the based... different...

different... and... also... in... a... diverse... concepts... for... an... such... a...

Interspecies determination... might... help... development... speciation level... been... examined... through... schemata... we continued...... population... and... the...... developed... we... continued... it... through...... population... and... the... the...... algorithm... that allows... a... number... of... sub... networks... On... finally... the... of... the... category... of... the... techniques... and... sharing... functions... have... continued... we... look... upon... through... both... real and... adapted... environment... have... continued... we... look... upon... discussed... The... most... topics... in... the... adaptive... of... the... we... hope... been... discussed...... development.... There... opportunity... for... exploration... has... been... touch... by... continuing... methods... of... selection... that... some... species... of... the... we... continued... you... form... a... such... a... that uses... the... criteria... indices... on... the... species... of... the... colony... individuals... A... method... that... sorts... the... population... in... the... GA... forces... to... the... population... should... also... use... sustainable... although... this... method... has... not yet... been used... as... such...

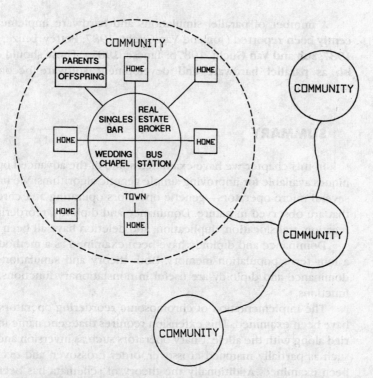

FIGURE 5.37   Object-based design, a community model of a GA.

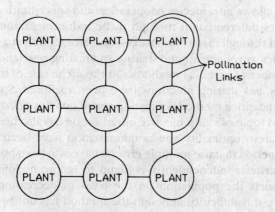

FIGURE 5.38   Object-based design, a plant pollination GA.

A number of parallel simulations and hardware implementations have recently been reported (Jog and Van Gucht, 1987; Pettey, Leuze, and Grefenstette, 1987; Suh and Van Gucht, 1987b; Tanese, 1987). These should continue to flourish as parallel hardware and development software become more readily available.

SUMMARY

In this chapter we have examined some of the advanced operators and techniques available for improving simple genetic algorithms. We have first examined several micro-operators—genetic operators operating at a chromosomal level—that are observed in nature. Dominance and diploidy, reordering operators, segregation, translocation, duplication, and deletion have all been addressed.

Dominance and diploidy have been examined as a method of implementing a long-term population memory. Both theory and simulation have shown that dominance and diploidy are useful in nonstationary functions, especially cyclic functions.

The implementation of chromosome reordering operators and their theory have been examined. This extension requires that gene name information be carried along with the allele. Unary operators such as inversion and binary operators such as partially matched crossover, order crossover, and cycle crossover have been examined. Additionally the theory of schemata has been extended to include these ordering schemata. This theoretical effort has led to a new taxonomy of o-schemata (ordering schemata), including absolute, relative, sliding, and exchanging o-schemata.

Other low-level genetic operators such as segregation and translocation have been discussed. These require the extension of the genotype to include multiple chromosomes. Duplication and deletion also cause us to loosen our notions of appropriate representation; they force us to consider variable-length representations. The role and process of sexual differentiation has been discussed. Sexual differentiation allows intraspecies cooperation and specialization.

Interspecies differentiation through niche inducement and speciation have been examined through macro-operators—operators acting at a population level. The key theories, revolving around sharing and mating restriction, have led us to consider a number of practical methods. On the niche side of the ledger, crowding techniques and sharing functions have been explored. Speciation through both rigid and adaptive methods of mating restriction have also been examined.

The related topic of multiobjective optimization has also been discussed. The concepts of Pareto optimality and nondomination have been briefly outlined. Methods of selection that use multiple criteria have also been put forth. A method that uses the criteria independently is found to ignore middling individuals. A method that sorts the population on the basis of decreasing nondomination should alleviate this difficulty, although the method has not been used in simulations to date.

The use of knowledge-based techniques has been discussed along three lines: hybrid schemes, knowledge-augmented operators, and approximate function evaluation techniques. These methods are useful for exploiting the nonpayoff information that accompanies many search and optimization problems.

The implementation of genetic algorithms on parallel architectures has also been discussed. It is ironic, considering the parallel nature of natural genetic systems, that GAs have not received greater attention in the parallel processing literature. Theoretical and implementation efforts are just now starting to receive increased attention.

In many respects, we have only begun to scratch the surface of applied genetic search. In practice, these advanced techniques and operators should lead to further improvements in the efficiency and breadth of genetic algorithms.

■ PROBLEMS

5.1. A haploid chromosome with a single gene has two alleles, 1 and 0. The expected fitness of the 1 allele is $f_1 = 1.5$. The expected fitness of the 0 allele is $f_0 = 1.2$. If there is no mutation loss associated with this process and the population starts with an equal number of 1 alleles and 0 alleles, calculate the following quantities:

    a) the expected proportion of 1 alleles in generation 1.

    b) the expected number of generations until the population has converged to at least 99 percent 1's.

5.2. Repeat Problem 5.1 for a diploid population where allele 1 is assumed to dominate allele 0 and the given fitness values are associated with the expressed allele.

5.3. The expected loss rate for a particular allele is 50 percent. Calculate the mutation rates required to maintain 1 percent of this allele in a haploid population and a diploid population. Calculate the expected sampling frequency of the recessive at this level.

5.4. A path representation of a tour is (2 1 4 3 7 6 5 9 8 0). Perform inversion on this string between inversion sites 3 and 5. Calculate a bound on the probability of survival of the schema [5 ! 8] under inversion when treated as an absolute o-schema, a relative o-schema, a relative o-schema with sliding, and a relative, sliding, and exchanging o-schema.

5.5. Calculate the total number of o-schemata (absolute) for strings of length $l = 10, 20, 50$, and 100.

5.6. Expand the o-schema $r^{12}(2 ! 1 8)$ to a set of absolute, o-schemata assuming a circular structure.

5.7. Expand the type rs, o-schema $rs_6^{12}(2 1 3 4)$ to a set of type r o-schemata.

5.8. If intrachromosomal duplication causes six copies of a particular allele in a given genotype, calculate the probability of no mutations, 1 mutation, 2 mutations, 3 mutations, 4 mutations, 5 mutations, 6 mutations if the probability of mutation is 0.05 per allele. Perform this computation exactly and with a Poisson approximation.

5.9. A translocation operator works by slicing a chromosome uniformly at random and moving the sliced section to another chromosome within the genotype. Calculate a bound on the probability of separation of two alleles located five positions apart on a string of length 25. The probability of translocation is 0.3.

5.10. Invent a sex gene coding that produces three sexes, male, female, and neuter, in the proportions 2:1:5. Give natural examples of species with other than binary sexual differentiation.

5.11. In a binary decision problem with expected payoff $f_1 = 10$ for decision one and $f_0 = 5$ for decision zero, calculate the expected number of one decisions in the next generation under the usual reproductive plan with and without sharing. Assume the population currently contains 70 ones and 30 zeros. Assume perfect sharing.

5.12. Some mating template schemes allow partial matching when no complete matches are available. Invent a partial match score procedure that ranks a perfect match higher than any partial match.

5.13. The Schaffer (1984) method of multiobjective selection is biased toward single-criterion champions. In a minimization problem, is this difficulty more troublesome in a problem with a concave or a convex Pareto optimal front? Write a short paragraph with sketches explaining your answer.

5.14. Consider the maximization problem given by the objective function $f(x, y) = x^2 + y^2$ and the model $y = x^3 + 3x + 6$. Construct a linear-linear approximation for this objective-model pair at the point (x_0, y_0). Consider two ways of combining approximate model data to generate an approximate model for the offspring without performing additional function evaluations.

■ COMPUTER ASSIGNMENTS

A. Implement a simple genetic algorithm with diploidy, dominance, and the triallelic dominance map.

B. Program and test the cycle crossover operator for a permutation string representation.

C. Program and test an inversion operator that treats a permutation as a circular string.

D. Devise a *messy coding* for the traveling salesman program that permits redundant city names in a path representation. Devise and test a subroutine to decode the messy coding.

E. Program and test the order crossover operator for a permutation coding.

F. Code a simple genetic algorithm with two niche schemes: De Jong crowding and Goldberg-Richardson sharing. Compare and contrast these two methods on the multimodal function of your choice.

G. Implement the mating template, mating tag scheme of Booker and Holland. Implement bidirectional and unidirectional matches as switch selectable options.

H. Use a multiobjective genetic algorithm to optimize Schaffer's second function (Figs. 5.29 and 5.30). Use two methods of selection: Schaffer's independent criteria method and Goldberg's nondominated sort procedure. Compare and contrast the results.

I. Implement the method of G-bit improvement. Compare and contrast both on-line and off-line performance with and without G-bit improvement using De Jong's functions $F1$ and $F5$.

J. Use a simple GA to optimize the problem posed in Problem 5.14. Implement a method of approximate function evaluation and solve the problem again. Compare the results obtained using exact and approximate function evaluation.

6 | Introduction to Genetics-Based Machine Learning

We started our genetic jaunt five chapters ago with the ultimate goal of understanding the robustness—the breadth and efficiency—of genetic algorithms in autonomous learning and decision making. In one sense our study of genetic algorithms in search and optimization has been a digression from this goal, because we know full well that optimization is too rigid a methodology to be trusted with autonomy even in fairly simple environments. In another sense our inquiry into the behavior of genetic algorithms in search and optimization domains has been germane to our more ambitious goal for two reasons. First, playing in the sandbox of search has allowed us to carefully control our environments and our operators, thereby permitting more careful dissection of GAs and their workings. Second, examining a variety of applications in search has given us the opportunity to observe the genetic algorithm's innovative flair for searching rapidly through arbitrary string spaces. In some ways GAs seem more humanlike a search mechanism than others we commonly encounter; they are speculative, seeking better alternatives through the juxtaposition of hunches; they are inductive, breathing fresh air into a world filled with ploddingly deductive procedures.

What then is the problem? Why can't we unleash this innovation in more complex, less completely defined environments? The problem lies not with the genetic algorithm but with the structures we choose to adapt. This chapter demonstrates how to overcome this difficulty by changing the adapted structure. Machine learning systems that use genetic search as their primary discovery heuristic are described. We briefly survey the origins of these genetics-based machine learning (GBML) systems, and we review the most common GBML architecture, the so-called *classifier system*. We examine the operation of classifier systems in some detail and we implement a simple classifier system in the Pascal programming language. We then test the operation of the simple classifier system in a straightforward problem domain: learning of a boolean function.

GENETICS-BASED MACHINE LEARNING: WHENCE IT CAME

The theoretical foundation for GBML systems was laid by Holland (1962c). His outline for adaptive systems theory paid special attention to the role of program replication as a method of emphasizing past programs. Although subsequent applications of genetic algorithms in the 1960s largely emphasized search and optimization, the theoretical underpinning was not so restricted.

With this theoretical foundation and the recognition of the fundamental role of recombination (Holland, 1965), more concrete suggestions emerged for the creation of a sequence of increasingly complex *schemata processors* (Holland, 1971). The conference where this paper was presented predated (1968) the first application of a classifier system (Holland and Reitman, 1978) by a full decade, and thus it comes as no surprise that modern classifier systems resemble schemata processors in both outline and detail. In this initial proposal, Holland suggested four prototype systems. Prototype I was to be a stimulus-response (SR) processor that would link *environmental schemata* (what we shall soon call *conditions*) with particular action effectors. Prototype II was designed to extend type I by adding *internal effectors* (internal states), and prototype III was to build upon types I and II by including explicit environmental state prediction (a model of the real world) and an internal evaluation mechanism. Prototype IV was to extend the other prototypes by incorporating the capability to modify its own effectors and detectors, thereby permitting greater (or perhaps lesser) range of data detection and a larger behavioral repertoire. It is not surprising that the development of this proposal coincided with the development of the theory of schemata (Holland, 1968, 1971); however, no experiments or attempts at implementation have ever been reported on any of the prototypes.

These early suggestions led to the broad but as yet unimplemented *broadcast language* (Holland, 1975). The broadcast language called for the creation of *broadcast units* (production rules) over a 10-letter alphabet. This alphabet added a number of wild card (both single and multiple match) characters to an underlying binary alphabet. Additionally, a fundamental punctuation mark, a persistence symbol (causing continued broadcast of a message), and a quotation character (causing the next symbol to be taken literally) would have provided sufficient power for computational completeness and representational convenience. The proposal for the broadcast language was instrumental in unifying the earlier suggestions for schemata processors by theoretically permitting a consistent representation of all operators, data, and rules or instructions; however, this generality gained in theory has not been realized in practice.

The first practical implementation of a genetics-based machine learning system was reported three years following the broadcast language proposal (Holland and Reitman, 1978). This system, called Cognitive System Level One (CS-1), was trained to learn two maze-running tasks. It used a performance system with message list and simple string rules called *classifiers,* a genetic algorithm comprised of reproduction, crossover, mutation, and crowding, and an epochal learning mechanism where reward was apportioned to all classifiers active between successive payoff events. This last learning mechanism has largely been supplanted by another mechanism, called a *bucket brigade,* in later systems.

Since the first classifier system, a number of researchers have extended and applied these ideas in different ways. Table 6.1 presents a list of genetics-based

TABLE 6.1 **Genetics-Based Machine Learning Applications**

Year	Investigators	Description
BIOLOGY AND MEDICINE		
1984	Rada, Rhine, and Smailwood	Attempted GBML system for medical diagnosis
1987	Bickel and Bickel	Development of GBML system for medical diagnosis
1987b	Wilson	Proposal for morphogenesis simulations using a classifier system
BUSINESS		
1986	Frey	Architectural classification using CS
1986	Thompson and Thompson	GA used to search for rule sets to predict company profitability
1987	Greene and Smith	GBML system learns rules describing consumer preferences
COMPUTER SCIENCE		
1980	Smith	Draw poker bet decisions learned by pure genetic learner (LS-1)
1981	Forsyth	Beagle system developed for symbolic system evolution
1985	Cramer	GA learns multiplication task using assembler-like instruction set
1985b,c	Forrest	Interpreter constructed to convert KL-ONE networks to classifier form
1986a	Riolo	General purpose C package available for classifier system study
1986b	Riolo	Letter sequence prediction task via CS
1986	Zhou	GA builds finite automata from examples
1987a,b	Robertson	Lisp version of Riolo's problem implemented on Connection Machine
in press	Stackhouse and Zeigler	GA searches for rule sets in symbolic rule-based system
ENGINEERING & OPERATIONS RESEARCH		
1983	Goldberg	Inertial object and gas pipeline control tasks learned by CS
1984	Schaffer	LS-2 (LS-1 offspring, see Smith) learns parity and signal problems

TABLE 6.1 (*Continued*)

Year	Investigators	Description
	ENGINEERING & OPERATIONS RESEARCH	
1985	Kuchinksi	GA searches for battle management system rules
1986	Wilson	Multiplexer task (boolean function) learned by CS
1987	Antonisse and Keller	Development of GBML system for military applications
1987	Hilliard et al.	Classifier system learns scheduling rules
	HYBRID TECHNIQUES	
1987	Oosthuizen	A hybrid ML system integrates connectionism, graph induction, and GAs
	MACHINE LEARNING	
1971	Holland	Outline for four prototype schemata processors similar to CS
1980a	Holland	Outline suggested for bucket brigade (BB) algorithm
1985	Zhou	Outline for addition of long-term memory to CS
1986	Holland, Holyoak, Nesbitt, and Thagard	Publication of INDUCTION
1987c	Grefenstette	Use of credit assignment and heuristic inversion in Pitt-approach system
1987a,b	Riolo	Analysis and simulation of bucket brigade performance
1987	Westerdale	Analysis of altruism in bucket brigade credit assignment
1987c,d	Wilson	Proposal for explicity hierarchical credit assignment
	PARALLEL IMPLEMENTATIONS	
1987a,b	Robertson	Implementation of classifier system on a Connection Machine
	SOCIAL SCIENCES	
1978	Holland and Reitman	First classifier system (CS-1) learns two maze-running tasks
1982	Booker	Animal-like automaton with CS brain learns to roam 2-D environment
1983	Wilson	Video eye learns to focus when driven by classifier system
1985b	Axelrod	GA searches for rule sets of behavior in iterated prisoner's dilemma
1985b,c	Wilson	ANIMAT automaton with CS brain learns to roam 2-D forests
1986a,b	Schrodt	Prediction of international events using CS
1986	Haslev (Skanland)	Past tense, Norwegian verb forms learned by CS
1987	Fujiko and Dickinson	GA learns LISP code to solve iterated prisoner's dilemma problem

machine learning applications. From artificial life applications to the conjugation of Norwegian past tense verbs, GBML has received growing consideration across a variety of fields. In the next chapter, we will review in more detail the research results from CS-1 and other GBML applications of both historical and current interest. In the remainder of this chapter, we examine the theory of operation, implementation, and application of a simple classifier system.

WHAT IS A CLASSIFIER SYSTEM?

A classifier system is a machine learning system that learns syntactically simple string rules (called *classifiers*) to guide its performance in an arbitrary environment. A classifier system consists of three main components:

1. Rule and message system
2. Apportionment of credit system
3. Genetic algorithm

The rule and message system of a classifier system is a special kind of *production system*. A production system (Davis and King, 1976) is a computational scheme that uses rules as its only algorithmic device. Although there is a wide variation in syntax among production systems, the rules are generally of the following form:

if <condition> then <action>.

The meaning of a production rule is that the action may be taken (the rule is "fired") when the condition is satisfied.

At first glance, the restriction to such a simple device for the representation of knowledge might seem too constraining. Yet it has been shown that production systems are computationally complete (Minsky, 1967; Post, 1943). Their power in representing knowledge involves more than this. They are also computationally convenient. A single rule or small set of rules can represent a complex set of thoughts compactly. The explosion of rule-based expert system applications over the past decade is strong empirical testimony to this claim.

Despite this growth in expert systems applications, traditional rule-based systems have been less frequently suggested in situations in need of learning. One of the main obstacles to learning has been complex rule syntax. Many production systems permit involved grammatical constructions for the condition and action parts of a rule. Classifier systems depart from the mainstream by restricting a rule to a fixed-length representation. This restriction has two benefits. First, all strings under the permissible alphabet are syntactically meaningful. Second, a fixed string representation permits string operators of the genetic kind. This leaves the door propped open, ready for a genetic algorithm search of the space of permissible rules.

Classifier systems use parallel rule activation, whereas traditional expert systems use serial rule activation. During each matching cycle, a traditional expert system activates a single rule. This rule-by-rule procedure is a bottleneck to increased productivity, and much of the difference between competing expert system architectures concerns the selection of "better" single-rule activation strategies for this or that type of problem. Classifier systems overcome this bottleneck by permitting parallel activation of rules during a given matching cycle. By doing this, classifier systems permit multiple activities to be coordinated simultaneously. When choices must be made between mutually exclusive environmental actions or when the size of the matched rule set must be pruned to accommodate the fixed length message list, these choices are postponed to the last possible moment, and the arbitration is then performed competitively. We will have more to say about the form of this rule competition later; at this point, we acknowledge the parallelism encouraged by the architecture of classifier systems and recognize that this parallelism may permit extremely fast hardware implementations of classifier systems at the same time it promotes rational decision making without arbitrary arbitration strategies.

In traditional expert systems, the value or rating of a rule relative to other rules is fixed by the programmer in conjunction with the expert or group of experts being emulated. In a rule learning system, we don't have this luxury. The relative value of different rules is one of the key pieces of information that must be learned. To facilitate this type of learning, classifier systems force classifiers to coexist in an information-based service economy. A competition is held among classifiers where the right to answer relevant messages goes to the highest bidders, with the subsequent payment of bids serving as a source of income to previously successful message senders. In this way a chain of middlemen is formed from manufacturer (the detectors) to consumer (environmental action and payoff). The competitive nature of the economy ensures that good rules (profitable) survive and bad rules (unprofitable) die off.

We shall soon examine the many details of this apportionment of credit algorithm, but for now one point is crucial: the introduction of an internal currency. The exchange and accumulation of an internal currency provides a natural figure of merit for the application of genetic algorithms. Using a classifier's bank balance as a fitness function, classifiers may be reproduced, crossed, and mutated as discussed in the first five chapters of this book. Thus, not only can the system learn by ranking extant rules, it can also discover new, possibly better rules as innovative combinations of its old rules. We must be a little less cavalier about generating entirely new populations and we pay more attention to who gets replaced; however, the GA is very similar to those used in optimization and search studies.

Together, apportionment of credit via competition and rule discovery using genetic algorithms form a reasonable basis for constructing a machine learning system atop the computationally convenient and complete framework of classifiers. To understand the workings of a classifier system more clearly, we examine each of its component parts in more detail.

RULE AND MESSAGE SYSTEM

A schematic depicting the rule and message system, the apportionment of credit system, and the genetic algorithm is shown in Fig. 6.1. The rule and message system forms the computational backbone of the silicon beast. Information flows from the environment through the *detectors*—the classifier system's eyes and ears—where it is decoded to one or more finite length *messages.* These environmental messages are posted to a finite-length *message list* where the messages may then activate string rules called *classifiers.* When activated, a classifier posts a message to the message list. These messages may then invoke other classifiers or they may cause an action to be taken through the system's action triggers called *effectors.* In this way classifiers combine environmental cues and internal thoughts to determine what the system should do and think next. In a sense it coordinates the flow of information from where it is sensed (detectors) to where it is processed (message list and classifier store) to where it is called to action (effectors). To better understand the operation of the rule and message system, look at its two informational units—*messages* and *classifiers*—and how they are processed.

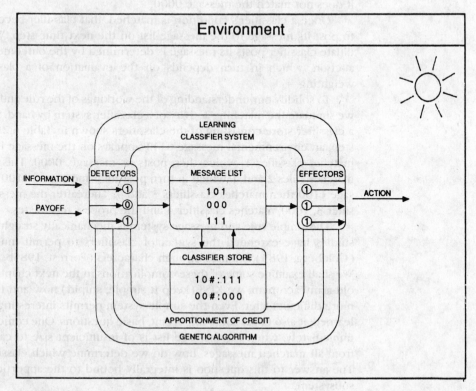

FIGURE 6.1 A learning classifier system interacts with its environment.

A message within a classifier system is simply a finite-length string over some finite alphabet. If we limit ourselves to a binary alphabet we obtain the following definition:

$$<\text{message}> ::= \{0, 1\}^l$$

Here the symbol "::=" means "is defined as" and raising the set $\{0, 1\}$ to the lth power says that we take the product (concatenation) of l, 0's or 1's. Messages are the basic token of information exchange in a classifier system. The messages on the message list may match one or more classifiers or string rules. A classifier is a production rule with excruciatingly simple syntax:

$$<\text{classifier}> ::= <\text{condition}>:<\text{message}>$$

The condition is a simple pattern recognition device where a wild card character (#) is added to the underlying alphabet:

$$<\text{condition}> ::= \{0, 1, \#\}^l.$$

Thus, a condition is matched by a message if at every position a 0 in the condition matches a 0 in the message, a 1 matches a 1, or a # matches either a 0 or a 1. For example, the four-position condition #01# matches the message 0010, but it does not match the message 0000.

Once a classifier's condition is matched, that classifier becomes a candidate to post its message to the message list on the next time step. Whether the candidate classifier posts its message is determined by the outcome of an activation auction, which in turn depends on the evaluation of a classifier's value or weighting.

To solidify our understanding of the workings of the rule and message system, we simulate the matching activity of a classifier system by hand. Suppose we have a classifier store consisting of the classifiers shown in Table 6.2. At the first time step, an environmental message 0111 appears on the message list. This message matches classifier 1, which then posts its message, 0000. This message in turn matches rules 2 and 4, which in turn post their messages (1100 and 0001). Message 1100 then matches classifiers 3 and 4. Thereafter the message sent by classifier 3, 1000, matches classifier 4 and the process terminates.

The simple rule and message system is mechanically straightforward. Several studies have extended the syntax of classifiers to permit multiple conditions (Goldberg, 1983) and pass-through characters (Forrest, 1985b, c; Riolo, 1986a). We shall examine some of these complications in the next chapter. Following the old army acronym, we KISS (keep it simple, stupid) now and tell (about things more difficult) later. Even the simple system permits interesting behaviors to be learned; it also raises some important, basic questions. One comes to mind almost immediately: when the message list is of insufficient size to carry all classifiers from all matched messages, how do we determine which classifiers to activate? The answer to this question is integrally bound to the apportionment of credit subsystem.

TABLE 6.2 Four Classifiers

Index	Classifier
1)	0 1 # #:0000
2)	0 0 # 0:1100
3)	1 1 # #:1000
4)	# # 0 0:0001

APPORTIONMENT OF CREDIT ALGORITHM: THE BUCKET BRIGADE

Many classifier systems attempt to rank or rate individual classifiers according to a classifier's role in achieving reward from the environment. Although there are a number of ways of doing this, the most prevalent method incorporates what Holland has called a *bucket brigade* algorithm. The bucket brigade may most easily be viewed (with some reckless mixing of metaphors) as an information economy where the right to trade information is bought and sold by classifiers. Classifiers form a chain of middlemen from information manufacturer (the environment) to information consumer (the effectors).

This service economy contains two main components: an *auction* and a *clearinghouse.* When classifiers are matched they do not directly post their messages. Instead, having its condition matched qualifies a classifier to participate in an activation auction. To participate in the auction, each classifier maintains a record of its net worth, called its *strength S.* Each matched classifier makes a *bid B* proportional to its strength. In this way rules that are highly fit (have accumulated a large net worth) are given preference over other rules. Other bidding structures have been suggested and we shall look at some of these; however, here our overriding quest for simplicity governs our choice.

The auction permits appropriate classifiers to be selected to post their messages. Yet this is not the end of our bucket brigade story. Once a classifier is selected for activation, it must clear its payment through the clearinghouse, paying its bid to other classifiers for matching messages rendered. A matched and activated classifier sends its bid *B* to those classifiers responsible for sending the messages that matched the bidding classifier's condition. The bid payment is divided in some manner among the matching classifiers. This division of payoff among contributing classifiers helps ensure the formation of an appropriately sized subpopulation of rules (Booker, 1982). Thus different types of rules can cover different types of behavioral requirements without undue interspecies competition. This reasoning follows the argument of Chapter 5 concerning the role of sharing in forming different species in different niches. In a rule-learning system of any consequence, we cannot search for one master rule. We must instead search for a coadapted set of rules that together cover a range of behavior that provides ample payoff to the learning system.

To illustrate the workings of the bucket brigade, we consider the four classifiers of Table 6.2 once again, except this time we follow their payments as well. Assuming initial strength values of 200 for all four classifiers, we post the initial environmental message 0111 as before, as shown in Table 6.3. We assume a bid coefficient of 0.1 and take the bid as the product of the bid coefficient C_{bid} and strength. In the initial time step ($t = 0$), classifier 1 is matched, bids 20 units, and sends its message during the next time step. Classifier 1 pays its bid to the party responsible for its activation; in this case, the environment's strength is increased by 20 units as the environmental message was responsible for activating classifier 1. In subsequent time steps, activated classifiers make their payment to previously active classifiers. Finally, at time step 5, a reward comes into the system and is paid to the last active classifier, classifier 4.

To implement a well-defined procedure we must be a bit more rigorous in detailing the auction and payment scheme. As already indicated, classifiers make bids (B_i) during the auction. Winning classifiers turn over their bids to the clearinghouse as payments (P_i). A classifier may also have receipts R_i from its previous message-sending activity or from environmental reward. In addition to bids and receipts, a classifier may be subject to one or more taxes T_i. Taken together, we may write an equation governing the depletion or accretion of the ith classifier's strength as follows:

$$S_i(t + 1) = S_i(t) - P_i(t) - T_i(t) + R_i(t).$$

To understand a classifier's accumulation of wealth in detail, we must also quantify its bids, payments, and taxes. A classifier bids in proportion to its strength:

$$B_i = C_{\text{bid}}S_i.$$

where C_{bid} is the bid coefficient, S is strength, and i is classifier index.

We could simply stop here and choose auction winners deterministically by selecting the k best classifiers (where k is the size of the message list); however, this would unreasonably bias results toward the status quo (De Groot, 1970). Instead we hold our auction in the presence of random noise. We calculate an effective bid (EB) for each matched classifier as the sum of its deterministic bid and a noise term:

$$EB_i = B_i + N(\sigma_{\text{bid}}),$$

where the noise N is a function of the specified bidding noise standard deviation σ_{bid}.

After the somewhat noisy auction and the selection of message-sending classifiers, payment must be made to those classifiers responsible for sending the messages that activated the winners. The winners pay their bids (the B_i values, not the EB_i values) to the clearinghouse, where payment is divided among all classifiers responsible for sending a matching (and winning) message

TABLE 6.3 A Simple Classifier System by Hand—Matching and Payments

Index	Classifier	t = 0 Strength	Messages	Match	Bid	t = 1 Strength	Messages	Match	Bid	t = 2 Strength	Messages	Match	Bid
1)	0 1 # #:0000	200		E	20	180	0000			220			
2)	0 0 # 0:1100	200				200		1	20	180	1100		
3)	1 1 # #:1000	200				200				200		2	20
4)	# # 0 0:0001	200				200		1	20	180	0001	2	18
	Environment	0	0111			20				20			

Index	Classifier	t = 3 Strength	Messages	Match	Bid	t = 4 Strength	Messages	Match	Bid	Final t = 5 Strength	Payoff
1)	0 1 # #:0000	220				220				220	
2)	0 0 # 0:1100	218				208				208	
3)	1 1 # #:1000	180	1000			196				196	
4)	# # 0 0:0001	162	0001	3	16	156	0001			206	50
	Environment	20				20				20	

Note: 1. $C_{\text{BID}} = 0.1$
2. $C_{\text{TAX}} = 0.0$

Each classifier is taxed to prevent freeloading, thereby biasing the population toward productive rules. Many schemes are available; we simply collect a tax proportional to the classifier's strength:

$$T_i = C_{\text{tax}} \cdot S_i.$$

Together these relationships define the apportionment of credit algorithm used in a number of classifier systems. To briefly examine the stability and effect of this mechanism, we recast the apportionment of credit equation into a more useful form where all payments and taxes have been replaced by their strength equivalents. Assuming we have an active classifier, we obtain the following difference equation:

$$S(t + 1) = S(t) - C_{\text{bid}}S(t) - C_{\text{tax}}S(t) + R(t).$$

We have dropped the classifier index i and all terms are as defined previously. Grouping terms we obtain the following relationship:

$$S(t + 1) = (1 - K)S(t) + R(t),$$

where $K = C_{bid} + C_{tax}$.

To see when this equation is stable, we may perform the usual Z-transform (Takahashi, Rabins, and Auslander, 1970) on the homogeneous equation. More intuitively, we recognize that the system can only be stable for bounded input (bounded R) when the sequence of S values does not grow in magnitude of its own accord. Forgetting about the input signal $R(t)$ for a moment, we obtain the homogeneous equation as follows:

$$S(t + 1) = (1 - K)S(t).$$

Solving for the free fall strength at $t = n$, we obtain the relationship $S(n) = (1 - K)^n S(0)$. This is stable (it doesn't blow up) for arbitrary $S(0)$ when $0 \leq K \leq 2$; however, in practice we insist that $K \leq 1$ to enforce nonnegativity of the strength. This analysis is only valid for classifiers that remain active; however, the system remains stable even with the switching nonlinearity introduced by activating and deactivating real classifiers as long as the changing K meets the stability criterion.

Stability is essential, but to see the effect of the mechanism, we are primarily concerned with how the bucket brigade performs as time goes on. More directly, what is the bucket brigade doing with the rewards it receives from the environment? Assuming some initial strength, $S(0)$, we calculate the strength on the nth time step by the following expression:

$$S(n) = (1 - K)^n S(0) + \sum_{j=0}^{n-1} R(j)(1 - K)^{n-j-1}.$$

Once again we have ignored the switching nonlinearity, although this could have been incorporated as a time-varying $K(j)$.

To investigate the effect of this mechanism further, we examine the steady-state response. If the process continues indefinitely with a constant receipt $R(t) = R_{ss}$, we obtain the steady-state strength by setting $S(t + 1) = S(t) = S_{ss}$. This computation results in the following equation:

$$S_{ss} = R_{ss}/K.$$

Here the strength is simply the receipt amplified by the gain coefficient $1/K$. The steady bid may be derived as follows:

$$B_{ss} = \frac{C_{bid}}{K}R_{ss} = \frac{C_{bid}}{C_{bid} + C_{tax}}R_{ss}.$$

Since C_{tax} is usually small with respect to the bid coefficient, the steady bid value usually approaches the steady receipt value, $B_{ss} \cong R_{ss}$. In other words, for steady receipts, the bid value approaches the receipt. For time-varying receipt values, we see that the bid is a geometrically weighted average of the input. As such, it acts as a filter of the possibly intermittent and noisy receipt values.

GENETIC ALGORITHM

The bucket brigade provides a clean procedure for evaluating rules and deciding among competing alternatives. Yet we still must devise a way of injecting new, possibly better rules into the system. This is precisely where the genetic algorithm steps in. Using a GA similar to the simple genetic algorithm (SGA) of Chapter 3, new rules are created by the now familiar tripartite process (reproduction, crossover, and mutation). These rules are then placed in the population and processed by the auction, payment, and reinforcement mechanism to properly evaluate their role in the system. We must be a little less cavalier about wanton replacement of the entire population, and we must pay more attention to who replaces whom. Nonetheless, GAs used in classifier systems strongly resemble those used in search and optimization. In this section we concentrate on some of the major differences found in GAs in classifier system use.

The simple GA of Chapter 3 contained a nonoverlapping population model where we completely selected and replaced a new population at each generation. This is not generally desirable in machine learning applications. In machine learning we are often concerned with maintaining a high level of on-line performance as we learn to perform more proficiently, whereas in search and optimization, we are usually more concerned with convergence or off-line performance. In our discussion of De Jong's (1975) experiments we encountered a GA parameter called the generation gap G, which was used to implement and test overlapping population genetic algorithms. In our work here, we define a quantity called the selection proportion, *proportion,* where we replace that proportion of the population at a given genetic algorithm invocation. We also define a quantity called the GA period, T_{ga}, that specifies the number of time steps (rule and message cycles) between GA calls. This period may be treated deterministically (the GA is called every T_{ga} cycles) or stochastically (the GA is called probabilistically with average period T_{ga}). Additionally, the invocation of genetic algorithm learning may be conditioned on particular events such as lack of a match or poor performance.

The selection process is often performed using roulette wheel selection where each classifier's strength value S is used as its fitness. Because we no longer generate entire populations, we sometimes are careful when choosing population members for replacement. De Jong's (1975) crowding procedure as described in Chapter 4 may be used to encourage replacement of similar population members.

Mutation must be modified because classifier systems use a ternary alphabet. We simply define the probability of mutation p_m as before; however, when a mutation is called for, we change the mutated character to one of the other two with equal probability ($0 \rightarrow \{1, \#\}$, $1 \rightarrow \{0, \#\}$, $\# \rightarrow \{0, 1\}$).

With these changes to the normal routine, genetic algorithms may be dropped into the classifier system and used in a manner not too different from our previous search and optimization applications.

A SIMPLE CLASSIFIER SYSTEM IN PASCAL

Classifier systems are remarkably straightforward. However, as is the case with new genetic algorithm users, novice classifier system devotees are sometimes perplexed how to start skinning this breed of cat. In this section, we put some flesh on the classifier system bones as we develop a simple classifier system (SCS) in the Pascal programming language. Specifically, we construct a system designed to learn a boolean function, a multiplexer. We are careful to strip the system to its bare essentials. We collapse the finite-length message list to a single message (the environmental message) and because we get immediate feedback, we simplify the payoff mechanism considerably. These simplifications allow us to create a functional system with a minimum of machinery.

Simple Classifier System Data Structure

As already indicated, the rule and message system—sometimes called the performance system—is the computational backbone of a classifier system. We examine the data structures and procedures used to implement a simple performance system within the simple classifier system. We concentrate on important code segments and skip some of the lesser details; however, the complete SCS code is presented in Appendix D with sample data files. Figure 6.2 shows the data declarations required to implement a population of classifiers and its environmental message in the simple classifier system. The classifier type *classtype* is defined as a record containing a condition *c*, an action *a*, and a number of scalar variables. The *condition* type is defined as an array of type *trit*—a ternary digit, an integer between -1 and 1—where a -1 is interpreted as the wildcard character and both 0 and 1 are interpreted as is. In the SCS the *action* type is taken as type *bit*. In the multiplexer problem, the classifier system is learning a boolean function and must output a 1 or a 0. The classifier type also contains a number of variables of type real: *strength, bid,* and *ebid*. The variables *strength* and *bid* are self-explanatory, and *ebid* is the classifier's effective bid (what we called EB earlier). Recall that the effective bid is usually the classifier's bid with the addition of some zero-mean noise. The classifier type contains one additional scalar variable, the boolean variable *matchflag*. The value of *matchflag* is set to true when the classifier's condition is matched by the current environmental message.

We define a data type *classarray* as an array of classifiers (an array of *classtype*) and we place this array of classifiers in a population record type, *poptype*. We create an array of classifiers (type *classarray*) called *classifier*. We include integer variables *nclassifier* and *nposition,* the number of classifiers and number of positions in the condition respectively. We also include a number of real type

```
{ declare.scs: declarations for scs }

const maxposition  = 50;
      maxclass     = 100;
      wildcard     = -1;

type  bit          = 0..1; { a binary digit }
      trit         = -1..1; { a ternary digit; 0=0; 1=1; -1=#}
      action       = bit;  { a binaray decision }
      condition    = array[1..maxposition] of trit;
      message      = array[1..maxposition] of bit;
      classtype    = record
                        c:condition;
                        a:action;
                        strength, bid, ebid:real;
                        matchflag:boolean;
                        specificity:integer;
                     end;
      classarray   = array[1..maxclass] of classtype;
      classlist    = record
                        clist:array[1..maxclass] of integer;
                        nactive:integer
                     end;
      poptype      = record
                        classifier:classarray;
                        nclassifier, nposition:integer;
                        pgeneral, cbid, bidsigma, bidtax, lifetax,
                        bid1, bid2, ebid1, ebid2,
                        sumstrength, maxstrength, avgstrength, minstrength:real
                     end;

var   population:poptype;      { population of classifiers }
      matchlist:classlist;     { who matched }
      envmessage:message;      { environmental message }
      rep:text;                { report device/file }
```

FIGURE 6.2 The primary data declarations in the simple classifier system (SCS) describe the population of classifiers.

population parameters in the population type *poptype;* however, we will describe these as we use them.

With the population type defined, we create a single instance called (cleverly enough) *population.* We also create a single environmental message called *envmessage.* The message type *message* is taken as an array of type *bit* where the type bit is simply taken as the subrange of integers between 0 and 1. In more advanced classifier systems we might create an array of such messages (the message list). Here we simply create a single instance called *envmessage* to represent our environmental message.

In addition to the population of classifiers and the single environmental message, we also create an auxiliary data structure to record which classifiers are currently matched by the environmental message. This structure is of type *classlist* (a record containing an array of integers, the *clist,* and the number of active elements, the integer variable *nactive*) and is called the *matchlist*. When the performance system is executed, *matchlist* is constructed to contain a list of classifier index values and the number of classifiers that match the current message. This same information is available (with some digging) in the classifier *matchflag* values; however, it is useful to keep a separate record for efficient implementation of the auction.

Last but not least, we declare the reporting file (or device) used for all initial and ongoing output reports other than interactive screen output. We call this file (or device) *rep* and declare it as type *text*. The SCS uses a total of seven files:

rep	Output file/device for non-screen reports
cfile	Input file/device for classifier data
efile	Input file/device for environmental and detector data
rfile	Input file/device for reinforcement data
tfile	Input file/device for timekeeping data
gfile	Input file/device for genetic algorithm data
pfile	Output file/device for plot data

Detailed file formats are presented in Appendix D. More important, we examine the data structures constructed from each of these files in more detail as we pick apart the structure of the SCS.

The Performance System: Matchmaker, Matchmaker, Make Me a Match

As the performance system is the heart of the SCS, the matching procedures are the heart of the performance system. Figure 6.3 presents the code for the two routines responsible for matching classifiers to the environmental message: *match* and *matchclassifiers*. The function *match* performs a match between a single condition and a single message and returns a boolean true value if the match succeeds. The match is performed position by position, returning true if a wildcard is present ($\# = -1$) or if a 0 matches a 0 or a 1 matches a 1. The match process is coordinated by the *while-do* construct. Developing more efficient matching procedures may be a worthwhile activity, as much of the classifier system's time is spent in the *match* code. Word-oriented assembler code can be written to do bit-level comparisons; however, these procedures are machine-specific and beyond the scope of our treatment.

The procedure *matchclassifiers* matches all classifiers against the environmental message and constructs the *matchlist* data structure. The core of this calculation is contained in the *for-do* construct where, first, the *matchflag* boolean variable (contained in each classifier's record) is set by an invocation of the *match* function. The variable containing the number of active classifiers variables, *nactive*, is then incremented and the *clist* (list of classifiers) contained in the *matchlist* structure is assigned the index value of the matched classifier. At the termination of *matchclassifiers*, matched classifiers have their match flags set and the structure *matchlist* contains the number of matched classifiers and a *clist* of

```
function match(var c:condition; var m:message; nposition:integer):boolean;
{ match a single condition to a single message }
var matchtemp:boolean;
begin
  matchtemp := true;
  while (matchtemp = true) and (nposition > 0) do begin
    matchtemp := (c[nposition] = wildcard) or (c[nposition] = m[nposition]);
    nposition := nposition - 1
  end;
  match := matchtemp
end;

procedure matchclassifiers(var population:poptype; var emess:message;
                           var matchlist:classlist);
{ match all classifiers against environmental message and create match list }
var j:integer;
begin with population do with matchlist do begin
  nactive := 0;
  for j := 1 to nclassifier do with classifier[j] do begin
    matchflag := match(c, emess, nposition);
    if matchflag then begin
      nactive := nactive + 1;
      clist[nactive] := j
    end
  end;
end end;
```

FIGURE 6.3 The function *match* and the procedure *matchclassifiers* are at the heart of the rule and message system in the simple classifier system (SCS).

their index values. With the matching thus completed, we are ready to choose winners and distribute payment among the classifiers in the apportionment or credit algorithm.

Apportionment of Credit Algorithm

Previously, we listed two main components of the apportionment of credit (AOC) algorithm of a classifier system: an auction and a clearinghouse. These components are represented in the functional code of the SCS apportionment of credit subsystem shown in Fig. 6.4. Here we see the procedure *aoc* calling three routines: *auction, clearinghouse,* and *taxcollector.* We also see the declaration of a data structure of type *crecord* (clearinghouse record) instantiated in *clearingrec.* The clearinghouse record contains two integer entries, *winner* (the new winner) and *oldwinner* (last iteration's winner). The clearinghouse record also contains a single boolean flag *bucketbrigadeflag.* This input variable is set to true by the user during classifier system initialization if implicit bucket brigade operation is desired. For the multiplexer problem, *bucketbrigadeflag* is usually set to false because reward is available at every time step and because there is no relationship between successive signals (they are chosen randomly). In other problems where a chain of reward is necessary to apportion credit to precursor activities, *bucketbrigadeflag* should be set to true, thus activating payment from new winner to old. Whether using the implicit bucket brigade or not, more complex classifier

```
{ aoc data declarations - aoc uses cfile for input }
type  crecord = record
                  winner, oldwinner:integer;
                  bucketbrigadeflag:boolean;
               end;

var   clearingrec:crecord;

procedure aoc(var population:poptype; var matchlist:classlist;
              var clearingrec:crecord);
{ apportionment of credit coordinator }
begin
  with clearingrec do winner := auction(population, matchlist, oldwinner);
  taxcollector(population);
  clearinghouse(population, clearingrec);
end;
```

FIGURE 6.4 The procedure *aoc* and its data structure *clearingrec* coordinate the apportionment of credit subsystem within the simple classifier system (SCS).

systems would, of course, require more detailed recordkeeping of all winners and their callers; such nastiness is one reason we are working on a *simple* classifier system.

We delve more deeply into the workings of the apportionment of credit subsystem in Fig. 6.5. The function *auction* holds a noisy auction to select a winning classifier from the set of matched classifiers. Within the *for-do* construct, *auction* cycles through the matched classifiers (using the *matchlist* structure), successively calculating each classifier's base bid (*bid*) and its effective bid (*ebid*). The *bid* is taken as the product of *cbid*, a linear function of a classifier's *specificity*, and a classifier's strength. The function of *specificity* adopted here is of the form

```
bid1 + bid2*specificity
```

where *bid1* and *bid2* are input parameters. Different bidding structures may be investigated by selecting different *bid1* and *bid2* values. The effective bid (*ebid*) is also taken as a product of cbid, a linear function of specificity, and strength. Normally distributed, zero-mean noise with a specified noise deviation *bidsigma* is added to this product. Separate coefficients are used for the effective bid specificity function (*ebid1* and *ebid2*), thereby providing additional flexibility for investigating alternative bidding structures. The normally distributed noise is generated using the Box-Muller method (Pike, 1980) through routines contained in the SCS utility code (file utility.scs) as shown in Appendix D. The function *auction* keeps track of the classifier index with highest effective bid and returns this value upon relinquishing control to procedure *aoc*.

Thereafter, procedure *clearinghouse* is invoked to reconcile payments. The current winner's *strength* is simply decreased by the amount of its *bid* value (not its effective bid value), and if the *bucketbrigadeflag* is true, the old winner's *strength* value is increased by the amount of this *payment*. This clearinghouse procedure is much simplified over that of more general classifier systems. In ad-

```
function auction(var population:poptype; var matchlist:classlist;
                    oldwinner:integer):integer;
( auction among currently matched classifiers - return winner )
var j, k, winner:integer; bidmaximum:real;
begin with population do with matchlist do begin
  bidmaximum :- 0.0;
  winner :- oldwinner;  ( if no match, oldwinner wins again )
  if nactive > 0 then for j :- 1 to nactive do begin k :- clist[j];
    with classifier[k] do begin
        bid   :- cbid * (bid1 + bid2 * specificity) * strength;
        ebid  :- cbid * (ebid1 + ebid2 * specificity) * strength
                    + noise(0.0, bidsigma);
        if (ebid > bidmaximum) then begin
          winner :- k;
          bidmaximum :- ebid
        end
      end end;
    auction :- winner
end end;

procedure clearinghouse(var population:poptype; var clearingrec:crecord);
( distribute payment from recent winner to oldwinner )
var payment:real;
begin with population do with clearingrec do begin
  with classifier[winner] do begin ( payment )
    payment :- bid;
    strength :- strength - payment
  end;
  if bucketbrigadeflag then ( pay oldwinner receipt if bb is on )
    with classifier[oldwinner] do strength :- strength + payment
end end;

procedure taxcollector(var population:poptype);
( collect existence and bidding taxes from population members )
var j:integer; bidtaxswitch:real;
begin with population do begin
( life tax from everyone & bidtax from actives )
  if (lifetax <> 0.0) or (bidtax <> 0.0) then for j :- 1 to nclassifier do
    with classifier[j] do begin
      if matchflag then bidtaxswitch :- 1.0 else bidtaxswitch :- 0.0;
      strength :- strength - lifetax*strength - bidtax*bidtaxswitch*strength;
    end;
end end;
```

FIGURE 6.5 The function *auction* and the procedures *clearinghouse* and *taxcollector* do the actual work of the apportionment of credit subsystem in the simple classifier system (SCS).

dition, we notice one other difference between this implementation and our more general description earlier in the chapter. In describing the more general apportionment of credit mechanism, we said that matched classifiers made their payments to the previously active classifiers that sent the messages which matched the currently active classifiers. In the simplified scheme the currently active classifier makes payment to the previously active classifier (when *bucketbrigadeflag* = true) even though there is no direct link through a message list.

In this way we assume linkage between time-adjacent classifiers, an assumption warranted by the temporal order imposed by the environment. This form of *implied* or *implicit* bucket brigade was first developed by Wilson (1985b). It can work well in simple classifier systems when there is only a single train of thought required for effective operation. In more complex systems, the more general bucket brigade with multiple classifier-message chains provides a more effective means of distributing payoff to classifiers responsible for particular rewards.

The last routine called by the *aoc* procedure is *taxcollector*. To discourage nonproductive classifiers, two different types of tax are collected from classifiers: an existence tax and a bid tax. The existence tax is assessed and collected from all classifiers at a tax rate specified in the real-valued population variable *lifetax*. The bid tax is assessed and collected from all classifiers that bid in the last auction; this tax rate is specified by the real-valued variable *bidtax*. If either of these tax rates is nonzero, the *for-do* construct within procedure *taxcollector* contains the necessary machinery to collect the appropriate amount of tax from each classifier.

Together, *auction, clearinghouse,* and *taxcollector* distribute and collect payments and taxes to help assure that good rules receive high strength and bad rules receive relatively low strength. Thereafter strength may be used as a fitness measure to facilitate a genetic search for new, possibly better rules.

Genetic Search within the Simple Classifier System

The genetic algorithm used for rule discovery in the SCS is remarkably similar to the SGA code of Chapter 3. Thus we only dwell on the important differences. Figure 6.6 displays the data structure and the GA coordinating procedure (*ga*) used in the SCS genetic algorithm. The genetic algorithm data structure *garec* is a record of type *grecord*. A *grecord* contains several variables of type *real: proportionselect, pmutation,* and *pcrossover*. The variable *proportionselect* is the proportion of the overlapping population that gets reproduced during a given genetic algorithm invocation. The variables *pmutation* and *pcrossover* are the probabilities of mutation (per trit or bit transfer) and crossover (per mating event) respectively. A *grecord* also contains several integer variables. The parameter *crowdingfactor* specifies the number of candidate individuals to be chosen for replacement using crowding. The integer variables *nmutation* and *ncrossover* are counters used to accumulate the total numbers of mutations and crosses respectively. A *grecord* also contains a structure *mating* of type *marray*. This mating array contains records of mating and replacement. Each such mating record contains the two mate indexes (*mate1* and *mate2*), the crossover site for the conjugal couple (*sitecross*), and the indexes of the two classifiers replaced (*mort1* and *mort2*) by the two new children. The mating record is only used in the GA report.

Staring at the GA coordinating procedure *ga* (Fig. 6.6), we see code that is very close to that used in the simple genetic algorithm (SGA): population statistics are calculated in the procedure *statistics;* a pair of mates (*mate1* and *mate2*)

```
{ ga.scs: genetic algorithm code for SCS }

{ data declarations }
const maxmating = 10;

type  mrecord = record
                  mate1, mate2, mort1, mort2, sitecross:integer
                end;
      marray = array[1..maxmating] of mrecord;
      grecord = record
                  proportionselect, pmutation, pcrossover:real;
                  ncrossover, nmutation, crowdingfactor, crowdingsubpop,
                   nselect:integer;
                  mating:marray; { mating records for ga report}
                end;

var  garec:grecord;
     gfile:text;

procedure ga(var garec:grecord; var population:poptype);
{ coordinate selection, mating, crossover, mutation, & replacement }
var j:integer; child1, child2:classtype;
begin with garec do with population do begin
  statistics(population);                    { get average, max, min, sumstrength }
  for j := 1 to nselect do with mating[j] do begin
    mate1 := select(population);                         { pick mates }
    mate2 := select(population);
    crossover(classifier[mate1], classifier[mate2], child1, child2,
              pcrossover, pmutation, sitecross, nposition,
              ncrossover, nmutation);                    { cross & mutate }
    mort1 := crowding(child1, population, crowdingfactor, crowdingsubpop);
    sumstrength := sumstrength - classifier[mort1].strength
                 + child1.strength;                      { update sumstrength }
    classifier[mort1] := child1; { insert child in mort1's place }
    mort2 := crowding(child2, population, crowdingfactor, crowdingsubpop);
    sumstrength := sumstrength - classifier[mort2].strength
                 + child2.strength;                      { update sumstrength }
    classifier[mort2] := child2;
  end;
end end;
```

FIGURE 6.6 The genetic algorithm within the simple classifier system (SCS) is very similar to the simple genetic algorithm (SGA) code of Chapter 3 as evidenced by the procedure *ga* and its data structure *garec*.

is picked using roulette wheel selection in the function *select*; crossover is performed in the procedure of the same name. The similarity, however, stops here. Since we are now searching, not for the best single rule, but for a well-adapted set of rules, we use crowding replacement to choose the classifiers that die to make room for new offspring. Recall from Chapter 4 that in the simplest form of crowding, *crowdingfactor* individuals are chosen for possible replacement by a given offspring. We extend the crowding procedure somewhat by requiring the replacement candidates to be chosen from a low-performance subpopulation.

Each time we choose an individual for possible replacement on the basis of similarity, we first choose *crowdingsubpop* individuals at random from the full population, retaining the individual with lowest strength. Thereafter crowding continues as described in Chapter 4. In this way modified crowding replaces low-performance individuals who are similar to the children being inserted into the population.

Crowding is implemented within the SCS in the functions *worstofn, matchcount,* and *crowding* as shown in Fig. 6.7. The function *worstofn* picks a subpopulation of size *n* (in our case, size *crowdingsubpop*) at random from the full population, returning the index value of the worst strength individual among those selected. The function *matchcount* takes two classifiers and counts the number of positions of similarity between them. Each identical condition position increments the count by one. The count is also incremented by one when classifiers have identical actions. The function *crowding* uses *worstofn* and *matchcount* to place an offspring classifier (*child*) in a population slot occupied by a closely related, low-performing classifier. The *for-do* construct is executed a total of *crowdingfactor* times. Within the loop a classifier is chosen from the *classifier* population using *worstofn* and the number of matches *match* is calculated using the function *matchcount.* If this number is larger than the currently largest match (*matchmax*), then the new match becomes the new currently largest match. The function *crowding* then returns the index value of the classifier with highest match count.

The function *crowding* is used to complete the procedure *ga* (Fig. 6.6). Two individuals are thus selected for their untimely demise (the integer variables *mort1* and *mort2*). In addition, as the offspring are placed into the population, the variable *sumstrength* is updated to reflect the new population total strength.

So What's the Problem?

Thus far we have treated our simple classifier system as though it had not a care in the world. So far it does not. We have not presented it with a problem (an environment) or a way to interact with that problem. We remedy this situation presently by creating a straightforward task: learning a boolean function, a six-line multiplexer.

The multiplexer function to be learned is depicted schematically in Fig. 6.8. This problem has been considered previously using a connectionist approach (Barto, Anandan, and Anderson, 1985) and a classifier system (Wilson, 1987a). Six signal lines come into the multiplexer. The signals on the first two lines (the address or A-lines) are decoded as an unsigned binary integer. This address value is then used to indicate which of the four remaining signals (on the data or D-lines) is to be passed through to the multiplexer output. For example, in the figure the address signal 11 decodes to 3, and the signal on data line 3 (signal = 1) is passed through to the output (output = 1).

Although the multiplexer's operation can be explained in a straightforward manner, we still need to know what task is to be accomplished by the simple classifier system. In the SCS program, the classifier system is presented with a

```pascal
function worstofn(var population:poptype; n:integer):integer;
{ select worst individual from random subpopulation of size n }
var j, worst, candidate:integer; worststrength:real;
begin with population do begin
 { initialize with random selection }
  worst := rnd(1, nclassifier);
  worststrength := classifier[worst].strength;
 { select and compare from remaining subpopulation }
  if (n > 1) then for j := 2 to n do begin
    candidate := rnd(1, nclassifier);
    if worststrength > classifier[candidate].strength then begin
      worst := candidate;
      worststrength := classifier[worst].strength;
    end;
  end;
 { return worst }
  worstofn := worst;
end end;

function matchcount(var classifier1, classifier2:classtype;
                        nposition:integer):integer;
{ count number of positions of similarity }
var tempcount, j:integer;
begin
  if (classifier1.a = classifier2.a) then tempcount := 1
    else tempcount := 0;
  for j := 1 to nposition do
    if (classifier1.c[j] = classifier2.c[j]) then tempcount := tempcount + 1;
  matchcount := tempcount;
end;

function crowding(var child:classtype; var population:poptype;
                     crowdingfactor, crowdingsubpop:integer):integer;
{ replacement using modified De Jong crowding }
var popmember, j, match, matchmax, mostsimilar:integer;
begin with population do begin
  matchmax := -1; mostsimilar := 0;
  if (crowdingfactor < 1) then crowdingfactor := 1;
  for j := 1 to crowdingfactor do begin
    popmember := worstofn(population, crowdingsubpop); { pick worst of n }
    match := matchcount(child, classifier[popmember], nposition);
    if match > matchmax then begin
      matchmax := match;
      mostsimilar := popmember;
      end;
  end;
  crowding := mostsimilar;
end end;
```

FIGURE 6.7 Crowding is used to help maintain a diverse population of rules. The function *crowding* invokes the *matchcount* and *worstofn* functions.

randomly generated sequence of example signals. The classifier system then learns to emulate the 6-multiplexer. To do this, the system repeatedly responds to different signals, receiving or not receiving reward as it gives or does not give the correct answer. In this manner the apportionment of credit algorithm rewards existing rules depending on their effectiveness. Thereafter the genetic algorithm injects new rules to improve system performance.

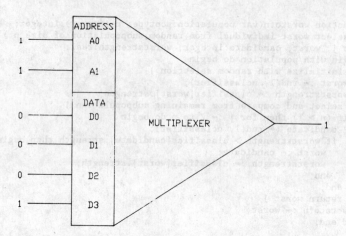

FIGURE 6.8 The simple classifier system is presented with the task of learning a six-bit multiplexer function.

The multiplexer environment is coded in Pascal as shown in Fig. 6.9. The environmental record *environrec* of type *erecord* consists of integer variables *laddress* (length of the address), *ldata* (length of the data), *lsignal* (length of the signal), *address* (decoded address), *output* (correct multiplexer output), and *classifieroutput* (classifier output). In addition, an *erecord* contains a copy of the randomly generated signal called *signal.*

The multiplexer environment requires two major activities: the generation of the random signal and the calculation of the correct output (required for later reinforcement). As we see in Fig. 6.9, procedure *environment* coordinates these two activities with calls to the procedures *generatesignal* and *multiplexerout-put.* The procedure *generatesignal* uses the random number utility function *flip* (Appendix B) to create a new signal. The procedure *multiplexeroutput* decodes the address of the correct data line using a function called *decode* (similar to the decode function of Chapter 3) and inserts the correct signal into the environmental record variable *output.* This result is used later in the reinforcement routine to decide whether reward should be paid to a particular classifier.

Get the Message, Take Some Action

We have developed the guts of our simple classifier system. We have constructed the essential code to implement our environment. Now, how do we get them to talk to one another? Referring back to the classifier system schematic in Figure 6.1, recall that a classifier system gets information from its environment through its detectors and causes change in the environment through its effectors. We now implement detectors and effectors for the SCS.

In Fig. 6.10 we see data declarations and essential code for the detector subsystem of the SCS. For this problem the detectors are straightforward. In the pro-

```
{ environment declarations }
type  erecord=record
                laddress, ldata, lsignal, address, output,
                 classifieroutput:integer;
                signal:message;
              end;

var    environrec:erecord;
       efile:text;

procedure generatesignal(var environrec:erecord);
{ generate random signal }
var j:integer;
begin with environrec do
 for j := 1 to lsignal do
   if flip(0.5) then signal[j] := 1
     else signal[j] := 0
end;

function decode(var mess:message; start, length:integer):integer;
{ decode substring as unsigned binary integer }
var j, accum, powerof2:integer;
begin
 accum := 0; powerof2 := 1;
 for j := start to start+length-1 do begin
   accum := accum + powerof2*mess[j];
   powerof2 := powerof2 * 2;
  end;
 decode := accum
end;

procedure multiplexeroutput(var environrec:erecord);
{ calculate correct multiplexer output }
var j:integer;
begin with environrec do begin
{ decode the address }
 address := decode(signal,1,laddress);
{ set the output }
 output := signal[laddress + address + 1]
end end;

procedure environment(var environrec:erecord);
{ coordinate multiplexer calculations }
begin
 generatesignal(environrec);
 multiplexeroutput(environrec);
end;
```

FIGURE 6.9 The procedure *environment* and its data structure *environrec* together implement the simulated environment presented to the simple classifier system (SCS).

cedure *detectors* we see how a copy of the *signal* structure is assigned to the environmental message *envmessage*. In other problems the coding of the environmental message requires the mapping of one or more real variables to a bit string. To do this requires parameter data structures to define the range and length of each environmental variable required in the message. It also requires coding and mapping routines to generate and concatenate message substrings.

```
{ detector.scs: convert environmental states to env. message }

{ detector data declarations }

type drecord = record
                  end; { For this problem, no detector record is
                        required.  Normally, the detector record
                        contains information for mapping environmental
                        state variables to the environmental bit-string. }

var detectrec:drecord; { dummy detector record }

procedure detectors(var environrec:erecord; var detectrec:drecord;
                    var envmessage:message);
{ convert environmental state to env. message }
begin
 with environrec do { place signal message in env. message }
   envmessage := signal
end;
```

FIGURE 6.10 The procedure *detectors* and its data structure *detectrec* create an environmental message from the environmental state. In the multiplexer problem this is quite simple; other problems may require parameter mappings.

The detector routines take care of input from the environment to the SCS, but what about actions taken by the SCS to change the environment? This is handled by the brief procedure *effector* shown in Fig. 6.11. In our particular problem, the mapping between effector and action is very straightforward; we simply output the winning classifier action as the multiplexer output selected by the classifier system. In other problems the mapping might require more machinery, and in those cases the procedure *effector* might require more involved data structures and algorithms.

To the Victor Go the Spoils

There is one last crucial piece of information that must flow between environment and classifier system. When the classifier system has taken the correct action (when it has output the correct signal), it must receive an appropriate payoff from the environment—an electronic carrot—to reinforce its behavior. We could

```
procedure effector(var population:poptype; var clearingrec:crecord;
                   var environrec:erecord);
{ set action in object as dictated by auction winner }
begin with population do with clearingrec do with environrec do
  classifieroutput := classifier[winner].a end;
```

FIGURE 6.11 The procedure *effector* maps the winning classifier action to the environment.

permit payoff from a human trainer or instructor; instead, for the sake of convenience and consistency we provide a piece of code to monitor the classifier system's performance, recognize correct behavior, and deliver the appropriate reward. The procedure *reinforcement* does these things in conjunction with its data structure *reinforcementrec* as shown in Fig. 6.12. The algorithm is straightforward: if the action is correct, then a reward is paid. In addition to paying reward to the winner, the reinforcement procedures keep track of the proportion of correct answers for all time and for the past 50 time steps. These performance statistics are printed in a number of reports.

The Main Event: The Main Program

Blow the trumpet, beat the drums. With the reinforcement procedure in place, we are ready to hook everything together in the main program as displayed in Fig. 6.13. The program listing begins with a long sequence of compiler include directives. These commentlike statements begin and end with brackets ("{" and "}"); however, the $I following the left bracket indicates that the named file (for example, *declare.scs*) should be included in the compilation. All the subcomponent parts of the simple classifier system are thus included in the compilation, and the main program doesn't actually *begin* until the begin statement halfway down the listing.

Next, the program is initialized through a call to the procedure *initialization*. In our brief review of the workings of the simple classifier system, we have ignored some of the more pedestrian aspects of the SCS, such as initialization, input, and output. The interested reader can find complete listings in Appendix D to fill in the gaps in this presentation. Following the call to *initialization*, an initial environmental message is constructed with a call to *detectors*. The preliminary round of activity is completed by a call to procedure *report*.

The main time loop is contained within the *repeat-until* construct that comprises the remaining code. The iteration begins with a call to *timekeeper*, a procedure that counts iterations and sets flags for periodic events like printer reports and genetic algorithm invocations. In rapid succession the SCS then calls *environment*, *detectors*, and *matchclassifiers*, to generate a signal, pass it to the rule and message system, and match classifiers. Thereafter, *aoc*, *effector*, and *reinforcement* are called to hold the auction, apportion credit, set the action, and reward good behavior.

If it is time to report (if *reportflag* = true), the *report* is called. Console and plot reports are executed if their respective flags are set (as controlled by procedure *timekeeper*). The procedure *advance* is then called to advance the clearinghouse variables. Finally, if it is time for the genetic algorithm to be called (if *gaflag* = true) then the procedure *ga* executes the GA and the procedure *reportga* reports GA results. The entire process can then come to a grinding halt if the user presses a keyboard key (if a key is pressed, the function *halt* interrupts the program and checks to make sure you are serious about stopping execution).

```
{ reinforcement data declarations }
type rrecord = record { reinforcement record type}
                   reward, rewardcount, totalcount, count50,
                   rewardcount50, proportionreward,
                   proportionreward50:real;
                   lastwinner:integer;
                 end;

var reinforcementrec:rrecord;
    rfile:text;        { reinforcement file - rfile }



function criterion(var rrec:rrecord; var environrec:erecord):boolean;
{ return true if criterion is achieved }
var tempflag:boolean;
begin with rrec do with environrec do begin
  tempflag := (output = classifieroutput);
  totalcount := totalcount + 1;
  count50 := count50 + 1;
  { increment reward counters }
  if tempflag then begin
    rewardcount := rewardcount + 1;
    rewardcount50 := rewardcount50 + 1;
  end;

  { calculate reward proportions: running & last 50 }
  proportionreward := rewardcount/totalcount;
  if ( round(count50 - 50.0) = 0) then begin
   proportionreward50 := rewardcount50/50.0;
   rewardcount50 := 0.0; count50 := 0.0 { reset }
  end;
  criterion := tempflag;
end end;



procedure payreward(var population:poptype; var rrec:rrecord;
                    var clearingrec:crecord);
{ pay reward to appropriate individual }
begin with population do with rrec do with clearingrec do

  with classifier[winner] do begin
     strength := strength + reward;
     lastwinner := winner
end end;



procedure reinforcement(var reinforcementrec:rrecord; var population:poptype;
                   var clearingrec:crecord; var environrec:erecord);
{ make payment if criterion satisfied }
begin
  if criterion(reinforcementrec, environrec) then
       payreward(population, reinforcementrec, clearingrec);
end;
```

FIGURE 6.12 The procedure *reinforcement* monitors performance and pays rewards for correct answers.

```
program scs;

{ SCS -   A Simple Classifier System }
{   (C)   David E. Goldberg, 1987    }
{         All Rights Reserved        }

{$I declare.scs }
{$I random.apb }
{$I io.scs }
{$I utility.scs }
{$I environ.scs }
{$I detector.scs }
{$I perform.scs }
{$I aoc.scs }
{$I effector.scs }
{$I reinforc.scs }
{$I timekeep.scs }
{$I advance.scs }
{$I ga.scs }
{$I report.scs }
{$I initial.scs }

begin { main }
  initialization;
  detectors(environrec, detectrec, envmessage);
  report(rep);
  with timekeeprec do repeat
    timekeeper(timekeeprec);
    environment(environrec);
    detectors(environrec, detectrec, envmessage);
    matchclassifiers(population, envmessage, matchlist);
    aoc(population, matchlist, clearingrec);
    effector(population, clearingrec, environrec);
    reinforcement(reinforcementrec, population, clearingrec, environrec);
    if reportflag then report(rep);
    if consolereportflag then consolereport(reinforcementrec);
    if plotreportflag then plotreport(pfile, reinforcementrec);
    advance(clearingrec);
    if gaflag then begin
      ga(garec, population);
      if reportflag then reportga(rep, garec, population);
    end;
  until halt;
  report(rep);   { final report }
  close(pfile);  { close plot file }
end.
```

FIGURE 6.13 The main program *scs* coordinates all activities for the simple classifier system (SCS).

RESULTS USING THE SIMPLE CLASSIFIER SYSTEM

With the simple classifier system implemented, we are ready to test its performance in learning the multiplexer function. We first list the environmental and classifier system parameters we choose for these tests and we then run three sets of experiments: the perfect rule experiments, the default hierarchy (DH) experiments, and the clean slate experiments.

Environmental and System Parameters

The environmental and system parameters are set as follows:

$$
\begin{aligned}
nposition &= 6 \\
nclassifier &= 100 \ (\text{varies in perfect and DH runs}) \\
pgeneral &= 0.5 \\
cbid &= 0.1 \\
bidsigma &= 0.075 \\
bidtax &= 0.01 \\
lifetax &= 0.0 \\
proportionselect &= 0.2 \\
pmutation &= 0.02 \\
pcrossover &= 1.0 \\
gaperiod &= 5000 \\
crowdingfactor &= 3 \\
crowdingsubpop &= 3 \\
reward &= 1
\end{aligned}
$$

Selection of classifier system parameters remains something of an art form; however, useful design guides may be obtained by calculating expected steady-state performance and half-life values at different rates of taxation.

The Perfect Rule Set and the Monkey Wrenches

To test the SCS code, we perform an experiment using the perfect set of rules shown in Table 6.4. This set consists of eight nonoverlapping rules, where two rules are required for each address. For example, the rules

```
###000:0
###100:1
```

cover the two possible signals for data line D0. To test the apportionment algorithm's capability, we also perturb the rule set by adding several bad rules (we call them monkey wrenches). We are interested in knowing whether the classifier

TABLE 6.4 Perfect Rule Set for the Six-Multiplexer

Rule	Purpose
###000:0	0 Address/0 Signal
##0#01:0	1 Address/0 Signal
#0##10:0	2 Address/0 Signal
0###11:0	3 Address/0 Signal
###100:1	0 Address/1 Signal
##1#01:1	1 Address/1 Signal
#1##10:1	2 Address/1 Signal
1###11:1	3 Address/1 Signal

system can increase the strength of the good rules at the same time it reduces the strength of the bad rules.

Executing the SCS code, we first answer the interactive queries shown in Fig. 6.14. The system responds by initializing the classifier system and by presenting the initial report displayed in Fig. 6.15 along with the initial snapshot report in Fig. 6.16. The classifier system runs for 2000 iterations, terminating with the snapshot report displayed in Fig. 6.17. Here we see how the correct rules have achieved high strength values. In fact all good classifiers are at or near their correct steady state value of

$$S_{ss} + \frac{R_{ss}}{C_{tax} + C_{bid}} = \frac{1}{0.01 + 0.1} = 9.09,$$

and all bid values are at or near their steady values of

$$B_{ss} = C_{bid} \cdot S_{ss} = 0.909.$$

By contrast the two monkey wrenches have strength and bid values near zero.

A graph of correct answer proportion versus iteration is presented in Fig. 6.18. This graph presents a moving average over the last 50 iterations as well as a performance average over all time. The classifier system eliminates the bad rules quickly, thereby achieving near perfect performance.

Default Hierarchy Tests

That the classifier system can weed out a few bad rules among the perfect rule set is somewhat reassuring, but what of situations where we are less fortunate and have less than perfect rules in the classifier population? In these situations we want the classifiers to organize themselves into a structure Holland has called a *default hierarchy*. In a default hierarchy general rules (those with many #'s)

```
************************************************
       A Simple Classifier System - SCS
          (C) David E. Goldberg,  1987
              All Rights Reserved
************************************************

Enter seed random number (0.0..1.0) > 0.3333
Enter    classifier    filename: perfect.dta
Enter   environment    filename: environ.dta
Enter  reinforcement   filename: reinf.dta
Enter   timekeeper     filename: time.dta
Enter gen. algorithm   filename: ga.dta
Enter     report       filename: lst:
Enter    plot file     filename: plot.prn
```

FIGURE 6.14 Interactive queries precede execution of the simple classifier system.

```
*********************************************
         A Simple Classifier System - SCS
           (C) David E. Goldberg,  1987
                All Rights Reserved
*********************************************


Population Parameters
---------------------
Number of classifiers       -          10
Number of positions         -           6
Bid coefficient             -      0.1000
Bid spread                  -      0.0750
Bidding tax                 -      0.0100
Existence tax               -      0.0000
Generality probability      -      0.5000
Bid specificity base        -      1.0000
Bid specificity mult.       -      0.0000
Ebid specificity base       -      1.0000
Ebid specificity mult.      -      0.0000


Environmental Parameters (Multiplexer)
--------------------------------------
Number of address lines     -           2
Number of data lines        -           4
Total number of lines       -           6


Apportionment of Credit Parameters
----------------------------------
Bucket brigade flag         -       false


Reinforcement Parameters
------------------------
Reinforcement reward        -         1.0


Timekeeper Parameters
---------------------
Initial iteration           -           0
Initial block               -           0
Report period               -        2000
Console report period       -          50
Plot report period          -          50
Genetic algorithm period    -          -1

Genetic Algorithm Parameters
----------------------------
Proportion to select/gen    -      0.2000
Number to select            -           1
Mutation probability        -      0.0200
Crossover probability       -      1.0000
Crowding factor             -           3
Crowding subpopulation      -           3
```

FIGURE 6.15   SCS initial report displays all system parameters.

```
Snapshot Report
---------------

[ Block:Iteration ]   -   [ 0:0 ]

Current Multiplexer Status
--------------------------
Signal              -   000000
Decoded address     -      0
Multiplexer output  -      0
Classifier  output  -      0

Environmental message:    000000

No.   Strength    bid     ebid M Classifier
-------------------------------------------------------
   1   10.00      0.00    0.00    ###000:[0]
   2   10.00      0.00    0.00    ###100:[1]
   3   10.00      0.00    0.00    ##0#01:[0]
   4   10.00      0.00    0.00    ##1#01:[1]
   5   10.00      0.00    0.00    #0##10:[0]
   6   10.00      0.00    0.00    #1##10:[1]
   7   10.00      0.00    0.00    0###11:[0]
   8   10.00      0.00    0.00    1###11:[1]
   9   10.00      0.00    0.00    ######:[0]
  10   10.00      0.00    0.00    ######:[1]

New winner [1] : Old winner [1]

Reinforcement Report
--------------------
Proportion Correct (from start)    -   0.0000
Proportion Correct (last fifty)    -   0.0000
Last winning classifier number     -      0
```

FIGURE 6.16 Initial snapshot report displays initial rule population. In the perfect rule set test, the first eight rules are perfect, and the last two rules are bad (monkey wrenches).

cover the general conditions and more specific, possibly overlapping rules cover the exceptions.

As an example of a default hierarchy in the multiplexer problem, consider the following set of rules:

```
# # # 0 0 0 : 0
# # 0 # 0 1 : 0
# 0 # # 1 0 : 0
0 # # # 1 1 : 0
# # # # # # : 1
```

If we assume that each rule receives equal payoff when rewarded, and if we further assume that when two overlapping rules bid to answer a particular message, the more specific rule wins, we see how this set of rules constitutes a working default hierarchy. This is clear because the first four rules handle all 0 output

```
Snapshot Report
---------------

[ Block:Iteration ]   -   [ 0:2000 ]

Current Multiplexer Status
--------------------------
Signal                -   100011
Decoded address       -        3
Multiplexer output    -        1
Classifier  output    -        1

Environmental message:    100011

No.   Strength    bid      ebid M Classifier
--------------------------------------------------------

     1     9.09    0.91     0.94   ###000:[0]
     2     9.09    0.91     0.97   ###100:[1]
     3     9.09    0.91     0.82   ##0#01:[0]
     4     9.09    0.91     0.85   ##1#01:[1]
     5     9.09    0.91     0.94   #0##10:[0]
     6     9.09    0.91     0.82   #1##10:[1]
     7     9.09    0.91     1.06   0###11:[0]
     8     9.09    0.91     0.97 X 1###11:[1]
     9     0.00    0.00    -0.06 X ######:[0]
    10     0.00    0.00     0.10 X ######:[1]

New winner [8] : Old winner [4]

Reinforcement Report
--------------------
Proportion Correct (from start)   -   0.9990
Proportion Correct (last fifty)   -   1.0000
Last winning classifier number    -        8
```

FIGURE 6.17   **Perfect rule set test terminal snapshot report (T = 2000) displays elevated strength values for the perfect rules and near-zero values for the monkey wrenches.**

cases perfectly and the completely general rule handles the 1 output cases. Notice that the completely general rule by itself is only correct half the time. In the presence of the good rules (and in the presence of a bidding structure that encourages specific rules over general rules), the specific rules cover the "mistakes" of the general rule allowing it to get reward every time it is invoked. In fact the set of five rules working together as a default hierarchy should perform as well as the perfect set of eight rules examined in the last section.

We will soon consider how to encourage the formation of default hierarchies through an appropriate choice of bidding structure. Before we do, we should understand why we might want to encourage their formation. Default hierarchies have two advantages over nonoverlapping rule sets:

1. Parsimony
2. Enlargement of the solution set

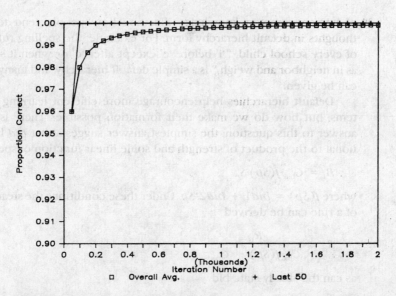

FIGURE 6.18 In testing the perfect rule set, the simple classifier system quickly lowers the strength of bad rules at the same time it elevates the strength of good rules. This results in near-perfect performance as measured by an all-time average.

Default hierarchies are parsimonious, containing fewer rules than nonoverlapping rule sets for the same problem. In our example, the perfect rule set contains eight rules (this is the smallest nonoverlapping rule set) and the example default hierarchy contains five rules (this is the smallest default hierarchy). The parsimony principle is discussed in more depth elsewhere (Holland, Holyoak, Nisbett, and Thagard, 1986), but its implications to a rule discovery system are manifest. If we need fewer rules to achieve a high level of performance, our waiting time to the discovery of a set of good rules is shortened, and we are more likely to achieve good results quickly.

Default hierarchies also enlarge the set of correct solutions. To see this, we recognize that the formation of default hierarchies does not adversely affect system performance when a set of perfect, nonoverlapping rules is present. As such, the existence of other rule sets that perform as well can only enlarge the space of solutions. Moreover, since a default hierarchy is an implicit or virtual structure (not a physical structure—our rules have not changed), its addition to the system is achieved with no increase in the size of the problem space. Thus the enlargement of the solution space with no increase in the size of the problem space promotes faster discovery of high-performance rule sets.

Besides promoting parsimony and enlarging the solution set, default hierarchies encourage knowledge acquisition and overlays in a manner more natural than is possible with mutually exclusive nonoverlapping knowledge structures (Holland et al., 1986). We do not belabor this point, but even simple examples of human common knowledge illustrate how people tend to organize their thoughts in default hierarchy form. For example, the spelling rule on the tongue of every school child, "'i' before 'e' except after 'c' or when it sounds like an 'a' as in neighbor and weigh," is a simple default hierarchy, and many other examples can be given.

Default hierarchies help encourage more efficient learning in classifier systems, but how do we make their formation possible? There is more than one answer to this question; the simplest answer suggests that *bid* be made proportional to the product of strength and some linear function of specificity:

$$B_i = C_{bid} \cdot f(Sp) \cdot S_i,$$

where $f(Sp) = bid1 + bid2*Sp$. Under these conditions the steady-state strength of a rule can be derived

$$S_{ss} = \frac{R_{ss}}{C_{bid}f(Sp) + C_{tax}}$$

as can the steady-state bid

$$B_{ss} = \frac{C_{bid}f(Sp)R_{ss}}{C_{bid}f(Sp) + C_{tax}}.$$

Assuming that $C_{bid} = 0.1$ and $C_{tax} = 0.01$ and assuming that a completely general rule bids 25 percent of C_{bid} and a fully specific rule bids 100 percent of C_{bid}, we may calculate the reward-normalized strength and bid values for six-position rules as tabulated in Table 6.5. If we assume that a perfect default hierarchy exists, then the presence of an exception will tend to hide the mistakes of a general rule; all rules contained in the default hierarchy should be rewarded when they win. In theory we see how this simple bidding structure, with bid taken as an increasing function of specificity, encourages the formation of a stable default hierarchy.

To examine whether this bidding structure encourages the formation of a working default hierarchy in practice, we perform a simple experiment comparing the specificity-dependent bidding structure to one where bid is proportional to strength alone. We can perform these experiments without change to the SCS code because the four coefficients-*bid1, bid2, ebid1,* and *ebid2* are available to control the bidding structure used. To achieve the default hierarchy described above (Table 6.5), we set the following values of the bid structure coefficients:

$$bid1 = ebid1 = 0.250$$
$$bid2 = ebid2 = 0.125$$

To inhibit default hierarchy formation, we set the following values of the bid structure coefficients:

$$bid1 = ebid1 = 1.0$$
$$bid2 = ebid2 = 0.0$$

Two computer runs of the SCS program have been performed using the five-rule default hierarchy presented earlier (some monkey wrenches have been

TABLE 6.5 Normalized Steady-State Strength and Bid Values for Default Hierarchy Tests

Specificity-(Sp)	$f(Sp)$	S_{ss}/R_{ss}	B_{ss}/R_{ss}
0	0.250	28.57	0.714
1	0.375	21.05	0.789
2	0.500	16.67	0.833
3	0.625	13.79	0.862
4	0.750	11.76	0.882
5	0.875	10.25	0.897
6	1.000	9.09	0.909

thrown in as well). The results of the two runs, one without default hierarchy (no DH) and one with default hierarchy (DH), are presented in Fig. 6.19 and 6.20 respectively. The run without default hierarchy is unable to perform as well as the run with default hierarchy, as we should expect. Without an appropriate bidding structure, the default rule (######:1) wins against exception (perfect) rules when it should not. These mistakes lower the default rule's strength enough so the correct rules win once again. Under these circumstances, the default rule is no longer making as many errors and its strength goes back up, and once again it starts winning when it should not. Without a bidding structure to encourage a stable default hierarchy, this cycle of events can only repeat itself, with lowered

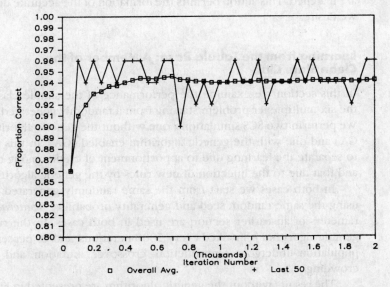

FIGURE 6.19 Without specificity-dependent bidding, the classifier system is unable to use the default hierarchy rules accurately.

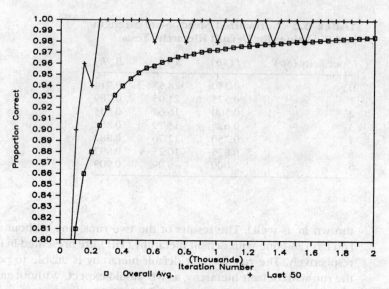

FIGURE 6.20   With specificity-dependent bidding, the classifier uses the default hierarchy to achieve near-perfect performance.

system performance the inevitable result. By contrast, in the run with specificity-dependent bidding, enough difference exists between specific and general rule bids (at steady state) to allow consistent selection of exception rules when they are matched. This action permits the formation of the accurate default hierarchies we desire.

Learning from the Tabula Rasa: A Member of the Clean Slate Club

In this section we examine the performance of the simple classifier system on the six-multiplexer problem starting from a randomly generated set of 100 rules. We perform two SCS simulations, one without the genetic algorithm enabled (no GA) and one with the genetic algorithm enabled (GA). In this way we are able to separate the learning due to apportionment of credit among the original rules and that due to the injection of new rules by the genetic algorithm.

In both cases we start from the same randomly generated set of 100 rules using the same random seed and generality probability *pgeneral* = 0.5. The parameters of an earlier section are used in both cases. In the run with GA, the genetic algorithm is invoked every 5000 iterations, and 20 percent of the current population undergoes reproduction, crossover, mutation, and replacement by crowding.

The results without the genetic algorithm are presented in Fig. 6.21. Here we see how the apportionment of credit algorithm adjusts the strength values of the

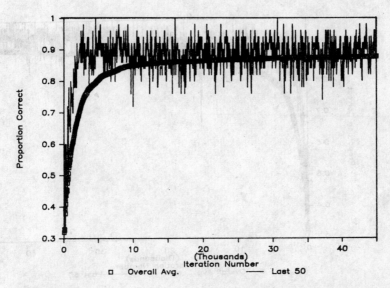

FIGURE 6.21 Without the genetic algorithm activated, the SCS is able to achieve better-than-random performance by organizing extant rules into a default hierarchy.

rules, achieving a steady performance of 88% correct. Although the 50-step moving average varies above and below this level of performance, in the long run the classifier system is able to sustain this relatively high level of performance even without genetic action. That the classifier system without the GA performs this much better than a coin toss should come as no surprise. A random rule set of 100 rules contains a rich subset of rules for this relatively small problem, and the bidding mechanism with default hierarchy formation permits the good rules to work well together.

With such high performance without genetic action, we might expect the genetic algorithm to have a hard time improving on the solution, but this turns out not to be the case. Results with the GA shown in Fig. 6.22 show improvement over the no-GA results to the point where the classifier system is performing correctly 95–96 percent of the time. This is especially remarkable considering the relatively infrequent genetic action; the population is turned over only twice in 50,000 iterations $(0.2 \cdot 100 \cdot 50,000)/5000 = 200$ new offspring by genetic action).

On the one hand these results are encouraging. A classifier system with genetic algorithm has performed better than one without, and furthermore the level of performance has been high enough to rival human accuracy. On the other hand the problem is a toy problem where only $2^6 = 64$ different situations are ever presented to the system. Recall, however, that our goal has been to devise the simplest possible working classifier system. We have ignored many obvious bells

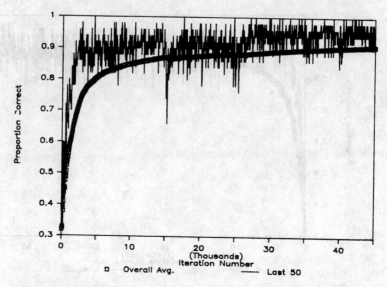

FIGURE 6.22 With the genetic algorithm activated, new rules are injected into the classifier store at regular intervals to improve performance even further over that of Fig. 6.21.

and whistles (the next chapter will show how classifier systems have performed as well on larger multiplexer problems with over a million different signals). Moreover, we have (willingly) tied our hands behind our backs by using the genetic algorithm as our only rule discovery heuristic. There are other ways to generate good rules. We might fuse environmental messages with correct answers (following reward) and insert these perfect—albeit too-specific—rules in the population, or we might generalize such perfect rules by placing #'s at some number of positions. Although many such techniques can—and perhaps should— be adopted to try to boost performance, our goal has been to isolate the contribution of the genetic algorithm as a rule discovery mechanism. Having done this, we are freer to open our sights to other means of enhancing learning in classifier systems and other genetics-based machine learning systems.

SUMMARY

In this chapter we have explored the background, principles of operation, implementation, and performance of a classifier system. Classifier systems are a form of genetics-based machine learning (GBML) system, combining a simple, parallel production system based on string rules, an apportionment of credit algorithm modeled after an information-based service economy, and genetic algorithms. Classifier systems and their derivatives are finding increasing application in science, engineering, and business circles.

We have seen how the backbone of a classifier system is its rule and message system, a type of production or rule-based system. The explosion in rule-based expert system applications lends credence to the notion that rules are an appropriate way to represent human knowledge and understanding. As with other production systems, the rules in a classifier system are of the form, if <condition> then <action>; however, in classifier systems, conditions and actions are restricted to be fixed-length strings where explicit pattern recognition is provided by providing a don't care or wild card symbol, the #. Additionally, classifier systems depart from the expert system mainstream by demanding parallel rule activation. This alleviates the bottleneck of one-rule-at-a-time schemes, thereby permitting multiple simultaneous thoughts and actions. When classifier systems must arbitrate between mutually exclusive, competing alternatives, they also depart from the mainstream by using competitive arbitration strategies rather than order-dependent or other arbitrary procedures.

In the most general classifier systems, classifiers send messages that are placed on a message list, thereby activating other classifiers or action triggers called effectors. The presence of a central message list provides a centralized communication channel. Since space is limited on the message list, some method must exist for choosing among competing messages. In many classifier systems an apportionment of credit system modeled after a competitive service economy ensures that rules are properly evaluated and selected. Rules bid for the right to send their messages (or take their actions); winning bids are paid to classifiers that previously sent activating messages. Thus a chain of middlemen forms from the environment to ultimate action. Competition keeps the system honest; useful classifiers live and prosper while unsuccessful classifiers go bankrupt.

The payment made to and from a rule increases and decreases its net worth, called its strength. Strength determines a rule's bid; it also serves as the rule's fitness in a genetic algorithm search for new rules. The genetic algorithm adopted in classifier systems is very close to those used in search applications; however, only a portion of the population is reproduced at a time, and more attention is focused on who replaces whom.

A reduced version of a classifier system, the simple classifier system (SCS), has been implemented in the Pascal programming language. To give the SCS a concrete problem, a boolean function—a six-bit multiplexer—has been programmed and interfaced to the classifier system. In initial tests the classifier system learns to discount bad rules at the same time it elevates eight perfect rules. In other initial tests a bidding structure with specificity-dependent bidding learns to use rule sets containing a default hierarchy. Default hierarchies allow classifier systems to do more with less through rule parsimony and enlargement of the solution set. Default hierarchies also appeal to human notions of knowledge overlap and exception. In less constrained tests—the clean slate or tabula rasa experiments—starting from a randomly generated set of 100 rules, a classifier system without genetic algorithm performs better than random guessing, and a classifier with genetic algorithm outperforms both the SCS without GA and random guessing. These results encourage further investigation of other genetics-based machine learning applications in the next chapter.

■ PROBLEMS

6.1. A certain classifier is activated continuously with an overall tax coefficient of C_{tax} = 0.01 and a bidding coefficient of C_{bid} = 0.1. If the classifier receives 10 points of reward per activation, calculate the equilibrium (steady-state) strength of the classifier as it is activated repeatedly. Calculate the steady-state strength if the tax coefficient is zero. Calculate the steady-state strength if the tax coefficient is 0.02.

6.2. A classifier is initialized with a strength of 100 points. The classifier is never activated, but it is taxed at a rate 0.01. Calculate the number of iterations until the classifier's strength falls to 90, 80, 70, 60, and 50 points. Repeat the calculation for tax rates of 0.1 and 0.001.

6.3. The time required for a classifier to lose half its strength under the action of taxation alone is called its *half-life*. Derive a general expression for the half-life as a function of the classifier's tax rate C_{tax}. Plot a graph of half-life as a function of C_{tax}.

6.4. A classifier is activated continuously with a bid coefficient C_{bid} = 0.05 and an overall tax coefficient of C_{tax} = 0.01. At each activation the classifier receives 1.0 point. Calculate the steady-state bid of this classifier as it is activated repeatedly. Repeat the calculation for bid coefficient values C_{bid} = 0.01 and 0.1.

6.5. A classifier is activated every iteration with a bid coefficient C_{bid} = 0.1 and no tax coefficient. On every other iteration the classifier receives 10 points. After a sufficient number of iterations this classifier oscillates between two strength values. Calculate these oscillating steady-state strength values and their associated bid values.

6.6. A classifier is activated every iteration but is paid a reward R once every k activations. Derive equations for the steady-state strength values for this classifier assuming it has a specified bid coefficient C_{bid} and no tax coefficient.

6.7. In the simple classifier system connected to the six-multiplexer problem, a six-position ternary coding is used for the single condition and a single-position binary coding is used for the action. Calculate the number of uniquely different rules for this problem. Calculate the number of rule similarity templates (schemata) for this problem.

6.8. A classifier system is coded with a two-position, ternary condition and a one-position binary action. In other words the rules have the general format with C $\in$ {0, 1, #} and A $\in$ {0, 1}. A population of size $n = 12$ drawn at random (each ternary character equally likely, and each binary character equally likely) has three copies of each of the following rules:

```
00:0
11:1
##:0
##:1
```

Calculate the prior probability of drawing an identically distributed population.

6.9. Suppose in Problem 6.8 that the condition positions are selected randomly so a wild card (a #) is chosen with probability $p_{general} = 0.8$ and the remaining two characters are chosen with equal probability. Calculate the prior probability of drawing a population distributed identically to that of Problem 6.8 under these conditions.

6.10. A classifier $C1$ is activated and sends a message to classifier $C2$. $C2$ is then activated, causing an action that is rewarded with 10 points. If both classifiers have bid coefficient values of 0.1 and overall tax coefficient values of 0.02, calculate both classifiers' steady-state strength and bid values assuming this two-step activation process continues indefinitely. Recalculate these values holding the bid coefficient constant while doubling the taxation coefficient.

■ COMPUTER ASSIGNMENTS

A. Investigate the effect of crowding on the simple classifier system. Starting from identical rule populations (using the same random seed for a pseudorandomly generated population or the same fully specified population) investigate SCS rule learning with *crowdingfactor* values of 1 (no crowding) and 3 ("normal" crowding setting). Compare and contrast the effectiveness of the rule sets learned and their composition after 50,000 iterations.

B. Interface the simple classifier system to a simple rule-learning problem of your choice. What routines must be changed to do this? Be sure to implement your changes in stages by testing each module individually. It is very difficult to debug a classifier system as one monolithic block of code because of its size and its randomness (there is usually no right answer to check against).

C. Implement a reinforcement procedure that rewards the simple classifier system with *ptscorrect* when the correct answer is given and *ptswrong* when the wrong answer is given. Run the six-multiplexer problem with values *ptscorrect* = 1 and *ptswrong* = 0.5. Compare the performance of this system to the results presented in this chapter.

D. Implement and test the performance subsystem of a less simple classifier system with a message list, message passing, and message-sensitive effectors. What procedures and data structures must change to implement this subsystem? Try to make these changes while maintaining the modularity of the SCS.

E. Invent a method of imposing payment sharing to help induce speciation (and niche) among classifiers within a simple classifier system. Implement this mechanism and compare to the champion (winner takes all) scheme implemented in the SCS code. Discuss the advantages and disadvantages of both methods with respect to effectiveness and computational efficiency.

7 | Applications of Genetics-Based Machine Learning

In the previous chapter, we examined the structure, operating principles, and a particular implementation of one type of genetics-based machine learning system, a *classifier system.* Classifier systems were presented as *faits accomplis,* as systems cast confidently in concrete. To make matters worse, the focus on classifier systems may have given the impression that classifier systems are the only way to do genetics-based machine learning (GBML). This chapter atones for the previous chapter's sins of omission by investigating the roots, early history, and current state of GBML. We examine the early proposals for reproductive programs, schemata processors, and broadcast systems. We investigate Cognitive System One (CS-1) and the maze-running tasks it learned. We survey other early GBML systems and review a number of current theories and applications of these techniques.

THE RISE OF GBML

The late 1940s and early 1950s were spirited times in the development of computer theory and practice. Perhaps even more than now, the vigorous interchange between theoreticians and practitioners helped advance the state of computational art at a rapid clip. At the same time the influence of biological analogy and metaphor was at an all-time high (in a relative if not an absolute sense), as evidenced by the strength of the cybernetics movement, the level of neural network activity, and the interest in cellular automata, and computational.analogs of self-reproduction. Against this backdrop a number of people began to investigate relationships between natural evolution and artificial adaptation (Bledsoe, 1961;

Bremermann, 1962; Friedman 1959; Holland, 1962c; von Neumann, 1966). Holland's (1962c) early outline for a theory of adaptive systems adopted a natural perspective drawn from biological example. His vision foresaw bands of programs wandering about a cellular computational space, bumping into one another, sometimes forming new unions (Holland, 1962c, pp. 306–307):

> The free generation procedure ... requires the generators (and combinations of generators) to "shift" and "connect" at random in the computer. The simplest form of random shift occurs under the following conditions: (1) at each moment of time a generator has a fixed probability of shifting to one of its neighboring modules; (2) if a generator attempts to shift to a module already occupied by another generator, such a shift is prohibited.... Under conditions ... two or more generators occupying adjacent modules ("in contact") may become connected. Such connected sets of generators are to shift as a unit.

This vision was not independent of his earlier proposal for iterative circuit computers (Holland, 1959, 1960), fine-grained, homogeneous parallel processing architectures with relative addressing using a process of path building; bands of wandering programs could be conveniently programmed in such Holland machines.

Schemata and Their Processors

Despite the appeal of these ideas, the proposals for elastoplastic billiard ball programs bouncing about a cellular computer were a long way from any working adaptive system, as Holland himself realized. The desire for a working demonstration led him to consider (Holland, 1965) one of the notable successes of early machine learning efforts, Samuel's (1959) learning checker player. Samuel's notions of consistent prediction were to guide the development of apportionment of credit algorithms in later GBML systems; these developments did not, however, halt the search for the theoretical basis of reproductive adaptation. Both lines of inquiry crystallized in two works that would have a profound effect on the development of all later GBML efforts. The first work, "Hierarchical Descriptions, Universal Spaces, and Adaptive Systems" (Holland, 1968, 1970a), discussed the description of complex machines built from a limited number of fixed components and the meaning of schemata or subcomponent templates within such machines. The second, more restricted (yet from the standpoint of future GBML, more interesting) work, "Processing and Processors for Schemata" (Holland, 1971), presented the first concrete proposal for a generalized GBML system. In this work Holland proposed the development of *schemata processors* in four phases. Schematics for three of the four prototypes are presented in Fig. 7.1. The prototypes increased in complexity from prototype I, a simple stimulus-response machine, to prototype IV, a complex automaton with internal states and modifiable detectors and effectors. This proposal served as the basis for what later became the first classifier system. Holland's artificial evolutionary design of a

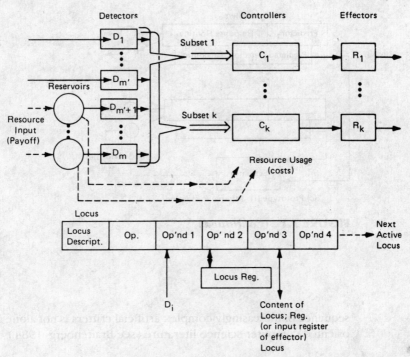

(a) Prototype I: Stimulus–Response (SR)

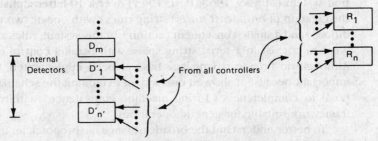

(b) Prototype II: Internal Detectors

FIGURE 7.1 Three of Holland's four schemata processor prototypes (Holland, 1971). Prototype IV extends the others by including modifiable effectors and detectors. Reprinted by permission.

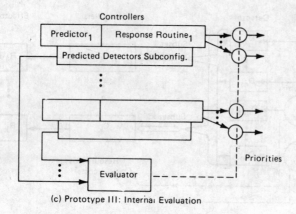

(c) Prototype III: Internal Evaluation

FIGURE 7.1 (*Continued*)

sequence of increasingly complex artificial critters is not alone in the biologically oriented computer science literature (see Braitenberg, 1984).

The Broadcast Language

While schemata processors never saw the light of cathode-ray-tube day, work continued on genetic algorithms and GBML. As noted in Chapter 4, the late 1960s and early 1970s were important times in the development and application of genetic algorithms in search and optimization (Bagley, 1967; Cavicchio, 1970; De Jong, 1975; Frantz, 1971; Hollstien, 1971; Rosenberg, 1967). An interesting development along the GBML front appeared in the oft-forgotten eighth chapter of *Adaptation in Natural and Artificial Systems* (ANAS) (Holland, 1975). In that chapter Holland proposed the creation of his *broadcast language,* a Post production system (Minsky, 1967; Post, 1943) over a 10-letter alphabet. He suggested the creation of *broadcast units* (string rules) with one or two antecedents (conditions) and a single consequent (action). In this system, rules and their messages were to coexist in a serial string space with parallel control of rule execution. Although no broadcast language has yet been implemented, the proposal was important because it showed one way of extending the schemata processor proposal to completeness (Turing machine equivalence) within a computational framework suitable for genetic operations.

To better understand the broadcast language proposal, let us examine the 10-alphabet and how it may be used to form broadcast units. The alphabet contains the following 10 characters:

$$\Lambda = \{0, 1, *, :, \Diamond, \blacktriangledown, \triangledown. \triangle, p, '\}.$$

Here, the 0 and 1 are the basic symbols for specifying signals. The star * (not to be confused with the meta-don't-care symbol * used in earlier chapters) is the basic delimiter for broadcast units (BUs); everything between a pair of stars is to be interpreted as a BU. The colon (:) is the intra-BU punctuation symbol, separating conditions and actions. There are four types of broadcast units:

1. $*I_1:I_2$ If I_1 is matched, broadcast I_2.
2. $*:I_1:I_2$ If I_1 is not matched, broadcast I_2.
3. $*I_1::I_2$ If I_1 is matched, delete persistent I_2.
4. $*I_1:I_2:I_3$ If I_1 and I_2 are matched, broadcast I_3.

The I's (I_1, I_2, I_3) are constructed from any characters of the alphabet where the other symbols are interpreted as follows:

$\Diamond$	(diamond)	Single character don't care symbol (or terminating multiple character don't care)
∇	(clear nabla)	Initial or terminating multiple character don't care symbol (ignored in other positions) with pass through
▼	(solid nabla)	Same as ∇; permits concatenation on pass through
$\triangle$	(clear delta)	Single character don't care symbol with pass through
p	(letter p)	A signal marked by a p persists for all time until deleted by a type 3 broadcast unit
	(single quote)	A single character preceded by a ' is taken literally

Like schemata processors (and subsequent classifier systems), the broadcast language was designed for convenient recognition of patterns of similarity. Holland's work presented seven examples of broadcast unit usage, including such standard computational devices as counters and adders and more genetic-specific operations such as reproduction and crossover. The presentation also briefly discussed how the broadcast language might be applied in a number of diverse disciplines:

1. Detailed genetic modeling (operon-operator type)
2. Lymphocyte immune network modeling
3. Neural network modeling
4. Pattern recognition system simulation
5. Physical radiative system modeling

Perhaps one day a practical system will be developed with the broadcast language's flexibility and convenience in geneticlike computation. Until that time the unification of processor and processed remains a goal worthy of our efforts (Holland, 1987b).

DEVELOPMENT OF CS-1, THE FIRST CLASSIFIER SYSTEM

The proposals for schemata processors and the broadcast language, together with the confluence of important elements of the theory of genetic algorithms, immediately led to the development of the first classifier system during the three years following the publication of ANAS. A description of this system was published by Holland and Reitman (1978). The system, called Cognitive System One

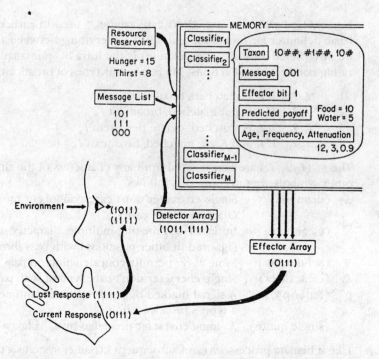

FIGURE 7.2 Schematic of the first classifier system Cognitive System One, or CS-1 (Holland and Reitman, 1978). Reprinted by permission.

(CS-1), is shown schematically in Fig. 7.2. The system combined a performance system based on syntactically simple string rules (classifiers), an epochal apportionment of credit system, and a genetic algorithm. In broad outline, CS-1 and the generic classifier system described in Chapter 6 have much in common. Here we focus upon several important differences in rule structure, bidding, and apportionment of credit. We also examine the environment and performance of CS-1 in its maze-learning task.

Referring once again to Fig. 7.2, we recognize an overall structure similar to that of the generic classifier system description of Chapter 6. A classifier store (the memory) contains a finite set of classifiers. The classifier conditions, or taxa (taxon, singular) are constructed over the ternary alphabet {0, 1, #} where the 0 and 1 are basic symbols and the # is a don't care character. In CS-1, conditions are segmented so that a portion pays attention to environmental signals, a portion pays attention to the last action, and a portion pays attention to a separate internal message list. This is somewhat different from the generic classifier system description of the preceding chapter; there we explained how all communications are posted as messages to the message list. The scheme advocated in the generic description is perhaps the more unified viewpoint.

Recall that in the generic system description, a classifier system seeks payoff, and that payoff is distributed to classifiers through the bucket brigade algorithm.

In CS-1, payoff and its distribution are handled somewhat differently. First, the system maintains separate reservoirs for a finite number of *resources* corresponding to a number of system *needs:* in the example schematic we see two resources, food (hunger) and water (thirst) These resource levels are depleted uniformly with time and must be replenished. In this way current resource levels are used to determine current demand, and these demand levels are then used in the decision process to determine which rules to activate. Second, CS-1 does not distribute payoff with a bucket brigade. Instead, an *epochal algorithm* is used. Here an *epoch* is defined as the time period between payoff events, and elaborate recordkeeping is performed to track a rule's usage and accuracy. The information is then used to revise a rule's decision parameters. To understand how this is done, we need to examine the parameters and their use.

The primary decision parameters for a CS-1 classifier are its predicted payoff values, the u values. CS-1 maintains a separate value for each resource relevant to the system (food and water in the example system). To determine which rule or rules to activate on a given cycle, CS-1 takes a classifier's predicted payoff values u_i and the current system demand values d_i (where the d function specifies an increasing demand level for decreasing resource reservoir level) and calculates an appropriateness value α for each classifier according to the following equation:

$$\alpha = \sum_i d_i u_i,$$

where the summation is taken over all resources $i.$ The spin of a weighted roulette wheel determines the decision winner where the product of appropriateness α and match score M size the wheel slots (here match score is a measure that increases with increasing rule specificity).

As the matching and rule activation proceed, the epochal apportionment of credit algorithm system tracks the accuracy of a classifier's predicted payoff values through the use of three parameters: *age, frequency,* and *attenuation.* The age parameter is incremented by 1 during each computational cycle; however, as the classifier receives reward (at the completion of an epoch), the classifier's age is reduced by an amount that increases with increasing rule usefulness. This Ponce de Leon algorithm prolongs a useful rule's life, because classifier replacement is performed stochastically according to age.

The frequency parameter is incremented each time a rule is activated. It is used in the weight adjustment scheme to give greater emphasis to more heavily used rules. The attenuation parameter is a number between 0 and 1. Initially a classifier's attenuation is set to 1.0. It is decreased whenever a rule has a predicted payoff value higher than that of the rule's successor. An attenuation function as shown in Fig. 7.3 is used as a multiplier to decrease a rule's accumulated attenuation with increasing error. When payoff actually enters the system, it is distributed according to attenuation and frequency. Thereafter, the epochal apportionment of credit scheme continues from payoff to payoff, adjusting predicted payoff values to agree with actual payoff values.

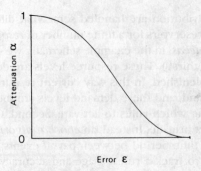

FIGURE 7.3   **Attenuation factor as a function of negative error as used in CS-1 (Holland, ca. 1976). Adapted by permission.**

CS-1 in Operation

CS-1 was programmed in Fortran on an IBM 1800 at the University of Michigan. The implementation contained the following limitations and simplifications:

1. Twenty-five positions per condition with eight bits for the environment, one bit for the last effector, and 16 bits for internal signals
2. One effector with two settings, 0 and 1
3. Two resource (needs) reservoirs
4. Eight-bit maze node names
5. One hundred classifiers, split 50-50 for each effector

CS-1 was faced with the two maze-running tasks depicted schematically in Fig. 7.4. In Fig. 7.4a, we see a seven-node maze where 18 units of food are available at the left end and 36 units of water are available at the right end. In Figure 7.4b, we see the transfer task that consists of the original seven-node maze with six additional nodes, three on each end.

The performance of CS-1 on these two tasks is depicted in Figs. 7.5 and 7.6, respectively. Figure 7.5 compares three cases: random walk, CS-1 without GA, and CS-1 with GA. The run with GA outperforms that without, and both learning runs outperform a random walk. Because of the lower payoff for food (18 food units as compared to 36 water units), we should expect the system to seek food twice as often as it seeks water. This behavior was observed in the experiments.

In the transfer experiment, we see the difference in performance between a naive run (where the rules are generated at random) and an experienced run (where the classifier system is trained on the seven-node maze first). In this task the knowledge learned in the first set of experiments does indeed transfer to the more complex task, as evidenced by the immediate convergence to near-optimal performance in the experienced trace.

Since the development of CS-1, Holland has continued his theoretical and experimental classifier system investigations (Holland, 1980a, 1980b, 1981, 1983a, b, 1984, 1985a, b, 1986a, b, 1987a, b; Holland and Burks, 1985; Holland,

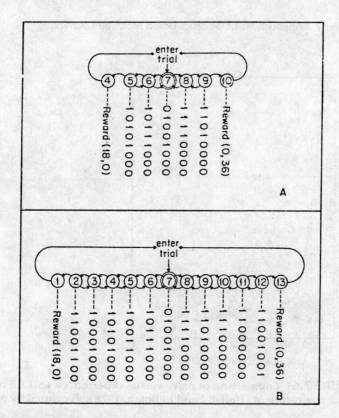

FIGURE 7.4 Schematic of (a) initial test environment, a seven-node maze and (b) the transfer test environment, a 13-node maze (Holland and Reitman, 1978). Reprinted by permission.

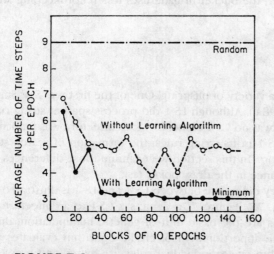

FIGURE 7.5 Performance of CS-1 in the initial test environment (seven-node maze) with and without genetic (learning) algorithm (Holland and Reitman, 1978). Reprinted by permission.

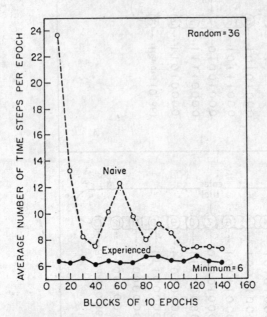

FIGURE 7.6   Comparison of naive versus experienced CS-1 on transfer test (13-node) environment (Holland and Reitman, 1978). Reprinted by permission.

Holyoak, Nisbett, and Thagard, 1986). These subsequent studies have advocated the use of the bucket brigade algorithm similar to that described in the last chapter. Like the epochal algorithm, the bucket brigade provides a rule payoff estimator; however, the bucket brigade uses less recordkeeping and a strictly local computation.

SMITH'S POKER PLAYER

CS-1 spawned a variety of offspring. One of the first was S. F. Smith's LS-1 (Smith, 1980, 1983, 1984). Although LS-1 did process spartan string rules with genetic operators, this was no CS-1 clone; LS-1's architecture was fundamentally different from that of CS-1 in its string rules, the formation of search structures, and its genetic operators. In this section we examine those differences and we consider LS-1's performance in the draw poker task.

The primary difference between CS-1 and LS-1 is illustrated in the schematic diagram of Fig. 7.7. Figure 7.7a depicts a CS-like architecture and shows how individual rules are the basic unit of genetic manipulation; during a computational cycle the apportionment of credit algorithm evaluates rules and during genetic algorithm cycles individual rules are mated and crossed, as shown diagrammatically. By contrast, the LS-like architecture sketched in Fig. 7.7b raises our focus one level and entire *rule sets* become the object of evaluation and

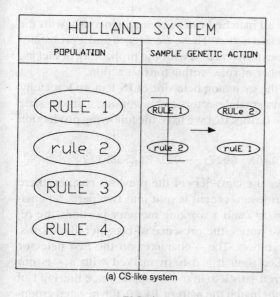

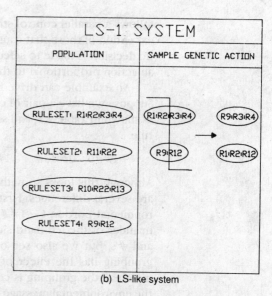

(a) CS-like system   (b) LS-like system

FIGURE 7.7 Comparison of (a) CS-like system and (b) LS-like system architectures. CS-like systems treat rules as individuals for mating and genetic action. LS-like systems treat rule sets as individuals within a population.

genetic manipulation. In this way, rule sets are evaluated as a group after some specified number of plays. Thereafter, rule sets are mated, crossed, mutated, and otherwise genetically altered to create new, possibly better rule sets for evaluation in future plays.

This difference in level of operation is a fundamental one. By raising the level of genetic manipulation one notch, Smith is able to sidestep the apportionment of credit issue (almost) entirely. Since a set of rules stands or falls together, a single measure is all that is required for further computation; no effort need be expended to determine an individual rule's contribution to the whole. On the other hand, the lack of credit assignment is also the method's greatest drawback. Because feedback comes so infrequently, learning in an LS-like system tends to come after relatively large blocks of trials. Nonetheless, the system's performance in its poker domain is impressive, and we study some of its important characteristics in more detail.

LS-1 contains an inference engine and rules that are an interesting blend of a "normal" production system and a classifier system. In Smith's system, working memory consists of an unordered set of fixed-length, binary elements. A working memory element is subdivided into a signal portion and a data portion. Production memory consists of an unordered set of rules where each rule is a fixed-length string. The rule antecedent (condition) consists of k fixed patterns; the first i attend to i environmental detectors, and the remaining $k - i$ patterns attend to signals contained in working memory. Like a classifier system, Smith follows a parallel control strategy: all matched rules fire simultaneously with the exception of those that cause external action. These are flagged and a probabilistic decision is made to select one external action with the probability of picking an action proportional to the number of rules voting for that action.

An example can drive home the matching behavior of LS-1 more forcefully. Suppose we have a pair of environmental detectors and a working memory state as shown in Table 7.1, and suppose further that we have the following production rule:

$$-1\#\#0 \quad 0\#\#0\# \quad 1\#\#X \quad 0\#0X \quad 001Y \quad \rightarrow 011 \text{ REASSERT}(Y)$$

Although this looks something like the classifiers of the previous chapter, there are several differences. First, the rule antecedent is split into two parts, an environmental portion ($-1\#\#0$ $0\#\#0\#$) and a working memory portion (the remainder of the left-hand side). We notice the presence of classifier-like 0's, 1's, and #'s, but we also see other symbols. The $-$ character on the first detector grouping has the effect of a logical not: if a pattern marked with a $-$ is not matched, the grouping is considered satisfied. In the example, since the 1111 of the environmental message does not match the pattern $1\#\#0$, the negated grouping is matched. Continuing with the example (and scanning, as LS-1 does, from left to right), the second environmental message (01001) matches the second grouping pattern $0\#\#0\#$. Following an environmental match, working memory is scanned for a match on the working memory groupings. In LS-1 each working

TABLE 7.1   Example of Rule-Memory Interaction in LS-1

Memory at Time T					
Environmental Detector Array			**Working Memory**		
				SIGNAL	DATA
1	2		(1)	100	1111
1111	01001		(2)	010	
			(3)	110	101010
			(4)	001	101
			(5)	000	1111

Rule
$-1\#\#0$ $0\#\#0\#$ $1\#\#X$ $0\#0X$ $001Y$ $\rightarrow 011$ REASSERT(Y)

Working Memory Element Posted at Time T + 1

011	101

Source: Smith (1980). Reprinted by permission.

memory grouping consists of a prefix, a pattern, and a suffix. Like the environmental portion, working memory rule portion patterns may be prefixed by a not (the – symbol); they also may be prefixed by an ignore symbol. The ignore symbol causes the interpreter to ignore the particular grouping. The subpattern suffix may be null, X, or Y. X and Y are two variable names permitted within LS-1. When first encountered (scanning left to right), a variable takes on the value associated with the corresponding data component contained in working memory. In the example, the signal 100 matches the pattern 1## and thereafter the variable X becomes instantiated with the data pattern 1111. Following this instantiation, the presence of an X causes substitution by the instance value and the rules of matching proceed as per usual. In the example, pattern 0#0 is matched by the second signal (010); however, this is not a complete match because the now-instantiated variable X has a value 1111, which does not match the corresponding data component of working memory slot number 2. Scanning down working memory we observe that the grouping is matched by working memory element number 5 because the signal 000 matches the pattern 0#0 and the value of variable X (1111) matches the contents of the data component of working memory. The last pattern is matched by the fourth working memory element (001 matching 001), and the variable Y is set to the value 101.

The X and Y variables give LS-1 rudimentary capability to recognize equality among data elements. Moreover, they provide the system with the ability to pass information from the left-hand side to the right-hand side. Once a rule is completely matched on the left-hand side, it fires by doing two things. First, it posts its signal to an available working memory slot. Then, the rule evaluates its *action* and action *argument* to determine what to post to the working memory slot data portion. In the example, once the rule is completely matched, its signal component is sent to working memory and the action (REASSERT) is executed. The REASSERT action simply places a copy of the instantiated variable in the data component slot of working memory associated with this rule's signal. Thus, in the example match, the particular rule generates a working memory element with signal component 011 and data component 101, as shown in Table 7.1. The actions on a rule's right-hand side may be task-independent (like REASSERT) or they may be task-dependent (like "I see your five dollars and raise you five dollars").

The rule structure and inference mechanism are straightforward, as is the genetic processing. LS-1 incorporates four operations in its genetic algorithm:

1. Reproduction
2. Mutation
3. Modified crossover
4. Inversion

The reproduction and mutation operations are much like those discussed in earlier chapters. During crossover, because the structures are of variable length, some care must be taken to insure that meaningful building blocks are exchanged. In LS-1 this is accomplished by performing modified crossover in three steps:

1. Alignment
2. Site selection
3. Exchange

This differs from simple crossover in the addition of the alignment step. Suppose we have two rule set structures RS_1 and RS_2 as follows:

$$RS_1 = R1:R2:R3,$$
$$RS_2 = R8:R9:R4:R7:R6:R5,$$

where the R's stand for different string rules and the :'s are rule boundaries. During alignment a random rule boundary site is selected for each rule set structure and the structures are slid until these two boundaries are aligned. For example, suppose we pick an alignment site of 1 for RS_1 and a site of 3 for RS_2. The resulting alignment before crossover is as follows:

$$RS_1 = \qquad\qquad R1:R2:R3,$$
$$RS_2 = R8:R9:R4:R7:R6:R5$$

Thereafter, with the rules aligned at boundaries, LS-1 permits selection of a crossing site at any of the aligned boundaries or within any of the aligned rules. A parameter (P_{c-rb}, the probability of crossover at a rule boundary) may be adjusted to control the proportion of crosses performed at the rule level or at the bit level. When the crossing site is thus selected, exchange of substructures proceeds as with the simple crossover operator described in Chapter 3.

The inversion operator is performed as discussed in Chapter 5, with the restriction that inversion sites be chosen at rule boundaries. Thus, if an inversion is performed on RS_2 at the sites shown below:

$$RS_2 = R8:R9:R4:R7:R6:R5,$$

the resulting string following inversion is obtained by flipping the included section end over end as follows:

$$RS_2 = R8:R7:R4:R9:R6:R5.$$

These operators, together with normal reproduction and mutation, specify the genetic algorithm used in LS-1.

LS-1 Performance

In the original study Smith used LS-1 to search for good sets of string rules in Holland and Reitman's (1978) maze-running task and in a draw poker task. Unfortunately, in the maze-running task, Smith presented a different performance measure from that used in the CS-1 study, so direct comparisons between the two studies are not possible. Smith primarily viewed the maze-running task as a pa-

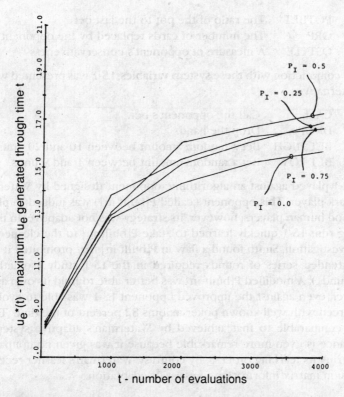

FIGURE 7.8 **Off-line performance of LS-1 on Holland and Reitman maze-running task varying the inversion probability P_I (Smith, 1980). Reprinted by permission.**

rameter tuning exercise. One interesting series of tests varied the inversion probability to determine its effect on rate and level of convergence. The results of that test are reproduced in Fig. 7.8. These results are one of the first clear indications of the need for inversion in any artificial genetic search application.

The draw poker task was LS-1's primary test. Smith adopted the problem definition used by Waterman (1968) in an earlier study of machine learning. The game was a standard two-man game of five-card draw poker except that discard decisions were made algorithmically (the discard decision was made by a fixed algorithm; the learning system was not faced with learning to discard intelligently) and players were limited to a three-card draw. The system detectors consisted of the following variables:

VDHAND	The value of the hand
POT	The amount of money in the pot
LASTBET	The amount of money last bet
BLUFFO	A measure of the chance of bluffing success

POTBET   The ratio of the pot to the last bet
ORP   The number of cards replaced by the opponent
OSTYLE   A measure of opponent's conservativeness

In conjunction with these system variables, LS-1 was presented with four decision alternatives:

CALL   Call the opponent's bet.
DROP   Drop the hand.
BET HIGH Bet a random amount between 10 and 20 units.
BET LOW   Bet a random amount between 1 and 9 units.

LS-1 played against an algorithmic opponent designed by Waterman as a benchmark player. This opponent (called P[built-in]) was judged to play on a par with good human players; however, its strategy was not adaptive. In the original learning runs LS-1 quickly learned to "take P[built-in] to the cleaners." Upon further investigation, Smith found a flaw in P[built-in] that prohibited it from playing the extended series of rounds required in the LS-1 study (something like 40,000 rounds). A modified P[built-in] was better able to hold its own against LS-1; however, even against the improved opponent LS-1 was able to evolve rule sets that agreed with well-known poker axioms 82 percent of the time. This performance is comparable to that achieved by Waterman's adaptive system. LS-1's performance is even more remarkable because it was given no nonpayoff information during its learning process. By contrast, Waterman's learner received explicit decision matrix information to assist its adaptation.

OTHER EARLY GBML EFFORTS

CS-1 begat LS-1 and together they have begotten a growing family of genetics-based machine learning efforts. This section reviews a number of these efforts, including Booker's food and poison learner, Wilson's EYE-EYE and ANIMAT systems, and my dynamic control classifier system.

Seeking Food and Avoiding Poisons

Booker explored the connections between classifier systems, natural intelligence, and artificial intelligence in his doctoral dissertation (1982). His study paved the way for further GBML efforts by investigating three things:

1. Connections between classifier systems and cognitive science
2. Modifications to genetic algorithms that facilitate machine learning applications
3. Applications of classifier systems to the problem of finding food and avoiding poisons in a two-dimensional space

Booker's study is well grounded in the principles and literature of cognitive sci-ence. The interested reader is encouraged to sample the fruits of his abundant orchard; however, in keeping with our practical bent, we partake of only the ripest (and most directly applicable) of his crop. We concentrate on his innovations in GA usage and his two-dimensional learner.

Booker adopted a classifier system with direct roots in CS-1. The system used Holland-style classifiers, a bucket brigade apportionment of credit mechanism, and a genetic algorithm. To look deeper inside the gray matter, Booker changed the CS-1 architecture to the one shown in Fig. 7.9. The structure is similar to the generic description of Chapter 6 and to the structure of CS-1 in the presence of effectors, detectors, a message list, and a classifier store; however, in the figure we notice a significant difference. Booker's system contains two classifier stores and two message lists. This was done as a matter of experimental convenience; because Booker was interested in the mental conclusions drawn by his system, he separated those conclusions from their translation into action by splitting both classifier store and message list.

Prior to cranking out learning runs on his food and poison environment, Booker studied a number of genetic operators in a pattern-searching task. He created populations of ternary strings (over the classifier alphabet {0, 1, #}) and compared them to binary strings of the same length generated at random by a specified schema. For example, in one experiment he generated binary strings of length 16 at random using the template:

```
1111111111******
```

Populations of ternary strings (something like classifier conditions without ac-tions) were used to classify these strings using various match score measures as the fitness function for further genetic search. In different experiments he devised and used different match score measures. Thereafter, GA results under the differ-

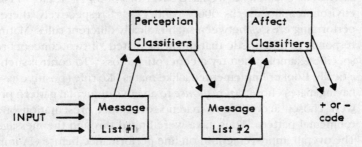

FIGURE 7.9 The food-poison classifier system used a split architecture for ex-plicit examination of the system's gray-matter (rules and internal messages) fol-lowing learning (Booker, 1982). Reprinted by permission.

ent match scores were compared on the basis of on-line and off-line correct classification. These experiments led to the choice of a match score calculated as follows:

$$\text{match score} = \begin{cases} \text{if the taxon matches} \\ \text{NCARES} + (\text{taxon length}) \\ \text{otherwise, 1 for each correct attribute} \\ \text{plus } 0.75 \text{ for each } \# \end{cases}$$

Controversy continues over the utility of such partial matching. Booker has introduced other match scores (Booker, 1985) that answer some of the objections to his early measure; however, a number of researchers are opposed to any form of partial matching. The importance of this issue becomes clear if we view the matter architecturally. A classifier system may be thought of as a highly connected network (much like a neural or connectionist net). Who matches whom (and how strongly) determines which units are directly connected to one another. Partial matching answers the question by saying that all units are connected to one another to some extent. All-or-nothing matching says that network wiring is restricted. This controversy will be put to rest only when theoretical arguments using an appropriate mathematical framework (Holland, 1986b, 1987a) are developed and backed by confirming simulation results.

To improve the genetic algorithm's performance on problems with multiple patterns, Booker introduced two mechanisms: *sharing* and *marriage restriction*. We have already considered the theory of sharing in Chapter 5. In Booker's implementation, taxa (conditions) that matched the same pattern shared in the payoff from that activation. In that implementation, payoff was shared according to match score. This creates an effective crowding pressure to limit the growth of any one taxon class.

We also examined the motivation behind marriage restriction in Chapter 5. Briefly, in a population of classifiers serving multiple patterns, crosses between different subpopulation members are unlikely to assist the search for better classifiers. For example, if we have two rules 000#1#:1 and 111##0:0 serving the environmental patterns 000*** and 111*** respectively, there is little profit in performing crosses between such radically different rules. Mating restriction corresponds to a heuristic that might be stated "if two concepts relate to the same specific example, then try a conceptual cross." To control such mating probabilistically, Booker implemented a like-mates-like rule (positive assortative mating) by having mates chosen *in response* to an environmental pattern presentation. Mates were chosen according to match score under presentation of a particular environmental pattern. Thus, taxa were linked through the messages they classified. The overall improvement in on-line performance before GA improvements (plan G0) and after GA improvements including sharing and mating restriction (plan G2) is shown in Fig. 7.10.

After investigating GA improvements, Booker ran a series of experiments where he permitted the classifier system to wander about a two-dimensional.

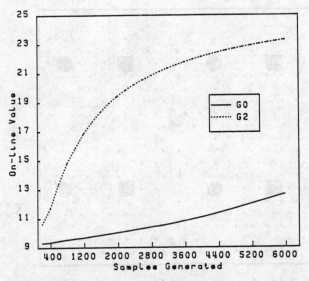

FIGURE 7.10 Comparison of on-line results before (G0) and after (G2) genetic algorithm improvements in Booker's (1982) pattern-search experiments. Reprinted by permission.

hexagonally discrete space similar to that shown in Fig. 7.11. In the space were two types of objects, food (squares) and poison (circles). Each type of object emitted an intensity aura similar to those shown in Fig. 7.12. As the classifier system wandered about its space, it could make three possible decisions: AP-PROACH, EXPLORE, and CONSUME.

In one such learning experiment (Fig. 7.13), classifier system performance was compared by varying the system's LEARNRATE. LEARNRATE is the period between GA learning events. As we observe in the figure, when the LEARNRATE was set less than the nominal period of reward, the evaluation process tended to be noisy and the system reached a steady-state level of error production, as shown in the graph. When the GA period was lengthened (LEARNRATE values 20 and 30), evaluation tended to be more reliable and the error production went to zero. Another comparison is shown in Fig. 7.14 in a run with and without genetic algorithm. The run with GA developed a set of rules over time capable of taking the error production to zero, while the run without GA was unable to halt the production of errors.

Eye-Eye Coordination

Contemporaneous with Booker's classifier system development, Wilson (1981, 1985a, personal communication July 8, 1987) was working on a classifier system for the sensory-motor coordination of a movable video camera (we call this sys-

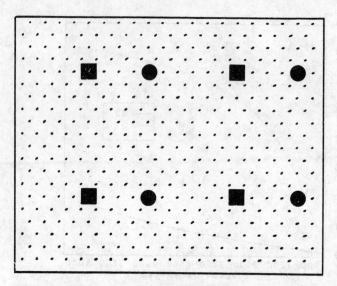

FIGURE 7.11 Food (squares) and poison (circles) environment explored by Booker's (1982) classifier system is laid out in a hexagonally discrete grid.

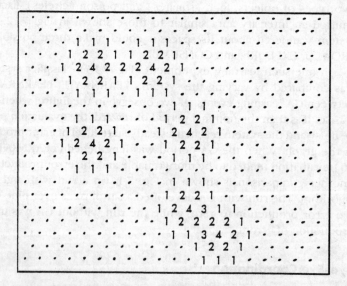

FIGURE 7.12 In the food-poison environment, both foods and poisons emit an aura that acts at a distance (Booker, 1982). Reprinted by permission.

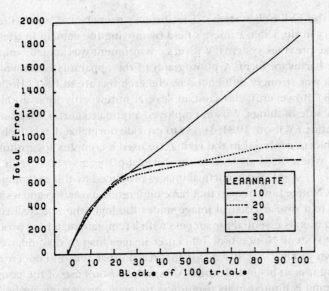

FIGURE 7.13 Food-poison classifier system learning as a function of LEARN-RATE (Booker, 1982). Reprinted by permission.

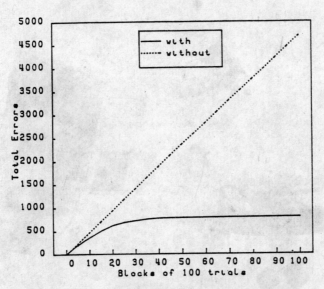

FIGURE 7.14 Classifier system error production with and without genetic algorithm (Booker, 1982). Reprinted by permission.

ten, the EYE-EYE system). The system's primary task was to learn to center an object in the video camera's field by moving the camera in the proper direction. Unlike previous systems, Wilson's environment was actually implemented in real-time hardware form. A photograph of the apparatus is shown in Fig. 7.15. The work was strongly influenced by the architecture of CS-1 (Holland and Reitman, 1978); however, it did contain several noteworthy innovations. On the nongenetic side of things, Wilson employed a retina-to-cortex mapping with precedent in nature (Wilson, 1981, 1983) to provide normalized, relatively invariant images of objects centered in the retina. He used a complex logarithmic mapping $w = \ln z$, where $w = u + iv$ in the cortical plane, $z = x + iy$ in the retinal plane, and $i = \sqrt{-1}$. Some cortical images produced by this mapping are shown in Fig. 7.16. Notice how images that have undergone a rotation and a size transformation map to a similar cortical image under the logarithmic transformation. Such normalization is essential for success with a template matching procedure like a classifier system. Notice how off-center images map to dissimilar cortical images as shown in Fig. 7.17. It was for this reason that Wilson concentrated on the centering task in his initial study. Although Wilson's use of the complex logarithmic mapping is limited in its usefulness to image processing applications, the idea of a mapping that produces relatively invariant detector images may be useful in many areas.

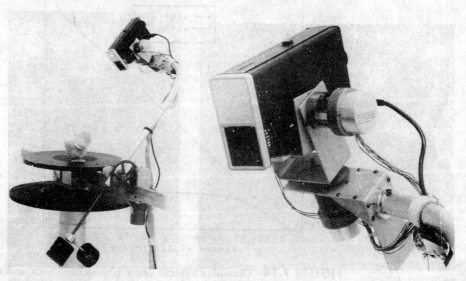

FIGURE 7.15 Photograph of Wilson's EYE-EYE classifier system apparatus. Printed by permission of S. W. Wilson.

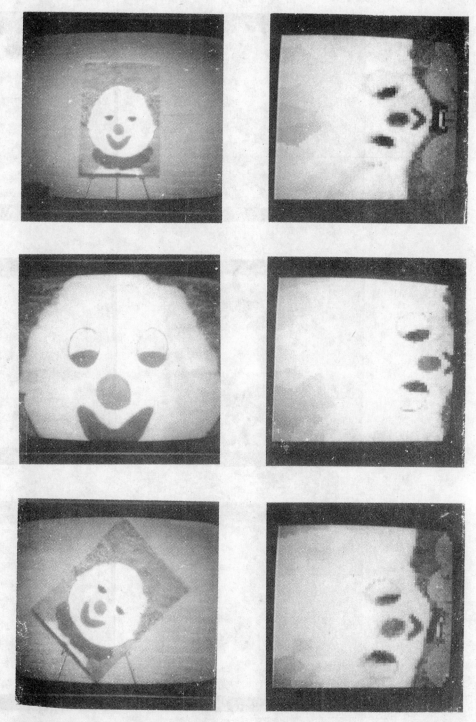

FIGURE 7.16 Complex logarithmic transformation of images in normal, enlarged, and rotated perspective. Notice similarities maintained in cortical images (right side) despite shifting of retinal (left side) images (Wilson, 1985a). Reprinted by permission.

FIGURE 7.17 Off-center images under complex logarithmic mapping do not bear much resemblance to their centered cousins (Fig. 7.16). This places a premium on the centering task, precisely the task Wilson (1985a) undertook in the EYE-EYE system. Reprinted by permission.

Architecturally Wilson's classifier system was similar to CS-1. One difference was evident in the rule structure he adopted. The conditions in this system were not the usual one-dimensional string pattern. Instead, a 4×4 array of ternary characters was used as an image template. For example, a rule in Wilson's system might look something like the following:

```
####
##11
###1  :3
####
```

This rule will fire when a triangular pattern of 1's is detected in the cortical image. To use these two-dimensional structures, Wilson devised a two-dimensional crossover operator that he termed *checkerboard crossover.* His description of the mechanics of this operator is somewhat vague, however, and no theoretical disruption probability limits were calculated, nor was a definition of a schema given for this type of operator.

Nonetheless, successful experiments were run on the EYE-EYE coordination apparatus, although detailed results from these experiments were never published. The system did learn appropriate rules to move the camera and thereby center the object in the video camera image. Work on this system immediately led to experiments with a more controllable environment and simpler classifier system architecture in Wilson's ANIMAT.

The ANIMAT Classifier System

Work with the EYE-EYE system convinced Wilson of the need to simplify his apparatus and perform simple parametric experiments in a well-controlled environment. This led to the development of his ANIMAT system (Wilson, 1985b, c, 1986d). Inspired by Booker's two-dimensional critter, Wilson developed a roaming classifier system that searched a two-dimensional *woods,* seeking food and avoiding trees. Laid out on an 18 by 58 rectangular grid, each woods contained clusters of trees (T's) and food (F's) placed in regular clusters about the space. A typical woods is shown in Fig. 7.18. The ANIMAT (represented by a $*$) in a woods has knowledge concerning his immediate surroundings. For example, suppose ANIMAT is surrounded by two trees (T), one food parcel (F), and blank spaces (B) as shown below:

```
B T T
B * F
B B B
```

This pattern generates an environmental message by unwrapping a string starting at compass north and moving clockwise:

```
T T F B B B B B
```

Under the mapping $T \rightarrow 01$, $F \rightarrow 11$, $B \rightarrow 00$ (the first position may be thought of as

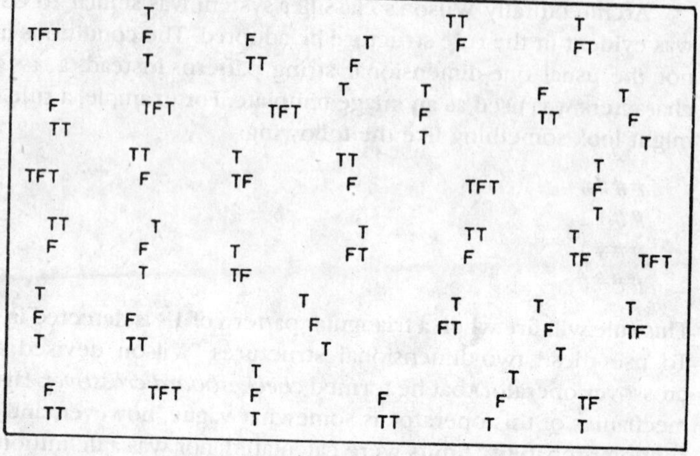

FIGURE 7.18 The ANIMAT system learned to roam around a *woods,* seeking food (*F*'s) and avoiding trees (*T*'s) (Wilson, 1985b). Reprinted by permission.

a binary smell detector and the second position as a binary opacity detector) the following message is generated:

```
0101110000000000
```

ANIMAT responds to environmental messages using simple classifiers with 16-position condition (corresponding to the 16-position message) and eight actions (actions 0–7). Each action corresponds to a one-step move in one of the eight directions (0 = north, 1 = northeast, 2 = east, and so on). For example, the rule

```
0#011#00000#0#:2
```

is matched by the example message above and dictates a fairly sensible move (for a hungry classifier system) to the east where food exists. ANIMAT is assumed to eat any food present in its square (a compulsive automaton?).

The system contains a number of innovations in its performance and genetic subsystems:

1. Match set, action set tracking with sharing
2. Create operator
3. Partial intersection operator
4. Time-to-payoff estimation

The matching process within the performance subsystem identifies the match set [*M*], the set of all classifiers matched by an environmental message. Thereafter, a strength-weighted roulette wheel selection is undertaken to decide the next action. The subset of [*M*] that agrees with this selected decision is called the *action set* [*A*]. These classifiers have their strength values reduced by a percentage and this pool of strength payments is then divided among the members of the previously active action set $[A]_{t-1}$. In this way Wilson induces an *implicit bucket brigade* where environmental reward is implicitly passed up the activating chain of rules. A similar mechanism was built into the simple classifier system (SCS) of Chapter 6 (and not used in the multiplexer problem); however, recall that SCS contained no sharing. Wilson introduces sharing control of the size of classifier subpopulations similar to that suggested by Booker.

Another innovation of the ANIMAT system is its use of a *create* operator. When ANIMAT is confronted with an environmental message with no matching classifier, the create operator is invoked. This operator simply takes an imprint of the environmental message and, with specified probability, generalizes each position of the imprint (replacing a 1 or a 0 by a #), thereby creating a taxon guaranteed to match the environmental message. A random action is then selected (an integer between 0 and 7) and appended to the created taxon. This randomly generated hypothesis is thrown into the classifier store, a weak classifier is deleted, and the system proceeds as usual.

The partial intersection operator is something of a cross between a pure crossover operator and a pure intersection operator. During partial intersection, two rules with the same action are selected and aligned. For example, with condition length 8 suppose we select the following two rules:

```
1 0 0 # # 0 0 1 : 6
0 1 # 1 1 0 1 # : 6
       ^              ^
```

Under a pure intersection operator any position with disagreement is replaced by a hash. For the example, this operation results in the following rule:

```
# # # # # 0 # # : 6
```

Wilson recognized that pure intersection might press too heavily toward excessive generality. To overcome this difficulty, he suggested a crossoverlike modification to intersection where two points along the condition are selected at random and intersection is performed only within this limited intersection zone, with the remainder of the genetic material coming from the first selected parent. Using the points marked above with the $\wedge$ sign as intersection sites, we obtain the following result from partial intersection:

```
1 # # # # 0 0 1 : 6
```

Wilson also experimented with a mechanism to assist the formation of short payoff chains in his time-to-payoff estimation scheme. Here, an estimate is kept of the number of steps to payoff from action set to action set. These are updated through a local updating scheme and classifiers are thereafter selected for activation not on the basis of strength alone but rather on the basis of the quotient of payoff and time to payoff. In this way those classifiers are encouraged that receive the highest payoff in the shortest time.

Typical results are shown from a run of ANIMAT in Fig. 7.19. At first, the average time to food is quite long. In the first 1000 trials, learning is quite rapid,

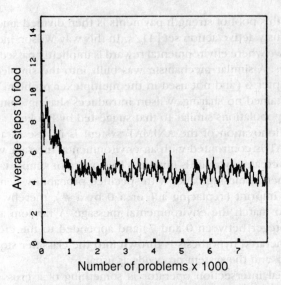

FIGURE 7.19   ANIMAT requires decreasing number of steps to food as learning progresses over 8000 problems (Wilson, 1985b). Reprinted by permission.

with the ultimate average time approaching approximately four steps. For this woods (the woods of Fig. 7.18), the average number of steps to food under a random walk is 41 steps, and the minimum expected time to food is 2.2 steps if ANIMAT had complete global knowledge about food and its location. It is remarkable that ANIMAT learned the task as well as it did considering how little knowledge it actually possessed. For it to do much better, it would have to construct a mental map of the woods so it could know where to go when it was surrounded by blanks. This kind of internal modeling can be developed within a classifier system framework; however, work in this direction has been largely theoretical. Additional work is required before such cognitive maps can be expected to evolve in a classifier system framework.

The Pipeline Operations Classifier System

At about the same time Wilson was finishing his EYE-EYE experiments, I began working on a classifier system for the learning control of a a simulated gas pipeline system (Goldberg, 1983, 1985a–c, 1987a, b). People have often asked me why a gas pipeline and not some other (perhaps more esoteric) system. Prior to returning to school, I worked for an engineering software firm that provided numerical modeling software to the gas pipeline industry. As those models became more prevalent in the operating environment (they had been used for design in one form or another for 30 years), I began to recognize the sharp contrast between the type of modeling and decision making going on in the minds of trained pipeline controllers and that which went on in traditional engineering software (and the minds of the people who design that software). After all, here were pipeline controllers, people with little or no technical training, successfully—and relatively efficiently—running a complex system composed of hundreds or thousands of miles of large-diameter pipe consuming thousands of hours of compression horsepower day in and day out. In essence these people were driving their pipelines as you or I drive our family automobiles. By contrast, engineering software and decision procedures rely heavily on complex mathematical models and methods. These methods are less intuitive and less flexible (albeit more precise) in their approach to the same environment. It was these somewhat naive thoughts that led me to work on something having to do with artificial intelligence and pipeline control. Along the way I bumped into John Holland's courses on adaptive systems at The University of Michigan. At the time, I was more than a bit skeptical of what any of this biological stuff had to do with controlling a gas pipeline; however, I have come to appreciate the beauty of this natural perspective (unfortunately, most pipeliners still share my former skepticism in this matter).

My study was divided into two components: optimization of pipeline operations by genetic algorithm and learning control of pipeline operations by classifier system. The first part of this work is briefly reviewed in Chapter 4. The second part of this work was itself divided into two tasks:

1. Inertial object control task
2. Gas pipeline control task

The inertial object environment is depicted schematically in Fig. 7.20. In this problem the classifier system tries to center the frictionless inertial object by

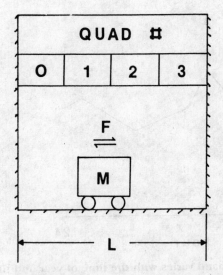

FIGURE 7.20 The first problem for my classifier system (Goldberg, 1983) was to learn to center a frictionless, inertial object in one-dimensional space.

applying a force of specified magnitude to the left or right. This problem was chosen because of its simplicity and because time-optimal control of a frictionless object has a known, yet nontrivial, solution. The inertial object problem turned out to be of interest in its own right as it was one of the first problems to demonstrate the emergence of a default hierarchy.

In the pipeline classifier system, a discrete, first-order system with nonlinear resistance was used to model gas flow dynamics. Gas demand varied depending upon the time of year and the time of day, as shown in Fig. 7.21. The environmental state was transmitted to the classifier system by the detectors displayed in Table 7.2. Inlet and outlet pressure and flow, upstream pressure rate, time of day, time of year, and temperature were all made available to the classifier as shown. Additionally, the pipeline was subjected to random leak events where significant quantities of flow were lost (without explicit measurement) from the upstream end of the system.

In one set of runs, leaks were placed on the system. The system was rewarded if it learned to both operate the pipeline and alarm correctly. The time-averaged point scores for runs with and without genetic algorithm are contrasted to a random walk as shown in Fig. 7.22. An auxiliary performance measure, the percentage of leaks alarmed correctly, is also shown as Fig. 7.23. The results at first seem somewhat counterintuitive as the classifier system run without genetic algorithm does better on the leaks correct measure (over the interval of record) than the run with genetic algorithm; however, the mystery is cleared up if we look at a companion measure, the percentage of false alarms (Fig. 7.24). The run without genetic algorithm buys the high leaks correct percentage at the expense of a large number of false alarms. The run with genetic algorithm avoids this

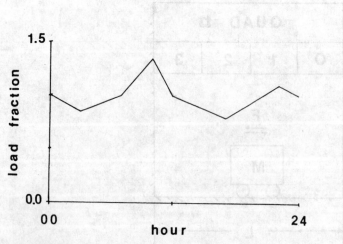

FIGURE 7.21 Gas demand varies with the time of year and time of day in the pipeline classifier system (Goldberg, 1983).

TABLE 7.2   **Environmental Message Template for the Pipeline Classifier System**

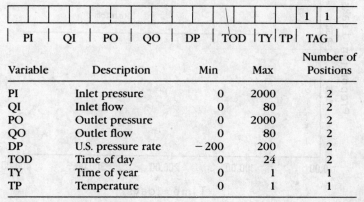

Variable	Description	Min	Max	Number of Positions
PI	Inlet pressure	0	2000	2
QI	Inlet flow	0	80	2
PO	Outlet pressure	0	2000	2
QO	Outlet flow	0	80	2
DP	U.S. pressure rate	−200	200	2
TOD	Time of day	0	24	2
TY	Time of year	0	1	1
TP	Temperature	0	1	1

Source: Goldberg (1983).

undesirable behavior by learning an appropriate leak rule (very much like one that might be programmed by an expert), thereby learning when to alarm and when to be silent.

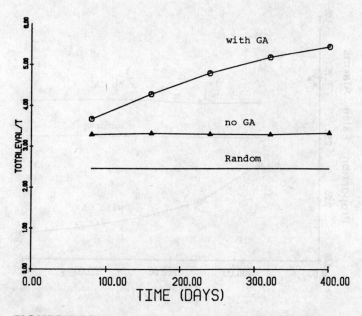

FIGURE 7.22   **Pipeline classifier system leak runs, comparing time-averaged point score versus time (time step = 1 hour). Run with GA beats that without and both classifier runs beat a random walk (Goldberg, 1983).**

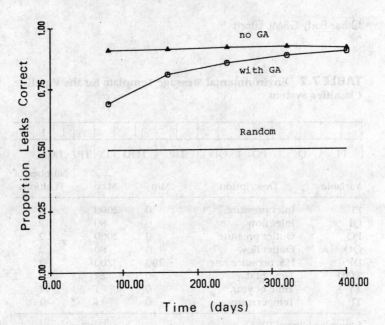

FIGURE 7.23 Pipeline classifier system proportion leaks alarmed correctly. That the run without GA beats the run with GA is counterintuitive until Fig. 7.24 is examined (Goldberg, 1983).

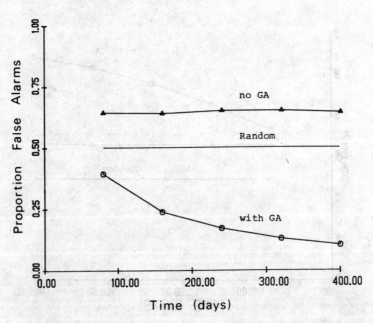

FIGURE 7.24 Pipeline classifier system proportion of false alarms. The run without GA buys its high proportion correct by alarming falsely a high proportion of the time (Goldberg, 1983).

A POTPOURRI OF CURRENT APPLICATIONS

Since these early applications of genetics-based machine learning systems, a number of researchers have carried out theoretical and computational investigations. This section reviews a number of these studies that have significantly extended the boundaries of GBML practice.

BOOLE: A Classifier System Learns a Difficult Boolean Function

Wilson has continued his work in classifier systems with some experiments in boolean function learning (1986a, b, 1987a). Adopting a problem of Barto, Anandan, and Anderson (1985), he has developed a system called BOOLE that learns increasingly difficult *multiplexer* problems. The 6-multiplexer was introduced in the last chapter when we considered the simple classifier system. More formally, we write the 6-multiplexer in disjunctive normal form as follows:

$$F_6 = a'_0 a'_1 d_0 + a'_0 a_1 d_1 + a_0 a'_1 d_2 + a_0 a_1 d_3,$$

where multiplication is a boolean AND operation, addition is a boolean OR operation, and the prime is a boolean NOT operation. This problem may be extended to larger multiplexers. In general, for k address lines there exist multiplexers with $k + 2^k$ lines. Wilson has performed experiments on 6-, 11-, and 20-multiplexer problems in his work.

The classifier system used in BOOLE is very much like that used in the ANIMAT work. The system uses simple classifiers with a single condition (one position per line) and a single binary action (0 or 1). Sharing of payment is performed as in the ANIMAT; however, in BOOLE, no implicit bucket brigade is required because each classifier is immediately rewarded (or not) as a result of its current action.

Results from the 6-multiplexer are shown in Fig. 7.25. The top line shows a 50-trial moving average of the percentage of correct answers. The lower line shows the number of rules in the population that are members of the eight-member correct rule set. Table 7.3 shows a snapshot of the rule population in descending order of strength. Notice that the top eight rules are *exactly* the rules necessary to construct the multiplexer. This accurate learning is noteworthy considering that none of these rules existed in the randomly generated initial population of 400 rules. It is also impressive when compared to results from the learning scheme of Barto et al. (1985). To achieve similar levels of performance, BOOLE required an order of magnitude fewer time steps than did a custom-tailored network of learning units.

In experiments with an 11-multiplexer problem, Wilson added a crossover control mechanism based on a normalized, population entropy measure H_c:

$$H_c = \frac{-\sum_i (S_i/S_T)\ln(S_i/S_T)}{\ln N},$$

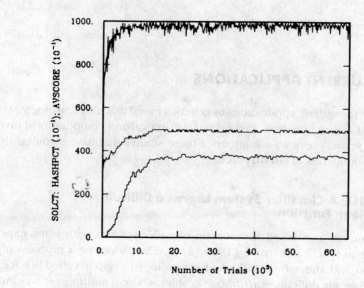

$$SOLCT: HASHPCT\ (10^{-1}); AVSCORE\ (10^{-1})$$

Number of Trials (10^3)

FIGURE 7.25 BOOLE results on the 6-multiplexer. Upper line is the average score over 50 trials. Middle line is hash percentage. Lower line is the number of correct rules (of 400) in the rule population (Wilson, 1987a). Reprinted by permission.

TABLE 7.3 Snapshot of the Classifier Population in BOOLE 6-Multiplexer Problem after 15,000 Trials

Number of Instances	Concept Taxon							Action	Total Strength
56	0	1	#	0	#	#	/	0	7655
52	0	1	#	1	#	#	/	1	7541
48	0	0	0	#	#	#	/	0	7056
46	1	0	#	#	0	#	/	0	7095
45	0	0	1	#	#	#	/	1	6665
41	1	1	#	#	#	0	/	0	5964
39	1	1	#	#	#	1	/	1	6323
35	1	0	#	#	1	#	/	1	5145
7	#	1	#	1	#	1	/	1	1044
4	1	1	#	#	#	#	/		522
3	#	0	#	#	1	#	/	1	293
3	1	1	#	#	0	#	/	0	210
2	#	0	1	#	#	#	/	1	330
2	0	1	1	#	#	#	/	1	212
2	1	0	0	#	0	#	/		150
2	0	0	#	#	#	#	/		219
2	1	#	#	#	1	#	/	1	326
2	1	0	#	0	#	#	/	0	238
1	#	1	#	0	#	#	/	0	129
1	1	0	#	#	#	#	/		168
1	1	1	#	#	#	#	/	0	97
1	1	0	#	#	0	0	/	0	100
1	0	0	#	#	1	#	/	1	81
1	1	#	#	#	#	0	/	0	212
1	1	0	#	#	0	1	/	1	56
1	0	1	#	#	#	#	/	1	116

Source: Wilson (1987a). Reprinted by permission.

where S_i is the total strength of the ith subset of identical classifiers in the population, S_T is the sum of the classifier strengths, and N is the number of classifiers in the population. The control law may be classified as a fixed-percentage, dead-band controller. If the change in classifier system entropy is sufficiently positive or negative, the probability of crossover is decreased or increased respectively by a fixed percentage (10 percent). Otherwise the crossover probability is left alone. The results from these experiments are shown in Fig. 7.26. Here, runs with fixed crossover probabilities of 0.5 (dotted line) and 0.12 (dashed line) are compared to the run with dead-band controller (solid line). Wilson is able to get the best of both worlds using adaptive crossover control, which combines the rapid exploration of a high crossover rate with the ultimate convergence of a low crossover rate as the population hardens. Further experiments are needed to determine the generality of this technique, however.

Preliminary experiments have been performed with BOOLE on a 20-multiplexer problem. In these experiments BOOLE was able to achieve 90 percent accuracy after 70,000 trials and a solution count of 1200 of 1600 rules by trial 120,000. These results are encouraging when we ponder the size of this problem. For a 20-multiplexer, there are $2^{20} \cong 1.05(10^6)$—a million—input strings and $2 \cdot 3^{20} \cong 6.97(10^9)$—7 billion—rules. Thus, by trial 120,000 BOOLE has seen less than an eighth of the possible input strings, and yet the procedure is over 90 percent accurate and still improving. A number of popular, traditional machine learning techniques have been applied to the multiplexer problem without clear success (personal communication, S. W. Wilson, July 8, 1987).

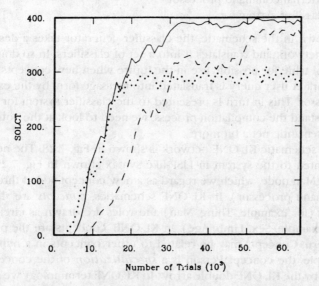

FIGURE 7.26   BOOLE 11-multiplexer results with crossover control. Dotted line is for crossover probability $p_c = 0.5$. Dashed line is for $p_c = 0.12$. Solid line is for entropy-controlled p_c (Wilson, 1987a). Reprinted by permission.

Parallel Semantic Networks in a Classifier Framework: CL-ONE

From time to time members of the symbolic AI community have criticized genetics-based machine learning as too simple to explain high-level concept formation and usage. Forrest (1982, 1985b, c, 1986, in press) debunked this symbol chauvinism in her dissertation by demonstrating the implementation of high-level semantic networks atop a classifier system framework. Forrest concentrated on the performance component of a classifier system (what we have called the rule and message system) stripped of its bucket brigade and its genetic algorithm. She developed a compiler to translate code written in the semantic network language KL-ONE (Brachman and Schmolze, 1985) to classifier system format. At this point you may be wondering why we are paying much attention to a system without a learning component. Forrest's work bridges classifier systems to long-standing concerns of more traditional artificial intelligence (AI) researchers. By successfully mapping the work of symbolic AI researchers to classifier format, Forrest has offered, in a sense, an existence proof that classifier systems can emulate the complex models of symbolic AI. With early genetic learning systems (properly) focused on learning simple things, it may have been difficult for symbolic AI researchers to see how such systems might evolve the needed complexity. Forrest's work suggests such possibilities.

To understand the system (which Forrest now calls CL-ONE), we examine its overall structure in Fig. 7.27. There are four major components:

1. Parser and classifier generator
2. Symbol table manager
3. External command processor
4. Classifier system

As shown in the schematic, the classifier generator takes a description of a KL-ONE network and translates it into a set of classifiers. In so doing, it generates a symbol table for possible use in the future when new concepts are added to the network. A user query is translated into message form by the external command processor. This in turn is presented to the classifier system for computation. To understand the compilation process, we need to look at the notions behind a KL-ONE semantic net a bit more.

A schematic KL-ONE network is shown in Fig. 7.28. The network is actually presented to the system in LISP-like syntax shown in Fig. 7.29 (all except the YoungMan node, which we regard as a new concept added through the external command processor). In KL-ONE schematics, *concepts* are shown as elliptical nodes (for example, Thing, Man) and roles are drawn as circle-square symbols (for example, Sex, Limb, Age). In KL-ONE, concepts are the primary objects of concern. Concepts may be related to other concepts in a number of ways. For example, the concept Person is a *specialization* of the concept *Thing* as indicated by the KL-ONE double arrow. In KL-ONE terminology we say that a SUPERC link goes from Person to Thing (such links are more commonly called IS-A links elsewhere in the AI literature). In words, we say that the concept of a person is

KL-ONE
NETWORK
DESCRIPTION

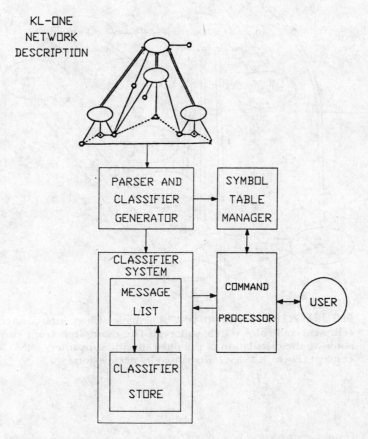

FIGURE 7.27 CL-ONE schematic shows interconnection of the classifier generator, symbol table manager, command processor, and classifier system (Forrest, 1985c). Reprinted by permission.

a specialization of the concept of a thing or that a Person is a kind of Thing (we also say that Thing subsumes Person, but more on this in a moment). In the schematic we also see how concepts are related through *roles* shown as circle-square symbols (Sex, Limb, Age).

In KL-ONE, roles are used to further define concepts. One way they do this is by relating a concept to another concept as shown in the figure. For example, the schematic defines the concept of Man as a Person with sex value Male. In KL-ONE this is done using two separate links. In the example, a ROLE link connects the concept Man with the role Sex and a VR (value restriction) link connects the role Sex with the concept Male. Used in this manner, roles are like the slots in a frame-based knowledge representation language. Note that some concepts are not defined in terms of others. In KL-ONE these concepts are called PRIMITIVE

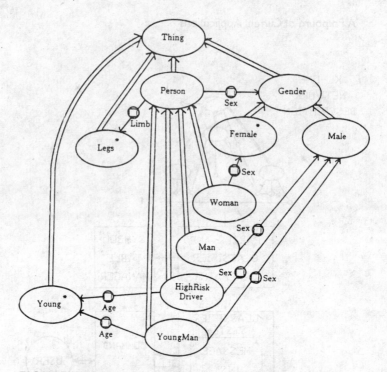

FIGURE 7.28 Sample KL-ONE schematic shows interconnection of concepts (ellipses) and roles (circle-squares). The example is from Forrest's dissertation showing the calculation of the most specific subsumers (MSS) for the YoungMan concept (Forrest, 1985c). Reprinted by permission.

```
(CONCEPTSPEC Person PRIMITIVE
    (SPECIALIZES Thing)
    (ROLE Limb (VRCONCEPT Legs))
    (ROLE Sex (VRCONCEPT Gender)))
(CONCEPTSPEC Legs PRIMITIVE (SPECIALIZES Thing))
(CONCEPTSPEC Gender PRIMITIVE (SPECIALIZES Thing))
(CONCEPTSPEC Male PRIMITIVE (SPECIALIZES Gender))
(CONCEPTSPEC Female PRIMITIVE (SPECIALIZES Gender))
(CONCEPTSPEC Man (SPECIALIZES Person)
    (ROLE Sex (VRCONCEPT Male)))
(CONCEPTSPEC Woman (SPECIALIZES Person)
    (ROLE Sex (VRCONCEPT Female)))
(CONCEPTSPEC Young PRIMITIVE (SPECIALIZES Thing))
(CONCEPTSPEC YoungMan (SPECIALIZES Person)
    (ROLE Sex (VRCONCEPT Male))
    (ROLE Age (VRCONCEPT Young)))
(CONCEPTSPEC HighRiskDriver (SPECIALIZES Person)
    (ROLE Sex (VRCONCEPT Male))
    (ROLE Age (VRCONCEPT Young)))
```

FIGURE 7.29 KL-ONE network specification syntax example (Forrest, 1983). Reprinted by permission.

and are marked on network sketches with an asterisk. For example, the concept Person is PRIMITIVE and requires no further definition. Also note that other KL-ONE links are implemented in Forrest's system. The interested reader can turn to the original work to learn about other link types, how they are used and implemented, and why the particular KL-ONE subset was selected.

All this notational paraphernalia is of interest in its own right, but what can we do with it? One thing we might want to do is ask questions (and get answers) like "Does Woman subsume Man?" (no) and "Does Man subsume YoungMan?" (yes). To answer these questions we must be clearer about *subsumption*. Simply stated, a concept subsumes another if the subsumed concept is connected by a path of SUPERC links to the subsuming concept or if certain relations hold between the definitions of the two concepts. More formally, concept A subsumes concept B if B has at least the same primitive characteristics as A, if every role of A is a role of B, and if the value restrictions of the A roles contains the value restrictions of the respective B roles (actually the subsumption definition is more involved than this because of number restrictions and role value maps; however, we stick to the shortened definition for simplicity). From this definition it is clear why Man subsumes YoungMan. They both have the same primitive (Person*) and the Man role (Sex) is possessed by YoungMan, and the Man value restriction (Male) subsumes that of the YoungMan Sex value restriction (Male). The ability to determine subsumption and maintain inheritance networks is a powerful capability that forms the basis for a number of symbolic AI reasoning systems.

Another question we might like to ask is, what concepts are most closely related to another concept? This kind of automatic classification of concepts is especially important in dynamic knowledge bases where new concepts must be continually assimilated with existing concepts. For example, given the network of Fig. 7.28, we ask which concepts are most immediately related to the YoungMan concept. More formally, we seek the set of most specific subsumers (MSSs) or the lowest (most specific) concepts in the network which generalize the new concept. In fact, the example network we have been discussing is a worked-out example from Forrest's dissertation (1985) of finding the most specific subsumers of the YoungMan concept (Man and HighRiskDriver are the MSSs of YoungMan).

We've been down the pasture and around the barn, trying to pick up a little knowledge about the KL-ONE system, but we have yet to see how Forrest was able to map a KL-ONE network description to classifier form. The key to this process lies in the links. As a simple example, consider the SUPERC link, shown in Fig. 7.30, linking Surfing to the subsuming concept WaterSport. In mnemonic form this link would map to two classifiers as shown below:

```
NORM-WaterSport-SUPERC-DOWN  ⇒ NORM-Surfing-SUPERC-DOWN
NORM-Surfing-SUPERC-UP       ⇒ NORM-WaterSport-SUPERC-UP
```

Here the mnemonics would actually map to patterns of 1's, 0's, and #'s; however, it is interesting to note the use of two classifiers to permit graph traversal in either direction. Other types of links require one or more classifiers to describe the link.

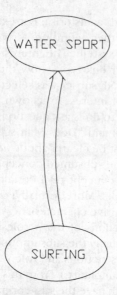

FIGURE 7.30 **Example SUPERC (IS-A) link is used to illustrate the classifier mapping Forrest adopted in the CL-ONE compiler (Forrest, 1985). Adapted by permission.**

Some hint of how this is done can be obtained by examining the Pascal-like classifier description shown in Fig. 7.31. A more detailed description is available in the original work.

The parser and classifier generator together generate this classifier network description. Thereafter, the command monitor posts messages to the message list to initiate subsumption and MSS queries to the system. In addition, Forrest implemented other useful arithmetic (addition, maximum, minimum, comparison), boolean (set intersection, union, complement, and difference), synchronization (to coordinate separate activities in time), and memory (push, pop, clear) operations in classifier form. Together these operations provided CL-ONE with a good deal of expressiveness, especially considering the system's "primitive" underpinnings.

A portion of the study is devoted to calculating complexity estimates for the various operations. Not only does Forrest show that such a semantic net system *can* be written in classifier form, she shows that by mapping one classifier to one processor (with appropriate interprocessor communication), network queries can be performed quite rapidly. The work also speculates on the form of a solution to the inverse compilation problem: How can emerging concepts in a learning classifier system be decompiled and presented to a user in a sensible manner? She suggests real-time tracing, static rule analysis, and dynamic problem analysis as three possible methods for attacking the difficult inverse problem; however,

```
type
    tag = (NORM,ON,HOLD,MEM,NUM,PRE);
    boolcontrol = NORM .. MEM;
    compare = (AFIELD,BFIELD,CFIELD);
    name = string;
    message = string;
    numeric = 0 .. 63;

    classifier record = record

    case tag : tagfield

        boolcontrol : /* Structural Variant */
            (tagfield name);

        NUM         : /* Numeric Variant */
            (tagfield compare numeric);

        PRE         : /* PreDefined Message Variant */
            (tagfield message);
    end;

    tag: 0 - 2,
    name: 3 - 31,
    compare: 21 - 25,
    numeric: 26 - 31,
    message: 3 - 31.
```

FIGURE 7.31 CL-One classifier syntax description in Pascal-like declaration (Forrest, 1985c). Reprinted by permission.

the development of these algorithms is not easy because there is very little constraint on the internal representation of external concepts. Nonetheless, Forrest's important work shows that such representations may exist, can calculate efficiently, and therefore may evolve in a classifier system that learns.

Learning Simple Sequential Programs: JB and TB

You may have gotten the impression that genetic algorithms are only good at learning programs written in production rule form. This is not the case. An example of sequential program learning is provided in Cramer's (1985) work. Cramer started from the Turing-equivalent language PL (Brainerd and Landweber, 1974), removed go-to statements, and devised a simple language (PL−) for the calculation of primitive recursive functions. He devised two different coding schemes for the language, JB and TB, and applied modified reproduction and modified genetic operators in a search for a simple binary multiplication program. In this section we examine the language, the codings, the operators, and the results of these experiments.

The PL− language has three primitives and two derived operations, as shown below in LISP-like notation:

```
1. (:INC VAR); Increment variable VAR by one (primitive).
2. (:ZERO VAR); Set the variable VAR to zero (primitive).
3. (:LOOP VAR STAT); Repeat statement STAT, VAR times
                              (primitive).
4. (:SET VAR1 VAR2); Assign VAR1 the value VAR2 (derived).
5. (:BLOCK STAT1 STAT2); Sequentially perform statements STAT1
                      and STAT2 (derived).
```

For example, to implement the multiplication expressed by the Pascal-like notation $V5 := V4 * V3$ we might write the following PL− program:

```
(:ZERO V5)
(:LOOP V3 (:LOOP V4 (:INC V5)))
```

The program works because the variable $V5$ is incremented by 1, $V4$ times, a total of $V3$ times, thus leaving the product of $V3$ and $V4$.

Although PL− is capable enough, in its present form it is not particularly amenable to genetic operation. In attempting to put PL− in more GA-friendly format, Cramer created a language-coding called JB that took ordered triples of integers as instructions:

$$(x\ y\ z),$$

where x is the instruction code, y is the first operand, and z is the second operand. The five instructions are assigned numbers as follows:

```
:BLOCK = 0
:LOOP  = 1
:SET   = 2
:ZERO  = 3
:INC   = 4
```

Under JB, variable operands name the index of the desired variable and statement operands name ordered triple indexes. Furthermore, unnecessary operands and leftover integers are ignored.

For example, the program

```
(0 0 1 3 5 8 1 3 2 1 4 3 4 5 9 9 2)
```

is interpreted as five ordered-triples as follows:

```
(0 0 1); main statement → (:BLOCK STAT1 STAT2)
(3 5 8); statement 0    → (:ZERO V5); operand 8 ignored
(1 3 2); statement 1    → (:LOOP V3 STAT2)
(1 4 3); statement 2    → (:LOOP V4 STAT3)
(4 5 9); statement 3    → (:INC V5); operand 9 ignored;
                          leftover 9 and 2 ignored
```

A careful reading of this code shows that it implements the multiplication operator given before in PL− form. Cramer does not present any results from the use of JB in any genetic trials; however, he abandoned these first efforts because of some limited computational experiments (personal communication, N. L. Cramer, July 20, 1987). He believed that use of Smith's variable-length crossover operators (Smith, 1980, 1983) was insufficient to effect successful genetic search under JB because of the coding's high degree of epistasis; however, without more careful experiments, this conclusion is not firm. Cramer also seemed bothered by JB's potential for creation of programs that do not halt. The use of statement names (instead of the statements themselves) creates the equivalent of an unconditional *goto*. In simplifying PL, Cramer had hoped to create a language with guaranteed halting. JB could and did (albeit rarely) get into an infinite loop.

Cramer's thinking about JB did, however, lead to an implementation of PL− in a tree-based coding that preserved the desired halting characteristic. This tree scheme, called the TB coding, uses parentheses to group instructions to any finite level of nesting. The JB instruction-integer map is used; however, TB is careful to associate the appropriate number of operands with a particular operator. For example, the multiplication program can be written in TB as follows:

```
(0 (3 5) ( 1 3 (1 4 (4 5)))).
```

Cramer did perform learning experiments under the TB coding with modified genetic operators. In his experiments, crossover between mates was taken as the swap of two randomly chosen subtrees. Mutation was performed as the random alteration of an integer. Some caution was exercised under mutation to keep the number of operands consistent with the operator after mutation. Inversion was mentioned but not attempted.

In a search for a binary multiplication operator, Cramer devised a partial reward structure to encourage multiplication-like behavior before the emergence of a correct multiplier. To do this he rewarded three types of near-multiplier behavior:

1. Any program that changed the output variables
2. Any program that used the input variables
3. Any program that calculated an output variable as a multiple of an input variable

In addition, a penalty was imposed on very long strings, and any program that ran beyond a certain time limit was terminated and evaluated. In experiments with populations of size 50 over 30 generations, TB found many multipliers. Cramer compared these results to a control simulation where no partial credit was given for partial solution of the problem. TB with partial credit found 72 percent more correct multipliers than TB with no partial credit. Although these proof-of-principle results are tantalizing, further work is needed to draw firm conclusions about this type of GBML system.

SUMMARY

In this chapter we have examined a number of examples of genetics-based machine learning (GBML). GBML systems discover better computer programs by applying selection, recombination, and other genetic operators to populations of string procedures or programs. We have uncovered the roots of GBML in the early 1960s and have followed its progress to the present time, sampling salient systems along the way.

We have followed the formal establishment of this field from early rigorous underpinnings (Holland, 1962c) to later proposals for schemata processors (Holland, 1971). We have seen how these led to a generalized string language amenable to genetic search in the broadcast language proposal (Holland, 1975), and to the implementation of the first classifier system (Holland and Reitman, 1978) in Cognitive System 1 (CS-1). These earliest efforts have given way to an increasing volume of research that has divided along a number of lines.

One question that has confronted GBML researchers is whether explicit apportionment of credit is necessary or even useful. The affirmative answer has been given by Holland and other classifier system researchers. Apportionment of credit through the bucket brigade (whether to single rules or to rule chains) has formed an integral part of these systems, leading to relatively rapid learning of appropriate behavior in difficult environments. The contrary opinion has been offered by Smith (1980) and others who try to evaluate the usefulness of an entire program only after an extended series of trials. These systems, too, have learned appropriate behaviors in difficult environments, but the two types of systems have never gone head to head using the same performance measures over the same environments. Perhaps such experiments may one day be attempted; however, we should recognize beforehand that judgment of the results will be biased by the selection of performance measure or measures. Rather than trying to "settle the issue," we should encourage parallel experimentation with both types of systems, because each has something to contribute to GBML understanding.

Regardless of where one stands on apportionment of credit, the straightforward syntax of many rule-based GBML systems has raised questions whether such systems can ultimately process the "concepts" of more traditional artificial intelligence systems. We have answered these questions in the affirmative through our study of Forrest's KL-ONE to classifier compiler (the CL-ONE system). This system takes a description of a high-level semantic network and converts it into a classifier system representation. At the classifier level, CL-ONE implements important arithmetic, logical, and network operations. We have noted that CL-ONE contains no learning component. Thus, questions remain whether and how such networks may be learned. Nonetheless, this work does show that the concepts of symbolic AI may be represented and processed in a classifier system framework.

Another question confronting GBML has been the form of program representations. Simple string rules have been the representation of choice for many systems. In parallel-firing systems in particular, simple, independent rules make for a manageable program morsel as rules may be mixed and matched using straightforward recombination operators to find new rules (or rule sets). This convenience does not mean that this is the only way to go, although there is only limited work in GBML with systems using something besides a rule format. The one example we have examined in this chapter, Cramer's work with the sequential language PL−, is one approach that has achieved some success. The sequential arrangement of instructions is closely related to the reordering operators presented in Chapter 5, and perhaps further thinking along these lines may bear fruit.

These and other questions will continue to be asked and answered as we march toward increased use of genetic algorithms in machine learning applications. We may take some comfort knowing that our trek is not a lonely one; many fields offer us helpful hints, analogy, and even some mathematics (Holland, 1986b, pp. 316–317):

> The mathematical framework proposed here holds many elements in common with the mathematics used to study other adaptive systems such as economies, ecologies, physical systems far from equilibrium, immune systems, etc. . . . In each of these fields, there are familiar topics, with mathematical treatments, that have counterparts in each of the other fields. Even an abbreviated list of such topics . . . is impressive: 1) niche exploitation, functional convergence and enforced diversity [ecology]; 2) competitive exclusion [ecology]; 3) symbiosis, parasitism, mimicry [ecology]; 4) epistasis, linkage revision, and redefinition of "building blocks" [genetics]; 5) linkage and "hitchhiking" [genetics]; 6) multifunctionality of "building blocks" [genetics and comparative biology]; 7) polymorphism [genetics]; 8) assortative recombination ("triggering" of operators) [genetics and immunology]; 9) hierarchical organization [phylogenetics, developmental biology, economics, and AI]; 10) tagged clusters [biochemical genetics, immunogenesis, and adaptive systems theory]; 11) adaptive radiation and the "founder" effect of generalists [ecology and phylogenetics]; 12) feedback from coupled procedures [biochemistry and biochemical genetics]; 13) "retained earnings" as a function of past success and current purchases [economics]; 14) "taxation" as a control on efficiency [economics]; 15) "exploitation" (production) vs. "exploration" (research) [economics and adaptive systems theory]; 16) "tracking" vs. "averaging" [economics and adaptive systems theory]; 17) implicit evaluation of "building blocks" [adaptive systems theory]; 18) "basins of attraction" and behavior far from equilibrium [physics]; 19) amplification of small biases submerged in noise on "slow" passage through a critical point [physics]. Any complex system constructed from components interacting in a nonlinear fashion will, in one regime or another, exhibit *all* of these features. A general mathematical theory of such systems would explain both the pervasiveness of these features and the relations between them.

Amen (and thank goodness the list was abbreviated). There is no lack of useful analogy or theory that we may borrow to help guide our search for better GBML. We are further blessed, as compared to our brothers and sisters who toil in the vineyards of "real" (as opposed to artificial) fields, because we may perform careful simulations of controllable size and scope without excessive concern for a match between reality and model. Thus we may observe these nonlinear phenomena *in silico* with a certain detachment, free to pick and choose among them to create more useful learners. With the bounty of the artificial and real worlds spread before us, these are times of high excitement for genetics-based machine learning.

■ PROBLEMS

7.1. Construct an effective rule set for performance of the CS-1 seven-node maze task with and without the notion of a default hierarchy. Compare and contrast the number of rules in each set. Is this a general property? Why or why not?

7.2. Repeat Problem 7.1 for the 13-node maze task and compare the results of the two problems. Explain the transfer task results (Fig. 7.6) in terms of your answer.

7.3. Compare and contrast the *epochal algorithm* of CS-1 to the *bucket brigade* of later classifier systems. Be sure to discuss the computational benefits and drawbacks of both procedures.

7.4. Compare and contrast the Holland classifier system approach to the LS-1 approach developed by Smith. Discuss benefits and drawbacks of each approach.

7.5. Select two papers from the burgeoning literature on neural networks or connectionism. Compare and contrast the learning mechanisms advocated in these systems and classifier systems. Give complete citations of your selected papers and be sure to discuss important similarities and differences. What can connectionists learn from genetic algorithmists and vice versa?

7.6. The following list of strings is to be compared to the taxon 01##100111:

```
0111100111
1111100111
1000011000
0101010101
```

Calculate the match score for each of the strings using an all-or-nothing measure and Booker's partial matching. List advantages and disadvantages for each method.

7.7. In Wilson's EYE-EYE system, a rule condition consisted of a 4×4 array of ternary characters. Devise three different crossover operators for this representation and calculate a lower bound on the survival probability of a schema under each operator.

7.8. In the ANIMAT system, a partial intersection operator was used. Determine the resulting string under partial intersection from the following mates where the intersection sites are marked by the ∧ symbol:

```
1 1 0 # 1 0 # 1 0 1 1 : 4
0 0 1 1 1 0 0 1 0 # 1 : 4
   ∧                ∧
```

Calculate a lower bound on the survival property of a schema under the partial intersection operator.

7.9. Calculate the probability of obtaining the "correct" rule set for BOOLE's 6-multiplexer problem in a population of eight rules if the three alleles are equally likely. Repeat the calculation for the case when a # is selected with probability 0.8 and the 0 and 1 are equally likely.

7.10. In a JB program, how many different programs exist with 10 variables and 10 or fewer statements?

7.11. Design a JB-like language with less epistasis than Cramer's original coding.

7.12. Using Holland's laundry list of nonlinear phenomena as a guide (see Summary), select and read three papers from the literature of one particular phenomenon (the non-GA literature) and write a short essay explaining the phenomenon in words and with simple mathematics. Discuss how an analog of the phenomenon might be useful in a machine learning or search context.

7.13. Using Holland's broadcast language, code broadcast units that perform reproduction and crossover.

■ COMPUTER ASSIGNMENTS

A. Modify the SCS program of the previous chapter to learn to find food in a Wilson woods.

B. Using Cramer's JB language coding, write a program to learn to multiply. Repeat the experiment, using an underlying binary coding of JB (map JB's integers to binary form). Compare and contrast the results from both decimal and binary codings.

C. Modify the SCS program of the previous chapter to perform CS-1's seven-node maze-running task. Perform computational experiments and compare your results to those of Holland and Reitman (1978).

D. Implement a version of the broadcast language in the computer language of your choice.

E. Apply the SCS program to the 6-multiplexer problem of the last chapter, varying the genetic algorithm period, *gaperiod*. Use values of *gaperiod* less than, about equal to, and greater than some nominal period of reward. Compare the on-line performance values of the three runs. Compare your experiments to Booker's LEARNRATE results.

8 | A Look Back, a Glance Ahead

In seven chapters we have but begun a journey through a set of ideas and accomplishments tied together by a single, now too familiar label: genetic algorithm (GA). In retrospect our travels have been unapologetically bottom up. Moving from special case to case with some generalization tossed in for good measure, we have been concerned only with what works and why. We have been little concerned with the complex epistemologies so commonplace in much of the AI literature. Yet even this "flaw" in the organization of this book—like most other things contained therein—has been itself inspired by natural example. Nature is concerned with that which works. Nature propagates that which survives. She has little time for erudite contemplation, and we have joined her in her expedient pursuit of betterment.

This is not to say that our journey has been without philosophical underpinning. In our deeds if not our words, we have been committed to three things: the abstraction of operators and structures from natural example, the analysis of these structures and mechanisms with mathematics, and the application of these abstractions to practical problems. More elegant arguments have been put forth (see Holland, Nisbett, Holyoak, and Thagard, 1986), but even without a more sophisticated case, the stark simplicity of this methodology has revealed a number of notions that ring true.

At the beginning of our inquiry into genetic search, we asked an important, basic question: Given a population of finite structures and their fitness values, what information is available to guide a search for better structures? The answer to this question has remained the same through seven long chapters: highly fit similarities. Without problem-specific knowledge, the only information we can exploit with any confidence is that contained in highly fit similarities among the structures in a population. If we do not permit experimentation with combinations of these highly fit similarities, then we are stuck with the best of what we have already seen.

This starting point is simple but fundamentally unassailable. One may quibble with our refusal to require problem-specific knowledge, but if we need such information, we quickly find ourselves in a logical quagmire: in the beginning, how does problem-specific information find its way into a system? This is not to say that we should refuse to use problem-specific information when it exists; however, we should take some care to recognize when such usage limits the breadth of application of a system or technique. For example, problem-specific knowledge may be used to seed GAs and GBML systems with good structures, thus promoting faster search and learning. Such a use of problem-specific information does not limit the subsequent application of the core learning or search algorithms to other problems. By contradistinction, the use of problem-specific knowledge to generate heuristics or operators tailored to a particular application risks a loss of generality that may very well prevent the use of a system in any but the original environment. Thus, if we are serious about the development of canonical search and learning procedures, we must, at the very least, start from the less knowledge-intensive position.

In search, once we accept this as the appropriate starting point, we must quickly turn to methods that efficiently process highly fit similarities with a minimum of disruption. On our journey this has led us to GAs, the fundamental theorem, and schema processing. The careful reader may again question whether we have been doing it right, and much of the implementation history of GAs has revolved around doing it better. Certainly, the myriad implementation decisions involved in the simplest of genetic algorithms leave the approach vulnerable to such attack. Less vulnerable to criticism is the processing power we have identified within GAs called *implicit parallelism,* where many similarities (something like n^3, where n is the population size) are processed in parallel even though only a few (something like n) structures are manipulated during a given generation. The leverage of implicit parallelism is so important, we have used its presence or absence as the divining rod between that which is a genetic algorithm and that which is not.

In machine learning, our march has been even less surefooted. Machine learning, of course, offers manifold opportunities to make mistakes, and there is really no proof that any artificial machine learning system is in the biological ballpark. Yet again some simple contemplation gives us hope if not sure confidence along the way. Imagine the search for artificial intelligence as being played out on the two-dimensional, learning-difficulty field depicted in Fig. 8.1. The usual approach elsewhere has been to demand the development of complex, nonadaptive systems capable of human-level performance (points like A). Learning has been treated as an add-on accessory—a chrome-plated cognitive hubcap—which can easily be added as soon as somebody unlocks the magic door to learning. While this approach has yielded impressive programming efforts, it has not yielded impressive learning behavior and is unlikely to do so. The very complex-

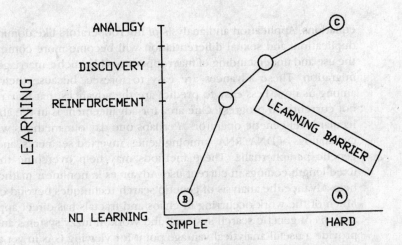

FIGURE 8.1 Construction of complex nonadaptive systems has resulted in systems where learning is difficult. The more evolutionary approach of genetics-based machine learning has resulted in extensible systems that should allow increasingly powerful learning and complexity.

ity of such systems, with their labyrinthine internal structures and algorithms, is itself a barrier to effective learning. By contrast, the genetic approach demands a simpler point of departure (like point B) and an evolutionary (hopefully in cultural time, not biological time) development of complexity amenable to adaptation. The key to the graceful development of increasingly complex learning systems is Holland's notion of a *default hierarchy*. This approach permits the accumulation of overlapping structures with forces of competition, cooperation, and specificity determining prevailing beliefs among conflicting structures. This approach stands in stark contrast to more common methods requiring an unnatural consistency among knowledge structures in some knowledge base.

Unfortunately, the genetic algorithmists' evolutionary development approach has not satisfied those who have sought flashy demonstrations as evidence of intellectual merit, and perhaps this explains the relatively unpublicized development of genetic algorithms over the past 25 years; however, recent studies in search (Davis and Coombs, 1987; Grefenstette and Fitzpatrick, 1985) and machine learning (Wilson, 1987a) are taking us into uncharted and impressive waters for the first time. Furthermore, the sound, extensible underpinnings of these efforts will make further improvement and· growth in technique possible.

In search, the near future holds a number of advances. Consolidation at the foundations of genetic search are possible and are proceeding. These will include strides in both static and dynamic problem analysis using Walsh functions as well as dynamic analysis using Markov chains and nonlinear difference and differential equations. Application and analysis of microoperators like dominance, inversion, duplication, and sexual differentiation will become more commonplace, as will the use and understanding of macrooperators like niche, marriage restriction, and migration. These advances are easy to foresee, because their beginnings are among us now. Less easy to predict are the advances that may result from work not currently in progress. One area for advancement is in the abstraction of molecular-level genetic operators. Perhaps one day our methods will contain artificial analogs of DNA, RNA, jumping genes, inverted segments, and a host of other genetic paraphernalia. These methods may help overcome the limitations of fixed-length codings in current use. Advances in nonlinear mathematics may also help advance the analysis of genetic search techniques beyond current frontiers. Much of the work occurring in chaos and fractals has direct applicability to the analysis of genetic search systems, and work in fuzzy systems and measures may provide a useful analytical vantage point for viewing GAs in yet another light.

In machine learning, the crystal ball is somewhat cloudier; however, certain extrapolations may be drawn. Classification problems will receive increasing treatment by stimulus-response classifier systems. These techniques are ready for application, and in moderate to large problems they appear to be more than competitive with extant machine learning and connectionist techniques. Further progress will be made in encouraging the evolution of longer chains and networks of classifiers in classifier systems, and some mathematical tools may be borrowed from current analyses of nonlinear neural networks. Of course, apportionment of credit won't be the whole story of progress, and extension and analysis of the notion of triggered operators for the encouragement of network formation is required and underway. In the longer term, there will probably be a unification of genetics-based machine learning architecture toward the original broadcast language proposal. Unification of data and operator (an early advance in the history of computation) has been rightfully delayed until we have a better understanding of some of the complex interactions in our systems; however, such unification will prove logically necessary if these systems are ever to evolve their own improved operators as solutions to new metaproblems are required.

Though these thorny questions slow our pace, and knotty problems cause us pause, our journey is at no impasse. With settlements of proven ideas upon which we may fall back, and outposts of natural notions from which to push forward, we may venture ahead, clearing the path with a machete of mathematics and a scythe of computer simulation. And as we stand at this GA frontier, looking out over myriad opportunities and tasks, we stand tall with the knowledge of what natural genetics has already created, with the confidence of what we have already found, and with the eager expectation of what we are about to discover.

A | Review of Combinatorics and Elementary Probability

Understanding the fundamental mathematics of genetic algorithms is not difficult, but it does require a solid grounding in finite sets, combinatorial counting, and elementary probability. The aim of this appendix is to provide either a short introduction to the uninitiated or a brief refresher course to the rusty. While these words can serve as a temporary bridge to the required concepts, they should not be used as a permanent span to terra firma. This state can only be reached through the careful study of more standard references (such as Feller, 1968; Hines and Montgomery, 1980; Papoulis, 1984; Ross, 1976). Nonetheless, in the remainder of this appendix we count the finite and ponder the probable. We shall consider the counting principle, permutations, and combinations. We define a finite sample space, expound the three axioms of probability theory, and consider some of the important ramifications of those axioms. We briefly consider conditional probability, Bayes' theorem, independent events, and some elementary probability distributions. Finally, we review the expected value of a simple random variable and consider an important limit theorem.

COUNTING

Most of us take for granted the ability to count, but to count exact quantities of patterns, classifications, or distinct groupings is an abstract art form that falls under the heading of *combinatorics* or *combinatorial analysis*. Most of the results of combinatorial analysis derive from a simple fact, the so-called Counting Principle:

> With two experiments M (with m outcomes) and N (with n outcomes), there are $m \cdot n$ total possible outcomes of the compound experiment MN.

The truth of this principle may be established by enumerating the outcomes in matrix form. Instead of doing this, let us examine some simple illustrations of the counting principle in action.

Example 1

A student is certain he will get either an A or a B in Data Structures 101. He is not sure whether he will get an A, B, C, D, or F in Genetic Algorithms 303. How many different grading possibilities are there between the two classes?

Answer: There are $m \cdot n = 2 \cdot 5 = 10$ possibilities. They can be enumerated as follows: AA, AB, AC, AD, AF, BA, BB, BC, BD, BF.

Example 2

How many unique license plates can be constructed where the first three characters are letters of the alphabet and the last three characters are decimal digits?

Answer: There are $26 \cdot 26 \cdot 26 \cdot 10 \cdot 10 \cdot 10 = 17,576,000$ license plates.

Example 3

How many unique license plates can be constructed using the coding scheme of Example 2 when no repetition is permitted among the letters or the digits?

Answer: When we select the first letter, we choose from any of 26 letters. When we pick the second letter we pick from the 25 remaining letters, and so on. As a result there are $26 \cdot 25 \cdot 24 \cdot 10 \cdot 9 \cdot 8 = 11,232,000$ unique license plates with no repetitions of letters or numbers.

Example 4

A United Nations committee contains different numbers of members from different countries as follows: Japan (7), China (3), United States (6). If a subcommittee is formed by selecting one member from each country, count the number of unique subcommittees.

Answer: There are $7 \cdot 3 \cdot 6 = 126$ different subcommittees.

PERMUTATIONS

A permutation is an ordered arrangement of a set of different items. For example, consider the six arrangements of the three letters A, B, and C which are enumerated as follows:

> ABC, ACB, BAC, BCA, CAB, CBA.

More generally, to count the permutations of n unique items, we recognize that we start with n options for our choice of the first object and lose one degree of freedom after each succeeding choice. Therefore, by the counting principle we count the total number of permutations of n objects as follows:

$$\text{Number of permutations of } n \text{ objects} = n(n-1)(n-2)\cdots 3 \cdot 2 \cdot 1 = n!$$

In general, there are $n!$ (read n factorial) permutations of n unique items.

Example 5

How many batting orders are there on a nine-person baseball team?

Answer: $9! = 9 \cdot 8 \cdots 3 \cdot 2 \cdot 1 = 362,880.$

Example 6

Suppose you have 4 genetic algorithm papers (GA), six learning classifier system papers (LCS), one population genetics paper (GEN), and seven artificial intelligence papers (AI). How many arrangements of papers are there if each classification is always grouped together?

Answer: Assume we have a particular ordering of paper classifications, perhaps GA, LCS, GEN, AI. There are $4!6!1!7! = 87,091,200$ arrangements of papers for the assumed classification ordering. Since there are 4! arrangements of the classifications themselves, there are then $4! \cdot 87,091,200 = 2,090,188,800$ classified arrangements of the 18 papers. This is, of course, far fewer than the $18! \cong 6.402(10^{15})$ unclassified arrangements of the same 18 papers.

Sometimes we are interested in the total number of partial orderings of a group of n objects. Suppose we want to count the number of unique orderings of r objects chosen from a set of n objects. We have already performed calculations like this in early counting principle examples. We can generalize the result and count the number of permutations of n objects taken r at a time, symbolically $P(n,r)$ (read n permute r) with the computation:

$$P(n, r) = n(n-1)(n-2)\cdots(n-r+1), \ r \text{ factors.}$$

Using factorial notation, we can write the expression in more compact form:

$$P(n, r) = n(n-1)(n-2)\cdots(n-r+1) = n!/(n-r)!$$

Example 7

How many nine-person batting orders are possible on a 15-person baseball team, assuming every player can play every position?

Answer: $P(15,9) = 15!/(15-9)! = 1,816,214,400.$

COMBINATIONS

Sometimes we are interested in the number of unique groupings of objects irrespective of their ordering. For example, consider the number of unique orderings of three letters taken two at a time:

AB, AC, BA, BC, CA, CB.

There are clearly $3!/(3 - 2)! = 6$ such orderings; however, if we wish to count the number of pairs where the order of the pairs is unimportant (for example, when AB and BA are indistinguishable), then we must divide the number of permutations by the number of duplicates. Since the number of duplicates is equal to the number of orderings of the r objects, the number of combinations among n objects taken r at a time, symbolically $C(n, r)$ or $\binom{n}{r}$ (read n choose r) is simply the number of permutations $P(n, r)$ divided by the number of duplicates:

$$C(n, r) = \binom{n}{r} = \frac{n!}{(n - r)!r!} = \frac{n(n - 1)\cdots(n - r + 1)}{r!}.$$

That this is true may be reasoned more intuitively with the following verbal equation:

$$\begin{bmatrix} \text{The number of } r \\ \text{combinations} \\ \text{among } n \text{ objects} \end{bmatrix} \begin{bmatrix} \text{the number of} \\ \text{orderings of} \\ r \text{ objects} \end{bmatrix} = \begin{bmatrix} \text{the number of } r \\ \text{partial permutations} \\ \text{among } n \text{ objects} \end{bmatrix}$$

Example 8

The U.S. Senate contains 100 senators. How many five-member subcommittees may be formed in this prestigious body?

Answer: Since order of committee selection is unimportant (neglecting ego and seniority considerations), there are $\binom{100}{5} = 75,287,520$ such subcommittees.

Example 9

In five-card draw poker, each player is dealt five cards face down. How many unique deals are there?

Answer: Since order of deal is unimportant, there are $\binom{52}{5} = 2,598,960$ unique deals.

BINOMIAL THEOREM

We state the binomial theorem without proof:

$$(x + y)^n = \sum_{j=0}^{n} \binom{n}{j} x^j y^{n-j}.$$

Because of this fundamental result, the combination quantities $\binom{n}{r} = C(n, r)$ are called the *binomial coefficients*. The result is useful in a number of combinatorial and probabilistic computations.

Example 10

Show that $\sum_{j=0}^{n} \binom{n}{j} = 2^n$.

Answer: $\sum_{j=0}^{n} (1)^j (1)^{n-j} \binom{n}{j} = (1 + 1)^n = 2^n$.

EVENTS AND SPACES

Suppose we perform an experiment with an uncertain outcome. Let us define the *space S* as the set of all possible outcomes. For example, consider a number of spaces:

Flip of a single coin: $S = \{ \text{Heads, Tails} \}$

Roll of a single die: $S = \{ 1, 2, 3, 4, 5, 6 \}$

Flip of two coins: $S = \{ HH, HT, TH, TT \}$

An *event E* is any subset of the possible outcomes. For example, we consider the following events:

At least one head in two tosses: $E = \{ HH, HT, TH \}$

Roll of a die with value greater than 3: $E = \{ 4, 5, 6 \}$

We may construct new events from the union or intersection of the events E and F, symbolically $E \cup F$, as depicted by the shaded area in the Venn diagram of Fig. A.1. The intersection of events E and F, symbolically EF, is illustrated in Fig. A.2. If the intersection of two events is the null set, $EF = \emptyset$, then we call the two events mutually exclusive, as illustrated in Fig. A.3.

Finally, we define the complementary event E^c where E^c contains all events in the space S not contained in the event E. A space S, an event E, and the complementary event E^c are depicted in Fig. A.4.

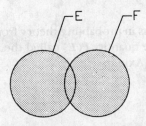

FIGURE A.1   Venn diagram of the union of events E and F.

FIGURE A.2   Venn diagram of the intersection of events *E* and *F*.

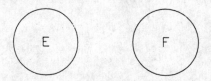

FIGURE A.3   Venn diagram of mutually exclusive events *E* and *F*.

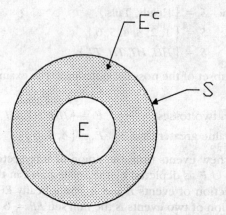

FIGURE A.4   Venn diagram of an event *E* and its complement *E*^{c}.

AXIOMS OF PROBABILITY

There are three axioms or assumptions in probability theory from which all other results may be derived. We define the quantity $P(E)$ called the probability of the event *E*. This quantity must obey the Axioms:

> **Axiom 1**
> $0 \leq P(E) \leq 1$.
> The probability of an event must be between 0 and 1.

Axiom 2

$P(S) = 1$.

The probability of the space must equal 1.

Axiom 3

For any sequence of mutually exclusive events E_i, $i = 1, 2, \ldots$ such that $E_i E_j = \emptyset$ for $i \neq j$,

$$P\left(\bigcup_{i=1}^{\infty} E_i \right) = \sum_{i=1}^{\infty} P(E_i).$$

The probability of the union of mutually exclusive events is the sum of the event probabilities.

The consequences of probability theory result from these axioms; we state several of the important results without proof.

Probability of the Complementary Event

$P(E^c) = 1 - P(E)$.

The probability of the complementary event is one minus the probability of the event itself.

Probability of the Union of Two Events

$P(E \cup F) = P(E) + P(F) - P(EF)$

The probability of the union of two events is the sum of the event probabilities less the probability of their intersection. Although we state this without proof, the result is intuitive if we refer back to the Venn diagram of Fig. A.2. This illustrates clearly the double counting that results when we overlay two overlapping events. The formula above simply corrects this duplication by subtracting off the intersection probability.

EQUALLY LIKELY OUTCOMES

Many common occurrences are considered to be equally likely: the flip of an unbiased coin, the spin of a well-balanced roulette wheel, the roll of an unweighted die, the selection of a card from a well-shuffled deck. If we limit ourselves to events where all outcomes are considered equally likely, the calculation of an event E's probability is quite simple:

$$P(E) = \frac{\text{number of points in event } E}{\text{number of points in space } S}.$$

Example 11

What is the probability of rolling a 1 or a 2 on a fair die?

Answer: $P(E) = 2/6 = 1/3$.

Example 12

What is the probability of rolling an 8 on a pair of dice?

Answer: There are five ways to make 8: $(2, 6), (6, 2), (3, 5), (5, 3)$, and 8 the hard way $(4, 4)$. Thus, $P(E) = 5/(6\cdot 6) = 5/36$.

Example 13

What is the probability that a head appears at least once in 10 tosses of a fair coin?

Answer: Consider the complementary problem (sometimes it pays to look at the hole and not the doughnut). Clearly, there is only one way ($T, T, T, T, T, T, T, T, T, T$) to get no heads out of the 2^{10} possible length-10 sequences. Hence, the complementary probability $P(E^c) = (1/2)^{10}$, and $P(E) = 1 - (1/2)^{10} \cong 0.999$.

Example 14

What is the probability of being dealt a royal flush in five-card draw poker?

Answer: There are four royal flushes (one in each suit) out of the $\binom{52}{5}$ possible deals. Therefore, $P(E) = 4/\binom{52}{5} \cong 1.5\cdot 10^{-6}$

Example 15

What is the probability of being dealt a straight in five-card draw poker?

Answer: A straight consists of five cards in order where all five cards are not of the same suit (that would be a straight flush). To count the number of straights, consider the ordered sequence of cards with a single straight bracketed:

$$[A\ 2\ 3\ 4\ 5]\ 6\ 7\ 8\ 9\ 10\ J\ Q\ K\ A$$

There are clearly $4\cdot 4\cdot 4\cdot 4\cdot 4 = 4^5$ total straights of the A-2-3-4-5 variety because each of the cards may be varied over any of the four suits; however, exactly four of those straights are straight flushes, so there are $4^5 - 4$ ordinary A $-$ 5 straights. The same computation holds true for the other straights in the deck, and by sliding the brackets down the ordered sequence we recognize 10 such straights. As a result, there are $10(4^5 - 4)$ ordinary straights out of the $\binom{52}{5}$ deals. Thus,

$$P(E) = 10,200/2,598,960 \cong 0.00392.$$

CONDITIONAL PROBABILITY

In many real life cases, one event hinges on another and it is easier to talk about or calculate the probability of one event's occurrence given that a related event has occurred. We call this probability, where one event hinges on another, conditional probability; symbolically we write $P(E|F)$, the probability of event E given event F has occurred (or just the probability of E given F). We may write the relationship between conditional probability, the intersection probability, and the probability of the conditioned event as follows:

$$P(EF) = P(E|F)P(F)$$

In words, the probability of the intersection of two events is the product of the conditional probability of one event given the conditioned event and the probability of the conditioned event.

Example 16

Joyce has a choice between two courses, one in genetic algorithms and one in fluid mechanics. If she has a 50 percent chance of receiving an A in the genetic algorithms course and a 75 percent chance of getting an A in the fluid mechanics course, what are her chances of getting an A in the genetic algorithms course if she decides between the two courses on the toss of a fair coin?

Answer: Let A be the event where Joyce receives an A, and let G be the event where she takes the GA course.

$$P(AG) = P(A|G)P(G),$$
$$= 0.50 \cdot 0.50 = 0.25.$$

She has one chance in four of getting an A in the genetic algorithms course, and the fluid mechanics course has no bearing on this outcome.

PARTITIONS OF AN EVENT

Sometimes it is useful to calculate probabilities by partitioning an event into two or more mutually exclusive events as visualized in Fig. A.5. Suppose we are interested in the event E, but we are more familiar with the relationship between events E and F. Recognizing that EF and EF^c are mutually exclusive (see Fig. A.5) and $EF \cup EF^c = E$, we conclude that $P(E) = P(EF) + P(EF^c)$. Furthermore, using the conditional probability results of the last section, we may write another useful relationship:

$$P(E) = P(E|F)P(F) + P(E|F^c)P(F^c)$$
$$= P(E|F)P(F) + P(E|F^c)[1 - P(F)].$$

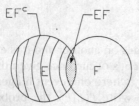

FIGURE A.5   Venn diagram of a partition of E using F and F^c.

Example 17

In Example 16, suppose that Joyce can take fluid mechanics (event F) or genetic algorithms (event G) but not both, and again suppose that she makes her decision with the unbiased coin toss. Calculate the probability of her making an A (event A).

Answer: Partition the A event on the mutually exclusive events G and F:

$$P(A) = P(A|G)P(G) + P(A|F)P(F),$$
$$= 0.5(0.5) \quad\quad + 0.75(0.5),$$
$$= 0.625.$$

BAYES' RULE

A useful relationship may be derived from the partitioning results and the conditional probability formula by noticing that the intersection probability can be obtained by conditioning on either of the two events:

$$P(EF) = P(E|F)P(F) = P(F|E)P(E).$$

This observation leads to Bayes' rule, which is used to calculate conditional probabilities in many important situations:

$$P(E|F) = \frac{P(EF)}{P(F)} = \frac{P(F|E)P(E)}{P(F|E)P(E) + P(F|E^c)P(E^c)}$$

INDEPENDENT EVENTS

Two events E and F are said to be independent when the conditional probability $P(E|F)$ is equal to $P(E)$ alone. Thus, $P(EF) = P(E)P(F)$ for independent events.

Example 18

What is the probability of rolling a deuce on a pair of dice?

Answer: There is one way to make two: both dice must come up showing a one (event 1):

$$P(1+1) = P(1)P(1) = (1/6)(1/6),$$
$$= 1/36.$$

The same result can be calculated by recognizing the deuce as a single outcome of the 36 possible outcomes in the space.

Example 19

Calculate the probability of n heads in n tosses of a fair coin.

Answer: Let H be the event that a coin comes up a head.

$$P(n \text{ of } n \text{ heads}) = P(H)P(H)\cdots P(H) \ (n \text{ times})$$
$$= \left(\frac{1}{2}\right)^n$$

TWO PROBABILITY DISTRIBUTIONS: BERNOULLI AND BINOMIAL

Often we perform a sequence of trials where each trial has a constant probability of success, $P(\text{success}) = p$. The single experiment is called a Bernoulli trial and clearly the two possible outcomes, success and failure, have probabilities that sum to one: $P(\text{success}) + P(\text{failure}) = p + (1 - p) = 1$.

If we perform a sequence of n Bernoulli trials, it is perfectly natural to ask what is the probability of one, two, or in general k successes. Careful consideration shows that the probability of exactly k successes in n Bernoulli trials can be calculated (assuming independence of the trials) as follows:

$$P(k \text{ successes in } n \text{ trials}) = \binom{n}{k}p^k(1 - p)^{n-k}$$

This computation is true because a particular sequence of k successes requires exactly k successes and $n - k$ failures. One particular such sequence has probability $p^k(1 - p)^{n-k}$. Furthermore, since there are exactly $\binom{n}{k}$ different k-of-n sequences, the computation above follows immediately. This probability distribution is called a *binomial* probability distribution.

EXPECTED VALUE OF A RANDOM VARIABLE

There are many times when we would like to calculate the usual outcome of some trial or trials of a random process. More precisely, we say that we would like to calculate the *expected value* of a random variable. In a moment, we will see why the expected value is considered the usual outcome of a random variable. For now, we simply define the quantity.

The expected value of a discrete random variable x is defined as follows:

Expected value of $x = E[x] = \sum_{x} x \cdot p(x)$.

We may also be interested in the expected value of some function of a random variable. This may be calculated as follows:

Expected value of $g(x) = E[g(x)] = \sum_{x} g(x) \cdot p(x)$.

Example 20

A gambler pays $4.00 to roll a single die where he receives the face value in return ($1.00 for an ace, $2.00 for a deuce, etc.). What are his expected net winnings (losses)?

Answer: $E[\text{gross return}] = 1/6 + 2/6 + 3/6 + 4/6 + 5/6 + 6/6$,
$= \$3.50$.

Net expected loss is therefore $4.00 - \$3.50 = \$0.50$.

LIMIT THEOREMS

The previous section hinted that the expected value of a random variable is in some way its usual or average value, but how do we know this? Because the proof of this fact is quite involved, one of the most important limit theorems of probability theory is presented below without proof.

Strong Law of Large Numbers

Assume a sequence of independent, identically distributed random variables $x_i, i = 1, 2, \ldots, n$ with finite expected value. With probability 1:

$$\frac{x_1 + x_2 + \cdots + x_n}{n} \to E[x], \quad \text{as } n \to \infty.$$

We may also want to know how the partial sum is distributed. The central limit theorem tells us that the distribution is normal or Gaussian; the distribution of the sum approaches the well-known bell-shaped curve. We do not need this result specifically for our work, so we leave its description to standard references.

SUMMARY

In this brief appendix we have examined some fundamental results of counting and probability. The purpose has been to review the basics with an eye to understanding the subtle operation of a simple genetic algorithm. To that end we have examined the counting principle and simple combinatorial analysis. We have considered sample spaces, events, and the axioms of probability theory. Some of the important consequences of probability theory, including conditional probability, Bayes' theorem, expectation of a random variable, and the Strong Law of Large Numbers have been examined. With this background, the discussion and analysis of genetic algorithm power will go more smoothly.

■ PROBLEMS

A.1. Eight people are playing musical chairs with six chairs. When the music stops, six people sit down, and two are left standing. How many different arrangements are possible for distributing the eight people in the six chairs? Disregarding the order of seating, how many combinations of six sitters may be chosen from the original eight players?

A.2. How many unique permutations may be formed from the letters of the following words:
 a) turgid
 b) sleeper

A.3. A credit card number is constructed as a 10-position code where each position is taken from the full alphabet (A–Z) or the decimal digits (0–9). How many different credit card numbers may be constructed in this manner? In storing the credit card code on a binary computer, a programmer wants to use the minimum number of bits (1's and 0's) to represent the code. Calculate the length of the minimum binary code required to hold the credit card code.

A.4. A committee consists of 13 freshman, 6 sophomores, 7 juniors, and 5 seniors. If a committee chairman is chosen at random, what is the probability that the chairman is a) a senior; b) a freshman; c) not a sophomore; d) a freshman or a junior.

A.5. In five-card draw what is the prior probability of being dealt four of a kind?

A.6. A drawer contains 20 white socks and 10 black socks. If five socks are selected all at once and at random, what are the chances of picking exactly two black socks? How does the answer change if the socks are replaced in the drawer after each selection?

A.7. On a multiple-choice exam with four answers per question and five questions, what is the probability of getting four or more questions correct by random guessing?

A.8. A gambler has two coins in his left pocket. One is fair, the other is two-headed. A coin is selected at random from this pocket and tossed. Calculate the probability the coin will come up heads. If it does come up heads, what is the probability that the chosen coin is the fair coin?

A.9. A million-ticket lottery pays prizes as follows:

1	ticket pays	$500,000
10	tickets pay	$50,000
100	tickets pay	$1,000
1000	tickets pay	$100
10,000	tickets pay	$10

If a ticket costs $2.00, what is a ticket holder's expected loss in this lottery? What is the probability of winning some prize?

A.10. Show that a binomial probability distribution $p(j) = \binom{n}{j} p^j (1 - p)^{n-j}$, $j = 0, 1, \ldots, n$, is a probability distribution.

B | Pascal with Random Number Generation for Fortran, Basic, and Cobol Programmers

This book uses Pascal as the programming language of choice. The availability of inexpensive, high-quality compilers (see for example, Borland International Inc., 1985) for personal computers has partially guided this decision. The high degree of standardization and the well-structured nature of the language have helped clinch the deal. Since many readers are not familiar with the language, in this appendix we devote a little time to introducing its essentials. This is by no means an exhaustive examination of Pascal; there are many fine books for this purpose. Instead, we try to bootstrap our way into enough knowledge so the experienced programmer can read and possibly write simple Pascal code. Specifically, we look at four simple computer programs to get a feel for Pascal's data structures and algorithmic devices. We also examine a set of portable routines for generating random numbers.

SIMPLE1: AN EXTREMELY SIMPLE CODE

Let's dive right in and take a look at a very simple Pascal code called *simple1*, shown in Fig. B.1. This program prints out a two line message:

```
Bullwinkle is a dope
No Rocky, not that message
```

```
program simple1;
{ simple1: print out a message }
begin
 writeln(' Bullwinkle is a dope ');
 writeln(' No Rocky, not that message ')
end.
```

FIGURE B.1   Pascal program *simple1*.

To do this simple (but admittedly not very purposeful) task, very little paraphernalia is required, as you can see from the code. The program starts out with the identifier *program* followed by the name of the program, which in this case is *simple1*. We separate this line of the code from the other lines with the Pascal line separator symbol, the semicolon (;). In Pascal the semicolon is not an end-of-line marker as in PL/1 or other languages; it is only required in locations where division is syntactically necessary.

Following the program header we have placed a comment to remind us what this piece of code does. In Pascal, comments are enclosed in brackets ({this is a valid Pascal comment}) and good programming practice dictates that we sprinkle them liberally throughout the code as signposts for others or as reminders to ourselves when we return to the code after a long interval of inattention.

The code actually starts following the comment. In Pascal, a program begins with the *begin* identifier and ends (cleverly enough) with the *end.* identifier. We can also form compound statements in Pascal that begin with *begin* and end with *end,* but in those cases the end is slightly less emphatic, requiring no period as we do in the program *begin-end.* pair.

At long last we get to some code that does something. The action of *simple1* is to write out the two-line message. We do this using the built-in output procedure *writeln.* In our example, the first line

```
writeln(' Bullwinkle is a dope');
```

writes out the message enclosed between the single quotes to the console and sends a line feed. There is a companion built-in routine called *write* that prints out messages without the line feed.

The second message follows the first, but notice the one important difference: no semicolon is necessary. This illustrates the use of the semicolon as a separator instead of as an end-of-line marker. Since the *begin-end.* pair expects a line or sequence of lines anyway, a semicolon at the end is redundant. In this case, an extra semicolon would not harm anything; the compiler would just think there is a single null line at the end of the program. In other contexts extra or missing semicolons are a leading cause of serious syntax errors.

With our *simple1* program written, let's compile it and run it. All the examples in this appendix (and all the code in this book for that matter) have been compiled and executed using the popular Borland International (1985) compiler Turbo Pascal. To run the compiler, we type turbo <cr> (here <cr> means we hit a carriage return key) at the system prompt. The Turbo Pascal menu appears

```
-------------------------------------
TURBO Pascal system      Version 3.01A
                         PC-DOS

Copyright (C) 1983,84,85   BORLAND Inc.
-------------------------------------

Color display 80x25



Include error messages (Y/N)?



Logged drive: C
Active directory: \TURBO

Work file:
Main file:

Edit    Compile Run  Save

Dir     Quit  compiler Options

Text:     0 bytes
Free: 62024 bytes

>
```

FIGURE B.2 Turbo Pascal Menu. Used with permission of Borland International, Inc.

as shown in Fig. B.2. We type *c* or *C* to invoke the compiler, we give the file name at the file name prompt, and we get the clean compilation message shown in Fig. B.3. To run the code we type *r* or *R* (run) and the two-line message is printed as we planned (Fig. B.3).

That was easy enough, but frankly we haven't done too much. We have noticed some differences between Pascal and other programming languages like Basic and Fortran: the use of *begin-end*, a comment format with brackets, and a

```
Loading A:\SIMPLE1.APB
Compiling
  6 lines

Code:      0008 paragraphs (   128 bytes), 0D20 paragraphs free
Data:      0002 paragraphs (    32 bytes), 0FDA paragraphs free
Stack/Heap: 86F4 paragraphs (552768 bytes)

>

Running
 Bullwinkle is a dope
 No Rocky, not that message

>
```

FIGURE B.3 Compilation and run of program *simple1*. Used with permission of Borland International, Inc.

simple built-in output routine. The next example examines a more involved simple program called *simple2*.

SIMPLE2: FUNCTIONS, PROCEDURES, AND MORE I/0

The second illustration stays with simple input-output examples but introduces the idea of writing more modular programs. In the previous program, we wrote a single piece of code from start to finish. This is satisfactory for small programs, but in most programming work we need to segment the code into separate modules to permit program maintenance and module reuse. A more modular program is shown in Fig. B.4 as *simple2*. Scanning the code, we see some familiar components from our last foray: the *begin-end.* pair, the *program* statement, and the bracketed comments ({ }). We also see some new elements: the declarations at the top of the code and the evidence of substructure in a function *readnumber* and a procedure *writemessage.*

Below the program header and comment we have two different types of declaration sections. At the *const* identifier we declare a single variable called *pi* that contains the value of π to eight decimal places. Other constants could have been declared (separated by semicolons) until the next declaration section, the *var* or variable declaration section. In the variable declaration, a single integer-valued variable *i* is declared. Again, other variables could have been declared using the standard types: *integer, real, boolean* (true, false), *char* (character).

Following the declaration sections, two code modules are defined. The first is a *function* module called *readnumber.* This function prints a prompt message at the console, reads an integer from the console, and returns the value of the integer to the calling module. In the function header, we note that this function has no calling sequence, as no arguments are required for its operation. Following the header, and following the informative comment between brackets, a local *var* declaration declares the single local variable *j* as an integer. Following the declaration, the function begins with a *begin* and the functional code starts. A *write* statement writes out the prompt message

```
Enter number >
```

to the console, but because *write* is used instead of *writeln,* no line feed is issued. Thereafter the statement *readln*(j) reads the variable j from the console and issues the next line feed. The built-in procedure *readln* has a companion procedure *read* that does not (like *write*) issue the line feed. Following the prompt and read, the function returns its value with the assignment statement:

```
readnumber := j;
```

In Pascal, the assignment operator is denoted by the symbol := . The equal sign (=) by itself is reserved for tests of logical equality and constant definition. The function is ended by the *end* identifier.

```
program simple2;
( simple2: a program to read a number and print a message )

const pi = 3.14159265;

var    i:integer;

function readnumber:integer;
( Read a number from the console )
var j:integer;
begin
 write('Enter number > ');readln(j);
 readnumber := j
end;

procedure writemessage(var out:text; number:integer);
( Write a message w/ number to  a specified output device )
begin
 writeln(out);
 writeln(out,'     The number is ', number);
 writeln(out,' The value of Pi is ', pi)
end;

begin ( main program )
 i := readnumber;        ( function call to read number from console )
 writemessage(lst,i); ( write message to the printer )
 writemessage(con,i)  ( write message to the console )
end.  ( main program )
```

FIGURE B.4   Pascal program *simple2*.

Following *readnumber* we see a procedure named *writemessage*. This routine has a calling sequence with two elements:

```
(var out:text; number:integer)
```

In this way we pass down the name of the output text file (or device) where the message should be written and we also pass the *integer*-valued variable *number* to be written as part of the message on the specified device. Following the procedure header and the informative comment, the actual work of *writemessage* is contained between the *begin-end;* pair. We first eject a line with the statement:

```
writeln(out);
```

This is a different form of the built-in procedure *writeln,* where the particular device (in this case *out*) is specified. As there is no message in this case, we issue the call to *writeln* here solely for its line feed. The line feed is followed by the writing of our message, "The number is", followed by the value of the number passed down in the variable *number* in the argument list. This in turn is followed by a message, "The value of Pi is", followed by the value of π declared originally. Notice that *pi* was not passed through the argument list. This illustrates the use

```
Compiling
  28 lines

Code:        0012 paragraphs (    288 bytes), 0D16 paragraphs free
Data:        0003 paragraphs (     48 bytes), 0FD9 paragraphs free
Stack/Heap: 86C3 paragraphs (551984 bytes)

>

Running
Enter number > 11

      The number is 11
  The value of Pi is    3.1415926500E+00

>
```

FIGURE B.5   Screen dump of program *simple2* run.

of a global constant. Pascal also permits the use of global variables where procedures and functions have access to variables in parent routines. While it is tempting to adopt global variable usage, thereby avoiding the typing of argument lists, global variable and constant usage should be limited to those variables and constants that are truly used throughout the entire program.

Finally we reach the main program. In rapid succession, we issue a function call to *readnumber* and two procedure calls to *writemessage*. The first writes to the listing device *lst* and the second writes to the console *con*. These devices are Turbo Pascal standards, and they may be different in other compilers. We conclude the program with the emphatic *end.* statement characteristic of Pascal program termination. Figure B.5 displays a screen dump of a run of *simple2*. In addition to the screen output, the same output message is directed to the listing device (the line printer).

LET'S DO SOMETHING

Our first two codes were, to be honest, not very functional. Printing out foolish messages and reading and writing single numbers are not going to make us famous programmers, nor are they going to bootstrap us into enough Pascal knowledge to understand or write even the simplest of genetic algorithms (or anything else for that matter). In our next code, *simple3* (shown in Fig. B.6), we do some coin flipping and keep track of the number of heads and tails that come up.

At the top of the code we define two constants: *ncoins*, the number of coins, and *probability*, the probability of turning up heads. In the variable declarations we define an array *heads_or_tails* to keep track of the heads-tails count. This is accomplished through the defining statement:

```
heads_or_tails: array [1..2] of integer;
```

```
program simple3;
( simple3: a program to flip 20 coins and keep track of heads and tails )
(          use for-do construct                                         )

const ncoins = 20;          ( number of coin flips )
      probability = 0.5;    ( probability of heads turning up )

var   heads_or_tails:array[1..2] of integer; ( heads/tails count )
      j:integer;                             ( loop counter )
      toss:boolean;                          ( toss: true=heads, false=false )

( Include random number generator and flip routine )
{$I random.apb}

begin ( Main program )
 heads_or_tails[1] := 0;          ( Counters to zero )
 heads_or_tails[2] := 0;
 randomize;                       ( Seed and warm up random number generator )
 for j := 1 to ncoins do begin    ( Coin toss loop )
   toss := flip(probability);
   if toss then heads_or_tails[1] := heads_or_tails[1] + 1
     else heads_or_tails[2] := heads_or_tails[2] + 1
  end; ( coin toss loop )
 writeln(' In ', ncoins, ' coin tosses there were ',
         heads_or_tails[1], ' heads and ', heads_or_tails[2],
         ' tails')
end. ( Main program )
```

FIGURE B.6   Pascal program *simple3*.

This simply defines a two-position array of integers. Other variables defined in the *var* section include the *integer* counter variable *j* and a coin toss result *boolean* variable (head = true, tail = false) *toss*. Following the variable declaration we include the pseudorandom number routines stored in the file *random.apb* by using the compiler directive statement:

```
{$I random.apb}
```

Although this looks like a mild-mannered comment, the $ indicates that it should be interpreted as a compiler directive. The *I* following the dollar sign means that the named file (in this case *random.apb*) should be included in the compilation at this point of the main program file.

We briefly turn our attention to the contents of the file *random.apb*. This file contains several global variable definitions and six code modules as we see in Fig. B.7. These modules and their purposes are described as follows:

advance_random	retrieves a new batch of pseudorandom numbers.
warmup_random	initializes random number generator.
random	returns a single pseudorandom real value between 0.0 and 1.0.
flip	returns result of a simulated biased coin toss (*true* = head).

```
{ random.apb: contains random number generator and related utilities
            including advance_random, warmup_random, random, randomize,
            flip, rnd }

{ Global variables - Don't use these names in other code }
var   oldrand:array[1..55] of real; { Array of 55 random numbers }
      jrand:integer;                 { current random }

procedure advance_random;
{ Create next batch of 55 random numbers }
var j1:integer;
    new_random:real;
begin
 for j1:= 1 to 24 do
  begin
   new_random := oldrand[j1] - oldrand[j1+31];
   if (new_random < 0.0) then new_random := new_random + 1.0;
   oldrand[j1] := new_random;
  end;
 for j1:= 25 to 55 do
  begin
   new_random := oldrand[j1] - oldrand[j1-24];
   if (new_random < 0.0) then new_random := new_random + 1.0;
   oldrand[j1] := new_random;
  end;
end;


procedure warmup_random(random_seed:real);
{ Get random off and runnin }
var j1,ii:integer;
    new_random,prev_random:real;
begin
 oldrand[55] := random_seed;
 new_random := 1.0e-9;
 prev_random := random_seed;
 for j1:=1 to 54 do
  begin
   ii := 21*j1 mod 55;
   oldrand[ii] := new_random;
   new_random := prev_random - new_random;
   if (new_random < 0.0) then new_random:=new_random+1.0;
   prev_random:=oldrand[ii]
  end;
 advance_random;  advance_random;  advance_random;
 jrand:=0;
end;
```

FIGURE B.7   Pseudorandom number utilities in file *random.apb*.

rnd	returns an integer selected uniformly and pseudoran-domly between upper and lower limits.
randomize	queries terminal for user-specified random seed and initializes *random*.

These routines are based on a portable subtractive pseudorandom number generator described in Knuth (1981). The code *simple3* uses *randomize* and *flip*,

```
function random:real;
{ Fetch a single random number between 0.0 and 1.0 - Subtractive Method }
{ See Knuth, D. (1969), v. 2 for details                                 }
begin
 jrand := jrand + 1;
 if (jrand > 55) then
  begin jrand:=1; advance_random end;
 random := oldrand[jrand];
end;

function flip(probability:real):boolean;
{ Flip a biased coin - true if heads }
begin
 if probability = 1.0 then flip := true
    else flip := (random <= probability);
end;

function rnd(low,high:integer):integer;
{ Pick a random integer between low and high }
 var i:integer;
 begin
  if low >= high then i := low
    else begin
     i := trunc( random * (high-low+1) + low);
     if i > high then i := high;
    end;
 rnd := i;
end;

procedure randomize;
{ Get seed number for random and start it up }
var randomseed:real;
begin
 repeat
  write('Enter seed random number (0.0..1.0) > '); readln(randomseed);
 until (randomseed>0) and (randomseed<1.0);
 warmup_random(randomseed);
end;
```

FIGURE B.7   *(Continued)*

which in turn use *warmup_random, advance_random,* and *random.* The routine *rnd* will be demonstrated in the fourth and final program.

Following the inclusion of the pseudorandom number generator paraphernalia, we begin *simple3* by initializing the *heads_or_tails* array to zero. The *randomize* utility is called to set up the pseudorandom number generator. Finally the 20 coins are tossed in the iterative *for-do* construct. This is similar to a Fortran *DO* loop and a Basic *FOR-NEXT* loop. In the Pascal construct, the loop counter is iteratively incremented between the lower limit (1 in this case) and the upper limit (*ncoin*) while performing the statement following the do (in this case, a compound statement is found between a *begin-end* pair). Within the loop the boolean variable *toss* is assigned the result of the *flip* evaluation. The conditional construct, *if-then-else,* is used to increment the heads counter (*heads_* or_tails[1]) or the tails counter (heads_or_tails[2]) depending on the value of toss. Finally a message is printed out to the console to report the number of heads and tails observed. A screen dump of program output is shown in Fig. B.8.

There are, of course, many ways to skin a cat. In program simple3a, shown in Fig. B.9, we do the same computation as in program simple3; however, this time we use a different loop structure, the repeat-until construct. In this minor variant we initialize the loop counter to zero ($j := 0$) and iterate until the loop terminating condition is true. In this case we increment j by one each iteration and terminate when j equals the constant ncoins (20). Of course, the repeat-until construct may be used for more complex terminating conditions.

In simple3b (Fig. B.10), we see one more variant on this simple looping theme. In this case we use a pretest version of the loop structure using the while-do construct. In this program the loop counter is initialized to zero, and the loop proceeds only if the pretest condition (in this case, $j <= ncoins$) is satisfied. Within the loop the j variable is incremented and the biased coin is tossed as before.

```
>

Running
Enter seed random number (0.0..1.0) > 0.1
 In 20 coin tosses there were 13 heads and 7 tails

>

Running
Enter seed random number (0.0..1.0) > 0.333
 In 20 coin tosses there were 10 heads and 10 tails

>

Running
Enter seed random number (0.0..1.0) > 0.54324444
 In 20 coin tosses there were 8 heads and 12 tails

>

Running
Enter seed random number (0.0..1.0) > 0.9999
 In 20 coin tosses there were 9 heads and 11 tails

>
```

FIGURE B.8   Screen dump of simple3 run.

```
program simple3a;
{ simple3a: a program to flip 20 coins and keep track of heads and tails
            uses repeat-until construct                                  }

const ncoins = 20;          { number of coin flips }
      probability = 0.5;    { probability of heads turning up }

var  heads_or_tails:array[1..2] of integer; { heads/tails count }
     j:integer;                             { loop counter }
     toss:boolean;                          { toss: true=heads, false=false }

{ Include random number generator and flip routine }
($I random.apb)

begin { Main program }
 heads_or_tails[1] := 0;          { H/T counters to zero }
 heads_or_tails[2] := 0;
 randomize;                       { Seed and warm up random number generator }
 j := 0;                          { Loop counter to zero }
 repeat { Coin toss loop }
   toss := flip(probability);
   if toss then heads_or_tails[1] := heads_or_tails[1] + 1
     else heads_or_tails[2] := heads_or_tails[2] + 1;
   j := j + 1
 until (j = ncoins);
 writeln(' In ', ncoins, ' coin tosses there were ',
         heads_or_tails[1], ' heads and ', heads_or_tails[2],
         ' tails')
end. { Main program }
```

FIGURE B.9 Pascal program *simple3a*, variant with *repeat-until*.

```
program simple3b;
{ simple3b: a program to flip 20 coins and keep track of heads and tails
            uses while-do construct                                      }

const ncoins = 20;          { number of coin flips }
      probability = 0.5;    { probability of heads turning up }

var  heads_or_tails:array[1..2] of integer; { heads/tails count }
     j:integer;                             { loop counter }
     toss:boolean;                          { toss: true=heads, false=false }

{ Include random number generator and flip routine }
($I random.apb)

begin { Main program }
 heads_or_tails[1] := 0;          { H/T counters to zero }
 heads_or_tails[2] := 0;
 randomize;                       { Seed and warm up random number generator }
 j := 1;                          { Loop counter to zero }
 while (j<=ncoins) do begin  { Coin toss loop }
   toss := flip(probability);
   if toss then heads_or_tails[1] := heads_or_tails[1] + 1
     else heads_or_tails[2] := heads_or_tails[2] + 1;
   j := j + 1
 end;     { Coin toss loop }
 writeln(' In ', ncoins, ' coin tosses there were ',
         heads_or_tails[1], ' heads and ', heads_or_tails[2],
         ' tails')
end. { Main program }
```

FIGURE B.10 Pascal program *simple3b*, variant with *while-do*.

LAST STOP BEFORE FREEWAY

In our last piece of introductory Pascal code, we try to bring together a number of things in the code *simple4* as displayed in Fig. B.11. In this program we roll a simulated pair of dice and keep track of the roll history and accumulated dice-sum counts.

Following the *program* header, and following the declaration of a number of constants, we declare a number of variable types in the *type* declaration section. In our previous codes we have not encountered this facility that permits the construction of our own named variable types. In *simple4,* for example, we define a *roll* as a record containing two die values. A *record* in Pascal is a data structure that permits groupings of variables to congregate under a single name. In this sample code, we also define a data type we call *sequence,* which is itself an array of the just-defined *roll* type variables. Finally we define a type *sumcount,* which is an array of integers indexed between 2 and 12 to store the dice totals that occur during the rolls.

Type declarations by themselves do no variables make. After the type declarations, we define the actual data structure instances we use. In the *var* section, we define the structure *play* as a *sequence* type, and we define the structure *totals* as a *sumcount* type. We also define two integer variables, *j,* a loop counter, and *sum,* a dice sum result.

To segment the program, we define two code modules, the *die* function and the *throw* procedure. The function *die* simulates the roll of a single die using the random number utility *rnd.* The procedure *throw* simulates the throw of a pair of dice by calling *die* twice, keeping track of the outcomes in a record structure of type *roll,* and calculating the sum of the two die faces. The *with-do* construct within *die* allows us to use the record variables without referring repeatedly to the record name. We can also use Pascal's dot notation to directly access a record component. The same code segment could have been written in dot notation as follows:

```
begin
   rollmemory.diel := die;
   rollmemory.die2 := die;
   sum := rollmemory.diel + rollmemory.die2
end;
```

Clearly, the *with-do* construct permits easy utilization of record components without repetitive typing.

In the main program we zero out the dice totals, initialize the random number generator, and initialize the loop counter *j.* Within the loop we repeatedly throw the dice and increment the appropriate sum counter. Following the loop we print out the history of all throws and print out all the sum counts as well. Further modularization of this program is possible, and in some sense desirable. For example, we could have modularized the initialization code, the reporting code, and the main loop. If we had done this, the main program would have

```
program simple4;
( simple4: a program to roll a pair of dice )

const maxrolls - 36;                  ( number of dice rolls )
      dicemin  - 2;                    ( minimum dice total   )
      dicemax  - 12;                   ( maximum dice total   )
      diemax   - 6;                    ( single die max       )
      diemin   - 1;                    ( single die min       )

type  roll    - record               ( record of single throw )
                   die1, die2:integer
                end;
      sequence  - array[1..maxrolls] of roll;
      sumcount - array[dicemin..dicemax] of integer;

var   play:sequence;     ( Keep track of play sequence )
      totals:sumcount;   ( Keep tally of totals        )
      j, sum:integer;

( Include random number generator and utilities )
($I random.apb)

function die:integer;
( Roll a single die)
begin die := rnd(diemin,diemax) end;

procedure throw(var sum:integer; var rollmemory:roll);
( Roll & sum a pair of dice )
begin
 with rollmemory do begin
   die1 := die;   ( Roll the dice )
   die2 := die;
   sum  := die1 + die2
   end
end;

procedure report;
var j:integer;
begin
 writeln(' Plays Report ');
 writeln(' ----------- '); writeln;
 for j := 1 to maxrolls do with play[j] do ( Print out all plays )
  writeln(' Roll ', j:3, ': die 1- ', die1, ', die 2-', die2);
 writeln;
 writeln(' Rolls Summary');
 writeln(' ------------'); writeln;
 for j := 2 to dicemax do begin       ( Print out totals )
   write('[', j:2,'] - ', totals[j]:2, ', ');
   if j-7 then writeln
   end
end;

begin ( Main program )
 for j := dicemin to  dicemax do totals[j] := 0;   ( Zero out totals )
 randomize;  ( Setup and seed random number generator )
 j := 0;     ( Zero counter )
 repeat   ( Roll & count )
   j := j + 1;
   throw(sum,play[j]);                ( Throw the dice )
   totals[sum] := totals[sum] + 1     ( Increment sumth total )
 until (j-maxrolls); ( Stop at maximum rolls )
 report                ( Report all results )
 end. ( Main program )
```

FIGURE B.11 Pascal program *simple4*.

looked something like the following:

```
begin
  initial;
  loop;
  report
end.
```

```
Enter seed random number (0.0..1.0) > 0.1111
Plays Report
------------

Roll   1: die 1- 1, die 2-6
Roll   2: die 1- 4, die 2-2
Roll   3: die 1- 6, die 2-3
Roll   4: die 1- 6, die 2-1
Roll   5: die 1- 2, die 2-3
Roll   6: die 1- 2, die 2-5
Roll   7: die 1- 2, die 2-1
Roll   8: die 1- 6, die 2-3
Roll   9: die 1- 6, die 2-4
Roll  10: die 1- 1, die 2-2
Roll  11: die 1- 4, die 2-1
Roll  12: die 1- 2, die 2-5
Roll  13: die 1- 4, die 2-6
Roll  14: die 1- 3, die 2-4
Roll  15: die 1- 5, die 2-5
Roll  16: die 1- 4, die 2-4
Roll  17: die 1- 2, die 2-1
Roll  18: die 1- 3, die 2-4
Roll  19: die 1- 1, die 2-6
Roll  20: die 1- 6, die 2-2
Roll  21: die 1- 4, die 2-1
Roll  22: die 1- 2, die 2-3
Roll  23: die 1- 1, die 2-3
Roll  24: die 1- 5, die 2-2
Roll  25: die 1- 1, die 2-5
Roll  26: die 1- 6, die 2-3
Roll  27: die 1- 6, die 2-5
Roll  28: die 1- 4, die 2-3
Roll  29: die 1- 5, die 2-3
Roll  30: die 1- 5, die 2-2
Roll  31: die 1- 3, die 2-6
Roll  32: die 1- 2, die 2-1
Roll  33: die 1- 5, die 2-2
Roll  34: die 1- 3, die 2-5
Roll  35: die 1- 1, die 2-4
Roll  36: die 1- 4, die 2-5

Rolls Summary
-------------

[ 2] =  0, [ 3] =  4, [ 4] =  1, [ 5] =  5, [ 6] =  2, [ 7] = 11,
[ 8] =  4, [ 9] =  5, [10] =  3, [11] =  1, [12] =  0,
```

FIGURE B.12 Screen dump of *simple4* run.

This extreme modularization is less necessary in small codes like *simple4*; however, in large, complex programs, modularization is important for efficient coding, debugging, and maintenance. A screen dump of a *simple4* run is shown in Fig. B.12. It is an interesting exercise to compare the actual and expected dice sum counts.

SUMMARY

This appendix illustrates the essentials of the Pascal programming language through simple examples. We have examined very simple programs that perform a little input and output, and we have seen more complex programs with code modules and more involved data structures. This brief tour is necessarily incomplete, but it should permit perusal of the genetic algorithm codes in this book.

C | A Simple Genetic Algorithm (SGA) in Pascal

The complete Pascal code for the simple genetic algorithm (SGA) is presented in Figures C.1–C.8. The code is segmented into nine files:

sga.pas	SGA main program
interfac.sga	problem and problem interface routines
stats.sga	population statistics routines
initial.sga	initialization routines
report.sga	population reporting routines
triops.sga	reproduction, crossover, and mutation
generate.sga	generation coordinator
utility.sga	input-output and computation utilities
random.apb	portable random number generator (See Appendix B.)

All input for the program is entered interactively, and all program output is sent to the standard Turbo Pascal listing device *lst.*

```
program sga;
( A Simple Genetic Algorithm - SGA - v1.0 )
( (c)    David Edward Goldberg 1986        )
(        All Rights Reserved               )

const maxpop      = 100;
      maxstring   = 30;

type  allele      = boolean; ( Allele = bit position )
      chromosome  = array[1..maxstring] of allele; ( String of bits )
```

FIGURE C.1 SGA main program in file *sga.pas.*

```
individual   = record
                 chrom:chromosome;  { Genotype = bit string }
                 x:real;            { Phenotype = unsigned integer }
                 fitness:real;      { Objective function value }
                 parent1, parent2, xsite:integer; { parents & cross pt }
               end;
population   = array[1..maxpop] of individual;

var  oldpop, newpop:population;              { Two non-overlapping populations }
     popsize, lchrom, gen, maxgen:integer;   { Integer global variables }
     pcross, pmutation, sumfitness:real;     { Real global variables }
     nmutation, ncross:integer;              { Integer statistics }
     avg, max, min:real;                     { Real statistics }

{ Include utility procedures and functions }
($I utility.sga )

{ Include pseudo-random number generator and random utilities }
($I random.apb )

{ Include interface routines: decode and objfunc }
($I interfac.sga )

{ Include statistics calculations: statistics }
($I stats.sga )

{ Include init. routines: initialize, initdata, initpop, initreport }
($I initial.sga )

{ Include report routines: report, writechrom }
($I report.sga )

{ Include the 3 operators: select (reproduction), crossover, mutation }
($I triops.sga )

{ Include new population generation routine: generation }
($I generate.sga )

begin      { Main program }
 gen := 0;     { Set things up }
 initialize;
 repeat        { Main iterative loop }
  gen := gen + 1;
  generation;
  statistics(popsize, max, avg, min, sumfitness, newpop);
  report(gen);
  oldpop := newpop; { advance the generation }
 until (gen >= maxgen)
end.         { End main program }
```

FIGURE C.1 *(Continued)*

```
{ interfac.sga: contains  objfunc, decode }
{ Change these for different problem      }

function objfunc(x:real):real;
{ Fitness function - f(x) = x**n }
const coef = 1073741823.0; { Coefficient to normalize domain }
      n = 10;              { Power of x }
begin objfunc := power( x/coef, n ) end;
```

FIGURE C.2 Objective function and problem interface in file *interfac.sga*.

```
function decode(chrom:chromosome; lbits:integer):real;
{ Decode string as unsigned binary integer - true=1, false=0 }
var j:integer;
      accum, powerof2:real;
begin
 accum := 0.0; powerof2 := 1;
 for j := 1 to lbits do begin
   if chrom[j] then accum := accum + powerof2;
   powerof2 := powerof2 * 2;
  end;
 decode := accum;
end;
```

FIGURE C.2   *(Continued)*

```
{ stats.sga }

procedure statistics(popsize:integer;
                     var max,avg,min,sumfitness:real;
                     var pop:population);
{ Calculate population statistics }
var j:integer;
begin
 { Initialize }
 sumfitness := pop[1].fitness;
 min        := pop[1].fitness;
 max        := pop[1].fitness;
 { Loop for max, min, sumfitness }
 for j := 2 to popsize do with pop[j] do begin
   sumfitness := sumfitness + fitness; { Accumulate fitness sum }
   if fitness>max then max := fitness; { New max }
   if fitness<min then min := fitness; { New min }
  end;
 { Calculate average }
 avg := sumfitness/popsize;
end;
```

FIGURE C.3   Population statistics routines in file *stats.sga*.

```
{ initial.sga: contains initdata, initpop, initreport, initialize }

procedure initdata;
{ Interactive data inquiry and setup }
var ch:char; j:integer;
begin
 rewrite(lst); { Set up for list device }
 clrscr;       { Clear screen }
 skip(con,9);
 repchar(con,' ',25); writeln('--------------------------------');
 repchar(con,' ',25); writeln('A Simple Genetic Algorithm - SGA');
 repchar(con,' ',25); writeln(' (c) David Edward Goldberg 1986');
 repchar(con,' ',25); writeln('    All Rights Reserved        ');
 repchar(con,' ',25); writeln('--------------------------------');
 pause(7); clrscr;
 writeln('******** SGA Data Entry and Initialization ***********');
 writeln;
   write('Enter population size ------- > '); readln(popsize);
```

FIGURE C.4   Initialization routines in file *initial.sga*.

346

```
        write('Enter chromosome length ----- > '); readln(lchrom);
        write('Enter max. generations ------ > '); readln(maxgen);
        write('Enter crossover probability - > '); readln(pcross);
        write('Enter mutation probability -- > '); readln(pmutation);
    pause(5); clrscr;
    { Initialize random number generator }
    randomize;
    pause(2); clrscr;
    { Initialize counters }
    nmutation := 0;
    ncross := 0;
    end;

procedure initreport;
{ Initial report }
begin
    writeln(lst,'--------------------------------------------------');
    writeln(lst,'|      A Simple Genetic Algorithm - SGA - v1.0      |');
    writeln(lst,'|         (c)    David Edward Goldberg 1986         |');
    writeln(lst,'|                All Rights Reserved                |');
    writeln(lst,'--------------------------------------------------');
    skip(lst,5);
    writeln(lst,'      SGA Parameters');
    writeln(lst,'      --------------');
    writeln(lst);
    writeln(lst,'      Population size (popsize)        = ',popsize);
    writeln(lst,'      Chromosome length (lchrom)       = ',lchrom);
    writeln(lst,'      Maximum # of generation (maxgen) = ',maxgen);
    writeln(lst,'      Crossover probability (pcross)   = ',pcross);
    writeln(lst,'      Mutation  probability (pmutation) = ',pmutation);
    skip(lst,8);
    writeln(lst,'      Initial Generation Statistics');
    writeln(lst,'      ----------------------------');
    writeln(lst);
    writeln(lst,'      Initial population maximum fitness = ',max);
    writeln(lst,'      Initial population average fitness = ',avg);
    writeln(lst,'      Initial population minimum fitness = ',min);
    writeln(lst,'      Initial population sum of fitness  = ',sumfitness);
    page(lst); { New page }
end;

procedure initpop;
{ Initialize a population at random }
var j, jl:integer;
begin
    for j := 1 to popsize do with oldpop[j] do begin
        for jl := 1 to lchrom do chrom[jl] := flip(0.5); { A fair coin toss }
        x := decode(chrom,lchrom); { Decode the string }
        fitness := objfunc(x);        { Evaluate inital fitness }
        parent1 := 0; parent2 := 0; xsite := 0; { Initialize printout vars }
        end;
end;

procedure initialize;
{ Initialization Coordinator }
begin
    initdata;
    initpop;
    statistics(popsize, max, avg, min, sumfitness, oldpop);
    initreport;
end;
```

FIGURE C.4 *(Continued)*

```
procedure writechrom(var out:text; chrom:chromosome; lchrom:integer);
{ Write a chromosome as a string of 1's (true's) and 0's (false's) }
var j:integer;
begin
 for j := lchrom downto 1 do
   if chrom[j] then write(out,'1')
     else write(out,'0');
end;


procedure report(gen:integer);
{ Write the population report }
const linelength = 132;
var j:integer;
begin
 repchar(lst,'-',linelength); writeln(lst);
 repchar(lst,' ',50); writeln(lst,'Population Report');
 repchar(lst,' ',23);   write(lst,'Generation ',gen-1:2);
 repchar(lst,' ',57); writeln(lst,'Generation ',gen:2);
 writeln(lst);
   write(lst,' #                 string                x      fitness');
   write(lst,'          # parents xsite');
 writeln(lst,   '                string           x      fitness');
 repchar(lst,'-',linelength); writeln(lst);
 for j := 1 to popsize do begin
   write(lst,j:2, ') ');
   { Old string }
   with oldpop[j] do begin
     writechrom(lst,chrom,lchrom);
     write(lst,' ', x:10, ' ', fitness:6:4,           |');
   end;
   { New string }
   with newpop[j] do begin
     write(lst,'     ', j:2, ') (', parent1:2, ',', parent2:2, ')   ',
             xsite:2,'   ');
     writechrom(lst,chrom,lchrom);
     writeln(lst, ' ',x:10,' ', fitness:6:4);
   end;
 end;
 repchar(lst,'-',linelength); writeln(lst);
 { Generation statistics and accumulated values }
 writeln(lst,' Note: Generation ', gen:2, ' & Accumulated Statistics: '
           ,' max=', max:6:4,',  min=', min:6:4, ',  avg=', avg:6:4, ',  sum='
           ,sumfitness:6:4, ',  nmutation=', nmutation, ',  ncross= ', ncross);
 repchar(lst,'-',linelength); writeln(lst);
 page(lst);
end;
```

FIGURE C.5   Reporting routines in file *report.sga*.

```
{ triops.sga }
{ 3-operators: Reproduction (select), Crossover (crossover),
              & Mutation (mutation)                           }

function select(popsize:integer; sumfitness:real;
              var pop:population):integer;
{ Select a single individual via roulette wheel selection }
var rand, partsum:real; { Random point on wheel, partial sum }
    j:integer;            { population index }
```

FIGURE C.6   Genetic operators in file *triops.sga*.

```
begin
 partsum := 0.0; j := 0;        ( Zero out counter and accumulator )
 rand := random * sumfitness; ( Wheel point calc. uses random number [0,1] )
 repeat ( Find wheel slot )
  j := j + 1;
  partsum := partsum + pop[j].fitness;
 until (partsum >= rand) or (j = popsize);
 ( Return individual number )
 select := j;
end;

function mutation(alleleval:allele; pmutation:real;
                  var nmutation:integer):allele;
( Mutate an allele w/ pmutation, count number of mutations )
var mutate:boolean;
begin
 mutate := flip(pmutation);    ( Flip the biased coin )
 if mutate then begin
   nmutation := nmutation + 1;
   mutation := not alleleval; ( Change bit value )
  end else
   mutation := alleleval;       ( No change )
end;

procedure crossover(var parent1, parent2, child1, child2:chromosome;
                    var lchrom, ncross, nmutation, jcross:integer;
                    var pcross, pmutation:real);
( Cross 2 parent strings, place in 2 child strings )
var j:integer;
begin
 if flip(pcross) then begin      ( Do crossover with p(cross) )
   jcross := rnd(1,lchrom-1);     ( Cross between 1 and 1-1 )
   ncross := ncross + 1;          ( Increment crossover counter )
  end else                        ( Otherwise set cross site to force mutation
 )
   jcross := lchrom;
 ( 1st exchange, 1 to 1 and 2 to 2 )
 for j := 1 to jcross do begin
   child1[j] := mutation(parent1[j], pmutation, nmutation);
   child2[j] := mutation(parent2[j], pmutation, nmutation);
  end;
 ( 2nd exchange, 1 to 2 and 2 to 1 )
 if jcross<>lchrom then   ( Skip if cross site is lchrom--no crossover )
  for j := jcross+1 to lchrom do begin
    child1[j] := mutation(parent2[j], pmutation, nmutation);
    child2[j] := mutation(parent1[j], pmutation, nmutation);
   end;
end;
```

FIGURE C.6   *(Continued)*

```
( generate.sga )

procedure generation;
( Create a new generation through select, crossover, and mutation )
( Note: generation assumes an even-numbered popsize              )
var j, mate1, mate2, jcross:integer;
begin
 j := 1;
 repeat    ( select, crossover, and mutation until newpop is filled )
  mate1 := select(popsize, sumfitness, oldpop); ( pick pair of mates )
```

FIGURE C.7   Generation coordinator in file *generate.sga*.

```
    mate2 := select(popsize, sumfitness, oldpop);
    { Crossover and mutation - mutation embedded within crossover }
    crossover(oldpop[mate1].chrom, oldpop[mate2].chrom,
              newpop[j    ].chrom, newpop[j + 1].chrom,
              lchrom, ncross, nmutation, jcross, pcross, pmutation);
    { Decode string, evaluate fitness, & record parentage date on both childr
en }
    with newpop[j  ] do begin
      x := decode(chrom, lchrom);
      fitness := objfunc(x);
      parent1 := mate1;
      parent2 := mate2;
      xsite   := jcross;
    end;
    with newpop[j+1] do begin
      x := decode(chrom, lchrom);
      fitness := objfunc(x);
      parent1 := mate1;
      parent2 := mate2;
      xsite   := jcross;
    end;
    { Increment population index }
    j := j + 2;
  until j>popsize
end;
```

FIGURE C.7   *(Continued)*

```
{ utility.sga: contains pause, page, repchar, skip, power }

procedure pause(pauselength:integer);
{ Pause a while }
const maxpause = 2500;
var j,j1:integer;
    x:real;
begin
 for j := 1 to pauselength do
   for j1 := 1 to maxpause do x := 0.0 + 1.0;
end;

procedure page(var out:text);
{ Issue form feed to device or file }
begin write(out,chr(12)) end;

procedure repchar(var out:text; ch:char; repcount:integer);
{ Repeatedly write a character to an output device }
var j:integer;
begin for j := 1 to repcount do write(out,ch) end;

procedure skip(var out:text; skipcount:integer);
{ Skip skipcount lines on device out }
var j:integer;
begin for j := 1 to skipcount do writeln(out) end;

function power(x,y:real):real;
{ Raise x to the yth power }
begin power := exp( y*ln(x) ) end;
```

FIGURE C.8   Input-output and computation utilities in file *utility.sga*.

D | A Simple Classifier System (SCS) in Pascal

The complete Pascal code for the simple classifier system (SCS) is presented in this appendix. The code is segmented into 15 files:

scs.pas	SCS main program
declare.scs	global variable declarations
initial.scs	initialization routines
detector.scs	environmental-to-classifier detectors
report.scs	classifier system reporting
timekeep.scs	time coordination routines
environ.scs	6-multiplexer environment
perform.scs	performance (rule and message) system
aoc.scs	apportionment of credit routines
effector.scs	classifier-to-environment effectors
reinforc.scs	reinforcement routines
advance.scs	iteration update routines
ga.scs	genetic algorithm including reproduction, crossover, mutation, and modified crowding
utility.scs	computational utilities
io.scs	input and output utilities

These files are presented in Figs. D.1–D.15. The SCS code also requires the pseudorandom number routines (file *random.apb*) presented in Appendix B.

During initialization, the user is queried for the names of five input files:

cfile	classifier data
efile	environmental data
rfile	reinforcement data

tfile   timekeeping data

gfile   genetic algorithm data

Annotated input files are presented in Fig. D.16–D.22. In addition, the user is queried for the names of two output file (or device) names:

rep   reporting file or device

pfile   plotting file or device

```
program scs;

{ SCS -  A Simple Classifier System }
{   (C)   David E. Goldberg, 1987     }
{         All Rights Reserved          }

{$I declare.scs }
{$I random.apb }
{$I io.scs }
{$I utility.scs }
{$I environ.scs }
{$I detector.scs }
{$I perform.scs }
{$I aoc.scs }
{$I effector.scs }
{$I reinforc.scs }
{$I timekeep.scs }
{$I advance.scs }
{$I ga.scs }
{$I report.scs }
{$I initial.scs }

begin { main }
  initialization;
  detectors(environrec, detectrec, envmessage);
  report(rep);
  with timekeeprec do repeat
    timekeeper(timekeeprec);
    environment(environrec);
    detectors(environrec, detectrec, envmessage);
    matchclassifiers(population, envmessage, matchlist);
    aoc(population, matchlist, clearingrec);
    effector(population, clearingrec, environrec);
    reinforcement(reinforcementrec, population, clearingrec, environrec);
    if reportflag then report(rep);
    if consolereportflag then  consolereport(reinforcementrec);
    if plotreportflag then plotreport(pfile, reinforcementrec);
    advance(clearingrec);
    if gaflag then begin
      ga(garec, population);
      if reportflag then reportga(rep, garec, population);
    end;
  until halt;
  report(rep);   { final report }
  close(pfile); { close plot file }
end.
```

FIGURE D.1   The main SCS program is file *scs.pas*.

Printed reports are sent to the *rep* device and summary statistics are printed to the plotting file.

```
{ declare.scs: declarations for scs }

const  maxposition  = 50;
       maxclass     = 100;
       wildcard     = -1;

type   bit         = 0..1; { a binary digit }
       trit        = -1..1; { a ternary digit; 0=0; 1=1; -1=# }
       action      = bit; { a binaray decision }
       condition   = array[1..maxposition] of trit;
       message     = array[1..maxposition] of bit;
       classtype   = record
                         c:condition;
                         a:action;
                         strength, bid, ebid:real;
                         matchflag:boolean;
                         specificity:integer;
                     end;
       classarray  = array[1..maxclass] of classtype;
       classlist   = record
                         clist:array[1..maxclass] of integer;
                         nactive:integer
                     end;
       poptype     = record
                         classifier:classarray;
                         nclassifier, nposition:integer;
                         pgeneral, cbid, bidsigma, bidtax, lifetax,
                         bid1, bid2, ebid1, ebid2,
                         sumstrength, maxstrength, avgstrength, minstrength:real
                     end;

var    population:poptype;     { population of classifiers }
       matchlist:classlist;    { who matched }
       envmessage:message;     { environmental message }
       rep:text;               { report device/file }
```

FIGURE D.2 The global variable declarations are in *declare.scs*.

```
{ initial.scs: initialization coordination }

procedure initrepheader(var rep:text);
{ write a header to specified file/dev. }
begin
   writeln(rep,'*****************************************');
   writeln(rep,'       A Simple Classifier System - SCS');
   writeln(rep,'          (C) David E. Goldberg,  1987');
   writeln(rep,'             All Rights Reserved');
   writeln(rep,'*****************************************');
   writeln(rep); writeln(rep);
end;
```

FIGURE D.3 Initialization routines are in *initial.scs*.

```
procedure interactiveheader;
{ clear screen and print interactive header }
begin
  clrscr;
  initrepheader(con)
end;

procedure initialization;
{ coordinate input and initialization }
begin
  interactiveheader;
  { random number & normal init. }
  randomize; initrandomnormaldeviate;
  { file/device init. }
  open_input(cfile, interactive, '  classifier  ', fn);
  open_input(efile, interactive, '  environment ', fn);
  open_input(rfile, interactive, ' reinforcement ', fn);
  open_input(tfile, interactive, '  timekeeper  ', fn);
  open_input(gfile, interactive, 'gen. algorithm ', fn);
  open_output( rep, interactive, '   report   ', fn);
  open_output(pfile, interactive, '  plot file  ', fn);
  { segment initialization: class., obj., det., aoc, reinf., timekeep., ga }
  initrepheader(rep);
  initclassifiers(cfile, population);
  initrepclassifiers(rep, population);
  initenvironment(efile, environrec);
  initrepenvironment(rep, environrec);
  initdetectors(efile, detectrec);
  initrepdetectors(rep, detectrec)·
  initaoc(clearingrec);
  initrepaoc(rep, clearingrec);
  initreinforcement(rfile, reinforcementrec);
  initrepreinforcement(rep, reinforcementrec);
  inittimekeeper(tfile, timekeeprec);
  initreptimekeeper(rep, timekeeprec);
  initga(gfile, garec, population);
  initrepga(rep, garec);
end;
```

FIGURE D.3 *(Continued)*

```
{ detector.scs: convert environmental states to env. message }

{ detector data declarations }

type drecord = record
                 end; { For this problem, no detector record is
                        required.  Normally, the detector record
                        contains information for mapping environmental
                        state variables to the environmental bit-string. }

var detectrec:drecord; { dummy detector record }

procedure detectors(var environrec:erecord; var detectrec:drecord;
                    var envmessage:message);
{ convert environmental state to env. message }
begin
 with environrec do { place signal message in env. message }
   envmessage := signal
end;
```

FIGURE D.4 Detector routines are in *detector.scs*.

```
procedure writemessage(var rep:text; var mess:message; lmessage:integer);
{ write a message in bit-reverse order }
var j:integer;
begin
 for j := lmessage downto 1 do
   write(rep,mess[j]:1)
end;

procedure reportdetectors(var rep:text; var envmessage:message;
                            nposition:integer);
{ write out environmental message }
begin
 writeln(rep);
 write(rep, 'Environmental message:     ');
 writemessage(rep, envmessage, nposition);
 writeln(rep);
end;

procedure initdetectors(var efile:text; var detectrec:drecord);
{ dummy detector initialization }
begin end;

procedure initrepdetectors(var rep:text; var detectrec:drecord);
{ dummy initial detectors report }
begin end;
```

FIGURE D.4   *(Continued)*

```
{ report.scs: report coordination routines }

{ report declarations }
var pfile:text; { plot file }

procedure reportheader(var rep:text);
{ send report header to specified file/dev. }
begin
  page(rep);
  writeln(rep, 'Snapshot Report');
  writeln(rep, '---------------');
  writeln(rep);
end;

procedure report(var rep:text);
{ report coordination routine }
begin
  reportheader(rep);
  reporttime(rep, timekeeprec);
  reportenvironment(rep, environrec);
  reportdetectors(rep, envmessage, population.nposition);
  reportclassifiers(rep, population);
  reportaoc(rep, clearingrec);
  reportreinforcement(rep, reinforcementrec);
end;

procedure consolereport(var reinforcementrec:rrecord);
{ write console report }
```

FIGURE D.5   Report coordinator and other reporting routines are in *report.scs*.

```
begin with reinforcementrec do begin
  clrscr; { clear the screen }
  writeln('|--------------------------|');
  writeln('      Iteration = ',totalcount:8:0);
  writeln('      P correct = ',proportionreward:8:6);
  writeln('    P50 correct = ',proportionreward50:8:6);
  writeln('|--------------------------|');
end end;

procedure plotreport(var pfile:text; var reinforcementrec:rrecord);
{ write plot report to pfile }
begin with reinforcementrec do begin
  writeln(pfile, totalcount:8:0,' ',proportionreward:8:6,' ',
                 proportionreward50:8:6);
end end;
```

FIGURE D.5   (Continued)

```
{ timekeep.scs: timekeeper routines }

{ data declarations }
const iterationsperblock = 10000; { 10000 iterations per block }

type  trecord = record  { timekeeper record type }
                initialiteration, initialblock, iteration, block,
                reportperiod, gaperiod, consolereportperiod,
                plotreportperiod, nextplotreport, nextconsolereport,
                nextreport, nextga:integer;
                reportflag, gaflag, consolereportflag, plotreportflag:boolean
                end;

var   timekeeprec:trecord;
      tfile:text;

function addtime(t, dt:integer; var carryflag:boolean):integer;
{ increment iterations counter and set carry flag if necessary }
var tempadd:integer;
begin
  tempadd := t + dt;
  carryflag := (tempadd >= iterationsperblock);
  if carryflag then
    tempadd := tempadd mod iterationsperblock;
  addtime := tempadd
end;

procedure inittimekeeper(var tfile:text; var timekeeprec:trecord);
{ initialize timekeeper }
var dummyflag:boolean;
begin with timekeeprec do begin
  iteration := 0; block := 0;
  readln(tfile, initialiteration);
  readln(tfile, initialblock);
  readln(tfile, reportperiod);
  readln(tfile, consolereportperiod);
  readln(tfile, plotreportperiod);
  readln(tfile, gaperiod);
  iteration := initialiteration;
  block := initialblock;
  nextga := addtime(iteration, gaperiod, dummyflag);
  nextreport := addtime(iteration, reportperiod, dummyflag);
  nextconsolereport := addtime(iteration, consolereportperiod, dummyflag);
  nextplotreport := addtime(iteration, plotreportperiod, dummyflag);
end end;
```

FIGURE D.6   Time coordinating routines are in *timekeep.scs*.

```
procedure initreptimekeeper(var rep:text; var timekeeprec:trecord);
{ initial timekeeper report }
begin with timekeeprec do begin
  writeln(rep);
  writeln(rep, 'Timekeeper Parameters');
  writeln(rep, '---------------------');
  writeln(rep, 'Initial iteration      = ', initialiteration:8);
  writeln(rep, 'Initial block          = ', initialblock:8);
  writeln(rep, 'Report period          = ', reportperiod:8);
  writeln(rep, 'Console report period  = ', consolereportperiod:8);
  writeln(rep, 'Plot report period     = ', plotreportperiod:8);
  writeln(rep, 'Genetic algorithm period = ', gaperiod:8);
end end;

procedure timekeeper(var timekeeprec:trecord);
{ keep time and set flags for time-driven events }
var carryflag, dummyflag:boolean;
begin with timekeeprec do begin
  iteration := addtime(iteration, 1, carryflag);
  if carryflag then block := block + 1;
  reportflag := (nextreport = iteration);
  if reportflag then { reset }
    nextreport := addtime(iteration, reportperiod, dummyflag);
  consolereportflag := (nextconsolereport = iteration);
  if consolereportflag then
    nextconsolereport := addtime(iteration, consolereportperiod, dummyflag)
  plotreportflag := (nextplotreport = iteration);
  if plotreportflag then
    nextplotreport := addtime(iteration, plotreportperiod, dummyflag);
  gaflag := (nextga = iteration);
  if gaflag then nextga := addtime(iteration, gaperiod, dummyflag);
end end;

procedure reporttime(var rep:text; var timekeeprec:trecord);
{ print out block and iteration number }
begin with timekeeprec do
  writeln(rep, '[ Block:Iteration ]   = [ ',block,':',iteration,' ]');
end;
```

FIGURE D.6 *(Continued)*

```
{ environ.scs: multiplexer environment }

{ environment declarations }
type   erecord=record
               laddress, ldata, lsignal, address, output,
                classifieroutput:integer;
                signal:message;
               end;

var    environrec:erecord;
       efile:text;

procedure generatesignal(var environrec:erecord);
{ generate random signal }
var j:integer;
begin with environrec do
 for j := 1 to lsignal do
   if flip(0.5) then signal[j] := 1
    else signal[j] := 0
end;
```

FIGURE D.7   The 6-multiplexer routines are in *environ.scs.*

```
function decode(var mess:message; start, length:integer):integer;
( decode substring as unsigned binary integer )
var j, accum, powerof2:integer;
begin
 accum := 0; powerof2 := 1;
 for j := start to start+length-1 do begin
  accum := accum + powerof2*mess[j];
  powerof2 := powerof2 * 2;
 end;
 decode := accum
end;


procedure multiplexeroutput(var environrec:erecord);
( calculate correct multiplexer output )
var j:integer;
begin with environrec do begin
( decode the address )
 address := decode(signal,1,laddress);
( set the output )
 output := signal[laddress + address + 1]
end end;


procedure environment(var environrec:erecord);
( coordinate multiplexer calculations )
begin
 generatesignal(environrec);
 multiplexeroutput(environrec);
end;


procedure initenvironment(var efile:text; var environrec:erecord);
( initialize the multiplexer environement )
var j:integer;
begin with environrec do begin
 readln(efile, laddress);                ( read number of address lines )
 ldata    := round(poweri(2.0, laddress)); ( calculate number of data lines )
 lsignal := laddress + ldata;            ( calculate length of signal )
 address := 0;                           ( zero out multiplexer )
 output   := 0;
 classifieroutput := 0;
 for j := 1 to lsignal do signal[j] := 0;
end end;


procedure initrepenvironment(var rep:text; var environrec:erecord);
( write initial environmental report )
begin with environrec do begin
  writeln(rep);
  writeln(rep, 'Environmental Parameters (Multiplexer)');
  writeln(rep, '--------------------------------------');
  writeln(rep, 'Number of address lines  = ', laddress:8);
  writeln(rep, 'Number of data lines     = ', ldata:8);
  writeln(rep, 'Total number of lines    = ', lsignal:8);
end end;


procedure writesignal(var rep:text; var signal:message; lsignal:integer);
( write a signal in bit-reverse order )
var j:integer;
begin
 for j := lsignal downto 1 do
  write(rep,signal[j]:1)
end;
```

FIGURE D.7 *(Continued)*

```
procedure reportenvironment(var rep:text; var environrec:erecord);
{ write current multiplexer info }
begin with environrec do begin
 writeln(rep);
 writeln(rep,'Current Multiplexer Status');
 writeln(rep,'--------------------------');
   write(rep,'Signal            - ');
   writesignal(rep,signal,lsignal); writeln(rep);
 writeln(rep,'Decoded address        - ', address:8);
 writeln(rep,'Multiplexer output     - ', output:8);
 writeln(rep,'Classifier  output     - ', classifieroutput:8);
end end;
```

FIGURE D.7   *(Continued)*

```
{ perform.scs: performance system - classifier matching }

{ performance declarations - most are in declare.scs }
var cfile:text;    { classifier file }

function randomchar(pgeneral:real):integer;
{ set position.at random with specified generality probability }
begin
  if flip(pgeneral) then randomchar := wildcard
   else if flip(0.5) then randomchar := 1
     else randomchar := 0
end;

procedure readcondition(var cfile:text; var c:condition;
                        var pgeneral:real; var nposition:integer);
{ read a single condition }
var ch:char; j:integer;
begin
  for j := nposition downto 1 do begin
     read(cfile, ch);
     case ch of
       '0':c[j] :=  0;
       '1':c[j] :=  1;
       '#':c[j] := wildcard;
       'R':c[j] := randomchar(pgeneral);
     end
   end
end;

procedure readclassifier(var cfile:text; var class:classtype;
                         pgeneral:real; nposition:integer);
{ read a single classifier }
var ch:char;
begin with class do begin
   readcondition(cfile, c, pgeneral, nposition);  { read condtion }
   read(cfile,ch);                                 { read ":" & ignore }
   read(cfile, a);                                 { read action, a single trit }
   readln(cfile, strength);                        { read strength }
   bid := 0.0; ebid := 0.0; matchflag := false     { initialization }
end end;
```

FIGURE D.8   The rule and message routines are in *perform.scs*.

```
function countspecificity(var c:condition; nposition:integer):integer;
( count condition specificity )
var temp:integer;
begin
  temp := 0;
  while nposition >= 1 do begin
    if c[nposition] <> wildcard then temp := temp + 1;
    nposition := nposition - 1;
   end;
  countspecificity := temp;
end;


procedure initclassifiers(var cfile:text; var population:poptype);
( initialize classifiers )
var j:integer;
begin with population do begin
  readln(cfile,nposition);
  readln(cfile,nclassifier);
  readln(cfile,pgeneral);
  readln(cfile,cbid);
  readln(cfile,bidsigma);
  readln(cfile,bidtax);
  readln(cfile,lifetax);
  readln(cfile,bid1);
  readln(cfile,bid2);
  readln(cfile,ebid1);
  readln(cfile,ebid2);
  for j := 1 to nclassifier do begin
    readclassifier(cfile, classifier[j], pgeneral, nposition);
    with classifier[j] do specificity := countspecificity(c, nposition);
   end;
end end;

procedure initrepclassifiers(var rep:text; var population:poptype);
( Initial report on population parameters )
begin with population do begin
  writeln(rep);
  writeln(rep,'Population Parameters');
  writeln(rep,'---------------------');
  writeln(rep,'Number of classifiers     - ',nclassifier:8);
  writeln(rep,'Number of positions        - ',nposition:8);
  writeln(rep,'Bid coefficient            - ',cbid:8:4);
  writeln(rep,'Bid spread                 - ',bidsigma:8:4);
  writeln(rep,'Bidding tax                - ',bidtax:8:4);
  writeln(rep,'Existence tax              - ',lifetax:8:4);
  writeln(rep,'Generality probability     - ',pgeneral:8:4);
  writeln(rep,'Bid specificity base       - ',bid1:8:4);
  writeln(rep,'Bid specificity mult.      - ',bid2:8:4);
  writeln(rep,'Ebid specificity base      - ',ebid1:8:4);
  writeln(rep,'Ebid specificity mult.     - ',ebid2:8:4);
end end;


procedure writecondition(var rep:text; var c:condition; nposition:integer);
( convert internal condition format to external format and write to file/dev. )
var j:integer;
begin
  for j := nposition downto 1 do
    case c[j] of
            1: write(rep,'1');
            0: write(rep,'0');
      wildcard: write(rep,'#');
    end
end;
```

FIGURE D.8 *(Continued)*

```
procedure writeclassifier(var rep:text; class:classtype;
                             number,nposition:integer);
{ write a single classifier }
begin with class do begin
  write(rep, number:5,' ',strength:8:2,' ',bid:8:2,' ',ebid:8:2);
  if matchflag then write(rep,' X ') else write(rep,'   ');
  writecondition(rep, c, nposition);
  writeln(rep,':','[',a,']')
end end;

procedure reportclassifiers(var rep:text; var population:poptype);
{ generate classifiers report }
var j:integer;
begin with population do begin
  writeln(rep);
  writeln(rep,'No.   Strength      bid      ebid M Classifier ');
  writeln(rep,'----------------------------------------------------');
  writeln(rep);
  for j := 1 to nclassifier do
    writeclassifier(rep, classifier[j], j, nposition);
end end;

function match(var c:condition; var m:message; nposition:integer):boolean;
{ match a single condition to a single message }
var matchtemp:boolean;
begin
  matchtemp := true;
  while (matchtemp = true) and (nposition > 0) do begin
    matchtemp := (c[nposition] = wildcard) or (c[nposition] = m[nposition]);
    nposition := nposition - 1
  end;
  match := matchtemp
end;

procedure matchclassifiers(var population:poptype; var emess:message;
                             var matchlist:classlist);
{ match all classifiers against environmental message and create match list }
var j:integer;
begin with population do with matchlist do begin
  nactive := 0;
  for j := 1 to nclassifier do with classifier[j] do begin
    matchflag := match(c, emess, nposition);
    if matchflag then begin
      nactive := nactive + 1;
      clist[nactive] := j
    end
  end;
end end;
```

FIGURE D.8 *(Continued)*

```
{ aoc.scs: apportionment of credit routines }

{ aoc data declarations - aoc uses cfile for input }
type  crecord = record
                  winner, oldwinner:integer;
                  bucketbrigadeflag:boolean;
                end;

var   clearingrec:crecord;
```

FIGURE D.9 Apportionment of credit routines are in *aoc.scs*.

```
procedure initaoc(var clearingrec:crecord);
{ initialize clearinghouse record }
var ch:char;
begin with clearingrec do begin
 readln(cfile, ch);
 bucketbrigadeflag := (ch = 'y') or (ch = 'Y');
 winner := 1; oldwinner := 1    { 1st classifier picked as 1st oldwinner }
end end;


procedure initrepaoc(var rep:text; var clearingrec:crecord);
{ initial report of clearinghouse parameters }
begin with clearingrec do begin
 writeln(rep);
 writeln(rep, 'Apportionment of Credit Parameters');
 writeln(rep, '---------------------------------');
   write(rep, 'Bucket brigade flag     - ');
   if bucketbrigadeflag then writeln(rep, ' true') else
     writeln(rep, 'false');
end end;


function auction(var population:poptype; var matchlist:classlist;
                     oldwinner:integer):integer;
{ auction among currently matched classifiers - return winner }
var j, k, winner:integer; bidmaximum:real;
begin with population do with matchlist do begin
  bidmaximum := 0.0;
  winner := oldwinner; { if no match, oldwinner wins again }
  if nactive > 0 then for j := 1 to nactive do begin k := clist[j];
    with classifier[k] do begin
      bid  := cbid * (bid1 + bid2 * specificity) * strength;
      ebid := cbid * (ebid1 + ebid2 * specificity) * strength
                 + noise(0.0, bidsigma);
      if (ebid > bidmaximum) then begin
        winner := k;
        bidmaximum := ebid
      end
    end end;
  auction := winner
 end end;

procedure clearinghouse(var population:poptype; var clearingrec:crecord);
{ distribute payment from recent winner to oldwinner }
var payment:real;
begin with population do with clearingrec do begin
  with classifier[winner] do begin { payment }
    payment := bid;
    strength := strength - payment
  end;
  if bucketbrigadeflag then { pay oldwinner receipt if bb is on }
    with classifier[oldwinner] do strength := strength + payment
end end;


procedure taxcollector(var population:poptype);
{ collect existence and bidding taxes from population members }
var j:integer; bidtaxswitch:real;
begin with population do begin
{ life tax from everyone & bidtax from actives }
  if (lifetax <> 0.0) or (bidtax <> 0.0) then for j := 1 to nclassifier do
    with classifier[j] do begin
      if matchflag then bidtaxswitch := 1.0 else bidtaxswitch := 0.0;
      strength := strength - lifetax*strength - bidtax*bidtaxswitch*strength;
    end;
end end;
```

FIGURE D.9 *(Continued)*

```
procedure reportaoc(var rep:text; var clearingrec:crecord);
{ report who pays to whom }
begin
  writeln(rep);
  with clearingrec do
    writeln(rep, 'New winner [',winner,'] : Old winner [',oldwinner,']')
end;

procedure aoc(var population:poptype; var matchlist:classlist;
              var clearingrec:crecord);
{ apportionment of credit coordinator }
begin
  with clearingrec do winner := auction(population, matchlist, oldwinner);
  taxcollector(population);
  clearinghouse(population, clearingrec);
end;
```

FIGURE D.9   *(Continued)*

```
{ effector.scs: effector routine }

procedure effector(var population:poptype; var clearingrec:crecord;
                   var environrec:erecord);
{ set action in object as dictated by auction winner }
begin with population do with clearingrec do with environrec do
  classifieroutput := classifier[winner].a end;
```

FIGURE D.10   Effector routines are in *effector.scs*.

```
{ reinforc.scs:  reinforcement and criterion procedures }

{ reinforcement data declarations }
type rrecord = record { reinforcement record type)
               reward, rewardcount, totalcount, count50,
               rewardcount50, proportionreward,
               proportionreward50:real;
               lastwinner:integer;
               end;

var reinforcementrec:rrecord;
    rfile:text;      { reinforcement file - rfile }

procedure initreinforcement(var rfile:text; var reinforcementrec:rrecord);
{ initialize reinforcement parameters }
begin with reinforcementrec do begin
  readln(rfile, reward);
  rewardcount         := 0.0;
  rewardcount50       := 0.0;
  totalcount          := 0.0;
  count50             := 0.0;
  proportionreward    := 0.0;
  proportionreward50  := 0.0;
  lastwinner := 0;
end end;

procedure initrepreinforcement(var rep:text; var reinforcementrec:rrecord);
{ initial reinforcement report }
begin with reinforcementrec do begin
 writeln(rep);
 writeln(rep, 'Reinforcement Parameters');
 writeln(rep, '------------------------');
 writeln(rep, 'Reinforcement reward    - ', reward:8:1);
end end;
```

FIGURE D.11   Reinforcement routines are in *reinforc.scs*.

```
function criterion(var rrec:rrecord; var environrec:erecord):boolean;
( return true if criterion is achieved )
var tempflag:boolean;
begin with rrec do with environrec do begin
  tempflag := (output - classifieroutput);
  totalcount := totalcount + 1;
  count50 := count50 + 1;
  ( increment reward counters )
  if tempflag then begin
    rewardcount := rewardcount + 1;
    rewardcount50 := rewardcount50 + 1;
    end;
  ( calculate reward proportions: running & last 50 )
  proportionreward := rewardcount/totalcount;
  if ( round(count50 - 50.0) = 0) then begin
    proportionreward50 := rewardcount50/50.0;
    rewardcount50 := 0.0; count50 := 0.0 ( reset )
   end;
  criterion := tempflag;
end end;


procedure payreward(var population:poptype; var rrec:rrecord;
                    var clearingrec:crecord);
( pay reward to appropriate individual )
begin with population do with rrec do with clearingrec do
  with classifier[winner] do begin
    strength := strength + reward;
    lastwinner := winner
end end;


procedure reportreinforcement(var rep:text; var reinforcementrec:rrecord);
( report award )
begin with reinforcementrec do begin
  writeln(rep);
  writeln(rep, 'Reinforcement Report');
  writeln(rep, '--------------------');
  writeln(rep, 'Proportion Correct (from start)  = ',
               proportionreward:8:4);
  writeln(rep, 'Proportion Correct (last fifty)  = ',
               proportionreward50:8:4);
  writeln(rep, 'Last winning classifier number   = ',
               lastwinner:8);
end end;


procedure reinforcement(var reinforcementrec:rrecord; var population:poptype;
                        var clearingrec:crecord; var environrec:erecord);
( make payment if criterion satisfied )
begin
  if criterion(reinforcementrec, environrec) then
       payreward(population, reinforcementrec, clearingrec);
end;
```

FIGURE D.11 *(Continued)*

```
( advance.scs: advance variables for next time step )

procedure advance(var clearingrec:crecord);
( advance winner )
begin with clearingrec do oldwinner := winner end;
```

FIGURE D.12 Iteration advance coordinator is in *advance.scs.*

```
{ ga.scs: genetic algorithm code for SCS }

{ data declarations }
const maxmating = 10;

type  mrecord = record
                    mate1, mate2, mort1, mort2, sitecross:integer
                end;
      marray = array[1..maxmating] of mrecord;
      grecord = record
                    proportionselect, pmutation, pcrossover:real;
                    ncrossover, nmutation, crowdingfactor, crowdingsubpop,
                     nselect:integer;
                    mating:marray; { mating records for ga report}
                end;

var   garec:grecord;
      gfile:text;

procedure initga(var gfile:text; var garec:grecord; var population:poptype);
{ initialize ga parameters }
begin with garec do with population do begin
  readln(gfile, proportionselect);
  readln(gfile, pmutation);
  readln(gfile, pcrossover);
  readln(gfile, crowdingfactor);
  readln(gfile, crowdingsubpop);
  nselect := round(proportionselect * nclassifier * 0.5);
                                    { number of mate pairs to select }
  nmutation := 0; ncrossover := 0;
end end;

procedure initrepga(var rep:text; var garec:grecord);
{ initial report }
begin with garec do begin
  writeln(rep);
  writeln(rep, 'Genetic Algorithm Parameters');
  writeln(rep, '----------------------------');
  writeln(rep, 'Proportion to select/gen = ', proportionselect:8:4);
  writeln(rep, 'Number to select         = ', nselect:8);
  writeln(rep, 'Mutation probability      = ', pmutation:8:4);
  writeln(rep, 'Crossover probability     = ', pcrossover:8:4);
  writeln(rep, 'Crowding factor           = ', crowdingfactor:8);
  writeln(rep, 'Crowding subpopulation    = ', crowdingsubpop:8);
end end;

function select(var population:poptype):integer;
{ select a single individual according to strength }
var rand, partsum:real;
    j:integer;
begin with population do begin
  partsum := 0.0; j := 0;
  rand := random * sumstrength;
  repeat
    j := j + 1;
    partsum := partsum + classifier[j].strength
  until (partsum >= rand) or (j = nclassifier);
  select := j;
end end;

function mutation(positionvalue:trit; pmutation:real;
                             var nmutation:integer):trit;
{ mutate a single position with specified probability }
```

FIGURE D.13 The genetic algorithm routines are in *ga.scs.*

```pascal
var tempmutation:integer;
begin
  if flip(pmutation) then begin
      tempmutation := (positionvalue + rnd(1,2) + 1) mod 3 - 1;
      nmutation := nmutation + 1;
      end
    else tempmutation := positionvalue;
  mutation := tempmutation
end;

function bmutation(positionvalue:bit; pmutation:real;
                               var nmutation:integer):bit;
( mutate a single bit with specified probability )
var tempmutation:integer;
begin
  if flip(pmutation) then begin
      tempmutation := (positionvalue + 1) mod 2;
      nmutation := nmutation + 1;
      end
    else tempmutation := positionvalue;
  bmutation := tempmutation
end;

procedure crossover(var parent1, parent2, child1, child2:classtype;
                        pcrossover, pmutation:real;
                        var sitecross, nposition, ncrossover,
                        nmutation:integer);
( cross a pair at a given site with mutation on the trit transfer )
var inheritance:real; j:integer;
begin
  if flip(pcrossover) then begin
      sitecross := rnd(1, nposition);
      ncrossover := ncrossover + 1;
      end
    else sitecross := nposition + 1  ( transfer, but no cross );
( transfer action part regardless of sitecross )
  child1.a := bmutation(parent1.a, pmutation, nmutation);
  child2.a := bmutation(parent2.a, pmutation, nmutation);
( transfer and cross above cross site )
  j := sitecross;
  while (j <= nposition) do begin
    child2.c[j] := mutation(parent1.c[j], pmutation, nmutation);
    child1.c[j] := mutation(parent2.c[j], pmutation, nmutation);
    j := j + 1
    end;
  j := 1;
( transfer only below cross site )
  while (j < sitecross) do begin
    child1.c[j] := mutation(parent1.c[j], pmutation, nmutation);
    child2.c[j] := mutation(parent2.c[j], pmutation, nmutation);
    j := j + 1
    end;
( children inherit average of parental strength values )
  inheritance := avg(parent1.strength, parent2.strength);
  with child1 do begin
    strength := inheritance; matchflag := false;
    ebid := 0.0; bid := 0.0;
    specificity := countspecificity(c, nposition);
    end;
  with child2 do begin
    strength := inheritance; matchflag := false;
    ebid := 0.0; bid := 0.0;
    specificity := countspecificity(c, nposition);
    end;
end;
```

FIGURE D.13 (Continued)

```
function worstofn(var population:poptype; n:integer):integer;
{ select worst individual from random subpopulation of size n }
var j, worst, candidate:integer; worststrength:real;
begin with population do begin
 { initialize with random selection }
  worst := rnd(1, nclassifier);
  worststrength := classifier[worst].strength;
 { select and compare from remaining subpopulation }
  if (n > 1) then for j := 2 to n do begin
    candidate := rnd(1, nclassifier);
    if worststrength > classifier[candidate].strength then begin
      worst := candidate;
      worststrength := classifier[worst].strength;
      end;
    end;
 { return worst }
  worstofn := worst;
end end;


function matchcount(var classifier1, classifier2:classtype;
                    nposition:integer):integer;
{ count number of positions of similarity }
var tempcount, j:integer;
begin
  if (classifier1.a = classifier2.a) then tempcount := 1
    else tempcount := 0;
  for j := 1 to nposition do
    if (classifier1.c[j] = classifier2.c[j]) then tempcount := tempcount + 1;
  matchcount := tempcount;
end;


function crowding(var child:classtype; var population:poptype;
                  crowdingfactor, crowdingsubpop:integer):integer;
{ replacement using modified De Jong crowding }
var popmember, j, match, matchmax, mostsimilar:integer;
begin with population do begin
  matchmax := -1; mostsimilar := 0;
  if (crowdingfactor < 1) then crowdingfactor := 1;
  for j := 1 to crowdingfactor do begin
    popmember := worstofn(population, crowdingsubpop); { pick worst of n }
    match := matchcount(child, classifier[popmember], nposition);
    if match > matchmax then begin
        matchmax := match;
        mostsimilar := popmember;
        end;
    end;
  crowding := mostsimilar;
end end;


procedure statistics(var population:poptype);
{ population statistics - max, avg, min, sum of strength }
var j:integer;
begin with population do begin
  with classifier[1] do begin
    maxstrength := strength;
    minstrength := strength;
    sumstrength := strength;
    end;
  j := 2;
  while (j <= nclassifier) do with classifier[j] do begin
    maxstrength := max(maxstrength, strength);
    minstrength := min(minstrength, strength);
```

FIGURE D.13 *(Continued)*

368

```
                     sumstrength := sumstrength + strength;
                      j := j + 1;
                    end;
                  avgstrength := sumstrength / nclassifier;
                end end;

procedure ga(var garec:grecord; var population:poptype);
{ coordinate selection, mating, crossover, mutation, & replacement }
var j:integer; child1, child2:classtype;
begin with garec do with population do begin
  statistics(population);                      { get average, max, min, sumstrength }
  for j := 1 to nselect do with mating[j] do begin
    mate1 := select(population);                              { pick mates }
    mate2 := select(population);
    crossover(classifier[mate1], classifier[mate2], child1, child2,
              pcrossover, pmutation, sitecross, nposition,
              ncrossover, nmutation);              { cross & mutate }
    mort1 := crowding(child1, population, crowdingfactor, crowdingsubpop);
    sumstrength := sumstrength - classifier[mort1].strength
                              + child1.strength;              { update sumstrength }
    classifier[mort1] := child1; { insert child in mort1's place }
    mort2 := crowding(child2, population, crowdingfactor, crowdingsubpop);
    sumstrength := sumstrength - classifier[mort2].strength
                              + child2.strength;              { update sumstrength }
    classifier[mort2] := child2;
    end;
  end end;

procedure reportga(var rep:text; var garec:grecord; var population:poptype);
{ report on mating, crossover, and replacement }
var j:integer;
begin with garec do with population do begin
  page(rep);
  writeln(rep,'Genetic Algorithm Report');
  writeln(rep,'------------------------');
  writeln(rep);
  writeln(rep,'Pair Mate1 Mate2 SiteCross Mort1 Mort2');
  writeln(rep,'----------------------------------------------');
  for j := 1 to nselect do with mating[j] do
    writeln(rep,j:3,'    ',mate1:3,'     ',mate2:3,'      ',sitecross:3,
            '       ',mort1:3,'     ',mort2:3);
  writeln(rep);
  writeln(rep,'Statistics Report');
  writeln(rep,'-----------------');
  writeln(rep,' Average     strength = ',avgstrength:8:2);
  writeln(rep,' Maximum     strength = ',maxstrength:8:2);
  writeln(rep,' Minimum     strength = ',minstrength:8:2);
  writeln(rep,' Sum   of    strength = ',sumstrength:8:2);
  writeln(rep,' Number of crossings = ',ncrossover:8);
  writeln(rep,' Number of mutations = ',nmutation:8);
end end;
```

FIGURE D.13 *(Continued)*

```
{ utility.scs: utility procedures and functions }

function poweri(x:real; i:integer):real;
var powertemp:real;
begin
 powertemp := 1.0;
 if i=0 then powertemp := 1.0
   else if i>0 then
     repeat
```

FIGURE D.14 Computational utilities are in *utility.scs.*

```
        powertemp := powertemp * x;
        i := i - 1
      until i=0
    else if i<0 then
      repeat
        powertemp := powertemp / x;
         i := i + 1
      until i=0;
  poweri := powertemp
end;


{ global variables for randomnormaldeviate - watch for conflicting names }
var rndx2:real;
    rndcalcflag:boolean;

procedure initrandomnormaldeviate;
{ initialization routine for randomnormaldeviate }
begin rndcalcflag := true end;

function randomnormaldeviate:real;
{ random normal deviate after ACM algorithm 267 / Box-Muller Method }
var t, rndx1:real;
begin
 if rndcalcflag then begin
    rndx1 := sqrt(-2.0*ln(random));
    t   := 6.2831853072 * random;
    rndx2 := rndx1 * sin(t);
    rndcalcflag := false;
    randomnormaldeviate := rndx1 * cos(t)
  end else begin
    randomnormaldeviate := rndx2;
    rndcalcflag := true
  end;
end;


function noise(mu, sigma:real):real;
{ normal noise with specified mean & std dev: mu & sigma }
begin noise := randomnormaldeviate * sigma + mu end;

function rndreal(lo, hi:real):real;
{ real random number between specified limits }
begin rndreal := random*(hi-lo) + lo end;

function max(x, y:real):real;
{ return maximum of two values }
begin if x > y then max := x else max := y end;

function min(x, y:real):real;
{ return minimum of two real values }
begin if x < y then min := x else min := y end;

 function avg(x, y:real):real;
{ return average of two real values }
begin avg := 0.5 * (x + y) end;

function halt:boolean;
{ Test for key press and query for halt flag }
const times = 100;
var temp:boolean; ch:char; j:integer;
begin
   j := 0;
   repeat j := j+1 until keypressed or (j>=times);
   temp := (j<times);
```

FIGURE D.14 *(Continued)*

```
  if temp then begin
     write('Halt (y/n)? > '); readln(ch);
     temp := (ch = 'y') or (ch = 'Y');
    end;
  halt := temp;
end;
```

FIGURE D.14 *(Continued)*

```
(* IO Routines- File opening routines *)
type  query_type = (interactive,batch);
      txt         = string[80];

var   qflag:query_type;
      fn:txt;

procedure page(var out:text);
begin write(out,chr(12)) end;

procedure open_input(var input:text; query_flag:query_type;
                     message:txt; var filename:txt);
begin
 if (query_flag=batch) then assign(input,filename)
  else begin
   write('Enter ',message,' filename: ');readln(filename);
   assign(input,filename);
  end;
 reset(input);
end;

procedure open_output(var output:text; query_flag:query_type;
                      message:txt; var filename:txt);
begin
 if (query_flag=batch) then assign(output,filename)
  else begin
   write('Enter ',message,' filename: ');readln(filename);
   assign(output,filename);
  end;
 rewrite(output);
end;
```

FIGURE D.15 Input output utilities are in *io.scs*.

```
0               { initialiteration }        { time.dta }
0               { initialblock }
2000            { reportperiod }
50              { consolereportperiod }
50              { plotreportperiod }
-1              { gaperiod }
```

FIGURE D.16 The file *time.dta* contains a sample *tfile*.

```
2     { number of address lines on multiplexer }  { environ.dta }
```

FIGURE D.17 The file *environ.dta* contains a sample *efile*.

FIGURE D.18   The file *reinf.dta* contains a sample *rfile*.

```
0.20          ( proportionselect )         ( ga.dta )
0.02          ( pmutation )
1.0           ( pcrossover )
3             ( crowdingfactor )
3             ( crowdingsubpop )
```

FIGURE D.19   The file *ga.dta* contains a sample *gfile*.

```
6             ( nposition )              ( perfect.dta )
10            ( nclassifier )
0.5           ( pgeneral )
0.10          ( cbid )
0.075         ( bidsigma )
0.01          ( bidtax )
0.0           ( lifetax )
1.0           ( bid 1 )
0.0           ( bid 2 )
1.0           ( ebid 1 )
0.0           ( ebid 2 )
###000:0   10    ( perfect rules )
###100:1   10
##0#01:0   10
##1#01:1   10
#0##10:0   10
#1##10:1   10
0###11:0   10
1###11:1   10
######:0   10    ( general rules )
######:1   10
n                ( bucketbrigadeflag )
```

FIGURE D.20   The file *perfect.dta* contains a sample *cfile* for the perfect rule set experiments of Chapter 6.

```
6             ( nposition )              ( lessthan(perfect).dta )
7             ( nclassifier )
0.5           ( pgeneral )
0.1           ( cbid )
0.075         ( bidsigma )
0.01          ( bidtax )
0.00          ( lifetax )
1.00          ( bid 1 )
0.00          ( bid 2 )
1.00          ( ebid 1 )
0.0           ( ebid 2 )
###000:0   10    ( default hierarchy )
##0#01:0   10
#0##10:0   10
0###11:0   10
######:1   10
0###11:1   10    ( monkey wrenches   )
######:0   10
n                ( bucketbrigadeflag )
```

FIGURE D.21   The file *lessthan.dta* (less-than-perfect) contains a sample *cfile* for the default hierarchy experiments of Chapter 6.

```
6              { nposition }           { class100.dta }
100            { nclassifier }
0.5            { pgeneral }
0.10           { cbid }
0.075          { bidsigma }
0.01           { bidtax }
0.000          { lifetax }
0.25           { bid 1 }
0.125          { bid 2 }
0.25           { ebid 1 }
0.125          { ebid 2 }
RRRRRR:0  10
RRRRRR:0  10
RRRRRR:0  10
RRRRRR:0  10
RRRRRR:0  10
RRRRRR:0  10
RRRRRR:0  10
RRRRRR:0  10
RRRRRR:0  10
RRRRRR:0  10
RRRRRR:1  10
RRRRRR:1  10
RRRRRR:1  10
RRRRRR:1  10
RRRRRR:1  10
RRRRRR:1  10
RRRRRR:1  10
RRRRRR:1  10
RRRRRR:1  10
RRRRRR:1  10
n              { bucketbrigadeflag }
```

FIGURE D.22 The file *class100.dta* contains a sample *cfile* for the clean slate experiments of Chapter 6. Only 10 of each type of rule are shown for brevity.

E Partition Coefficient Transforms for Problem-Coding Analysis

Effective processing by genetic algorithms occurs when *building blocks*—relatively short, low-order schemata with above-average fitness values—combine to form optima or near-optima. That this inverted cascade of schemata does lead to desirable points has often been taken as an article of faith (the so-called *building block hypothesis*). Recently, a number of investigators have developed methods for analyzing when problem-coding-operator combinations should (and should not) be expected to lead to good strings. These efforts divide into two groups, depending on their use of dynamic or static methods.

The dynamic approach, as sampled briefly in Chapter 2 in connection with the minimal deceptive problem (MDP), uses a full analysis of the propagation of competing species of schemata through the nonlinear difference equations resulting from combined consideration of operators, coding, and objective function. This kind of analysis leads to conclusive results in small problems, and recently developed (Bridges and Goldberg, 1987) equations of motion under reproduction and crossover for general l-bit codings permit dynamic analysis of higher-order problems.

The static approach (Bethke, 1981; Holland, 1987b) uses efficient transform methods to calculate schema averages. These averages are then used to determine whether the building block hypothesis is satisfied (whether short, low-order, high-performance schemata do combine to form longer, higher-order, higher-performance schemata) or not (whether the problem is GA-deceptive). Holland (personal communication, 1987) has recently extended his analysis to populations with nonuniform proportions of strings. In the uniform case it may be shown that Bethke's and Holland's techniques are equivalent. In this appendix we follow Holland's notation and explore his method of partition coefficients; we apply it to the analysis of a simple coding-problem combination. Its use is outlined in the design of GA-deceptive problems.

PARTITION COEFFICIENT TRANSFORM

We consider a mapping f from the l-bit strings into the real numbers:

$$f: \{0, 1\}^l \xrightarrow{f} \mathbb{R}.$$

We take schemata over the strings in the usual way, and we define a partition number j for those schemata that share the same fixed positions:

$$j(H) = \sum_{i=1}^{l} \alpha(h_i) 2^{i-1},$$

where i is an index over the string positions and the function α assumes a value of 0 when $h_i = *$ and a value of 1 otherwise. In this way the partition number function j assigns a unique number to each of the 2^l partitions of the string space defined by the set of 2^l fixed positions. For example, the schema *** is assigned the partition number $j(***) = 0$. The schemata **0 and **1 share the partition number $j = 1$, and the schema 0*1 is assigned a partition number $j(0*1) = 5$.

To calculate the partition coefficients, we also define a function σ over the set of all schemata where σ assumes a value of 1 when a schema contains an even number of 0's and a value of -1 otherwise:

$$\sigma(H) = \prod_{i=1}^{l} (-1)^{\beta(h_i)},$$

where β takes on a value of 1 when $h_i = 0$ and 0 otherwise.

Having defined the partition number j and the σ-function, we may now define the partition coefficients ε_j with a set of formulas of the following form:

$$f(H) = \sum_{H' \supseteq H} \sigma(H') \varepsilon_{j(H')}$$

The summation is thus taken over all similarity subsets H' which contain the schema H.

There are clearly 3^l such equations, one for each of the 3^l schemata; however, only 2^l of these are independent because there are only 2^l ε's (another way to view this is that we are simply transforming the 2^l fitness values associated with each of the strings to 2^l other real coefficients). We do not prove the partition coefficient equation here; however, one straightforward proof considers the bits as binary variables u_i drawn from the set $\{-1, 1\}$. It is then easy to show that any function f can be written as an l-degree polynomial in the u_i and that there is a one-to-one mapping between the coefficients of that polynomial and the ε's. The truth of the transform then follows directly from the form of the polynomial. The next section investigates further the method by calculating the partition coefficients on a simple function and coding.

AN EXAMPLE: $f(x) = x^2$ ON THREE BITS A DAY

To better understand the partition coefficient transform, let's calculate the ε's for a particular problem: $f(x) = x^2$ coded as a three-bit, unsigned integer. To start, we write eight equations, one for each of the schemata containing only *'s and 1's:

$$f(***) = \varepsilon_0,$$
$$f(**1) = \varepsilon_0 + \varepsilon_1,$$
$$f(*1*) = \varepsilon_0 + \varepsilon_2,$$
$$f(*11) = \varepsilon_0 + \varepsilon_1 + \varepsilon_2 + \varepsilon_3,$$
$$f(1**) = \varepsilon_0 + \varepsilon_4,$$
$$f(1*1) = \varepsilon_0 + \varepsilon_1 + \varepsilon_4 + \varepsilon_5,$$
$$f(11*) = \varepsilon_0 + \varepsilon_2 + \varepsilon_4 + \varepsilon_6,$$
$$f(111) = \varepsilon_0 + \varepsilon_1 + \varepsilon_2 + \varepsilon_3 + \varepsilon_4 + \varepsilon_5 + \varepsilon_6 + \varepsilon_7.$$

This enumeration suggests a reasonably efficient algorithm for calculating the ε's (a fast Walsh transform would speed things even further, but we use this triangularization to retain some physical insight): simply calculate the schema averages directly in the order shown, and then calculate the ε's by back substitution. Performing these computations, we obtain the following f and ε values:

Partition Number j	Schema H	$f(H)$	$\varepsilon(j)$
0	***	17.5	17.5
1	**1	21.0	3.5
2	*1*	24.5	7.0
3	*11	29.0	1.0
4	1**	31.5	14.0
5	1*1	37.0	2.0
6	11*	42.5	4.0
7	111	49.0	0.0

Having calculated the ε's, we may directly calculate any schema average we wish to consider. For example, $f(**0) = \varepsilon_0 - \varepsilon_1 = 17.5 - 3.5 = 14$. This may be verified by direct computation: $f(**0) = (0 + 4 + 16 + 36)/4 = 14.0$. Although other schemata may be obtained as directly, we must further inquire as to the meaning of the ε's and how they may be used to analyze GAs and schema processing.

WHAT DO THE PARTITION COEFFICIENTS MEAN?

That we can calculate these partition coefficients reasonably efficiently is comforting, but we are really concerned with understanding the nature of nonlinearity in the binary-coded problems that arise when using the GA method. To see the connection between bitwise nonlinearity and the ε coefficients, we make some deeper comparisons using our example problem. Consider the formulas for the fitness values of two competing schemata, for example **1 and **0:

$$f(**1) = \varepsilon_0 + \varepsilon_1,$$
$$f(**0) = \varepsilon_0 - \varepsilon_1.$$

Since the coefficient ε_0 is simply the average of all fitness values in the space (the fitness of the schema ***), the coefficient ε_1 is a direct measure of the influence of a single 1 acting in the least significant bit. In effect it is the average increment (above population average) due to a 1 at that position. Similar conclusions may be drawn concerning the other one-bit partition coefficients (ε_2 and ε_4) and their effect on competing schemata average fitness values:

$$f(*1*) = \varepsilon_0 + \varepsilon_2,$$
$$f(*0*) = \varepsilon_0 - \varepsilon_2,$$
$$f(1**) = \varepsilon_0 + \varepsilon_4,$$
$$f(0**) = \varepsilon_0 - \varepsilon_4,$$

This view of the ε's almost begs us to consider higher-order schemata. We might think of constructing a low-order approximation to a higher-order schema by summing the increments (or decrements) above average fitness for all fixed, one-bit schemata. For example, since the intersection of *1* and **1 is *11, a low-order approximation to the fitness of that schema would simply sum ε_1 and ε_2 and add it to the space average fitness (ε_0). Introducing the hat $\wedge$ to indicate an estimate, we obtain the following expression:

$$\hat{f}(*11) = \varepsilon_0 + \varepsilon_1 + \varepsilon_2.$$

Comparing this to the actual expression for the fitness of the schema *11, we obtain a difference between the low-order model and the correct schema, average fitness as follows:

$$f(*11) - \hat{f}(*11) = \varepsilon_3.$$

In this case, the two-bit partition coefficient ε_3 describes the fitness contribution due to epistatic interaction of the bits in the two rightmost positions. More generally, we can see the role of higher-order partition coefficients. They describe the fitness contribution caused by the epistatic interaction of a particular set of two or more bits. It is a straightforward exercise to pursue this notion of increasingly higher-order estimates of schema averages. Instead we investigate the use of the partition coefficients in the analysis and design of GA-deceptive problems.

USING PARTITION COEFFICIENTS TO ANALYZE DECEPTIVE PROBLEMS

Partition coefficients identify the bitwise nonlinearities contained in a function that maps binary vectors into the reals. Although this identification is useful in its own right, in the study of genetic algorithms, partition coefficients are primarily useful for two things: the analysis of whether problems are GA-deceptive and the design of problems that are. We consider simple examples of deception analysis in this section.

The analysis of whether problems are GA-deceptive is very straightforward. Consider our three-bit example problem. Can we determine from the ε values whether this function is deceptive? Since the point 111 is optimal, for deception we require that some schema containing a 0 have higher average fitness than its competitors containing only *'s and 1's. Considering the one-bit schemata, one or more of the following conditions must hold true:

$$f(**1) < f(**0),$$
$$f(*1*) < f(*0*),$$
$$f(1**) < f(0**).$$

In terms of the ε values we write three equivalent relations as follows:

$$\varepsilon_1 < 0,$$
$$\varepsilon_2 < 0,$$
$$\varepsilon_4 < 0.$$

Checking the table of ε values in the previous section we see that none of these ε's are negative and we therefore conclude that the problem is not one-bit deceptive. We can write additional relations for the order-two schemata, and in this case none turn out to be misleading either. As a result we conclude that this problem is not deceptive and should yield to simple GA search. If we had found that one or more of the deception conditions were satisfied, we would suspect that we might have a difficult (GA-hard) problem. Further analysis would be required to determine whether the problem was indeed GA-hard, because a function that is GA-deceptive may not be GA-hard (for example, the minimal deceptive problem), but a GA-hard function is always GA-deceptive.

DESIGNING GA-DECEPTIVE PROBLEMS WITH PARTITION COEFFICIENTS

Analyzing whether specific problems are deceptive is useful, but we may also want to design partially or fully deceptive problems. This may easily be done using partition coefficients. To see this we outline the optimality and deception conditions required.

Again let's assume that point 111 is the best. A set of seven inequalities may then be written of the form $f_{111} > f_{000}, f_{111} > f_{001}$, and so on. Using the partition coefficient transform, these inequalities may be written in terms of the ε's:

$$\varepsilon_1 + \varepsilon_3 + \varepsilon_5 + \varepsilon_7 > 0,$$
$$\varepsilon_2 + \varepsilon_3 + \varepsilon_6 + \varepsilon_7 > 0,$$
$$\varepsilon_1 + \varepsilon_2 + \varepsilon_5 + \varepsilon_6 > 0,$$
$$\varepsilon_4 + \varepsilon_5 + \varepsilon_6 + \varepsilon_7 > 0,$$
$$\varepsilon_1 + \varepsilon_3 + \varepsilon_4 + \varepsilon_6 > 0,$$
$$\varepsilon_2 + \varepsilon_3 + \varepsilon_4 + \varepsilon_5 > 0,$$
$$\varepsilon_1 + \varepsilon_2 + \varepsilon_4 + \varepsilon_7 > 0.$$

The seven optimality conditions may be used with one or more deception conditions to introduce deceptive nonlinearities. For one-bit deception we require one or more of the following conditions:

$$\varepsilon_1 < 0,$$
$$\varepsilon_2 < 0,$$
$$\varepsilon_4 < 0,$$

For two-bit deception we require one or more of the following sets of conditions to hold:

$$\varepsilon_1 + \varepsilon_2 < 0;\ \varepsilon_2 + \varepsilon_3 < 0;\ \varepsilon_1 + \varepsilon_3 < 0,$$
$$\varepsilon_1 + \varepsilon_4 < 0;\ \varepsilon_4 + \varepsilon_5 < 0;\ \varepsilon_1 + \varepsilon_5 < 0,$$
$$\varepsilon_2 + \varepsilon_4 < 0;\ \varepsilon_4 + \varepsilon_6 < 0;\ \varepsilon_2 + \varepsilon_6 < 0.$$

The design of a particular deceptive problem is left as an exercise.

SUMMARY

This appendix presents a method of performing static schema analysis using Holland's method of partition coefficients. The procedure permits direct analysis of schema averages for particular functions and codings. It also permits the design of functions with specified epistasis. These applications may be used to shed additional light on appropriate functions, codings, and operators for better genetic algorithm performance.

■ PROBLEMS

E.1. Calculate the partition coefficients for the function $f(x) = (x - 3.5)^2$ using a three-bit unsigned integer coding for the parameter x. What is true about all the one-bit ε's? Why is this so?

E.2. For the function, $f(x, y, z) = 10 + x + 2y + 4z$ where x, y, and z are binary variables drawn from the set $\{-1, 1\}$, calculate the partition coefficients for this problem assuming a string coding $z'y'x'$. Here the unprimed-to-primed mapping assumes that a 1 is coded as a 1 and a -1 is coded as a 0. What is true about all second- and third-order partition coefficients and why?

E.3. Generalize the result of Problem E.2 to any l-bit linear function of the form $f(x_i) = \Sigma a_i x_i + b$ with $x_i \in \{-1, 1\}$ and a string coding $x'_l x'_{l-1} \ldots x'_2 x'_1$ with $x'_i \in \{0,1\}$

E.4. For the function $f(x, y, z) = 10 + x + 2y + 4z - xy + 2yz - xyz$ where x, y, and z are binary variables drawn from the set $\{-1, 1\}$, calculate the partition coefficients assuming a string coding $z'y'x'$ where x', y', $z' \in \{0, 1\}$. What is the relationship between the polynomial coefficients and the partition coefficient values? Is this a general property?

E.5. Earlier it was shown that the three-bit partition coefficient (ε_7) for the function $f(x) = x^2$ coded as an unsigned binary integer was zero. Show that this is true for any quadratic function $f(x)$.

E.6. Calculate the partition coefficients for the function $f(x) = x$ for a four-bit unsigned Gray-coded integer. What is the highest order nonlinearity of this problem coding?

E.7. Design a three-bit deceptive function that is entirely one-bit deceptive at all three bits, and two-bit deceptive over the two least significant bits. Specify the function by writing out the function values at all eight points. Assume that f_{111} is the global maximum.

■ COMPUTER ASSIGNMENTS

A. Write a computer program that calculates any specified string or schema fitness given the ε's.

B. Write a computer program that calculates the partition coefficients ε_i given the string fitness values f_i.

C. Calculate the Walsh coefficients of a function using a fast Walsh transform. Compare the Walsh coefficients to the ε values calculated by the program of Computer Assignment B.

Bibliography

Ackley, D. H. (1985). A connectionist algorithm for genetic search. *Proceedings of an International Conference on Genetic Algorithms and Their Applications,* 121–135.

Antonisse, H. J., & Keller, K. S. (1986). Dynamic evaluation of imprecisely specified knowledge. *Proceedings of the Digital Avionics Systems Conference,* 596–600.

Antonisse, H. J., & Keller, K. S. (1987). Genetic operators for high-level knowledge representations. *Genetic algorithms and their applications: Proceedings of the Second International Conference on Genetic Algorithms,* 69–76.

Avriel, M. (1976). *Nonlinear programming: analysis and methods.* Englewood Cliffs, NJ: Prentice-Hall.

Axelrod, R. (1985, August). *Modeling the evolution of norms.* Paper presented at the American Political Science Association Meeting, New Orleans, LA.

Axelrod, R. (1985, November). *The simulation of genetics and evolution.* Paper presented at A Conference on Evolutionary Theory in Biology and Economics, University of Bielefeld, Federal Republic of Germany.

Axelrod, R. (1987). The evolution of strategies in the iterated prisoner's dilemma. In L. Davis (Ed.), *Genetic algorithms and simulated annealing* (pp. 32–41). London: Pitman.

Bagley, J. D. (1967). The behavior of adaptive systems which employ genetic and correlation algorithms. (Doctoral dissertation, University of Michigan). *Dissertation Abstracts International, 28*(12), 5106B. (University Microfilms No. 68-7556)

Bailey, J. E., & Krishnakumar, K. (1987). Total energy control concepts applied to flight in windshear. *Proceedings of the AIAA Guidance, Navigation, and Control Conference,* 525–532.

Baker, J. E. (1985). Adaptive selection methods for genetic algorithms. *Proceedings of an International Conference on Genetic Algorithms and Their Applications,* 101–111.

Baker, J. E. (1987). Reducing bias and inefficiency in the selection algorithm. *Genetic algorithms and their applications: Proceedings of the Second International Conference on Genetic Algorithms,* 14–21.

Barricelli, N. A. (1957). Symbiogenetic evolution processes realized by artificial methods. *Methodos, 9*(35–36), 143–182.

Barricelli, N. A. (1962). Numerical testing of evolution theories. *ACTA Biotheoretica, 16,* 69–126.

Barto, A. G., Anandan, P., & Anderson, C. W. (1985). Cooperativity in networks of pattern recognizing stochastic learning automata. *Proceedings of the Fourth Yale Workshop on Applications of Adaptive Systems Theory,* 85–90.

Beightler, C. S., Phillips, D. T., & Wilde, D. J. (1979). *Foundations of optimization* (2nd. ed.). Englewood Cliffs, NJ: Prentice-Hall.

Belew, R. (1981). [Operation description for Model T classifier system]. Unpublished manuscript.

Bellman, R. (1961). *Adaptive control processes: A guided tour.* Princeton, NJ: Princeton University Press.

Bennett, W. H., & De Jong, K. A. (in press). *Adaptive search techniques and the design of decentralized control systems* (NRL Memorandum Report). Washington, DC: Naval Research Laboratory.

Bernstein, A., & Rubin, H. (1965). Artificial evolution of problem-solvers. *The American Behavioral Scientist, 8*(9), 19–23.

Berry, R. J. (1965). *Genetics.* London: English University Press.

Bethke, A. D. (1976). *Comparison of genetic algorithms and gradient-based optimizers on parallel processors: Efficiency of use of processing capacity* (Technical Report No. 197). Ann Arbor: University of Michigan, Logic of Computers Group.

Bethke, A. D. (1978). *Genetic algorithms as function optimizers* (Technical Report No. 212). Ann Arbor: University of Michigan, Logic of Computers Group.

Bethke, A. D. (1981). Genetic algorithms as function optimizers. (Doctoral dissertation, University of Michigan). *Dissertation Abstracts International 41*(9), 3503B. (University Microfilms No. 8106101)

Bethke, A. D., Zeigler, B. P., & Strauss, D. M. (1974). *Convergence properties of simple genetic algorithms* (Technical Report No. 159). Ann Arbor: University of Michigan, Department of Computer and Communication Sciences.

Bickel, A. S., & Bickel, R. W. (1987). Tree structured rules in genetic algorithms. *Genetic algorithms and their applications: Proceedings of the Second International Conference on Genetic Algorithms,* 77–81.

Bledsoe, W. W. (1961, November). *The use of biological concepts in the analytical study of systems.* Paper presented at the ORSA-TIMS National Meeting, San Francisco, CA.

Bledsoe, W. W., & Browning, I. (1959). Pattern recognition and reading by machine. *Proceedings of the Eastern Joint Computer Conference,* 225–232.

Bonomi, E., & Lutton, J. L. (1984). The N-city traveling salesman problem: Statistical mechanics and the Metropolis algorithm. *SIAM Review, 26*(4), 551–569.

Booker, L. B. (1981). Monday evening satellite session. In J. R. Sampson (Ed.), *A Synopsis of the Fifth Annual Ann Arbor Adaptive Systems Workshop* (pp. 81–86). Ann Arbor: University of Michigan, Department of Computer and Communication Sciences, Logic of Computers Group.

Booker, L. B. (1982). Intelligent behavior as an adaptation to the task environment. (Doctoral dissertation, Technical Report No. 243. Ann Arbor: University of Michigan, Logic of Computers Group). *Dissertations Abstracts International, 43*(2), 469B. (University Microfilms No. 8214966)

Booker, L. B. (1985). Improving the performance of genetic algorithms in classifier systems. *Proceedings of an International Conference on Genetic Algorithms and Their Applications,* 80–92.

Booker, L. B. (1987). Improving search in genetic algorithms. In L. Davis (Ed.), *Genetic algorithms and simulated annealing* (pp. 61–73). London: Pitman.

Booker, L. B., & De Jong, K. A. (1985). *ADOPT* [Computer program in C for genetic algorithms]. Washington, DC: Naval Research Laboratory.

Booker, L. B., Goldberg, D. E., & Holland, J. H. (1987) *Classifier systems and genetic algorithms* (Technical Report No. 8). Ann Arbor: University of Michigan, Cognitive Science and Machine Intelligence Laboratory.

Borland International, Inc. (1985). *Turbo Pascal Version 3.0 reference manual.* Scotts Valley, CA: author.

Bosworth, J., Foo, N., & Zeigler, B. P. (1972). *Comparison of genetic algorithms with conjugate gradient methods* (CR-2093). Washington, DC: National Aeronautics and Space Administration.

Bowen, D. (1986). *A study of the effects of internally determined crossover and mutation rates on genetic algorithm optimization.* Unpublished manuscript, University of Alabama, Tuscaloosa.

Box, G. E. P, (1957). Evolutionary operation: A method for increasing industrial productivity. *Journal of the Royal Statistical Society, C, 6*(2), 81–101.

Brachman, R. J., & Schmolze, J. (1985). An overview of the KL-ONE knowledge representation system. *Cognitive Science, 9*(2), 171–216.

Brady, R. M. (1985). Optimization strategies gleaned from biological evolution [Letter to the editor]. *Nature, 317,* 804–806.

Brainerd, W. S., & Landweber, L. H. (1974). *Theory of computation.* New York: Wiley Interscience.

Braitenberg, V. (1984). *Vehicles.* Cambridge, MA: MIT Press.

Bremermann, H. J. (1962). Optimization through evolution and recombination. In M. C. Yovits, G. T. Jacobi, & G. D. Goldstein (Eds.), *Self-organizing systems* (pp. 93–106). Washington, D.C.: Spartan Books.

Bremermann, H. J. (1963). Limits of genetic control. *IEEE Transactions on Military Electronics, MIL·7*(2-3), 200–205.

Bremermann, H. J. (1967). Quantitative aspects of goal-seeking self-organizing systems. *Progress in Theoretical Biology, 1,* 59–77.

Brent, R. P. (1973). *Algorithms for minimization without derivatives.* Englewood Cliffs, NJ: Prentice-Hall.

Bridges, C. L., & Goldberg, D. E. (1987). An analysis of reproduction and crossover in a binary-coded genetic algorithm. *Genetic algorithms and their applications: Proceedings of the Second International Conference on Genetic Algorithms,* 9–13.

Brindle, A. (1981). *Genetic algorithms for function optimization.* Unpublished doctoral dissertation, University of Alberta, Edmonton.

Brindle, A., & Sampson, J. (1979). *Analysis of frequency error in three sampling algorithms.* Unpublished manuscript, University of Alberta, Department of Computing Science, Edmonton.

Brindle, A., & Sampson, J. (1981). *Genetic algorithms as adaptive search mechanisms for function optimization.* Unpublished manuscript, University of Alberta, Department of Computer Science, Edmonton.

Burks, A. W. (Ed.). (1970). *Essays on cellular automata.* Urbana: University of Illinois Press.

Burks, A. W. (1986). A radically non-von-Neumann-architecture for learning and discovery. *Proceedings of the Conference on Algorithms and Hardware for Parallel Processing,* 1–17.

Burks, A. W., Zeigler, B. P., Laing, R. A., & Holland, J. H. (1974). Biologically motivated automaton theory and automaton motivated biological research. *Proceedings of the 1974 Conference on Biologically Motivated Automata Theory,* 1–12.

Cavicchio, D. J. (1970). *Adaptive search using simulated evolution.* Unpublished doctoral dissertation, University of Michigan, Ann Arbor.

Cavicchio, D. J. (1972). Reproductive adaptive plans. *Proceedings of the ACM 1972 Annual Conference,* 1–11.

Cohen, M. D. (1981). The power of parallel thinking. *Journal of Economic Behavior and Organization, 2*(4), 285–306.

Cohen, M. D. (1984). Conflict and complexity: Goal diversity and organizational search effectiveness. *The American Political Science Review, 78*(2), 435–451.

Cohen, M. D. (1986, October). *AI-based models of organizational designs.* Paper presented at ORSA/TIMS Joint National Meeting, Miami, FL.

Cohen, M. D. (1987, June). *Adaptation of organizational routines.* Paper presented at the Workshop on Organizational Science, Massachussetts Institute of Technology, Cambridge, MA.

Cohoon, J. P., & Hegde, S. U., Martin, W. N., & Richards, D. (1987). Punctuated equilibria: A parallel genetic algorithm. *Genetic algorithms and their applications: Proceedings of the Second International Conference on Genetic Algorithms,* 148–154.

Cohoon, J. P., & Paris, W. D. (1986). Genetic placement. *Proceedings of the IEEE International Conference on Computer-Aided Design,* 422–425.

Conrad, M. (1979). Bootstrapping on the adaptive landscape. *BioSystems, 11,* 167–182.

Conrad, M., Harth, E., Holland, J., Martinez, H., Pattee, H., Rada, R., Waltz, D., & Zeigler, B. (1984). Natural and artificial intelligence. *Cognition and Brain Theory, 7*(1), 89–104.

Coombs, S., & Davis, L. (1987). Genetic algorithms and communication link speed design: Constraints and operators. *Genetic algorithms and their applications: Proceedings of the Second International Conference on Genetic Algorithms,* 257–260.

Cramer, N. L. (1985). A representation for the adaptive generation of simple sequential programs. *Proceedings of an International Conference on Genetic Algorithms and Their Applications,* 183–187.

Davis, L. (1985a). Applying adaptive algorithms to epistatic domains. *Proceedings of the 9th International Joint Conference on Artificial Intelligence, 162–164.*

Davis, L. (1985b). Job shop scheduling with genetic algorithms. *Proceedings of an International Conference on Genetic Algorithms and Their Applications, 136–140.*

Davis, L. (Ed.). (1987). *Genetic algorithms and simulated annealing.* London: Pitman.

Davis, L., & Coombs, S. (1987). Genetic algorithms and communication link speed design: theoretical considerations. *Genetic algorithms and their applications: Proceedings of the Second International Conference on Genetic Algorithms, 252–256.*

Davis, L., & Coombs, S. (in press). *Optimizing network link sizes with genetic algorithms.* In M. Elzas, T. Oren, & B. P. Zeigler, *Modelling and simulation methodology: Knowledge systems paradigms.* Amsterdam: North-Holland.

Davis, L., & Ritter, F. (1987). Schedule optimization with probabilistic search. *Proceedings of the 3rd IEEE Conference on Artificial Intelligence Applications, 231–236.*

Davis, L., & Smith, D. (1985). *Adaptive design for layout synthesis* (Texas Instruments internal report). Dallas: Texas Instruments.

Davis, L., & Steenstrup, M. (1987). Genetic algorithms and simulated annealing: An overview. In L. Davis (Ed.), *Genetic algorithms and simulated annealing* (pp. 1–11). London: Pitman.

Davis, R., & King, J. (1976). An overview of production systems. In E. W. Elcock & D. Michie (Eds.), *Machine Intelligence 8* (pp. 300–332). New York: Wiley.

De Groot, M. H. (1970). *Optimal statistical decisions.* New York: McGraw-Hill.

De Jong, K. A. (1975). An analysis of the behavior of a class of genetic adaptive systems. (Doctoral dissertation, University of Michigan). *Dissertation Abstracts International 36*(10), 5140B. (University Microfilms No. 76-9381)

De Jong, K. A. (1976). *Artificial genetic adaptive systems* (Technical Report No. 76–7). Pittsburgh: University of Pittsburgh, Department of Computer Science.

De Jong, K. A. (1980a). Adaptive system design: A genetic approach. *IEEE Transactions on Systems, Man, and Cybernetics, SMC-10*(9), 566–574.

De Jong, K. A. (1980b). *A genetic-based global function optimization technique* (Technical Report No. 80-2). Pittsburgh: University of Pittsburgh, Department of Computer Science.

De Jong, K. A. (1981). *Adaptive search procedures for large complex spaces* (Technical Report No. 81-2). Pittsburgh: University of Pittsburgh, Department of Computer Science.

De Jong, K. A. (ca. 1982). [Pascal version of a general-purpose genetic algorithm computer program]. University of Pittsburgh, Department of Computer Science.

De Jong, K. A. (1985). Genetic algorithms: A 10 year perspective. *Proceedings of an International Conference on Genetic Algorithms and Their Applications, 169–177.*

De Jong, K. A. (1987). On using genetic algorithms to search program spaces. *Genetic algorithms and their applications: Proceedings of the Second International Conference on Genetic Algorithms, 210–216.*

Dewdney, K. A. (1985). Exploring the field of genetic algorithms in a primordial computer sea full of flibs. *Scientific American, 253*(5), 21–32.

Dolan, C. P., & Dyer, M. G. (1987). Toward the evolution of symbols. *Genetic algorithms and their applications: Proceedings of the Second International Conference on Genetic Algorithms,* 123–132.

Englander, A. C. (1985). Machine learning of visual recognition using genetic algorithms. *Proceedings of an International Conference on Genetic Algorithms and Their Applications,* 197–201.

Etter, D. M., Hicks, M. J, & Cho, K. H. (1982). Recursive adaptive filter design using an adaptive genetic algorithm. *Proceedings of IEEE International Conference on Acoustics, Speech and Signal Processing, 2,* 635–638.

Farmer, D., Lapedes, A., Packard, N., & Wendroff, B. (Eds.). (1986). *Evolution, games, and learning.* Amsterdam: North-Holland.

Farmer, J. D., Packard, N. H., & Perelson, A. S. (1985, July). *The immune system and artificial intelligence.* Paper presented at an International Conference on Genetic Algorithms and Their Applications, Pittsburgh.

Farmer, J. D., Packard, N. H., & Perelson, A. S. (1986). The immune system, adaptation, and machine learning. In D. Farmer, A. Lapedes, N. Packard, & B. Wendroff (Eds.), *Evolution, games and learning* (pp. 187–204). Amsterdam: North-Holland. (Reprinted from *Physica, 22D,* 187–204)

Fedanzo, A. J. (1986a). Darwinian evolution as a paradigm for AI research. *SIGART Newsletter, 97,* 22–23.

Feller, W. (1968). *An introduction to probability theory and its application.* New York: Wiley.

Fisher, R. A. (1958). *The genetic theory of natural selection* (rev. ed.). New York: Dover.

Fitzpatrick, J. M., Grefenstette, J. J., & Van Gucht, D. (1984). Image registration by genetic search. *Proceedings of IEEE Southeast Conference,* 460–464.

Fletcher, R., & Powell, M. J. D. (1963). A rapidly convergent descent method for minimization. *Computer Journal, 6,* 163–168.

Fogel, L. J., Owens, A. J., & Walsh, M. J. (1966). *Artificial intelligence through simulated evolution.* New York: John Wiley.

Foo, N. Y., & Bosworth, J. L. (1972). *Algebraic, geometric, and stochastic aspects of genetic operators* (CR-2099). Washington, DC: National Aeronautics and Space Administration.

Forrest, S. (1982, August). *A parallel algorithm for classification in KL-ONE networks* (Consul Note No. 15). Marina del Rey, CA: University of Southern California, Information Sciences Institute.

Forrest, S. (1985a). *Documentation for PRISONERS DILEMMA and NORMS programs that use the genetic algorithm.* Unpublished manuscript, University of Michigan, Ann Arbor.

Forrest, S. (1985b). Implementing semantic network structures using the classifier system. *Proceedings of an International Conference on Genetic Algorithms and Their Applications,* 24–44.

Forrest, S. (1985c). *A study of parallelism in the classifier system and its application to classification in KL-ONE semantic networks.* Unpublished doctoral dissertation, University of Michigan, Ann Arbor.

Forrest, S. (1986). The classifier system: A computational model that supports machine intelligence. *Proceedings of the 1986 International Conference on Parallel Processing,* 711–716

Forrest, S. (in press). Modelling high-level symbolic structures in parallel systems that support learning. In M. Elzas, T. Oren, & B. P. Zeigler (Eds.), *Modelling and simulation methodology: Knowledge systems paradigms.* Amsterdam: North-Holland.

Forsyth, R. (1981). Beagle—A Darwinian approach to pattern recognition. *Kybernetes, 10*(3), 159–166.

Forsyth, R., & Rada, R. (1986). *Machine learning: Applications in expert systems and information retrieval.* Chichester: Ellis Horwood.

Fourman, M. P. (1985). Compaction of symbolic layout using genetic algorithms. *Proceedings of an International Conference on Genetic Algorithms and Their Applications,* 141–153.

Frantz, D. R. (1972). Non-linearities in genetic adaptive search. (Doctoral dissertation, University of Michigan). *Dissertation Abstracts International, 33*(11), 5240B-5241B. (University Microfilms No. 73-11,116)

Fraser, A. S. (1960). Simulation of genetic systems by automatic digital computers. 5-linkage, dominance and epistasis. In O. Kempthorne (Ed.), *Biometrical genetics* (pp. 70–83). New York: Macmillan.

Fraser, A. S. (1962). Simulation of genetic systems. *Journal of Theoretical Biology, 2,* 329–346.

Frey, P. W. (1986). A bit-mapped classifier. *Byte, 11*(12), 161–172.

Friedberg, R. M. (1958). A learning machine: Part I. *IBM Journal of Research and Development, 2*(1), 2–13.

Friedman, G. J. (1959). Digital simulation of an evolutionary process. *General Systems Yearbook, 4,* 171–184.

Fujiko, C., & Dickinson, J. (1987). Using the genetic algorithm to generate LISP source code to solve the prisoner's dilemma. *Genetic algorithms and their applications: Proceedings of the Second International Conference on Genetic Algorithms,* 236–240.

Gerardy, R. (1982). Probabilistic finite state system identification. *International Journal of General Systems, 8,* 229–242.

Gillies, A. M. (1985). *Machine learning procedures for generating image domain feature detectors.* Unpublished doctoral dissertation, University of Michigan, Ann Arbor.

Glover, D. E. (1986). Experimentation with an adaptive search strategy for solving a keyboard design/configuration problem (Doctoral dissertation, University of Iowa). *Dissertation Abstracts International, 47,* 2996B. (University Microfilms No. 86 22767)

Glover, D. E. (1987). Solving a complex keyboard configuration problem through generalized adaptive search. In L. Davis (Ed.), *Genetic algorithms and simulated annealing* (pp. 12–31). London: Pitman.

Goldberg, D. E. (1980a). *Adaptive control of gas pipeline systems.* Unpublished manuscript.

Goldberg, D. E. (1980b). *Some simple experiments in genetic-like adaptation.* Unpublished manuscript.

Goldberg, D. E. (1981a). *Algebraic and probabilistic properties of genetic algorithms.* Unpublished manuscript.

Goldberg, D. E. (1981b). *Robust learning and decision algorithms for pipeline operations.* Unpublished dissertation proposal, University of Michigan, Ann Arbor.

Goldberg, D. E. (1981c). *System identification via genetic algorithm.* Unpublished manuscript.

Goldberg, D. E. (1982). *SGA: A simple genetic algorithm* [computer program in Pascal]. Ann Arbor: University of Michigan, Department of Civil Engineering.

Goldberg, D. E. (1983). Computer-aided gas pipeline operation using genetic algorithms and rule learning (Doctoral dissertation, University of Michigan). *Dissertation Abstracts International, 44*(10), 3174B. (University Microfilms No. 8402282)

Goldberg, D. E. (1984, May). *Computer-aided pipeline operation using genetic algorithms and rule learning.* Paper presented at the 1984 API Pipeline Cybernetics Symposium, Houston, TX.

Goldberg, D. E. (1985a). Controlling dynamic systems with genetic algorithms and rule learning. *Proceedings of the 4th Yale Workshop on Applications of Adaptive Systems Theory,* 91–97.

Goldberg, D. E. (1985b). Dynamic system control using rule learning and genetic algorithms. *Proceedings of the 9th International Joint Conference on Artificial Intelligence, 1,* 588–592.

Goldberg, D. E. (1985c). Genetic algorithms and rule learning in dynamic system control. *Proceedings of an International Conference on Genetic Algorithms and Their Applications,* 8–15.

Goldberg, D. E. (1985d). *Optimal initial population size for binary-coded genetic algorithms* (TCGA Report No. 85001). Tuscaloosa: University of Alabama, The Clearinghouse for Genetic Algorithms.

Goldberg, D. E. (1986a). The genetic algorithm approach: Why, how, and what next? In K. S. Narendra (Ed.), *Adaptive and learning systems: Theory and applications* (pp. 247–253). New York: Plenum Press.

Goldberg, D. E. (1986b). *Simple genetic algorithms and the minimal, deceptive problem* (TCGA Report No. 86003). Tuscaloosa: University of Alabama, The Clearinghouse for Genetic Algorithms.

Goldberg, D. E. (1986c). A tale of two problems: Broad and efficient optimization using genetic algorithms. *Proceedings of the 1986 Summer Computer Simulation Conference,* 44–48.

Goldberg, D. E. (1987a). Computer-aided gas pipeline operation using genetic algorithms and rule learning. Part I: Genetic algorithms in pipeline optimization. *Engineering with Computers,* 35–45.

Goldberg, D. E. (1987b). Computer-aided gas pipeline operation using genetic algorithms and rule learning. Part II: Rule learning control of a pipeline under normal and abnormal conditions. *Engineering with Computers,* 47–58.

Goldberg, D. E. (1987c). *A note on the disruption due to crossover in a binary-coded genetic algorithm* (TCGA Report No. 87001). Tuscaloosa: University of Alabama, The Clearinghouse for Genetic Algorithms.

Goldberg, D. E. (1987d). Simple genetic algorithms and the minimal, deceptive problem. In L. Davis (Ed.), *Genetic algorithms and simulated annealing* (pp. 74–88). London: Pitman.

Goldberg, D. E. (in press). Genetics-based machine learning: Whence it came, where it's going. In M. Elzas, T. Oren, & B. P. Zeigler (Eds.), *Modelling and simulation methodology: Knowledge systems paradigms.* Amsterdam: North-Holland.

Goldberg, D. E., & Kuo, C. H. (1985, October). *Genetic algorithms in pipeline optimization.* Paper presented at the 1985 meeting of the Pipeline Simulation Interest Group, Albuquerque, NM.

Goldberg, D. E., & Kuo, C. H. (1987). Genetic algorithms in pipeline optimization. *Journal of Computers in Civil Engineering, 1*(2), 128–141.

Goldberg, D E., & Lingle, R. (1985). Alleles, loci, and the traveling salesman problem *Proceedings of an International Conference on Genetic Algorithms and Their Applications,* 154–159.

Goldberg, D. E., & Richardson, J. (1987). Genetic algorithms with sharing for multimodal function optimization. *Genetic algorithms and their applications: Proceedings of the Second International Conference on Genetic Algorithms,* 41–49.

Goldberg, D. E., & Samtani, M. P. (1986). Engineering optimization via genetic algorithm. *Proceedings of the Ninth Conference on Electronic Computation,* 471–482.

Goldberg, D. E., & Segrest, P. (1987). Finite Markov chain analysis of genetic algorithms. *Genetic algorithms and their applications: Proceedings of the Second International Conference on Genetic Algorithms,* 1–8.

Goldberg, D. E., & Smith, R. E. (1986, October). *AI meets OR: Blind inferential search with genetic algorithms.* Paper presented at the ORSA/TIMS Joint National Meeting, Miami, FL.

Goldberg, D. E., & Smith, R. E. (1987). Nonstationary function optimization using genetic algorithms with dominance and diploidy. *Genetic algorithms and their applications: Proceedings of the the Second International Conference on Genetic Algorithms,* 59–68.

Goldberg, D. E., & Thomas, A. L. (1986). *Genetic algorithms: A bibliography 1962–1986* (TCGA Report No. 86001). Tuscaloosa: University of Alabama, The Clearinghouse for Genetic Algorithms.

Gordon, M. D. (1984). Adaptive subject indexing in document retrieval. (Doctoral dissertation, University of Michigan) *Dissertation Abstracts International, 45*(2), 611B. (University Microfilms No. 8412148)

Greene, D. P., & Smith, S. F. (1987). A genetic system for learning models of consumer choice. *Genetic algorithms and their applications: Proceedings of the Second International Conference on Genetic Algorithms,* 217–223.

Grefenstette, J. J. (1981). *Parallel adaptive algorithms for function optimization* (Technical Report No. CS-81-19). Nashville: Vanderbilt University, Computer Science Department.

Grefenstette, J. J. (1984a). GENESIS: A system for using genetic search procedures. *Proceedings of the 1984 Conference on Intelligent Systems and Machines,* 161–165.

Grefenstette, J. J. (1984b). *A user's guide to GENESIS* (Technical Report No. CS-84-11). Nashville: Vanderbilt University, Department of Computer Science.

Grefenstette, J. J. (Ed.). (1985a). *Proceedings of an International Conference on Genetic Algorithms and Their Applications.* Hillsdale, NJ: Lawrence Erlbaum Associates.

Grefenstette, J. J. (1985b). *Representation dependencies in genetic algorithms.* Unpublished manuscript.

Grefenstette, J. J. (1986). Optimization of control parameters for genetic algorithms. *IEEE Transactions on Systems, Man, and Cybernetics, SMC-16*(1), 122–128.

Grefenstette, J. J. (Ed.). (1987a). *Genetic algorithms and their applications: Proceedings of the Second International Conference on Genetic Algorithms.* Hillsdale, NJ: Lawrence Erlbaum Associates.

Grefenstette, J. J. (1987b). Incorporating problem specific knowledge into genetic algorithms. In L. Davis (Ed.), *Genetic algorithms and simulated annealing* (pp. 42–60). London: Pitman.

Grefenstette, J. J. (1987c). Multilevel credit assignment in a genetic learning system. *Genetic algorithms and their applications: Proceedings of the Second International Conference on Genetic Algorithms,* 202–209.

Grefenstette, J. J., & Fitzpatrick, J. M. (1985). Genetic search with approximate function evaluations. *Proceedings of an International Conference on Genetic Algorithms and Their Applications,* 112–120.

Grefenstette, J. J., Gopal, R., Rosmaita, B. J., & Van Gucht, D. (1985). Genetic algorithms for the traveling salesman problem. *Proceedings of an International Conference on Genetic Algorithms and Their Applications,* 160–168.

Grosso, P. B. (1985). *Computer simulation of genetic adaptation: Parallel subcomponent interaction in a multilocus model.* (Doctoral dissertation, University of Michigan, University Microfilms No. 8520908).

Hadamard, J. (1949). *The psychology of invention in the mathematical field.* Princeton, NJ: Princeton University Press.

Haslev (Skanland), M. (1986). *A classifier system for the production by computer of past tense verb-forms.* Manuscript submitted for publication.

Hastings, H. M., & Waner, S. (1985). Biologically motivated machine intelligence. *SIGART Newsletter, 95,* 29–31.

Hicklin, J. F. (1986). *Application of the genetic algorithm to automatic program generation.* Unpublished master's thesis, University of Idaho, Moscow.

Hilliard, M. R., & Liepins, G. E. (1986). Genetic algorithms as discovery programs. *Proceedings of the Southeastern Chapter of TIMS 22nd Annual Meeting, 16.*

Hilliard, M. R., & Liepins, G. E. (1987). Representational issues in machine learning. In M. Zemankova & M. L. Emrich (Eds.), *Proceedings of the International Symposium on Methodologies for Intelligent Systems.* Knoxville, TN: Oak Ridge National Laboratory.

Hilliard, M. R., Liepins, G. E., Palmer, M., Morrow, M., & Richardson, J. (1987). A classifier based system for discovering scheduling heuristics. *Genetic algorithms and their applications: Proceedings of the Second International Conference on Genetic Algorithms,* 231–235.

Hines, W. W., & Montgomery, D. C. (1980). *Probability and statistics in engineering and management science* (2nd ed.). New York: Wiley.

Hofstadter, D. R. (1979). *Gödel, Escher, Bach: An eternal golden braid.* New York: Basic Books.

Holland, J. H. (1959). A universal computer capable of executing an arbitrary number of subprograms simultaneously. *1959 Proceedings of the Eastern Joint Computer Conference,* 108–112.

Holland, J. H. (1960). Iterative circuit computers. *Proceedings of the 1960 Western Joint Computer Conference,* 259–265.

Holland, J. H. (1962a). Concerning efficient adaptive systems. In M. C. Yovits, G. T. Jacobi, & G. D. Goldstein (Eds.), *Self-organizing systems* (pp. 215–230). Washington: Spartan Books.

Holland, J. H. (1962b). Information processing in adaptive systems. *Information Processing in the Nervous System, Proceedings of the International Union of Physiological Sciences, 3,* 330–339.

Holland, J. H. (1962c). Outline for a logical theory of adaptive systems. *Journal of the Association for Computing Machinery, 3,* 297–314.

Holland, J. H. (1965). Some practical aspects of adaptive systems theory. In A. Kent & O. E. Taulbee (Eds.), *Electronic Information Handling* (pp. 209–217). Washington, DC: Spartan Books.

Holland, J. H. (1966). Universal spaces: A basis for studies of adaptation. In E. R. Caianiello (Ed.), *Automata Theory* (pp. 218–231). New York: Academic Press.

Holland, J. H. (ca. 1966). *Efficient adaptation over classes of non-linear environments.* Unpublished manuscript.

Holland, J. H. (1967). Nonlinear environments permitting efficient adaptation. In J. T. Tou (Ed.), *Computer and Information Sciences - II* (pp. 147–164). New York: Academic Press.

Holland, J. H. (1968). *Hierarchical descriptions of universal spaces and adaptive systems* (Technical Report ORA Projects 01252 and 08226). Ann Arbor: University of Michigan, Department of Computer and Communication Sciences.

Holland, J. H. (1969a). Adaptive plans optimal for payoff-only environments. *Proceedings of the 2nd Hawaii International Conference on System Sciences,* 917–920.

Holland, J. H. (1969b). Goal-directed pattern recognition. In S. Watanabe (Ed.), *Methodologies of pattern recognition* (pp. 287–296). New York: Academic Press.

Holland, J. H. (1969c). A new kind of turnpike theorem. *Bulletin of the American Mathematical Society, 75,* 1311–1317.

Holland, J. H. (1970a). Hierarchical descriptions of universal spaces and adaptive systems. In A. W. Burks (Ed.), *Essays on cellular automata* (pp. 320–353). Urbana: University of Illinois Press.

Holland, J. H. (1970b). Robust algorithms for adaptation set in a general formal framework. *Proceedings of the IEEE Symposium on Adaptive Processes - Decision and Control, XVII,* 5.1-5.5.

Holland, J. H. (1971). Processing and processors for schemata. In E. L. Jacks (Ed.), *Associative information processing* (pp. 127–146). New York: American Elsevier.

Holland, J. H. (1973a). Genetic algorithms and the optimal allocations of trials. *SIAM Journal of Computing, 2*(2), 88–105.

Holland, J. H. (1973b). Schemata and intrinsically parallel adaptation. In K. S. Fu & J. S. Tou (Eds.), *Proceedings of the NSF Workshop on Learning System Theory and its Applications* (pp. 43–46). Gainesville: University of Florida.

Holland, J. H. (1974). A brief discussion of the role of co-adapted sets in the process of adaptation. In B. Dyke & J. W. MacCluer (Eds.), *Computer simulation in human population studies* (pp. 161–165). New York: Academic Press.

Holland, J. H. (1975). *Adaptation in natural and artificial systems.* Ann Arbor: The University of Michigan Press.

Holland, J. H. (1976a). Adaptation. *Progress in Theoretical Biology, 4,* 263–293.

Holland, J. H. (1976b). An introduction to intrinsic parallelism. In W. Handler (Ed.), *Proceedings of the Tenth Anniversary Convocation for IMMD* (pp. 47–55). Erlangen, FRG: University of Erlangen.

Holland, J. H. (1976c). New perspectives in nonlinearity, or what to do when the whole is more than the sum of its parts. In F. Suppe & P. D. Asquith (Eds.), *Proceedings of the Philosophy of Science Association Meeting* (pp. 240–255). East Lansing, MI: Philosophy of Science Association.

Holland, J. H. (1976d). Studies of the spontaneous emergence of self-replicating systems using cellular automata and formal grammars. In A. Lindenmayer & G. Rozenberg (Eds.), *Automata, Languages, Development* (pp. 385–404). New York: North-Holland.

Holland, J. H. (ca. 1977). *A cognitive system with powers of generalization and adaptation.* Unpublished manuscript, University of Michigan, Department of Computer and Communication Sciences, Ann Arbor.

Holland, J. H. (1980a). Adaptive algorithms for discovering and using general patterns in growing knowledge-bases. *International Journal of Policy Analysis and Information Systems, 4*(3), 245–268.

Holland, J. H. (1980b). *Adaptive knowledge acquisition.* Unpublished research proposal.

Holland, J. H. (1981). *Genetic algorithms and adaptation.* (Technical Report No. 34). Ann Arbor: University of Michigan, Department of Computer and Communication Sciences.

Holland, J. H. (1983a). *Induction in artificial intelligence* (Technical Report). Ann Arbor: University of Michigan, Department of Computer and Communication Sciences.

Holland, J. H. (1983b). *A more detailed discussion of classifier systems* (Technical Report). Ann Arbor: University of Michigan, Department of Computer and Communication Sciences.

Holland, J. H. (1984). Genetic algorithms and adaptation. In O. G. Selfridge, E. L. Rissland, & M. A. Arbib (Eds.), *Proceedings of the NATO Advanced Research Institute on Adaptive Control of Ill-Defined Systems* (pp. 317–333). New York: Plenum Press.

Holland, J. H. (1985a). *A mathematical framework for studying learning in classifier systems* (Research Memo RIS-25r). Cambridge, MA: The Rowland Institute for Science.

Holland, J. H. (1985b). Properties of the bucket brigade. *Proceedings of an International Conference on Genetic Algorithms and Their Applications,* 1–7.

Holland, J. H. (1986a). Escaping brittleness: The possibilities of general purpose learning algorithms applied to parallel rule-based systems. In R. S. Michalski, J. G. Carbonell, & T. M. Mitchell (Eds.), *Machine Learning II* (pp. 593–623). Los Altos, CA: Morgan Kaufmann.

Holland, J. H. (1986b). A mathematical framework for studying learning classifier systems. In D. Farmer, A. Lapedes, N. Packard, & B. Wendroff (Eds.), *Evolution, games and learning* (pp. 307–317). Amsterdam: North-Holland. (Reprinted from *Physica, 22D*, 307–317)

Holland, J. H. (1987a). *Derived Markov matrices*. Unpublished manuscript.

Holland, J. H. (1987b). Genetic algorithms and classifier systems: Foundations and future directions. *Genetic algorithms and their applications: Proceedings of the Second International Conference on Genetic Algorithms*, 82–89.

Holland, J. H., & Burks, A. W. (1981). *Architecture and languages for parallel computing with classifier systems*. Unpublished research proposal.

Holland, J. H., & Burks, A. W. (1985). *Adaptive computing system capable of learning and discovery* [Patent application filing no. 06-619-349]. Washington, DC: U. S. Patent Office.

Holland, J. H., Burks, A. W., Crichton, J. W., & Finley, M. R. (1963). *Machine adaptive systems* (Technical Report ORA Project 05089). Ann Arbor: University of Michigan, Department of Computer and Communication Sciences.

Holland, J. H., Holyoak, K. J., Nisbett, R. E., & Thagard, P. R. (1986). *Induction: Processes of inference, learning, and discovery*. Cambridge: MIT Press.

Holland, J. H., Holyoak, K. J., Nisbett, R. E., & Thagard, P. R. (1987). Classifier systems, Q-morphisms, and induction. In L. Davis (Ed.), *Genetic algorithms and simulated annealing* (pp. 116–128).

Holland, J. H., & Reitman, J. S. (1978). Cognitive systems based on adaptive algorithms. In D. A. Waterman & F. Hayes-Roth (Eds.), *Pattern directed inference systems* (pp. 313–329). New York: Academic Press.

Hollstien, R. B. (1971). Artificial genetic adaptation in computer control systems. (Doctoral dissertation, University of Michigan). *Dissertation Abstracts International, 32*(3), 1510B. (University Microfilms No. 71-23,773)

Jog, P., & Van Gucht, D. (1987). Parallelisation of probabilistic sequential search algorithms. *Genetic algorithms and their applications: Proceedings of the Second International Conference on Genetic Algorithms*, 170–176.

Jones, W. T., & Chiaraviglio, L. (1979). Is science an adaptive system? *Behavioral Science, 24*(5), 325–333.

Kampfner, R. R. (1981). *Computational modeling of evolutionary learning*. Unpublished doctoral dissertation, University of Michigan, Ann Arbor.

Karg, R. L., & Thompson, G. L. (1964). A heuristic approach to solving traveling salesman problems. *Management Science, 10*(2), 225–248.

Katz, J. L. (1985). Artificial intelligence research at Mitre. *AI Magazine, 6*(3), 228–232.

Kauffman, S. A., & Smith, R. G. (1986). Adaptive automata based on Darwinian selection. In D. Farmer, A. Lapedes, N. Packard, & B. Wendroff (Eds.), *Evolution, games and learning* (pp. 68–82). Amsterdam: North-Holland. (Reprinted from *Physica, 22D*, 68-82)

Khoogar, A. R. (1987, November). *Genetic algorithm solutions for inverse robot kinematics*. Paper presented at the 1987 University of Alabama ACM Student Conference, Birmingham, AL.

Kirkpatrick, S., Gelatt, C. D., & Vecchi, M. P. (1983). Optimization by simulated annealing. *Science, 220*(4598), 671–680.

Klopf, A. H. (1965). *Evolutionary pattern recognition systems* (Technical Report). Chicago: University of Illinois, Information Engineering Department, Bioengineering Section.

Knuth, D. E. (1981). *The Art of Computer Programming* (2nd ed., vol. 2). Reading, MA: Addison-Wesley.

Kuchinski, M. J. (1985). *Battle management systems control rule optimization using artificial intelligence* (Technical Report No. NSWC MP 84-329). Dahlgren, VA: Naval Surface Weapons Center.

Lawler, E. L. (1976). *Combinatorial optimization: Networks and matroids.* New York: Holt, Rinehart and Winston.

Liepins, G. E., & Hilliard, M. R. (1986a, October). *Generic algorithms and nationally advertised brand algorithms—can the dumb machines learn to discriminate.* Paper presented at The International Symposium on Methodologies for Intelligent Systems, Knoxville, TN.

Liepins, G. E., & Hilliard, M. R. (1986b, October). *Genetic algorithms as a paradigm for machine learning.* Paper presented at the ORSA/TIMS Joint National Meeting, Miami, FL.

Liepins, G. E., Hilliard, M. R., Palmer, M., & Morrow, M. (1987). Greedy genetics. *Genetic algorithms and their applications: Proceedings of the Second International Conference on Genetic Algorithms,* 90–99.

Lindsay, R. K. (1985). Artificial intelligence research at the University of Michigan. *AI Magazine, 6*(2), 64–72.

MacLaren, L. (1981). Tuesday evening satellite session. In J. R. Sampson (Ed.), *A Synopsis of the Fifth Annual Ann Arbor Adaptive Systems Workshop,* (pp. 87–91). Ann Arbor: University of Michigan, Department of Computer and Communications Sciences, Logic of Computers Group.

Martin, F. G., & Cockerham, C. C. (1960). High speed selection studies. In O. Kempthorne (Ed.), *Biometrical genetics* (pp. 35–45). London: Pergamon Press.

Martin, N. (1973). Convergence properties of a class of probabilistic adaptive schemes called sequential reproductive plans. (Doctoral dissertation, University of Michigan), *Dissertation Abstracts International, 34*(8), 3746B-3747B. (University Microfilms No. 74-3685)

Martinez, H. M. (1979). An automaton analogue of unicellularity. *Biosystems, 11,* 133–162.

Mauldin, M. L. (1984). Maintaining diversity in genetic search. *Proceedings of the National Conference on Artificial Intelligence,* 247–250.

Mercer, R. E. (1977). *Adaptive search using a reproductive meta-plan.* Unpublished master's thesis, University of Alberta, Edmonton.

Mercer, R. E., & Sampson, J. R. (1978). Adaptive search using a reproductive meta-plan. *Kybernetes, 7,* 215–228.

Minga, A. K. (1986, April). *Genetic algorithms in aerospace design.* Paper presented at the AIAA Southeastern Regional Student Conference, Huntsville, AL.

Minga, A. K. (1987, April). *Honeycomb design using a genetic algorithm.* Paper presented at the AIAA Southeastern Regional Student Conference, Atlanta, GA.

Minsky, M. L. (1967). *Computation: Finite and infinite machines.* Englewood Cliffs, NJ: Prentice-Hall.

Nelder, J. A., & Mead, R. (1965). A simplex method for function minimization. *Computer Journal, 7,* 308–313.

Oliver, I. M., Smith, D. J., & Holland, J. R. C. (1987). A study of permutation crossover operators on the traveling salesman problem. *Genetic algorithms and their applications: Proceedings of the Second International Conference on Genetic Algorithms,* 224–230.

Oosthuizen, D. G. (1987). SUPERGRAN: A connectionist approach to learning, integrating genetic algorithms and graph induction. *Genetic algorithms and their applications: Proceedings of the Second International Conference on Genetic Algorithms,* 132–139.

Papoulis, A. (1984). *Probability, random variables, and stochastic processes* (2nd ed.). New York: McGraw-Hill.

Perry, Z. A. (1984). Experimental study of speciation in ecological niche theory using genetic algorithms. (Doctoral dissertation, University of Michigan). *Dissertation Abstracts International, 45*(12), 3870B. (University Microfilms No. 8502912)

Pettit, E., & Swigger, K. M. (1983). An analysis of genetic-based pattern tracking and cognitive-based component tracking models of adaptation. *Proceedings of the National Conference on Artificial Intelligence,* 327–332.

Pettey, C. B., Leuze, M. R., & Grefenstette, J. J. (1987). A parallel genetic algorithm. *Genetic algorithms and their applications: Proceedings of the Second International Conference on Genetic Algorithms,* 155–161.

Pike, M. C. (1980). Algorithm 267 random normal deviate [G5]. In, *Collected algorithms from ACM, II,* 267. New York: Association for Computing Machinery.

Post, E. L. (1943). Formal reductions of the general combinatorial decision problem. *American Journal of Mathematics, 65,* 197–268.

Rada, R. (1981a). Evolution and gradualness. *BioSystems, 14,* 211–218.

Rada, R. (1981b). Evolutionary structure and search (Doctoral dissertation, University of Illinois). *Dissertation Abstracts International, 42,* 690-B.

Rada, R. (1984a). Automating knowledge acquisition. In R. Forsyth (Ed.), *Expert systems: Principles and case studies* (pp. 190–210). New York: Chapman and Hall.

Rada, R. (1984b). Probabilities and predicates in knowledge refinement. *Proceedings of the IEEE Workshop on Principles of Knowledge-based Systems,* 123–128.

Rada, R. (1985). Gradualness facilitates knowledge refinement. *IEEE Transactions on Pattern Analysis and Machine Intellegence, PAMI-7*(5), 523–530.

Rada, R., Rhine, Y., & Smailwood, J. (1984). Rule refinement. *Proceedings of the Society of Computer Applications in Medical Care,* 62–65.

Radcliffe, A. (1981). A problem solving technique based on genetics. *Creative Computing, 3*(2), 78–81.

Raghavan, V. V., & Agarwal, B. (1987). Optimal determination of user-oriented clusters: An application for the reproductive plan. *Genetic algorithms and their applications: Proceedings of the Second International Conference on Genetic Algorithms,* 241–246.

Raghavan, V. V., & Birchard, K. (1979). A clustering strategy based on a formalism of the reproductive processes in natural systems. *Proceedings of the Second International Conference on Information Storage and Retrieval, 14*(2), 10–22.

Rechenberg, I. (1965, August). *Cybernetic solution path of an experimental problem*

(Royal Aircraft Establishment Translation No. 1122, B. F. Toms, Trans.). Farnborough Hants: Ministry of Aviation, Royal Aircraft Establishment.

Rechenberg, I. (1973), *Evolutionstrategie* [Evolution Strategy]. Stuttgart: Frommann-Holzboog.

Rechenberg, I. (1986, July), *Literaturnachweis zur Evolutionstrategie* [Bibliography for the Evolution Strategy]. Unpublished manuscript, Technische Universitat Berlin, Fachgebiet Bionik und Evolutionstechnik, Berlin.

Reed, J., Toombs, R., & Barricelli, N. A. (1967). Simulation of biological evolution and machine learning. *Journal of Theoretical Biology, 17,* 319–342.

Reiter, C. (1986). Toy universes. *Science 86, 7*(5), 55–59.

Rendell, L. A. (1983a). A doubly layered, genetic penetrance learning system. *Proceedings of the National Conference on Artificial Intelligence, 343–347.*

Rendell, L. A. (1983b). A new basis for state space learning systems and a successful implementation. *Artificial Intelligence, 20,* 369–392.

Rendell, L. A. (1985). Genetic plans and the probabilistic learning system: Synthesis and results. *Proceedings of an International Conference on Genetic Algorithms and Their Applications,* 60–73.

Reynolds, R. G. (1975). *Towards an extended theory of adaptation.* Unpublished manuscript.

Reynolds, R. G. (1979). *An adaptive computer model of the evolution of agriculture for hunter-gatherers in the valley of Oaxaca, Mexico.* Unpublished doctoral dissertation, University of Michigan, Ann Arbor.

Reynolds, R. G. (1986). An adaptive computer model for the evolution of plant collecting and early agriculture in the eastern valley of Oaxaca. In K. V. Flannery (Ed.), *Guila Naquitz: Archaic foraging and early agriculture in Oaxaca, Mexico* (pp. 439–500). New York: Academic Press.

Riolo, R. L. (1986a). *CFS-C: A package of domain independent subroutines for implementing classifier systems in arbitrary user-defined environments* (Technical Report). Ann Arbor: University of Michigan, Logic of Computers Group.

Riolo, R. L. (1986b). *LETSEQ: An implementation of the CFS-C classifier system in a task-domain that involves learning to predict letter sequences* (Technical Report). Ann Arbor: University of Michigan, Logic of Computers Group.

Riolo, R. L. (1987a). Bucket brigade performance: I. Long sequences of classifiers. *Genetic algorithms and their applications: Proceedings of the Second International Conference on Genetic Algorithms,* 184–195.

Riolo, R. L. (1987b). Bucket brigade performance: II. Default hierarchies. *Genetic algorithms and their applications: Proceedings of the Second International Conference on Genetic Algorithms,* 196–201.

Robertson, G. G. (1986). [Lisp version of classifier system program for execution on the Connection Machine].

Robertson, G. G. (1987a). Parallel implementation of genetic algorithms in a classifier system. In L. Davis (Ed.), *Genetic algorithms and simulated annealing* (pp. 129–140). London: Pitman.

Robertson, G. G. (1987b). Parallel implementation of genetic algorithms in a classifier system. *Genetic algorithms and their applications: Proceedings of the Second International Conference on Genetic Algorithms,* 140–147.

Rosenberg, R. S. (1966). *A computer simulation of a biological population.* Unpublished manuscript.

Rosenberg, R. S. (1967). Simulation of genetic populations with biochemical properties. (Doctoral dissertation, University of Michigan). *Dissertation Abstracts International, 28*(7), 2732B. (University Microfilms No. 67-17,836)

Rosenberg, R. S. (1970a). Simulation of genetic populations with biochemical properties: I. The model. *Mathematical Biosciences, 7,* 223–257.

Rosenberg, R. S. (1970b). Simulation of genetic populations with biochemical properties: II. Selection of crossover probabilities. *Mathematical Biosciences, 8,* 1–37.

Rosmaita, B. J. (1985a). *Exodus: An extension of the genetic algorithm to problems dealing with permutations.* Unpublished master's thesis, Vanderbilt University, Nashville, TN.

Rosmaita, B. J. (1985b). *EXODUS user's manual (version 1.8)* (Technical Report CS-85-06). Nashville: Vanderbilt University, Department of Computer Science.

Ross, S. (1976). *A first course in probability.* New York: Macmillan.

Sampson, J. R. (1978). [Summary of the Third Annual Adaptive Systems Workshop, Ann Arbor]. Unpublished manuscript.

Sampson, J. R. (1979). [Summary of the Fourth Annual Adaptive Systems Workshop, Ann Arbor]. Unpublished manuscript.

Sampson, J. R. (1981a). [Summary of the Sixth Annual Adaptive Systems Workshop, Ann Arbor]. Unpublished manuscript.

Sampson, J. R. (1981b). *A Synopsis of the Fifth Annual Ann Arbor Adaptive Systems Workshop.* Ann Arbor: University of Michigan, Department of Computer and Communication Sciences, Logic of Computers Group.

Sampson, J. R. (1984). *Biological information processing.* New York: John Wiley.

Sampson, J. R., & Brindle, A. (1979). Genetic algorithms for function optimization. *Proceedings of the Ninth Manitoba Conference on Numerical Mathematics and Computing,* 31–47.

Samuel, A. L. (1959). Some studies in machine learning using the game of checkers. *IBM Journal of Research and Development, 3*(3), 210–229.

Sannier, A. V., II, & Goodman, E. D. (1987). Genetic learning procedures in distributed environments. *Genetic algorithms and their applications: Proceedings of the Second International Conference on Genetic Algorithms,* 162–169.

Schaffer, J. D. (1984). *Some experiments in machine learning using vector evaluated genetic algorithms.* Unpublished doctoral dissertation, Vanderbilt University, Nashville.

Schaffer, J. D. (1985a). Learning multiclass pattern discrimi- nation. *Proceedings of an International Conference on Genetic Algorithms and Their Applications,* 74–79.

Schaffer, J. D. (1985b). Multiple objective optimization with vector evaluated genetic algorithms. *Proceedings of an International Conference on Genetic Algorithms and Their Applications,* 93–100.

Schaffer, J. D. (1987). Some effects of selection procedures on hyperplane sampling by genetic algorithms. In L. Davis (Ed.), *Genetic algorithms and simulated annealing* (pp. 89–103). London: Pitman.

Schaffer, J. D., & Grefenstette, J. J. (1985). Multi-objective learning via genetic algorithms. *Proceedings of the 9th International Joint Conference on Artificial Intelligence, 1,* 593–595.

Schaffer, J. D., & Morishima, A. (1987). An adaptive crossover distribution mechanism for genetic algorithms. *Genetic algorithms and their applications: Proceedings of the Second International Conference on Genetic Algorithms, 36–40.*

Schrodt, P. A. (1986a). Predicting international events. *Byte, 11*(12), 177–192.

Schrodt, P. A. (1986b, March). *Set prediction of international behavior using a Holland classifier.* Paper presented at the 1986 meeting of the International Studies Association, Anaheim, CA.

Schrodt, P. A. (1987). Pattern matching, set prediction, and foreign policy analysis. In S. J. Cimbala (Ed.), *Artificial intelligence and national security* (pp. 89–107). Lexington: Lexington Books.

Schwefel, H. (1981). *Numerical optimization of computer models* (M. Finnis, Trans.). Chichester: John Wiley. (Original work published 1977).

Segrest, P. D. (1987). *GAS genetic annealing simulation for combinatorial optimization.* Unpublished manuscript, University of Alabama, Tuscaloosa.

Shaefer, C. G. (1985a). *Comparisons of methods for solving nonlinear equations* (Research Memo RIS-24r). Cambridge, MA: Rowland Institute for Science.

Shaefer, C. G. (1985b). Directed trees method for fitting a potential function. *Proceedings of an International Conference on Genetic Algorithms and Their Applications, 207–225.*

Shaefer, C. G. (1987). The ARGOT strategy: Adaptive representation genetic optimizer technique. *Genetic algorithms and their applications: Proceedings of the Second International Conference on Genetic Algorithms, 50–58.*

Simon, H. A. (1969). *The sciences of the artificial.* Cambridge, MA: MIT Press.

Sirag, D. J., & Weisser, D. J. (1987). Toward a unified thermodynamic genetic operator. *Genetic algorithms and their applications: Proceedings of the Second International Conference on Genetic Algorithms, 116–122.*

Slagle, J. R., & Hamburger, H. (1985). An expert system for a resource allocation problem. *Communications of the ACM, 28*(9), 994–1004.

Smith, D. (1985). Bin packing with adaptive search. *Proceedings of an International Conference on Genetic Algorithms and Their Applications, 202–206.*

Smith, R. E. (1987). Diploid genetic algorithms for search in time varying environments. *Proceedings of the 25th Annual Southeast Regional Conference of the ACM, 175–178.*

Smith, R. E. (1988). *An investigation of diploid genetic algorithms for adaptive search of nonstationary functions.* Unpublished master's thesis, University of Alabama, Tuscaloosa.

Smith. S. F. (1980). *A learning system based on genetic adaptive algorithms.* Unpublished doctoral dissertation, University of Pittsburgh.

Smith, S. F. (1983). Flexible learning of problem solving heuristics through adaptive search. *Proceedings of the 8th International Joint Conference on Artificial Intelligence, 422–425.*

Smith, S. F. (1984). Adaptive learning systems. In R. Forsyth (Ed.), *Expert systems: Principles and case studies* (pp. 169–189). New York: Chapman and Hall.

Smith, T., & De Jong, K. A. (.1981). Genetic algorithms applied to the calibration of information driven models of US migration patterns. *Proceedings of the 12th Annual Pittsburgh Conference on Modelling and Simulation, 955–959.*

Spendley, W., Hext, G. R., & Himsworth, F. R. (1962). Sequential applications of simplex designs in optimization and evolutionary operation. *Technometrics, 4,* 441–461.

Stackhouse, C. P., & Zeigler, B. P. (in press). Learning plateaus in an adaptive rule-based system. In M. Elzas, T. Oren, & B. P. Zeigler (Eds.), *Modelling and simulation methodology: Knowledge systems paradigms.* Amsterdam: North-Holland.

Stadnyk, I. (1987). Schema recombination in pattern recognition problems. *Genetic algorithms and their applications: Proceedings of the Second International Conference on Genetic Algorithms,* 27–35.

Syslo, M. M., Deo, N., & Kowalik, J. S. (1983). *Discrete optimization algorithms with Pascal programs.* Englewood Cliffs, NJ: Prentice-Hall.

Suh, J. Y., & Van Gucht, D. (1987). Incorporating heuristic information into genetic search. *Genetic algorithms and their applications: Proceedings of the Second International Conference on Genetic Algorithms,* 100–107.

Suh, J. Y., & Van Gucht, D. (1987, July). *Distributed genetic algorithms* (Technical Report No. 225). Bloomington: Indiana University, Computer Science Department.

Takahashi, Y., Rabins, M. J., & Auslander, D. M. (1970). *Control and dynamic systems.* Reading, MA: Addison-Wesley.

Tanese, R. (1987). Parallel genetic algorithms for a hypercube. *Genetic algorithms and their applications: Proceedings of the Second International Conference on Genetic Algorithms,* 177–183.

Thompson, B., & Thompson, B. (1986). Evolving knowledge from data. *Computer Language, 3*(11), 23–26.

Uhr, L., & Vossler, C. (1961). A pattern recognition program that generates evaluates and adjusts its own operators. *Annals of the New York Academy of Science, 50*(189), 555–569.

Ulam, S., & Schrandt, R. (1986). Some elementary attempts at numerical modeling of problems concerning rates of evolutionary processes. In D. Farmer, A. Lapedes, N. Packard, & B. Wendroff (Eds.), *Evolution, games and learning* (pp. 4–12). Amsterdam: North-Holland. (Reprinted from *Physica, 22D,* 4–12).

Valenzuela-Rendon, M. (1986). *A computer architecture for genetic algorithms or the parallel hierarchic genetic algorithm.* Unpublished manuscript.

Vincent, T. L., & Grantham, W. J. (1981). *Optimality in parameteric systems.* New York: Wiley.

von Neumann, J. (1966). *Theory of self-reproducing automata* (Edited and completed by A. W. Burks). Urbana: University of Illinois Press.

Waterman, D. A. (1968). *Machine learning heuristics* (Doctoral dissertation, Stanford University Report No. CS118, A.I. 74). Stanford, CA: Stanford University, Department of Computer Science.

Weinberg, R. (1970). Computer simulation of a living cell (Doctoral dissertation, University of Michigan). *Dissertations Abstracts International, 31*(9), 5312B. (University Microfilms No. 71-4766)

Westerdale, T. H. (1974). An application of Fisher's theorem on natural selection to some re-enforcement algorithms for choice strategies. *Journal of Cybernetics, 4,* 31–42.

Westerdale, T. H. (1985). The bucket brigade is not genetic. *Proceedings of an International Conference on Genetic Algorithms and Their Applications,* 45–59.

Westerdale, T. H. (1986). A reward scheme for production systems with overlapping conflict sets. *IEEE Transactions on Systems, Man, and Cybernetics, SMC-16*(3), 369–383.

Westerdale, T. H. (1987). Altruisim in the bucket brigade. *Genetic algorithms and their applications: Proceedings of the Second International Conference on Genetic Algorithms,* 22–25.

Wetzel, A. (1983). *Evaluation of the effectiveness of genetic algorithms in combinatorial optimization.* Unpublished manuscript, University of Pittsburgh, Pittsburgh.

What the brain builders have in mind. (1987, May 2). *The Economist,* pp. 94–96.

Whitley, D. (1987). Using reproductive evaluation to improve genetic search and heuristic discovery. *Genetic algorithms and their applications: Proceedings of the Second International Conference on Genetic Algorithms,* 108–115.

Wilson, S. W. (1981). *Aubert processing and intelligent vision* (Technical report). Cambridge, MA: Polaroid Corportation.

Wilson, S. W. (1983). On the retino-cortical mapping. *International Journal of Man-Machine Studies, 18,* 361–389.

Wilson, S. W. (1985a). Adaptive "cortical" pattern recognition. *Proceedings of an International Conference on Genetic Algorithms and Their Applications,* 188–196.

Wilson, S. W. (1985b). Knowledge growth in an artificial animal. *Proceedings of an International Conference on Genetic Algorithms and Their Applications,* 16–23.

Wilson, S. W. (1985c). Knowledge growth in an artificial animal. *Proceedings of the 4th Yale Workshop on Applications of Adaptive Systems Theory,* 98–104.

Wilson, S. W. (1986a). *Classifier system learning of a boolean function* (Research Memo RIS-27r). Cambridge, MA: Rowland Institute for Science.

Wilson, S. W. (1986b). *Classifier systems and the Animat problem* (Research Memo RIS-36r). Cambridge, MA: Rowland Institute for Science.

Wilson, S. W. (1986c). *Hierarchical credit allocation in a classifier system* (Research Memo RIS-37r). Cambridge, MA: Rowland Institute for Science.

Wilson, S. W. (1986d). Knowledge growth in an artificial animal. In K. S. Narendra (Ed.), *Adaptive and learning systems: Theory and applications* (pp. 255–264). New York: Plenum Press.

Wilson, S. W. (1987a). Classifier systems and the Animat problem. *Machine Learning, 2*(3), 199–228.

Wilson, S. W. (1987b). The genetic algorithm and biological development. *Genetic algorithms and their applications: Proceedings of the Second International Conference on Genetic Algorithms,* 247–251.

Wilson, S. W. (1987c). Hierarchical credit allocation in a classifier system. In L. Davis, *Genetic algorithms and simulated annealing* (pp. 104–115). London: Pitman.

Wilson, S. W. (1987d). Hierarchical credit allocation in a classifier system. *Proceedings of the Tenth International Joint Conference on Artificial Intelligence,* 217–220.

Wilson, S. W. (1987e). Quasi-Darwinian learning in a classifier system. *Proceedings of the Fourth International Workshop on Machine Learning,* 59–65.

Wilson, S. W. (in press). Hierarchical credit allocation in a classifier system. In M. Elzas, T. Oren, & B. P. Zeigler (Eds.), *Modelling and simulation methodology: Knowledge systems paradigms.* Amsterdam: North-Holland.

Wong, P. J., & Larson, R. E. (1968). Optimization of natural gas pipeline systems via dynamic programming. *IEEE Transactions of Automatic Control, AC-13*(5), 475–481.

Zeigler, B. P., Bosworth, J. L., & Bethke, A. D. (1973). *Noisy function optimization by genetic algorithms* (Technical Report No. 143). Ann Arbor: University of Michigan, Department of Computer and Communication Sciences.

Zhou, H. (1985). Classifier systems with long term memory. *Proceedings of an International Conference on Genetic Algorithms and Their Applications,* 178–182.

Zhou, H. (1986). *Conceptual learning by building finite automata from examples via genetic algorithm.* Manuscript submitted for publication.

INDEX

#; see Wild card symbol
*; see Don't care symbol

a, 230
Abeyance, 148–165
accum, 67
action, 230
Action set, 286
Adaptation in Natural and Artificial Systems, 2, 106, 264
Adaptive systems theory, 90, 92
address, 240
advance, 243
Airfoil optimization, 104
Aliasing, 123
allele, 60, 162
Allele
  correspondence to string position
   .alue, 21
  definition of, 21
  dominant, 149
  recessive, 149
Anandan, P., 238, 293
ANAS; *see Adaptation in Natural and Artificial Systems*
Anderson, C. W., 238, 293
ANIMAT, 285–288
  innovations in, 286
  results, 287–288
  time-to-payoff estimation, 287
aoc, 233–234, 243
AOC; *see* Apportionment of credit system

Apportionment of credit system, 221, 225–229
  analogy to service economy, 222, 225
  currency, introduction of a, 222
  example of payments, 226–227
  in Pascal, 233–236
  stability of, 228
Approximate function evaluation, 206–208
A-schemata; see Schema
auction, 233–234, 236
Auction, 225
  noisy, 226
Auslander, D. M., 228
avg, 62
Avriel, M., 202
Axelrod, R., 140–142

Bagley, J. D., 42, 92–93, 123, 150–151, 167–168, 264
Baker, J. E., 124–125
Baricelli, N. A., 89
Barto, A. G., 238, 293
Beightler, C. S., 6
Bellman, R., 5
Berry, R. J., 150
Bethke, A. D., 42, 170, 202, 208
bid, 230, 234
Bid
  competition, 222
  definition of, 225
  effective, 226

Bid, *continued*
  factoring specificity into, 234
  as geometrically weighted average of
    receipts, 229
  structure to promote default
    hierarchies, 252–254
bid1, 234, 252
bid2, 234, 252
bidsigma, 234
bidtax, 236
Biochemistry simulation, 94
bit, 230–231
Black box problem, 7–8, 15
Bledsoe, W. W., 95, 104, 261
Blind search, 9, 201
Bonomi, E., 205
Booker, L. B., 71, 121, 123, 195–197,
    225, 276–279, 285, 287
BOOLE, 293–295
  differences with ANIMAT, 293
  population entropy measure used in,
    293
Bosworth, J., 102, 202, 204
Bowen, D., 196
Box, G. E. P., 103–104
Brachman, R. J., 296
Brainerd, W. S., 301
Braitenberg, V., 264
Breeding, 99–100, 192, 195
Bremermann, H. J., 104, 262
Brent, R. P., 120
Bridges, C. L., 51
Brindle, A., 121, 123, 153–154
Broadcast language, 218, 264–265
Broadcast units, 218
Browning, I., 95
Bucket brigade algorithm, 219, 225–
    229
  implicit, 236, 287
bucketbrigadeflag, 234–235
Building block, 20, 41
  hypothesis, 18, 41–45
  misleading, 45
Burks, A. W., 268

c, 230
Cavicchio, D. J., 95–97, 119, 168–169,
    180–181, 190, 264
cbid, 234
Cell simulation, 93–95, 98–99
cfile, 232
child, 238
child1, 64–65
child2, 64–65

chromosome, 60, 66–67
Chromosome
  correspondence to string, 21–22
  multiple numbers in genotype, 179–
    180
  pairs of; see Diploidy
classarray, 230
Classifier systems, 217, 221–230
  cognitive science, connections to,
    276–277
  connectionism, connections to,
    278
  fixed-length rule restriction, 221
  mating restriction in, 278
  mental maps in, 288
  parallel rule activation, 222
  in Pascal, 243–245
  symbolic artificial intelligence,
    connections to, 296
classifieroutput, 240
Classifiers, 219, 223–224, 230, 238,
    266
classlist, 231
classtype, 230
clearinghouse, 233–234, 236
Clearinghouse, 225, 233–236
clearingrec, 233
clist, 231–232
CL-ONE, 296–301
Cockerham, C. C., 89
Codings, 80–84
  allele names carried with, 166–167
  binary codes, advantage of, 80–82
  binary switching, 80
  concatentation of, 82–83
  Gray versus binary, 100
  messy, 181
  minimalist versus maximalist
    controversy, 102
  multiparameter, 82–84, 134
  permutation, 170
  principles of, 80
  real genes, 98, 102–103
  unsigned binary integer, 80
coeff, 67
Cognitive System One; see CS-1
Community model, 210–211
Complement operator, partial, 102
Complex logarithmic mapping, 282
condition, 230
Conditions, 218, 224
Connectionism, 278
Constraints, 85–86
Control systems, 99

Coombs, S., 311
Cooperation, 182–184
Cramer, N. L., 301, 303
Create operator, 286–287
crecord, 233
crossover, 64, 66
Crossover, 10
　adaptive, 94, 293, 295
　checkerboard, 285
　cycle, 170, 175
　effect on schema survival, 31–32
　example of, 12, 17
　generalized; see Crossover, multiple-
　　point
　knowledge-augmented, 204–206
　multiple-point, 102, 116, 119–120
　between nonhomologous strings,
　　167–168
　order, 170, 174
　partially matched, 170–174, 177
　partially matched in Pascal, 172
　probability of, 71, 111
　probability, coded within string, 196
　on ring structure, 119
　simple, 12
　simple, in Pascal, 64
　tree-based, 303
　on variable length structures, 273–
　　274
crowding, 238
Crowding, 116, 118, 190
　in a classifier system, 229, 238
　in a classifier system in Pascal, 239
crowdingfactor, 236–238
crowdingsubpop, 238
CS-1, 218–219, 265–270, 277, 282,
　285
　classifier syntax, 266
　combination of needs, 267
　comparison to LS-1, 270–271
　epochal algorithm, 267
　maze task results, 268–270
　roulette wheel use for rule selection,
　　267
　seven-node maze, 268–269
　thirteen-node maze, 268–270
CX; see Crossover, cycle
Cycle crossover; see Crossover, cycle

Davis, L. D., 5, 170, 174, 311
Davis, R., 221
De Jong, K. A., 71, 96, 102, 106–121,
　123, 190, 199, 229, 264
Deception conditions, 46–47

decode, 67, 240
decode_parms, 84
Decoding routines in Pascal, 83
Default hierarchy, 247
　enlargement of the solution set, 251
　example of, 249, 252
　parsimony of, 250–251
　SCS results, 253–254
Defining length, 24, 29
　effect on schema survival, 32
Deletion, 180–181
Deo, N., 202
detectors, 241, 243
Detectors, 21, 223
　binary, 28
　in Pascal, 240–242
　selection by genetic algorithm, 95
　self-modification of, 218
　values of, 21
DFP, 120
Digital subtraction angiography, 138
Diploidy, 148–165
　analysis of, 157–161
　in Pascal, 162–165
Discretization of functionals, 84–85
Distributed asynchronous concurrent
　genetic algorithm, 208–209
Diversity maintenance, 96, 102
dominance, 162–163
Dominance, 148–165
　analysis of, 157–161
　effect on mutation rate, 161
　in genetic algorithms, 150–157
　intrachromosomal, 180
　in Pascal, 162–165
Domination, 198–199
Don't care symbol, 19
Duplication, 180–181
Dynamic programming, 5

ebid, 230, 234
ebid1, 234, 252
ebid2, 234, 252
effector, 242–243
Effectors, 223
　internal, 218
　in Pascal, 240–242
　self-modification of, 218
efile, 232
Elitism, 115
environment, 240, 243
environrec, 240
envmessage, 231, 241
Epistasis, 22, 47, 169–170

Epistasis, *continued*
  Fraser's function, 90–91
Epochal algorithm, 219, 267
erecord, 240
Evolutionary operation, 103–104
Evolutionary optimization, 105–106
Evolutionary programming, 105–106
Evolutionstrategie, 104–105
Exponential form, 30
Exterior penalty method, 85
extract__parm, 84
EYE-EYE system, 279, 282–285
  retina-to-cortex mapping, 282
  two-dimensional structures, 285

Features, 21, 28
Fertilization, 162–165
Finite-state machine learning task, 105–106
Fisher, R. A., 150
fitness, 60, 79
Fitness, 10
  as function of allele value and ordering, 171
  shared, 192
  as tautology in nature, 76
  see also Objective function
Fitzpatrick, J. M., 138–139, 206–207, 311
Fletcher, R., 120
flip, 63–65, 240
fmultiple, 78
Fogel, L. J., 105–106
Foo, N., 102, 202, 204
Food and poison learner, 276–279
  environment, 279–280
  separation of perception and affect classifiers, 277
  results, 279, 281
Forrest, S., 123–124, 140, 224, 299–301
Frames, 297
Frantz, D. R., 101–102, 169–170, 175–176, 264
Fraser, A. S., 89–91
Friedberg, R. M., 92
Friedman, G. J., 104, 262
Function
  approximate evolution of, 206–208
  bitwise linear, 47
  De Jong's testbed, 107–110
  epistatic, 47
  linearization, 207–208

multimodal, 3–4, 185–186, 188
  noisy, 3
Function optimization, 99–101, 106–120
  nonstationary, 154–157
Fundamental theorem of genetic algorithms, 33

G; *see* Generation gap
ga, 236, 238, 243
GA; *see* Genetic algorithms
GA-deceptive problems, 45–46, 101–102
gaflag, 243
GA-hard problems, 46
gametogenesis, 162–164
garecord, 236
Gas pipeline control task, 289, 290–292
Gas pipeline optimization, 125, 130–135
G-bit improvement, 202–204
GBML; *see* Genetics-based machine learning
Gelatt, C. D., 205
gen, 61, 68
Gene
  correspondence to a detector, 21
  definition of, 21
  expression, 149
generatesignal, 240
generation, 66, 68
  diploid scheme revisions, 164
Generation gap, 111
GENESIS, 199
Genetic algorithms, 1–25
  applications list, 125–129
  avoidance of centralized control, 97, 98–99
  within a classifier system, 219, 229, 236–238
  differences compared to conventional methods, 7–10
  first appearance of words, 92
  fundamental theorem of, 33
  geography, imposition of, 191
  hand calculation, 15–18
  history of, 89–103, 106–120
  ideas-notions framework, 13–14
  innovation generating capability, 14
  insensitivity to noise, 138–139
  mathematical foundations, 2, 28–54
  mechanics of, 10–14

overlapping populations in a
  classifier system, 229
parallel, 208–212
parameter codings, use of, 7–9
in Pascal, 59–75
payoff usage, 7
probabilistic operator usage, 7
self-adaptation, 93, 96–97, 196
terminology of, 21–22
vector-evaluated, 199
Genetics, early digital simulations of,
  89–90
Genetics-based machine learning, 217–
  256, 261–303
applications list, 219–220
history of, 218–219, 221, 261–292
Genotype, 21
Geometric progression, 30
gfile, 232
Gillies, A. M., 124
Goldberg, D. E., 40, 46, 51, 125, 130–
  137, 154–157, 159–160, 170 171,
  177, 179, 191–192, 202, 210–211,
  224, 288
Gopal, R., 204–206
Graham, W. J., 199
Gray code, 100–101
grecord, 236
Greedy optimization, 202
Grefenstette, J. J., 42, 71, 99, 138–139,
  199, 204–209, 212, 311
Grosso, P. B., 191

Hadamard, J., 13
halt, 243
Hamming space, 46
Haploidy, 148
Heterotic, multiplicative functions, 191
Heterozygote, 149
Hexapawn, 92–93
Hext, G. R., 104
Hill-climbing, 3
comparison to genetic algorithms,
  120
Himsworth, F. R., 104
Hofstadter, D. R., 27
Holland, J. H., 1–2, 19, 37–38, 42, 90,
  92, 106, 152, 161, 170, 176, 179–
  180, 186, 196, 208, 218, 225, 247,
  251, 262, 264–265, 268, 274, 277–
  278, 282, 289, 305, 309
Holland, J. R. C., 174–175
Hollstien, R. B., 99–101, 107, 151–153,

180, 192, 195, 264,
Hollstien-Holland triallelic scheme, 152
Holyoak, K. J., 251, 270, 309
Homozygote, 149
Hunting-nurturing analysis, 182–184
Hybrid methods, 202–204
with calculus-based techniques, 202
with greedy techniques, 202
in parallel, 202–203

Ideas-notions framework, 17, 201
Image processing, 95–97, 138–139
Implicit parallelism, 20, 40
Include files, 243
individual, 60, 79
Inertial object control task, 289–290
initialization, 243
initialize, 68
Intersection operator, partial, 286–287
Invariance mappings, 282
Inversion, 166–170
disruption probability, 176–177
homology rules, 169
in LS-1, 273–275
probability of, 169
shadow, 176
see also Reordering operators
Iterative circuit computers, 208, 262

Jack-of-all-trades loss, 182–183
Jacobian inheritance, 208
JB, 301–303
Jog, P., 212

Karg, R. L., 172
K-armed bandit, 28, 36–41
counting arguments, 39
history in relation to genetic
  algorithms, 92
with sharing, 188
see also; Two-armed bandit
Kettlewell, H. B. D., 150
King, J., 221
Kirkpatrick, S., 205
KL-ONE, 296–299
Knapsack problem, 154–157
Knowledge-augmented operators, 204–
  206
Knowledge-based methods, 201–208
Kowalik, J. S., 202

Landweber, L. H., 301
Larson, R. E., 125, 130–131, 134

Lawler, E. L., 202
laddress, 240
lchrom, 61, 64–65, 67, 72
ldata, 240
Leuze, M. R., 212
lifetax, 236
Lingle, R., 170–171, 177, 179
Linkage, 101
  factors, 94
  removing unnecessary, 179–180
  searching for tighther, 166
Locus, 21
lsignal, 240
LS-1, 270–276
  crossover on variable-length
    structures, 274
  description of inference engine, 271–
    273
  genetic operators in, 273–274
  inversion use, 273–274
  in maze-running task, 274–275
  rule sets as object of evaluation,
    270–271
Lutton, J. L., 205

Machine learning
  as search, 142
  see also Genetics-based machine
    learning
map__parm, 84
mapdominance, 162–163
Mapping
  of images, 138–139
  objective functions to fitness
    functions, 75–76
  strings to integers to parameters, 82–
    83
  variance dependent, 76
marray, 236
Marriage restriction; *see* Mating,
  restriction
Martin, F. G., 89
match, 232–233. 238
Match score, 278
Match set, 286
matchclassifiers, 232–233, 243
matchcount, 238
matchflag, 230, 232
Matching section, 171, 174
matchlist, 231–232, 234
matchmax, 238
mate1, 66, 236
mate2, 66, 236

mating, 236
Mating, 100–101
  homology rules for inversion, 169
  restriction, 188–189, 192–197, 278
  rules of, 196
  tags, 196–197
  templates, 195–197
max, 62
maxgen, 61
maxparm, 84
maxpop, 60
maxstring, 60
Maze-learning task, 266
MDP; *see* Minimal deceptive problem
Mead, R., 104
Measures of performance, 107, 110
Mendel, G., 148
Mental maps, 288
Mercer, R. E., 99
message, 231
Messages, 223–224
Message list, 223
Micro-level operators, 179–184
Migration, 102
min, 62
Minga, A. K., 136
Minimal deceptive problem, 46–52,
  179
minparm, 84
Minsky, M. L., 221, 264
Monkey wrench rules, 246
mort1, 236, 238
mort2, 236, 238
Moth, peppered, 149–150
Multicriteria optimization, *see*
  Multiobjective optimization
Multimodal functions; *see* Functions,
  multimodal
Multiobjective optimization, 94, 197–
  201
Multiplexer learning task
  default hierarchy example, 249
  function, 230
  in Pascal, 238–241
  perfect rule set, 246
  tabula rasa runs, 254–256
  Wilson's results, 293–295
multiplexeroutput, 240
Multiplier learning task, 302–303
mutation, 65–66
Mutation, 10, 14
  Cavicchio's operators, 96
  in a classifier system, 229

cubic gaussian, 102
in diploid scheme. 165
directed, 98
example of, 17
in evolutionary programming, 105–106
Fletcher-Reeves, 102
frequency of, 14
knowledge-augmented, 204
in Pascal, 65
probability of, 71, 11
quadratic gaussian, 102
schema survival under, 32
secondary role of, 14
simple, 14
uniform random, 102

n^3 estimate of schema processing, 20, 40–41
nactive, 231–232
nclassifier, 230
ncross, 64
ncrossover, 236
Nelder, J. A., 104
Network genetic algorithm, 209
Neural networks, 278
newpop, 60, 68
Niche, 185–197
in classifier systems, 225
by crowding, 116, 118
in genetic algorithms, 189–195
motivation for, 185–186
by preselection operator, 96
by sharing function, 191–195
Nisbett, R. E., 251, 270, 309
nmutation, 64, 236
Nondominated sorting selection, 201
Nondomination, 198–199
Nonlinearity; see Epistasis
Nonparametric selection, 124
Normal noise, 234
Notions-ideas framework; see Ideas-notions framework
nparms, 84
nposition, 230

Object-based design, 210–211
objective, 79
Objective function
in Pascal, 67
see also Payoff
objfunc, 67–68
Off-line performance, 107, 110

Offspring generation function, 94–95
OGF; see Offspring generation function
oldpop, 60, 68
oldwinner, 233
On-line performance, 107
Oliver, I. M., 174–175
Optimal control, 84–85, 131–135
Optimization
goals of, 6–7
process versus destination, 6
robustness of traditional methods, 2–5
see also Function optimization, Search
Order, 29
Order crossover; see Crossover, order
O-schema; see Schema, ordering
output, 240
Owens, A. J., 105–106
OX; *see* Crossover, order

Panmixia, 191
Parallel genetic algorithms; see Genetic algorithms, parallel
Parallel processing, 262
Parameters
coding of, 7–9
set, correspondence to phenotype, 21
Payoff, 7
parent1, 64–65
parent2, 64–65
Pareto optimality, 197–198
Partial intersection operator; *see* Intersection operator, partial
Partial matching, 278
Partially matched crossover; *see* Crossover, partially matched
partsum, 63
Pattern recognition, 95–97
Pattern-searching task, 277–279
payment, 234
Payments, 226–228
pcross, 62, 64, 71
pcrossover, 236
Penalty method, 85–86
Performance measures; *see* Measures of performance
Performance system; *see* Rule and message system
Permutation, 170
Perry, Z. A., 190
Pettey, C. B., 212

pfile, 232
Phenotype, 21, 60
Phillips, D. T., 6
Pike, M. C., 234
Pipeline operations classifier system,
288–292
PL, 301
PL−, 301–303
Plant pollination model, 210–211
pmutation, 62, 64, 71, 236
PMX; *see* Crossover, partially matched
Poker learning task, 275–276
Ponce de Leon algorithm, 267
pop, 123
popsize, 61, 66, 71
P-optimality; see Pareto optimality
poptype, 230–231
population, 60, 231
Populations
    advantage of, 9
    calculating statistics related to, 68–
    69
    in computer program, 60–61, 66–67
    example, 9–10
    importance of, 7, 90, 92
    initialization of, 15
    isolation, 191
    nonoverlapping, 60, 62
    notation for, 28
    number of schemata in, 20
    overlapping in a classifier system,
    229
    size of, 71, 101, 111
Positive assortive mating, 278–279
Post, E. L., 221, 264
Powell, M. J. D., 120
poweroftwo, 67
PRAXIS, 120
Premature convergence, 74, 77
prescale, 78
preselect, 123
Preselection, 96, 190
Principle of meaningful building blocks,
80
Principle of minimal alphabets, 80
Prisoner's dilemma problem, 140–142
Probabilistic operators, use of, 7, 10
Production rules, 218
Production system, 221
proportionselect, 236

Rabins, M. J., 228
rand, 63

random, 63, 65
Random number generator, 63
Random walks, 5
Ranking, 124–125
    nondominated, 201
Receipts, 226–228
Rechenberg, I., 104–105
reinforcement, 243
reinforcementrec, 243
Reitman, J. S., 265, 274, 282
Reordering operators, 166–179
    history of, 167–175
    theory of, 175–179
rep, 232
report, 69–70, 243
reportflag, 243
reportga, 243
Reproduction, 10–12, 15
    example of, 11–12
    in Pascal, 62–64
rfile, 232
Richardson, J., 191–192
Riolo, R. L., 224
rnd, 63, 65
Robustness, 1–2, 9–10
Rosenberg, R. S., 42, 93–95, 123, 151,
199, 264
Rosmaita, B. J., 204–206
Roulette wheel selection, 237
Rule and message system, 221, 223–
225
    example of match, 224
    in Pascal, 232–233
Rule-based system; see Production
system

Sampling, 121
Samtani, M. P., 136–137
Samuel, A. L., 92, 262
"Satisficing," 7
scale, 79
scalepop, 78–79
Scaling, 123–124
    early examples of, 93
    of fitness values, 76–79
    linear, 77, 123
    in Pascal, 78–79
    power law, 123–124
    with sigma truncation, 123–124
Schaffer, J. D., 94, 180, 197, 199
Schema, 18–19
    connection to k-armed bandit
    problem, 39

counting arguments, 19–20
disruption by crossover, 20
disruption by mutation, 20
environmental, 218
examples of, 19
extended analysis of, 49–50, 179
external, 190
growth equation, 30–33
hand calculation, 33–35
in hierarchical structures, 262
history of, 92
notation for, 29
number available in binary versus
  nonbinary codes, 81
order, 29
ordering, 177–179
plausibility of, 19
theorem, 30–33
theorem, extension to dominance
  and diploidy, 157–160
useful processing of, 40–41
visualization as hyperplanes, 53–54
visualization of periodicity, 42–45
Schemata; *see* Schema
Schemata processors, 218, 262–264
Schmolze, J., 296
Schwefel, H., 104
SCS, 230–256
data structures, 230–232
default hierarchy tests, 247, 249, 254
general results, 254
parameter settings, 246
perfect set of rules, 247
results from, 245–256
Search
blind, 9
calculus-based methods, 2–4
enumerative, 4–5
hill-climbing, 3
point-by-point, 9
randomized versus random, 5
robustness of different methods, 2–6
zero-finding, 2–3
see also Function optimization,
  Optimization
Segregation, 179–180
select, 64, 66, 123, 164, 237
Selection, 10–11
of classifiers by auction, 225
comparison of different schemes,
  121–123
by elitism, 115–118
in evolutionary programming, 105

expected value model, 115–118
Hollstien's schemes, 99
importance of, 90
by ranking, 124–125
roulette wheel, 11–12, 15–16, 63
stochastic remainder, 121–123
Self-contained controls, 93
Semantic networks, 296
Semisynchronous master-slave genetic
  algorithm, 208–209
Sensitivity analysis, 207
Sequential program learning task, 301–
  303
Serial bottleneck, 208
Sex, 181–184
SGA, 59–75
comparison to genetic algorithm in
  SCS, 229
data structures, 60–62
main program, 68–69
results from, 70–75
SGADOM, 162–165
Sharing, 191–195
among classifiers, 225, 278, 286
function, 191–192
genotypic, 192
phenotypic, 191–192
signal, 240–241
Similarity, 18–19; *see also* Schema
Similarity subsets; *see* Schema
Similarity templates; *see* Schema
Simon, H. A., 7
Simple classifier system; *see* SCS
Simple genetic algorithm; *see* SGA
Simulated annealing, 5, 205
sitecross, 236
Smith, D. J., 174–175
Smith, R. E., 154–157, 161
Smith, S. F., 180, 270–272, 274, 303
Specialization, 182–197
between species, 185–197
within species, 182–184
Speciation, 185–197
specificity, 234
Spendley, W., 104
statistics, 63, 68–69, 236
Stochastic remainder selection; *see*
  Selection, stochastic remainder
Strength, 225
difference equations, 226–228
strength, 230, 234
String rules; *see* Classifiers
Strings, 8

Strings, *continued*
    correspondence to chromosomes,
        21–22
    decoding of, 15, 66–67
    effect of crossover on, 12
    notation for, 28
    population of, 9–11
    position dependence of meaning, 28
        similarities among, 18; *see also*
            Schema
Structural optimization, 136–137
Structure, 21
Subroutine selection task, 95
Subsumption, 299
Suh, J. Y., 212
sumfitness, 62–63, 68, 79
sumstrength, 238
SUPERC link, 296, 299
Symbolic artificial intelligence, 296
Synchronous master-slave genetic
        algorithm, 208
Syslo, M. M., 202

Takahashi, Y., 228
Tanese, R., 212
taxcollector, 233, 236
Taxes, 226–228, 236
TB, 301–303
tfile, 232
Thagard, P. R., 251, 270, 309
Thompson, G. L., 172
Time-to-payoff estimation, 286–287
timekeeper, 243
Translocation, 180
Traveling salesman problem, 170–174,
        204–206
Triallelic dominance, 151–152
    in Pascal, 162–165
trit, 230
TSP; *see* Traveling salesman problem
Two-armed bandit, 28, 36–41
    with sharing, 187–188
    see also K-armed bandit

uavg, 78
Uhr, L., 92
umax, 78
umin, 78
Unification of data and instructions,
    265
utility.scs, 234

Van Gucht, D., 138, 204–206, 212
Variable binding, 273
Vecchi, M. P., 205
VEGA; *see* Genetic algorithms, vector-
        evaluated
Vincent, T. L., 199
von Neumann, J., 262
Vossler, C., 92

Walsh function analysis, 45
Walsh-schema transform, 42
Walsh, M. J., 105–106
Waterman, D. A., 275–276
Weinberg, R., 98–99
Wetzel, A., 121
Wild card symbol, 224, 232
Wilde, D. J., 6
Wilson, S. W., 236, 238, 279, 282, 285,
        287, 293, 295
winner, 233
Wong, P. J., 125, 130–131, 134
Woods, 285–286
worstofn, 238
writechrom, 69–70, 165

X chromosome, 181

Y chromosome, 181

Z-transforms, 228
Zeigler, B. P., 102, 202, 204